Red Conspirator

Red Conspirator

J. Peters and the American Communist Underground

THOMAS SAKMYSTER

UNIVERSITY OF ILLINOIS PRESS

Urbana, Chicago, and Springfield

Frontispiece: J. Peters at his deportation trial in 1948.
Courtesy of the Library of Congress and Associated
Press Images.

Publication of this book was supported in part by
a grant from the University of Cincinnati.

Library of Congress Cataloging-in-Publication Data
Sakmyster, Thomas L.
Red conspirator : J. Peters and the American communist
underground / Thomas Sakmyster.
p.   cm.
Includes bibliographical references and index.
ISBN-13: 978-0-252-03598-2 (hbk. : alk. paper)
ISBN-10: 0-252-03598-4 (hbk. : alk. paper)
1. Peters, J. (Josef). 2. Communism—United States—History—
20th century. 3. Espionage, Communist—United States—
History—20th century. 4. Communists—Hungary—Biography.
I. Title.
E743.5.S29   2011
335.4092—dc22 [B]   2010041903

Contents

Acknowledgments   vii

Abbreviations   ix

Introduction   xiii

1. Sándor Goldberger: From Hungary to the New World   1

2. The Making of J. Peters, 1931–32   25

3. J. Peters in the 1930s: The Organization Man   39

4. J. Peters and the Secret Apparatus   56

5. Whittaker Chambers and the "Washington Set-up"   74

6. J. Peters's Espionage Ring, 1934–38   91

7. From Peters to Stevens: Life in the Underground   111

8. Dueling with "the Feds," 1943–48   130

9. Trial and Deportation   149

Epilogue and Assessment   169

Notes   193

Bibliography   235

Index   245

Illustrations appear after page 90

Acknowledgments

I wish to express my gratitude to those individuals who agreed to interviews in which they shared their recollections of J. Peters, including Paul Lendvai, Dan Rosenberg, and Susan (Weinstock) Gould. The research for this book has been facilitated by numerous archivists, librarians, and historians in several countries, only a few of whom I can mention here. I wish to acknowledge in particular the assistance provided by John Fox, historian of the FBI, John Earl Haynes (Library of Congress), Tibor Frank (Eötvös Loránd University, Budapest), Erika Gottfried (Tamiment Library, New York University), Sally Moffitt (Langsam Library, University of Cincinnati), and Mikaila Corday (Interlibrary Loan Department, Langsam Library). I am also indebted to several of my colleagues in the History Department at the University of Cincinnati, particularly Willard Sunderland, Tom Lorman, and June Alexander. They helped me to procure archival material, offered helpful comments on the manuscript, and in general encouraged me in the project. The research for this project was made possible by grants from the Charles Phelps Taft Research Center of the University of Cincinnati.

Abbreviations

AAA	Agricultural Adjustment Administration
ACPFB	American Committee for the Protection of the Foreign Born
AFL	American Federation of Labor
AWP	Allen Weinstein Papers, Hoover Institution Archives
AWU	Automobile Workers Union
CCC	Central Control Commission
CPUSA	Communist Party of the United States
ECCI	Executive Committee of the Comintern International
FCPUSA	Files of the Communist Party of the United States
GPU	State Political Directorate
GRU	Main Intelligence Directorate of the Soviet General Staff
HUAC	House Committee on Un-American Activities
INS	Immigration and Naturalization Service
NKVD	People's Commissariat for Internal Affairs, successor to the OGPU
OGPU	Joint State Political Directorate, successor to the GPU
OMS	the Comintern's International Liaison Section
POLCOM	Political Committee of the CPUSA; also PolBuro
RGASPI	Russian State Archive of Social and Political History
RSACB	Records of the Subversive Activities Control Board
VN	Vassiliev Notebooks
YCL	Young Communist League

Red Conspirator

Introduction

On May 8, 1949, a Communist best known by the name J. Peters boarded a plane at New York International airport and departed for Hungary, where he had been born fifty-five years earlier. His departure was voluntary and with the knowledge and approval of the Immigration and Naturalization Service, which several months earlier had recommended that he be deported as an alien subversive. Born in Hungary in 1894 as Sándor Goldberger, Peters had used numerous other pseudonyms during his twenty-five-year sojourn in the United States, including József Péter for most of the 1920s, Joe Peter from 1929 to 1932, and Alexander Stevens in the 1940s. His expertise in the Communist movement had been in the areas of organization and cadre building, and his greatest accomplishments consisted of the development of an underground apparatus and the creation of an espionage operation in cooperation with Soviet intelligence organizations. Many of his colleagues in the leadership of the Communist Party of the United States (referred to hereafter as CPUSA) no doubt shared the admiration of Peters felt by Nathaniel Weyl, a Party member who called him "the most capable individual he had known in the Communist Party," a man "firm in his decisions and an excellent organizer."[1] Although most of Peters's activities were clandestine in nature and therefore not widely known, probably all American Communist Party members of the 1930s and

---

A major difficulty confronting the biographer of an individual like J. Peters, who in his long career used a bewildering number of aliases, is which one to use at a given point in the narrative. I have selected "J. Peters" as the default when referring to the subject in general, along with the generic term "red conspirator" or "man of mystery." Otherwise, I have used the alias he himself had assumed at the time of the events being described. In some cases this will require frequent shifting back and forth, even in the same paragraph.

1940s recognized the name "J. Peters," for he had been the author of an important textbook on Communist organization, *A Manual on Organization*,[2] which, when it appeared in 1935, was heavily promoted as an important handbook for all Party activists. Peters's abilities and accomplishments were much valued by party leaders. The entire Communist Party leadership attended a dinner in his honor a few days before his departure for Hungary. One of those present, John Williamson, declared that he could think of no other individual who had made a more significant contribution to the growth and development of the American Communist Party.[3]

At the time of J. Peters's arrest and his deportation trial in 1947 and 1948, anti-Communism, which had been present in American society all through the 1920s and 1930s, was becoming more virulent as the Cold War emerged. The testimony of a small group of ex-Communists convinced many Americans that the Soviet Union had taken advantage of its wartime alliance with the United States to engage in a perfidious campaign of espionage in which Soviet agents and spies had enlisted the support of American Communists. The Communist Party was coming to be regarded as an agent of "subversion, sabotage, and espionage."[4] Although for most of his twenty-five-year stay in the United States, J. Peters had been completely unknown to the public and, until the late 1930s, even to the FBI, this was to change dramatically when Peters was arrested in October 1947 by agents of the Immigration and Naturalization Service (INS). His arrest and his appearance less than a year later at an INS deportation hearing and before the House Committee on Un-American Activities (HUAC) received newspaper and magazine coverage in a sensationalist tone typified by the headline: "Another Stalin Agent Is Smoked Out."[5] Peters was described variously as a "Red Conspirator," "Kremlin Agent," "Top Stalin Spy," "Red Saboteur," and author of the "Red Textbook on Revolution." The most damaging accusations against Peters came in August and September 1948. Testifying at a session of HUAC, Whittaker Chambers described Peters as "the head of the whole underground of the American Communist Party" during the 1930s. Another ex-Communist, Louis Budenz, testified at Peters's deportation hearing that he was the chief underground link between Communists in the United States and the Soviet secret police.[6]

Although stories about J. Peters thus appeared frequently in the American national press in the period 1947–49, he nonetheless remained a man of mystery. American journalists were confounded by the many aliases Peters had used, and were never sure of his true name or how to refer to him in their stories. Likewise there was uncertainty about his national origin: was he Russian, Czech, German, or Hungarian? Peters himself did little to enlighten the public. When called before HUAC, he invoked the Fifth Amendment of the Constitution to refuse to answer most of the questions posed to him. The few brief statements Peters did provide to the press were largely uninformative and misleading.

After Peters's voluntary departure from the United States in May 1949, anti-Communists in the government and the media continued to cite his alleged underground activity as a sinister example of the subversive nature of the American Communist movement. In his autobiography, which appeared in 1952, Whittaker Chambers melodramatically declared that J. Peters had been "a lurking figure of fate in the lives of millions of Americans, who did not dream that he existed."[7] In the 1950s, House and Senate committees held hearings to investigate Communist activity and Soviet espionage,[8] and several witnesses, mostly former Communists, repeated Whittaker Chambers's claim that Peters had directed the underground activity of the Communist Party during the 1930s. In the dramatic confrontations between Whittaker Chambers and Alger Hiss at HUAC sessions and at the perjury trials of Alger Hiss, J. Peters's name was often mentioned. If Chambers's accusations were true, Peters was responsible for initiating and, at least in the 1930s, supervising the espionage activities that Chambers and Hiss had engaged in. However, Peters's role was never fully explored as part of the "Hiss case." As a result, although the Chambers-Hiss controversy would remain for many decades a frequent topic of often acrimonious debate among scholars and public intellectuals, J. Peters himself came in time to be regarded as simply a footnote to the bigger story. Those who believed that Hiss was innocent (and for nearly half a century most American historians were in this category) were convinced that Whittaker Chambers was a despicable, unsavory, and completely unreliable individual. For whatever personal reasons, he had concocted a story about espionage activity involving himself and Alger Hiss that had no basis in reality. And since Chambers had lied about his relationship with Hiss, there was no reason to believe he was being truthful in his testimony about J. Peters and his alleged work in the Communist underground.

From the start, it is true, a few scholars, particularly those interested in the history of national security and espionage, were convinced that J. Peters, though very much a "shadowy man,"[9] had indeed been an influential figure in the American Communist underground. In his extensive study of Soviet espionage activity, David Dallin asserted that Peters was "the most active, energetic, and resourceful man in those obscure depths of the underground where Soviet espionage borders on American Communism."[10] Still, not many historians and intellectuals were fully persuaded by Dallin's arguments, since, in the absence of pertinent American, Soviet, or Communist Party records, he had based his conclusions about the historical role of J. Peters largely on the testimony of former Communist Party members. In 1978, however, the American historian Allen Weinstein published a study of the Alger Hiss case based on important new evidence he had uncovered, including FBI records.[11] Although he had previously believed Hiss to be innocent, Weinstein now concluded that the evidence showed beyond a doubt that Whittaker Chambers had been right after all: both

Alger Hiss and J. Peters had engaged in espionage on behalf of Soviet intelligence agencies. Weinstein had even journeyed to Budapest to interview Peters, who was still active and alert at the age of eighty-four.[12] The evidence that Weinstein uncovered about Peters's career was significant, but in part still ambiguous and, especially concerning his espionage work, inconclusive. Nonetheless Weinstein confidently concluded that J. Peters had been a professional Soviet agent and a "gray eminence" in the American Communist movement.[13]

Although Weinstein's book changed the minds of many in the broader educated public who had previously been skeptical of Whittaker Chambers as a historical witness, many academics and writers on the Left remained unconvinced, believing that Weinstein had employed sloppy research methods and had misread or distorted the new evidence he had presented. For more than a decade after the appearance of *Perjury: The Hiss-Chambers Case,* most historians of the American Communist Party evinced little interest in alleged underground or espionage activities of American Communists. Underlying most of the academic monographs about the CPUSA that were published in the 1980s and much of the 1990s was the assumption that the Communist Party was a largely indigenous and progressive (albeit quite radical) political organization that had championed the rights of workers and minorities and had played an early and leading role in the world campaign against fascism. These historians were often called the "revisionists" because they were seeking to correct what they regarded as the distortions and omissions of historians who had emphasized the subservience of the American Communists to Moscow and their frequent adoption of Stalinist techniques.[14] The "revisionists," whom Maurice Isserman has called the "new historians of American Communism," preferred to focus on (and sometimes implicitly praise) the objectives and achievements of American Communists at the local level.[15] They either ignored or downplayed the significance of the ties between the CPUSA and the Comintern and the Soviet regime. Given this mindset and historiographical approach, one can understand why the "revisionists" showed no interest in (or simply denied the existence of) an underground in the CPUSA or collaboration between American Communists and Soviet intelligence agencies.

On the eve of his departure for Hungary in 1949, J. Peters had been praised by Party leaders for his significant contributions to the development of the American Communist Party. By the early 1990s, however, the "new historians of Communism," if they referred to him at all, regarded Peters as marginal and insignificant. Thus, in his important and well-regarded study of the Communist Party in the 1930s, the very period in which Peters was most active, Fraser Ottanelli made only one brief mention of him. He described Peters's *A Manual on Organization* as an exceedingly dull tract that reflected the former "dreariness of party life."[16] Nowhere in Ottanelli's work was there a discussion of illegal, conspiratorial, or underground activity, the role played by Peters in Party organization, or possible collaboration with Soviet intelligence agencies. In a similar vein, the editors of the first edition of the *Encyclopedia of the American Left*, an important reference guide, provided no entry for J. Peters or for such topics as the Communist underground or espionage.[17]

One reason for the lack of interest that the "revisionist" historians displayed in the CPUSA underground were the misleading statements made by American Communists who had played leading roles in the Party in the 1930s and 1940s. In his public comments J. Peters never wavered in his insistence that there was no such thing as an illegal or underground wing of the Communist Party, and that Whittaker Chambers's testimony was simply untrue. Other former leaders of the CPUSA not only issued similar denials, but also attempted to discredit the idea that J. Peters had played an important role of any kind in the Communist movement. In his memoir, Earl Browder, general secretary of the Party from 1932 to 1945, made no mention of J. Peters and asserted that the allegation that members of the CPUSA had engaged in espionage was "a lot of cloak and dagger nonsense."[18] Max Bedacht, whose career in the Communist movement spanned three decades and whom Chambers had identified as Peters's predecessor as the link between the CPUSA and Soviet intelligence agencies in the early 1930s, offered similar denials: "Never in these years did the Party have anything even faintly resembling an underground apparatus."[19] When questioned about J. Peters, Bedacht disingenuously claimed he knew him only slightly, "as one would know someone in a building you worked in."[20] In retrospect it would appear that Peters, Browder, Bedacht, and other former Communist leaders felt governed by what veterans of the movement sometimes called the "discipline of apparatus," according to which Communists who had engaged in or had knowledge of the Party's secret or underground activity were required to observe a code of silence and denial. American Communists had also long been instructed that when questioned by the authorities or the hostile media, the best approach was to "deny everything."[21]

At the same time, "revisionist" historians of the CPUSA and those on the non-academic Left were loathe even to acknowledge, let alone cite as reliable evidence, the testimony of those who had broken from the Communist movement and did not feel bound by the "discipline of apparatus." This was particularly true of Whittaker Chambers, whose melodramatic style and sometimes imperfect recall of specific events led skeptics to conclude that he was completely untrustworthy, indeed a despicable liar. Some of the other ex-Communist witnesses, such as Paul Crouch and John Lautner, had served as district leaders and presumably could have offered insights that would have been useful to those historians who were interested in Communist Party activity at the local level. But the recollections of Crouch, Lautner, and others, given typically before congressional committees at the height of the Cold War in the 1950s, tended to focus on the conspiratorial aspects of their work. They stated unequivocally that J. Peters had been the head of underground operations and had supervised a variety of conspiratorial activities. For the most part the "revisionists" dismissed these witnesses as embittered former Party members who were in thrall of anti-Communism and were determined at all cost to defame the Communist movement. However, I have found that the testimony of these ex-Communists as it related to the career of J. Peters, though at times exaggerated or simply mistaken because of faulty memory, was in fact largely accurate and independently corroborated by other kinds of evidence. This is a critical point, for John Lautner was Peters's closest friend in the community of Hungarian American Communists,[22] and Chambers his most intimate collaborator in conspiratorial work.

Beginning in the 1990s, important new documentary material on the history of the CPUSA became available. The collapse of Communist governments in Eastern Europe in 1989 and of the Soviet regime two years later soon made accessible to scholars primary sources from long-closed archives.[23] Most relevant for a study of J. Peters and his clandestine activity in the American Communist movement were the records of the Communist International (the Comintern), which included voluminous files of the national headquarters of the CPUSA from the 1920s and 1930s, and KGB material excerpted in lengthy notebooks by Alexander Vassiliev. Two American historians, John Haynes and Harvey Klehr, have made an extensive study of the newly available archival material and published many of the key documents.[24] On the basis of this new evidence they concluded that the "revisionist" position had been completely undermined: "It is no longer possible to maintain that the Soviet Union did not fund the American party, that the CPUSA did not maintain a covert apparatus, and that key leaders and cadres were innocent of connection with Soviet espionage operations."[25] Among the new documents uncovered were several that threw new light on the "illegal apparatus" of the CPUSA and the clandestine operations supervised by J. Peters. Important details about the life and career of Peters could now also be gleaned from the newly available Comintern records.[26]

Using the new evidence that became available in the 1990s, including messages of Soviet intelligence agencies intercepted by the United States as part of the Venona project,[27] historians have been able to revisit, and write with greater authority about, some of the controversies concerning the CPUSA that for decades had caused acrimonious debate. In the two volumes of documents that they edited, Haynes and Klehr provided extensive analysis of and commentary on the new evidence. In a thorough biography published in 1998, Sam Tanenhaus argued persuasively that Whittaker Chambers had by and large told the truth about his relationship with J. Peters and Alger Hiss.[28] Scholars have produced several new books about espionage and national security that contain more accurate, though still quite brief, treatments of the career of J. Peters.[29] Those historians who had been skeptical or agnostic about the alleged conspiratorial activities of Peters also had to take into account the new evidence. Maurice Isserman now declared that J. Peters's involvement "in a secret party apparatus" could no longer be disputed.[30] Other historians made similar concessions, but attempted to interpret the new material in a way that was least damaging to the "revisionist" view of the CPUSA. Thus, Paul Buhle, a coeditor of the *Encyclopedia of the American Left*, now acknowledged that Peters had been responsible for "secret work" that the Party had engaged in. However, Buhle described Peters as a kind of disruptive outsider, a Comintern representative whose "ham-fisted intervention" had a negative impact on the CPUSA. He was a member of the "conspiracy minded" bureaucracy in the Party's national headquarters that was alien to the majority of Party members and "catastrophic for the real social movement" that the Party represented.[31]

The historian who attempts to study and write about the career of J. Peters, who remained to many scholars a "shadowy Hungarian Communist,"[32] faces formidable challenges. The Comintern and CPUSA records now available throw new light on Peters's career, but reveal little of his personal life. Not surprisingly, he kept no diary, and almost none of his personal correspondence has survived. Very few of those who knew him well wrote about him in memoirs or are still alive and available for interviews. In the 1930s, when he was engaged in his most important conspiratorial work, Peters was assiduous in following Communist underground directives that stipulated that there should be little or no paper trail and that only a handful of other Party leaders should be apprised of his activity. Records that document his espionage activity for Soviet military intelligence, if they have survived at all, are safeguarded in Russian archives and are unlikely in the foreseeable future to be made available to researchers. On the other hand, I have been able to make use of an important new primary source, a short memoir that József Péter composed in the 1980s for deposit in the confidential archive of the Institute of the History of the [Hungarian] Communist Party (Párttörténeti Intézet).[33] No doubt confident that this document would only in the distant future (if ever) be scrutinized by those outside the Hungarian Communist Party, Péter here for the first time admitted that he had indeed been deeply involved in clandestine or underground operations. Péter's memoir is a particularly rich source for his family origins, education, participation in the work of the Hungarian and Czechoslovak Communist parties up to 1924, and his leading role in the Hungarian Federation of the CPUSA in the second half of the 1920s. Using this memoir, Peters's FBI and INS files, records of the Comintern and the CPUSA, and documents from numerous other sources, I have attempted in this work to reconstruct and offer an assessment of the career of this "man of mystery" who directed the CPUSA underground in the 1930s and specialized in such conspiratorial work as espionage and the production of fraudulent passports.

The career of the "red conspirator" can be studied from a number of perspectives. During his long life he took on many names and identities. His activity under the alias J. Peters in the 1930s is of course the most controversial and significant in terms of the history of the American Communist movement. As a historian who previously focused on Hungarian history,[34] I have come to the heated debates over J. Peters, Whittaker Chambers, Alger Hiss, and issues of conspiratorial activity and espionage without preconceived ideas or ideological certainties. I have attempted in this study to evaluate the relevant evidence carefully and objectively, hoping to answer key questions and offer insights into several aspects of the history of the CPUSA. It is now indisputable that Peters directed the "secret apparatus" of the Party during the 1930s. But what did this mean, and to whom did he report? What was the distinction between the "secret apparatus" and the "illegal apparatus"? In addition to supervising the forging of passports and making preparations for the Party to survive should the government attempt to suppress it, what other projects were part of Peters's underground operations?

The evidence now available shows that during the 1930s J. Peters was also intensively involved in the "above ground" activities of the Party's Organization Department. Indeed, it was his recognized expertise in issues of organization and cadre development that led Party leaders to select him to write what was intended to be the definitive handbook of Communist organization. I will address several important questions concerning the genesis and influence of Peters's *A Manual on Organization*. What were his motives in writing the *Manual* and what was his reaction when a change in direction ordered by Moscow rendered his pamphlet obsolete? Did ordinary American Communists actually read the pamphlet and try to adhere to the principles of organization Peters had outlined? Was it in fact used in Party schools and workshops? Finally, issues surrounding J. Peters's involvement in espionage have been and remain contentious, for the documentation is sparse. What was Peters's relationship with Whittaker Chambers, and what was the nature of the underground unit in the nation's capital that he called his "Washington set-up"? What connection did Peters have with the Comintern and other Soviet intelligence agencies? Is it correct to call him, as did so many American journalists and government investigators in the late 1940s, a "Kremlin agent" or one of "Stalin's spies"?

It is important to note that the "red conspirator's" persona as J. Peters represents only about fifteen years of his career. An examination of the many years during which he was known as József Péter can also offer important insights to the historian. Though he had only an imperfect knowledge of English when he arrived in the United States, it was comparatively easy for Péter to join the

Hungarian Federation of the CPUSA, and, despite his lack of training or experience, quickly become a journalist and editor for the Hungarian Communist daily newspaper, the *Új Előre*. Péter's shrewd political instincts and ability to establish a good relationship with non-Hungarian Party leaders enabled him to survive the bitter factional struggles that bedeviled the Hungarian language group. In a relatively short time he became secretary of the Hungarian Federation and by the late 1920s, having demonstrated his political and financial acumen by offering a plan to rescue the faltering Party newspaper, the *Daily Worker*, Péter was well poised to make the leap into the central leadership in New York. A study of Péter's career in the 1920s thus provides insights into the world of the ethnic federations that were so vital a part of the early American Communist movement.

In 1949 and for the remaining forty-one years of his life, this man of mystery reverted to the name József Péter. Although in these years he maintained ties with some former American comrades and followed with deep interest the Alger Hiss trial and other Cold War controversies, he quickly settled into a quiet late-life career in Party organizations dealing with cultural affairs. But these four decades, though a kind of footnote to his more colorful and controversial Party activity in the United States, were not without some suspense and mystery of their own. It appears that in 1949–50 Péter narrowly escaped becoming embroiled as a defendant in the first of the major Stalinist show trials in Eastern Europe. Instead he was consigned to editorial work for a variety of Party journals. Since he never spoke publicly about his career in the United States, Péter remained completely unknown to the public and the academic world in Hungary. His death in 1990, one year after the collapse of Communist regimes in Hungary and elsewhere in Eastern Europe, was barely noted in Hungarian newspapers, and few seemed to be aware that he was the J. Peters who had played such a significant and notorious role in American history of the 1930s and 1940s.[35]

Finally, the biographer of this Hungarian "man of mystery" must also grapple with important questions concerning the first thirty years of his life as Sándor Goldberger. Born in a small town in the far northeastern region of the Kingdom of Hungary into a poor, Jewish family, the young Sándor excelled in his school work, graduated from the gymnasium (high school), studied to become a lawyer, and served as an infantry officer in World War I. He had the good fortune to survive four years of combat, but the revolutionary events of 1918–19 stirred in him a previously dormant interest in political affairs. Encounters with Hungarian prisoners of war returning as fervent Communists from Russia and the shock of experiencing the virulent anti-Semitism that erupted at the end of the war soon radicalized him. By the end of 1918 he had become deeply involved in revolutionary activity and his career as an organizer and agitator in the Communist movement had begun.

As was the case with many other young Hungarians, especially those of Jewish background, Sándor Goldberger felt an immediate and powerful attraction to Marxist ideology and the newly established Soviet government in Russia. Although the great majority of Hungarian Jews rejected radical left-wing ideologies, it is true that the Hungarian Communist Party, as it emerged in 1918–19, had among its leaders and most zealous advocates a highly disproportionate number of men (and a few women) who had grown up in Jewish families and with at least a nominal attachment to Judaism.

During his career as a Communist functionary, he never once referred to his Jewish origins, but he never entirely succeeded in erasing this fact about his origins. As Sándor Goldberger he was instantly thought of as a Jew by his contemporaries, for Goldberger was a very common Jewish name in the Austro-Hungarian Empire. Even in the American Communist movement, when he no longer used the name Goldberger, most of his colleagues nonetheless identified him as a Hungarian Jew. A surprisingly large number of Hungarian Jews were to go on to play important roles in the world Communist movement, whether in Soviet Russia, Germany, the United States, or elsewhere. Even more striking is the disproportionate presence of Hungarians in such areas as propaganda, conspiratorial activity, and espionage. Sándor Goldberger/J. Peters was a member of this cohort, and a study of his career can provide important insights into the background and motivation of these émigré Hungarians who became loyal and very effective servants of world Communism.

1

Sándor Goldberger

From Hungary to the New World

In the five-decade period that began in 1880, about a half a million Hungarians emigrated to the United States. In the great migration before World War I, most of these were poor farm laborers seeking to escape the debilitating poverty of the Hungarian countryside. The second, much smaller wave after the Great War had a much different character. Although a substantial number of these émigrés were still from the ranks of the destitute, there was a notable increase in those who were urban and well educated.[1] Though small in number, many of the latter were to have dazzling success in the West, particularly in the United States, and would make remarkable contributions in such areas as science, classical music, the social sciences, and entertainment. The achievements of this cohort of Hungarians, most of them born between 1880 and 1905, have been noted by historians and other writers who have been moved to ponder and expound on the nature of what some would call the "Hungarian talent."[2] These Hungarian émigrés shared a number of traits: all of them benefited from what one historian has aptly called the "magnificent liberal educational system"[3] that had been established in Hungary by the late nineteenth century. In addition, they were innovative individuals who were open to "intellectual and artistic experimentalism."[4] Finally, and perhaps most remarkably, almost all of these émigrés were of Jewish origin, although they came primarily from assimilated and secular families. As adults most of them felt no connection to or identity with Judaism; indeed, many preferred to be silent about, or even to deny, their Jewish origins.[5]

Although his name is never mentioned in the studies that have chronicled the history of Hungarian Americans and their achievements, Sándor Goldberger was a member of this cohort of Hungarian émigrés. He was born of Jewish parents on August 11, 1894, in the Hungarian town of Csap and emigrated to the

United States in 1924. Like his more illustrious fellow émigrés of that period, Goldberger was to demonstrate considerable talent and creativity and to forge a remarkable career that left its mark on the American Communist movement and made him a central figure in one of the most important political controversies of twentieth-century American history. In the late 1940s, his name (or rather his various aliases) and his photograph appeared in national publications probably more often than that of any contemporary Hungarian American. Yet, in contrast to the brilliant contributions made to American society by other Hungarian Americans of his generation, Sándor Goldberger/J. Peters engaged in activities aimed at undermining American democratic institutions. His achievements as a professional Communist activist were largely hidden from the public or, when revealed, remained ambiguous and contested.

Csap, the birthplace of Sándor Goldberger, was a town of about three thousand people located in the northeastern region of the Kingdom of Hungary known as Ruthenia. There was a rich ethnic diversity in Ruthenia, including a substantial number of Jews who had fled persecution in the Russian Empire in the last half of the nineteenth century. By the turn of the twentieth century many of the Jews in Csap, and indeed throughout the Kingdom of Hungary, were using Hungarian as their primary language and were assimilating rapidly into Hungarian society. Although most Jews living in rural areas tended to cling to their Orthodox faith and remain traditional in their customs, speech, and dress, those living in Hungarian towns and cities were responding to powerful incentives to assimilate, to speak Hungarian rather than Yiddish, and in general to become "more Magyar than the Magyars themselves."[6] The subsequent rise in the social and economic status of Hungarian Jews was truly meteoric. By the turn of the century, Jews were graduating from high school (the gymnasium) and universities in numbers disproportionately far higher than their percentage in the population as a whole. On the eve of World War I, Jews represented 5 percent of the total population of the Kingdom of Hungary. Yet 85 percent of the leading bankers, 42 percent of the journalists, 49 percent of medical doctors, and 49 percent of lawyers were of Jewish origin.[7]

Sándor Goldberger was thus born at a time and in a country that offered to Jews a degree of civil equality, tolerance, and opportunity to advance that was perhaps unprecedented in European history. No records survive that document Sándor Goldberger's family origins, and he was silent on this subject in the brief autobiographical sketches he would later compose. His parents, József Goldberger and Rosalie Deutsch, were most likely emigrants, or the children of emigrants, from the Russian Empire. Sándor had two brothers, József and Imre. Hungarian was probably spoken in the home, but the parents no doubt were conversant in Yiddish and perhaps German.[8] In any case, as an adult, Sándor could communicate reasonably well in German, though he had not acquired any knowledge of Slovak or Ukrainian, the languages spoken by the majority of the inhabitants of Ruthenia.

Like most of the Jewish families who had emigrated to northeastern Hungary in the late nineteenth century, the Goldbergers were poor and, as Sándor Goldberger later recalled, his parents "always struggled to keep up the family."[9] Csap was (and remains today) an important railroad junction, and several members of the Goldberger family found employment in that industry. Sándor's father was employed for a time as a railroad brakeman, but at some point left that job and began to work with his wife in a restaurant. Later they opened their own small restaurant in Csap.[10] That they had hopes for the advancement of their sons through assimilation into Hungarian society is shown in their decision to give them authentic Magyar first names: Imre, József, and Sándor.

Given Sándor's later silence on the subject, it is difficult to determine to what extent the Goldbergers were religiously devout. Most likely they were secular in outlook, although they might have been nominal members of the thriving Neolog synagogue in Csap. It is certain that Sándor's parents were eager to make it possible for him to get the best secular schooling available. In 1899 they sent him to live with his grandfather in Debrecen, Hungary's second largest city, which enjoyed a reputation for having excellent elementary and secondary schools, many of them run by the Calvinist Church. It is possible that the parents felt they could not provide adequately for their three children, and welcomed an offer from Rosalie Deutsch's parents to take on one of the sons. Sándor might have been chosen because he showed the greatest aptitude of the three sons and would be the one who would derive the greatest benefits from the educational opportunities in Debrecen. The Goldbergers, like so many Hungarian-Jewish families in that era, clearly placed a great emphasis on education as a means to advance the family's fortunes and status. The result was that from the age of five Sándor lived most of the time with his grandparents and had only infrequent contact with his parents and brothers, since he was able to visit Csap only during school vacations.

Sándor Goldberger attended and graduated from a primary school in Debrecen and presumably performed well enough on the entrance examination to enroll, probably in 1904, in one of the city's secondary schools. Hungarian gymnasiums of that era offered a strict and demanding curriculum that emphasized the humanities, especially classical literature and history. Almost nothing is known of Sándor's life during the eight years he attended the gymnasium. He apparently took some interest in the workers movement at the urging of his grandfather and an uncle, who were active in the railroad and machinist unions. He attended some union meetings, and as a ten-year-old experienced one of the most impressive workers' protests of the pre-war era, the Hungarian rail-workers' strike of 1904.[11] But, so he later admitted, as a teenager he eventually lost interest in "these questions."[12] He apparently had no contact with the Social Democratic Party in Debrecen, and in fact showed no real interest in political affairs.

When he graduated from the gymnasium, probably in 1912, Sándor Goldberger could with justification feel that, despite his humble origins in a poor, Jewish family, he was now poised to embark on a professional career and make the great social leap into the bourgeoisie. Yet Goldberger, like many of his Jewish contemporaries, may also have noticed that legal equality for Jews had not insured their social acceptability. As events would later demonstrate, a strong current of popular anti-Semitism remained just below the surface. For many Christian Hungarians the parvenu Jews, even though they were fully assimilated, spoke excellent Hungarian, and strongly supported the national cause, could never really be accepted as authentic Magyars. They remained the easily identifiable "other," Magyar Jews but not truly Magyars.[13] Some Hungarian Jews sought to overcome this final obstacle by more drastic methods of erasing evidence of their Jewish origins. Before 1914 thousands of Hungarian Jews legally dropped their Jewish-sounding names and chose new Magyar names that they believed would reflect their personal metamorphosis into Hungarian patriots. Although "Goldberger" would have been instantly recognized by Hungarian Christians and Jews alike as a Jewish name, Sándor chose not to abandon it at this point. Perhaps he correctly sensed that such name changes did not fool the anti-Semites, as some of his contemporaries who later became important leaders of the Communist movement were to discover.[14]

After pondering the various career opportunities available to him, Sándor Goldberger decided he would become a lawyer. Since the University of Debrecen at that time had no law school, in 1913 he enrolled instead in the Law College at the University of Kolozsvár in Transylvania, some one hundred miles from Debrecen. He thus unconsciously followed the path of another Hungarian who later became a prominent Communist, Béla Kun, who had begun his legal studies in Kolozsvár ten years earlier.[15] However, he quickly realized that he could not afford the expense of actually attending classes in Kolozsvár. So he remained in Debrecen, presumably read law books on his own, and returned to Kolozsvár only when he was required to take an examination. To support himself he took an office job (perhaps provided by one of his uncles) and for a time taught classes in the lower grades of a gymnasium in Debrecen.[16]

By June 1914, Goldberger had completed three semesters of law school in this somewhat haphazard manner. The outbreak of war changed everything. Like hundreds of thousands of other men of his generation, he was immediately drafted into the Austro-Hungarian army, where he received several months of training as an infantry soldier. In his later memoirs Goldberger passed quickly over his participation in the Great War and revealed almost nothing about his own attitude toward that conflict. It may well be, however, that like many assimilated or partially assimilated Hungarian Jews he welcomed the war with some enthusiasm, seeing it as an opportunity to demonstrate his patriotism and to strike a blow against the Russian Empire, the bastion of anti-Semitism.[17]

By early 1915, the Austro-Hungarian military leadership realized that the war would not, as at first anticipated, end after just a few months with a glorious victory. In the rush to replace heavy losses in the opening campaigns, any recruit who had graduated from the gymnasium and knew some German was almost certain to be selected for officer training. Because many Jewish conscripts had these qualifications, the number of Jewish reserve officers rapidly increased. In this way, Sándor Goldberger was chosen for officer training and early in 1915 became a reserve infantry officer at the rank of lieutenant. That he was placed in the infantry was somewhat unusual: most Jewish officers were given assignments in the artillery, medical corps, or military administration.[18]

Goldberger was assigned to the Italian front, where he remained, except for a few short furloughs, for the duration of the war. The sparse surviving records that relate to Hungarian officers in the Great War reveal nothing remarkable about Goldberger's service, save that he was among the few fortunate officers to survive the four years of carnage. His apparent ability to avoid injury during enemy artillery attacks seemed to convince the soldiers under his command that he led a charmed life. Thus, in defiance of military practice and common sense, they attempted to cluster around him when such attacks occurred.[19]

Although the horrors and absurdities of the war no doubt had their impact on Sándor Goldberger, there is no evidence that during the conflict he was so radicalized by his experiences that he was ever inclined to shirk his duty or be insubordinate. Goldberger later told a Communist colleague that toward the end of the war, as the army was disintegrating, he had defiantly tossed his medals at his superior officer.[20] But this was a lie, perhaps invented by Goldberger to tell to fellow Communists who might otherwise have queried why he had loyally served as an officer to the bitter end of the imperialist war. In fact, Austro-Hungarian military records show that in early October 1918, just a month before the armistice, Goldberger was granted an unusual two-and-a-half month furlough so that he could resume his legal studies. Only an officer with an unblemished record would have received such an extended furlough at such a critical time in the war.[21]

Goldberger planned to resume his law studies not in Kolozsvár but at the newly established Law College in Debrecen. He found, however, that the city was experiencing severe social and political upheaval and that many of his former friends and classmates were involved in anti-war movements. He may also have been shocked to discover that there had been a notable resurgence of a virulent anti-Semitism on the home front. Goldberger is unlikely to have experienced outright prejudice against Jews in the Austro-Hungarian Army.

But among civilians, as the hopes of victory were diminishing, Jews were being widely accused of cowardice, war profiteering, and a general undermining of the war effort. Perhaps it was under the impetus of this discovery that a previously suppressed inclination toward political radicalism appeared. This would explain why Goldberger abruptly decided to abandon his studies and join his friends in their anti-war activities. Within weeks, however, the war was over and Goldberger continued on to Csap to reunite with his mother (his father had died in 1913) and brothers.

In Csap his new tendencies toward radicalism were strengthened by contact with some of the large number of Hungarian soldiers who were temporarily residing in or passing through this vital railway junction. Among them were some of Goldberger's former friends who were now returning from the prisoner of war camps in Russia. They related to Goldberger their experiences in Russia, their faith in Bolshevism, and their conviction that the most important political task for young men like themselves who had fought in the war was to help in building the Hungarian Communist Party.[22] Goldberger must have been highly receptive to their arguments and the lure of Marxist ideology, for, as he later wrote, his "conceptions about everything" now changed and he became a "class conscious fighter."[23] At this point he abandoned all thought of becoming a lawyer. In late October, with four former prisoners of war, he helped organize the first Communist unit in Csap, which immediately affiliated with the Hungarian Communist Party when it was formally established in Budapest in November. He was now prepared to make the advancement of Communism his life's work.

In 1918–19, Sándor Goldberger's band of Communist activists in Ruthenia was small and faced formidable challenges. Yet they had some modest successes. Not unnaturally, the Communists focused at first on the organization of rail workers, and here some inroads were made, perhaps because of Goldberger's previous experiences and useful family connections. The Party managed to gain support and influence "in every department of the railroad center."[24] Whenever troop trains stopped at Csap, Goldberger and his comrades were on the platforms, exhorting the soldiers to join in the workers' strikes and peasant revolts that they anticipated would soon be erupting all across Hungary. Although Hungarian peasants were to prove mostly indifferent or hostile to the Communists, Goldberger was successful in organizing a sit-down strike of farm laborers on a large estate located a few kilometers from Csap.[25]

In a broader sense, however, the Communist Party in Csap and other Ruthenian towns and cities was miniscule when compared with the major political parties. But the situation was transformed in March 1919, when Béla Kun and his collaborators were able to establish a Soviet Republic in Budapest. This gave an immediate, though artificial, boost to the small groups of Communists throughout the country. The Communist Party now gained control of the governing council for Ung County, in which Csap was located, and Goldberger was appointed a member. In Csap he joined eagerly in the far-reaching projects the Communists had for remaking society along Marxist lines.

According to the terms of the Treaty of Trianon, signed in June 1920, Ruthenia was assigned permanently to Czechoslovakia. Sándor Goldberger and his family thereby became citizens of a new state in which Hungarians were a small minority. Many Hungarians regarded the terms of the peace settlement as profoundly unjust and most of those who were transferred to Czechoslovakia or the other so-called Successor States harbored a deep resentment against those responsible for destroying the "thousand year kingdom of Hungary." However, for Sándor Goldberger and other Hungarian Jews this seemed for the most part a favorable development. The new Hungary, greatly reduced in size and population, was no longer a safe haven for Jews. Many Hungarians, outraged by the excesses of Béla Kun's Soviet Republic, had come to believe that Bolshevism was "a purely Jewish product."[26] In late 1919 and early 1920, detachments of military officers traveled freely throughout Hungary in a campaign to punish those who had participated in (or merely sympathized with) the Communist regime. The result was what came to be called the "White Terror," a series of atrocities that resulted in the execution of hundreds and the arrest and torture of thousands, most of them Jews. The regime that emerged in Hungary after defeat in war, political turmoil, and the traumatic peace settlement was guided by a program of anti-Communism, anti-Semitism, and a fervent nationalism.[27]

Had he remained a citizen of Hungary, Sándor Goldberger might well have been imprisoned, or even executed, during the "White Terror." In fact, one of his uncles who lived in Debrecen was arrested and briefly incarcerated by one of the officer detachments after the fall of the Communist regime.[28] But Czechoslovakia was a democratic state in which the Jews could expect a degree of tolerance and protection from outbursts of anti-Semitism. Furthermore, in Czechoslovakia, unlike Hungary, the Communist Party was legal and its members could operate openly. Goldberger was thus able to continue his work as a Communist activist, though now as a member of the Czechoslovak Communist Party. The fact that he had no ability to communicate in Slovak was not a serious handicap, since the Communist Party in Ruthenia was largely dominated by Hungarian Jews.[29]

From 1919 to 1921 Goldberger continued his Party work in and around Csap. He apparently had no regular job, so he must have relied on assistance from his family and the meager salary the Communist Party would have provided. He worked mainly among peasants, agricultural workers, railroad workers, and common laborers. At one point he and some comrades attempted to organize a strike among ditch diggers. However, according to Goldberger's later account, the strike was "broken by terror" and he and the strike leaders were arrested and spent several days in prison.[30] This would be the only time in his career as a professional Communist that Goldberger was ever arrested for participating in a public protest or social agitation. In Csap and its environs he also involved himself in efforts to organize youth and workers, serving for a time as head of the Communist Boy Scouts.

In 1921 the Party, wishing to take advantage of Goldberger's brief legal training, transferred him from Csap to Uzhhorod (Ungvár) to work as the assistant to the Party's attorney. When that attorney was arrested and had to spend time in jail, Goldberger served as his replacement.[31] In the early 1920s, the Communist Party continued its local electoral successes in the towns and small cities of Ruthenia. In Uzhhorod they captured a majority of delegates on the municipal council, and Goldberger was appointed the Party representative on one of the municipal committees. His stature in the Party was confirmed when, in 1923, he was appointed chairman of the Control Committee and a member of the executive committee of the Uzhhorod district.

In 1923, at the age of twenty-nine, Sándor Goldberger had thus achieved some prominence in the Communist Party of Ruthenia, but he must not have been optimistic about his long-term prospects in the area. Late in 1923 he (along with his mother and older brother) applied for a visa to emigrate to the United States. Goldberger's reasons for making this fateful decision remain unclear. In one later account he maintained that the Czechoslovak CP sent him to carry out Party work in America.[32] It is more probable, however, that Goldberger decided on his own to emigrate, and the Party had no objection. Perhaps he had aspirations as a professional Communist that could not be fulfilled in Ruthenia, which after all was one of the most remote provinces of Eastern Europe. Shortly after his political conversion to Communism in 1918 he had begun a diligent course of independent study of the classic works of Marxism, which he read in Hungarian and German. He focused on Marx, Engels, and the collected works of Lenin.[33] By 1923 his knowledge of Marxist and Communist theory was perhaps superior to any of his comrades in Uzhhorod. It was he who organized and led the first Marxist "study circle" there.

Other considerations might also have played a part in Goldberger's decision. Perhaps he sensed that in Czechoslovakia or Hungary he would always be thought of as a Jew and would suffer from the virulent anti-Semitism that had taken root and was spreading throughout Eastern Europe. Emigration would offer a way to escape from the prejudices of the Old World and forge a new identity as a Communist in the New World. He must also have received encouragement from his older brother, József, who, for his own personal reasons, had emigrated to the United States in 1921. There he had found a job and no doubt reported back to his family in favorable terms about life in America. He had been able to save enough money so that he could offer to pay for the required rail and ocean liner tickets that would enable his family in Csap to join him in the New World. This provided the final impetus that led to the application for visas that was sent to the American consulate in Prague. Procuring such visas had become very difficult after World War I, since the quotas for citizens in East European countries who wished to emigrate to America had been drastically reduced. In addition, the American consulate in Prague seemed particularly reluctant to grant visas to Jews, who were thought likely to "become public charges through an aversion to work."[34] In his visa application and subsequent immigration documents, Sándor Goldberger thus concealed his Jewish origins and identified himself as a medical doctor.[35] This ploy was based on the accurate assumption that the U.S. immigration authorities gave a preference to applicants who were professionals with advanced degrees. It must have worked, for on November 1, 1923, the Goldbergers' application was approved and they began the preparations to embark on their great journey in February of the following year.

One of the most puzzling events in the life of Sándor Goldberger occurred on December 1, 1923. On that date in the city of Uzhhorod he married a woman by the name of Francuska Amersak. There is no reference to this marriage in his later memoirs, and his wife did not accompany him on the voyage to America. Furthermore, upon arrival at Ellis Island, Goldberger declared himself to be unmarried. Thereafter he never mentioned to his American friends that he was married, and his wife never joined him in the United States. Perhaps she was unable to obtain an immigration visa, or for some reason Goldberger discouraged her by failing to provide the funds to pay for her ticket. This episode remains a mystery, and in fact the existence of Francuska Amersak would have been unknown had Goldberger, as Alexander Stevens, not traveled to Reno, Nevada, in 1942 in order to obtain a legal divorce from her so that he could marry another woman.

The Goldbergers shared the passage across the Atlantic Ocean with other emigrants, many of them Jews from Poland, Hungary, Czechoslovakia, and Romania. They arrived at Ellis Island on February 10, 1924. At this point many immigrants were filled with anxiety, fearful that at the last moment they would be rejected by customs officials for some reason, such as poor health, and would be forced to return to Europe. In supplying information for the ship manifest, Goldberger gave assurances that he, his mother, and brother were in the best of health. He again declared himself to be a medical doctor, and under the category of "race" suggested that the family was Hungarian. The hard-nosed customs officials at Ellis Island must have been used to this sort of prevarication by newly arrived immigrants. On the ship's manifest the word "Hungarian" was crossed out by hand and replaced with the word "Hebrew." There seemed no way for the Goldberger family to hide their Jewish origins. Sándor's credentials as a physician must also have been challenged, for the word "medical doctor" was crossed out and the word "lawyer" added. Perhaps he explained his way out of this difficulty by suggesting that there had been a misunderstanding. His title of "Doctor" referred to the doctorate he had earned not in medical, but in legal, studies.[36] If so, this would not be the only time during his sojourn in the United States that Sándor Goldberger would succeed in confounding the American authorities

Upon his arrival in New York, Sándor Goldberger knew little or no English. He realized, however, that to succeed as a Communist functionary in the United States he must learn English as rapidly as possible. Following the example of other Communist Hungarian immigrants, Goldberger enrolled in one of the many night schools offering intensive English language study. Equally important was the problem of finding a job that would enable him to begin to pay for the rent and food that in the beginning were provided by his brother József. Sándor Goldberger had few marketable skills. His rudimentary expertise in legal studies was of no value, especially since he could not communicate in English. On the other hand, he had no real training or experience as a craftsman or laborer. Fortunately, his brother managed to procure for him a job in the toy factory where he had been employed since his arrival in 1921. For his first eight months in America, Goldberger thus spent his work days painting faces on toy dolls.[37]

Sándor Goldberger had no intention of ever returning to Czechoslovakia or Hungary, so he wasted no time in beginning the process of becoming an American citizen. On February 16, just six days after his arrival, he declared his intention to seek naturalization by filing the "first papers" at the Supreme Court of New York County.[38] Goldberger also quickly introduced himself at the Yorkville branch of the Hungarian Federation of the Workers Party and requested a membership transfer from the Czechoslovak Party. His new comrades apparently found Goldberger to be a convivial fellow, eager to relate (although sometimes exaggerate) his exploits at the time of the Hungarian Soviet Republic.[39] Although he surely did not speak of his Jewish origins, the Hungarian Communists of Yorkville instantly identified him as such on the basis of his name, accent, and appearance. In later years, when asked about their former comrade by government agents or the media, they almost invariably began by noting that he was a Hungarian Jew. This was done casually and without malice or hint of anti-Semitism; after all, the majority of the Hungarian Communist activists in the United States were themselves of a Jewish background.

Twenty-nine years old at the time of his arrival in the United States, Sándor Goldberger did not have a commanding physical presence. He was five feet, four inches tall, with a dark complexion and black, bushy hair. He was not exactly fat, but he had a round face and a "pair of nice little fat hands." And his weight, centered in the lower part of his body, "seemed to be out of proportion to his height."[40] An American friend later described him as "built like a fire hydrant."[41] In general, Goldberger's affability and dedication made a good initial impression on his new colleagues. He was a "quiet and serious talker," did not smoke, drank alcohol in moderation, and had a calm demeanor. Moreover, his education and knowledge of Communist theory surpassed that of most of the current members of the Hungarian Federation. He was thus regarded as something of an intellectual, although he was careful not to emphasize his relatively advanced educational background.[42]

For eight months Goldberger dutifully attended meetings at the Yorkville branch and continued his efforts to gain a basic mastery of English. Amid the marvels, luxuries, and curiosities of the metropolis, he led a simple, even primitive, life in these early days. He later recalled the typical apartment, small, dingy, and bereft of furniture, in which members of the Hungarian Federation lived: "a narrow iron bed with iron wire box springs; one chair, and on it . . . a pitcher of water in a wash basin."[43] Goldberger realized that millions of workers and their families lived in such inadequate apartments and received wages that would never allow them to escape poverty. He was determined to work diligently as a Communist to promote the revolution that he firmly believed would liberate these workers.

Late in 1924, the leaders of the Hungarian Federation determined that Goldberger was ready to join them as a full-time functionary in the Workers Party. In the various language sections of the American Communist movement it was customary for those experiencing this "rite of passage" to choose a new name. The adoption of an alias, usually a generic, English-sounding name, was considered necessary to thwart police surveillance and to demonstrate that the individual was making a full break from his past life in the Old World and joining other comrades to advance the goals of the Communist Party in the United States. Many Hungarian émigrés followed a simple formula: they chose new first and last names that had the same initials as their original name. For example, József Pogány, who arrived in 1921 and soon was playing an important role in the leadership of the Workers Party, chose the name John Pepper.[44] However, in adopting the name József Péter, Sándor Goldberger did not follow this pattern. Péter (pronounced Pay-ter in Hungarian) could pass as either Hungarian or English. To American colleagues who would work with him in the future he would be known as Joe Peter, or, to friends, simply as "Pete." József Péter was probably relieved to rid himself of the name Sándor Goldberger, with its constant reminder of his Jewish origins. From this point he rarely found it necessary to use his former name, and most of his future comrades in the Communist movement would be unaware that he had once been called Goldberger.

In November 1924, József Péter was instructed to quit his job in the toy factory and was sent to Chicago, which he was to use as a base to travel throughout the Midwest and attempt to sell subscriptions to the Hungarian Communist newspaper, *Új Előre*, and agitate among Hungarian-speaking workers. For nine months he visited and revisited mineworkers in Southern Illinois, steelworkers in Gary, automobile workers in South Bend and Detroit, and factory workers in St. Louis.[45] There is no evidence that Péter had much success, at least when measured by the number of workers who agreed to become dues-paying members of the Hungarian Federation or took out subscriptions to the *Új Előre*. In fact, national membership in the Hungarian Federation, which peaked at a total of 550 in 1925, steadily declined for the rest of the decade and bottomed out at 205 in 1929.[46] Most of that membership was concentrated in Cleveland and New York.

At the very outset of his career, József Péter was thus confronted with a harsh reality, which as a dedicated and idealistic Communist he would never be able to understand or accept: the Communist movement had little appeal to most Hungarian American workers, let alone to those who hoped to make their way into the middle class. Whether because of devotion to their church, Hungarian patriotism, loyalty to their new homeland, or belief that their children would benefit from the "American dream" even though they themselves had to endure hardship, most Hungarian Americans remained indifferent if not hostile to those who were advocating the overthrow of the American government and a radical reordering of society. For many workers, the *Új Előre* was thus at best a curiosity, at worst a despicable, atheistic rag. Of course, Péter was perceptive enough to notice that the workers were not responding favorably to the message he was bringing. He probably rationalized this by concluding that the workers simply did not know what was in their best interests. History was on the side of the Communists. Eventually, the greed of the bourgeoisie and the oppressive and terrorist policies of the capitalists would become so unbearable that the workers would finally agree that the only solution was a violent revolution guided by the Communist Party.

During his sojourn in the Midwest, Péter gained a greater insight into the nature and practices of the Workers Party, which was at the time headquartered in Chicago. In August 1925 he attended the Fourth National Congress, which decided on important changes in the structure of the Party. Of greatest significance to Péter and his colleagues in the Hungarian Federation was the decision that the language federations would be turned into sections (later called bureaus) that would be much more fully integrated into the Party and would be closely supervised by the Central Committee. The Party leadership had become greatly concerned that the language federations, which in the mid-1920s comprised 86 percent of the Party's membership, had become too independent, prone to factionalism, and unwilling to break out of their linguistic insularity.[47] Shortly after the congress, Péter was recalled to New York so that he could participate in the refashioning of the Hungarian Section and join the editorial board of the *Új Előre*.[48]

The common assumption of the leaders of the CPUSA that factionalism was endemic to the language groups was certainly true of the Hungarian Federation, for Hungarian Communist émigrés, whether in Moscow, Berlin, New York, or Cleveland seemed unusually prone to the dreaded Communist sin of factionalism. Shortly after his arrival in 1924, Péter had noted that the two feuding camps were the "veterans," many of whom were former Social Democrats, and the "greenhorns" or "1919ers," whose world view was shaped by the Great War and the revolutions in Russia and Hungary. As a newcomer, Péter naturally gravitated toward the latter camp, for which he soon became the chief spokesman. Despite warnings from the Party's Central Committee, the factional struggle in the Hungarian Section persisted and even intensified. In early December 1926, William Weinstone, who had been appointed by the Central Committee to investigate the factional struggle, gave his support to the group headed by Péter, who shortly thereafter was named national secretary of what was now called the Hungarian Bureau.[49] He was to remain in this position until 1929, during which time he guided the Hungarian Bureau through renewed bouts of factionalism and ingratiated himself with the national leadership of the Party.

During his tenure as secretary of the Hungarian Bureau, Péter developed an effective leadership style that would gain him the admiration of many who would work with him during his career in the CPUSA. He proved to be a diligent and hardworking administrator, who was very devoted to the cause and never allowed his personal life to interfere with his Party work. He placed heavy demands on his subordinates, but had a knack for treating them with tact and encouragement. He had a "smooth manner in giving assignments in which he would suggest that things need to be done rather than rudely ordering them to be done."[50]

One of Péter's major objectives as secretary of the Hungarian Section was to enhance the image of the Party among Hungarian-American workers and to gain legitimacy for the Communist Party by engaging in some collaborative actions with other moderate and left-wing organizations in a united front against Horthy's Hungary. This was a formidable task, given the fact that the *Új Előre* had a poor reputation among Hungarian moderates and routinely contained personal invectives and vile accusations aimed at a whole range of individuals and groups on the left. As a result, leaders of more moderate left-wing Hungarian parties had nothing but scorn for the *Új Előre*, which they believed had "no serious following . . . [in New York] and even less in the countryside."[51] Against all odds, however, Péter and his comrades in the Hungarian Bureau did have one notable success in supporting the creation of a united front. In 1927, the Hungarian Communists joined other "anti-fascist elements" in forming the "Anti-Horthy League," which sought to alert Americans to the evils of the Horthy regime. It was perhaps the first anti-fascist front group organized in the United

States. As Péter reported at the time, the "nominal leaders" of the league were "artists, several editors, liberals," and other respected leaders in the Hungarian American community, but Hungarian Communists were the guiding force.[52] Péter and his colleagues were responsible for the most sensational demonstration organized by the Anti-Horthy League.

A number of nationalistic Hungarian American groups, in cooperation with the Hungarian government, began plans in 1927 to erect a statue of Lajos Kossuth in New York City. These groups asserted that no city with a Hungarian community as large as that of New York should be without a memorial to the great Hungarian statesman and national hero. From the start, the writers of *Új Előre* condemned this plan as a way of strengthening the Horthy regime by stoking the fires of chauvinism and treaty revisionism. The Anti-Horthy League held a series of rallies and demonstrations to protest the plans of the "Horthyites." The official ceremony dedicating the statue in March 1928 was disrupted by an event that Péter later recalled with great pride and delight in his memoir: "All the sidewalks were thronged with comrades and anti-fascists who were demonstrating against fascism. The ceremony of the unveiling of the statue had hardly begun when leaflets showered down on the ceremony from a low-flying airplane, which had been rented by the Hungarian Bureau and had taken off from the Jersey side of the river. Hugó Gellért, the famous painter, dispersed thousands of leaflets from the plane. For the press this was a sensation: they wrote not about the unveiling of the statue, but what had happened with the airplane."[53] The event was recounted in great detail in triumphal articles in *Új Előre* over the following several days, and even the *New York Times* noted the disturbance.[54]

During his tenure as secretary of the Hungarian Bureau, Péter also joined in all the activities expected of a Communist activist. He walked the picket lines of many strikes, attended countless rallies, and gave talks or engaged in debates on a range of topics before any Hungarian American group or club that would welcome him. His oratory was at times effective. After one lecture on the evils of Trotskyism, Péter was approached by a member of the audience who congratulated him on the persuasiveness of his thesis: "Never before have I heard such a convincing analysis of the meaning of Trotskyism." The speaker was none other than Béla Lugosi, who would in a few years gain fame as a Hollywood film star. Péter believed that it was his influence that made Lugosi a life-long sympathizer of the Communist Party.[55]

Péter's responsibilities as an editor and journalist for the newspaper of the Hungarian Federation also occupied much of his time from 1926 to 1929. His lack of any experience in working a newspaper turned out to be no great handicap, since few on the board of editors had any training as journalists, and most in fact had only a meager education. As a result, the *Új Előre* was an amateurish publication, filled with Communist jargon and grammatical lapses. The main purpose of *Új Előre* was, as one editor later admitted, "not the dissemination of news but agitation and propaganda."[56] Readers of the newspaper were provided, in issue after issue, with sensational and repetitive stories about the horrors of capitalism and fascism (especially in Hungary and the United States), the constant threat of political terror and oppression in all countries of the world except the Soviet Union, and the misery and suffering of Hungarian American workers. József Péter, of course, shared this view of world affairs and undertook his new assignment as a journalist with enthusiasm, determined to answer Lenin's call for a Communist press that would aid in Bolshevizing the masses.[57]

Although one of his colleagues would later remark that "he never made any mark as a writer,"[58] Péter in fact was one of the few journalists on the *Új Előre* who developed a degree of sophistication and creativity. Of course, he had to hew closely to the Party line as dictated by the Comintern, and to avoid fiery, revolutionary rhetoric that might catch the attention of the police or FBI. In time Péter developed a distinctive staccato writing style, characterized by a succession of short, sometimes one-word, sentences. Careful readers of the *Új Előre* were able to identify pieces written by Péter even when they were unsigned.[59] Most of what he wrote was a formulaic rehashing of the Communist Party "line" as revealed in the *Daily Worker*, but some of Péter's favorite themes and topics did show some originality. He did his best to try to demonstrate to Hungarian immigrants that their image of America as a land of opportunity, democracy, and social mobility was sadly mistaken. The "real America," he argued, was a place of grinding poverty, hopelessness, police oppression, and discrimination. Péter developed this theme in many articles that reflected a sincere empathy for impoverished Americans. For example, each year at Christmas time he published an essay that described how the holiday season aggravated the misery of the poor and revealed the arrogance and social irresponsibility of the capitalists and the bourgeoisie. In 1926, he observed that at a time when Wall Street newspapers were announcing the arrival of an age of prosperity for all Americans, the truth could be found if one took a Christmas stroll through the slums of New York. There one encountered pervasive destitution, poorly nourished and clothed children, rampant prostitution, and "mountains of garbage in front of each tenement."[60]

In August 1926, József Péter began to write a weekly column, "Ma" (Today), for the *Új Előre*. This gave him the opportunity to choose the topics he would explore and to further develop some of his favorite themes and personal concerns. In his columns Péter emphasized again and again that the duplicity and greed of American capitalists and the bourgeoisie would ensure that the wretched workers would never benefit properly from their hard work and improve their lot. Péter could find capitalist plots in the most unlikely places. When newspapers reported on the work of a scientist who was studying the possibility of eliminating the need for humans to sleep, Péter declared that the obvious purpose of this research was to find a way to lengthen the work day of the workers.[61]

The picture that emerges from the journalistic efforts of József Péter is that of a rigid and doctrinaire Communist. Yet there are hints in his writings that he at least realized that ordinary Americans, even some who were generally sympathetic to the Communist movement, found many of the Party positions very difficult to accept. In the interwar period, American Communists unflinchingly praised the Soviet Union as a land of real freedom and true democracy. At the same time, of course, the United States was denounced as a country of terror and oppression. In 1928, after a visit to Russia that will be described below, Péter gave a lecture tour in which he extolled the virtues of the new Soviet Russia, a true workers' paradise. More than once, apparently, members of his audience seemed puzzled about the sharp contrast he described between the country in which they lived and the Soviet utopia. On one occasion in Philadelphia a voice from the crowd asked: "But there is democracy in America too, isn't there?" Péter immediately "set the record straight." Yes, technically workers had the right to vote, but the two major parties were indistinguishable in their policies: unemployment remained high no matter which one was in power. Furthermore, unemployment (or its looming threat) taught the workers "that they can hold no political opinion than those of their bosses."[62]

József Péter's three-year stint as a journalist and editor of the *Új Előre* gave him a certain prominence among the small band of Communists in the Hungarian-American community, but it was unlikely to enhance his prospects for advancement in the hierarchy of the national party. No one in the national leadership of the Party could become familiar with Péter through his articles and column, which were all written in Hungarian. If József Péter was to make his mark in the American Communist movement, it would have to be on the basis of his dealings with Party leaders in his capacity as secretary of the Hungarian Section. In fact, one of Péter's first initiatives after assuming that position early in 1927 was to have a major impact not only on the Hungarian Section but on the national party as well.

For some time the *Daily Worker* had been experiencing severe financial difficulties, in large part because it did not operate its own printing plant. Péter was the first to come up with a creative solution that eventually solved the problem and helped the paper avoid bankruptcy. After winning over the Hungarian Bureau to his idea, he proposed to the Central Committee that the *Daily Worker* should share the printing press used by the *Új Előre* in a condominium that other ethnic Communist newspapers in New York might join.[63] The Central Committee approved this idea, and Péter was assigned to "reorganize the printing shop so that the *Daily Worker* and the other Party papers could be centralized in one printing plant."[64] In May 1928, the Party announced the opening of the new building on Union Square, which would house not only the combined printing press but the national headquarters of the Party as well.[65]

Péter's role in the financial rescue of the *Daily Worker* was of course much appreciated by the Party leadership, though less so by some of his colleagues in the Hungarian Bureau, who complained that Péter had signed over the assets of the *Új Előre* to a "new dummy corporation" controlled by the Party and saddled the Hungarian Bureau with a "fantastic mortgage" that it could never repay. They expressed their consternation to members of the Party's Central Committee, but were rebuffed. The Party secretary, Jay Lovestone, pointed out that Péter had acted properly and praised this "voluntary action by our generous Hungarian colleagues."[66] As a result of his creative solution to the financial problems of the *Daily Worker*, Péter found that his stature in the national Party was greatly enhanced and new opportunities were open to him. At the Fifth Congress of the Party in August 1927, with the support of Lovestone and his faction, he was elected an alternate member of the Central Committee.[67] In his capacity as manager of the joint print shop, Péter continued to address financial problems that occurred from time to time at the *Daily Worker* with clever "bookkeeping transactions."[68] Because of his close association with the Party newspaper, Péter came to know several individuals who would play important roles in his later career, including Earl Browder and Whittaker Chambers.

During this period Péter continued to live a simple and frugal life style, his sole luxury being frequent meals at one of the Hungarian restaurants on New York's Upper East Side. His whole life, both public and private, revolved around the Party. His only recreation seems to have been reading mystery novels, for which he developed a real passion. The salary he received was $35 a week, roughly comparable to what auto workers were making at the time. But Party salaries were not always paid on time and, at certain times of financial stringency, not at all. Moreover, a functionary was expected to give generously to all the Party fund drives. Thus, whenever the *Új Előre* had one of its frequent crises and faced imminent bankruptcy, Péter had to set an example by making large donations. A list of contributors during one such crisis in October 1929 shows Péter giving an entire week's salary of $35. That same list of contributors contains the name of Lilly Szirtes, a Party worker who gave half of her weekly salary.[69] At some point in the last half of the 1920s, Péter began to live together with Lilly Szirtes in a common-law marriage. Their combined income ensured that they would be able to avoid the kind of severe poverty about which Péter often wrote in his newspaper column.

Since he was now in the good graces of the majority faction in the CPUSA leadership, the Lovestone group, Péter sought to obtain another, highly desirable reward: the opportunity to attend the Sixth World Congress of the Communist International, held during the summer of 1928. He applied for and was granted a three-month leave of absence in order to travel to Russia and attend the congress as a representative of the *Új Előre*. He departed on June 19, using a legal reentry visa under the name Alexander Goldberger.[70] There are no records directly documenting Péter's activities in the U.S.S.R., and he did not describe his visit in his memoir. But on the basis of his lectures and articles upon his return to the United States, it appears that in addition to attending the congress he also toured factories and various Soviet institutions in and near Moscow. Clearly he was elated by the experience and felt confirmed in his faith that the Soviet Union was on its way to becoming a workers' paradise. From September to December 1928, Péter went on a speaking tour to describe to Hungarian-Americans the glories of the "homeland of socialism." He crisscrossed the Midwestern states and appeared also in Montreal and Toronto. In these lectures and in articles in the *Új Előre* he scoffed at reports in the "bourgeois press" about terror or oppression in Soviet Russia. It was true, he admitted, that firm action was taken against those who organized against the "power of the peasants and workers" and plotted to restore the tsarist regime. But that was "justified state-sanctioned violence."[71]

Although it did not begin auspiciously, the year 1929 was to represent a major turning point in József Péter's career as a Communist activist. Given the viciousness of the infighting that had bedeviled the Hungarian Bureau throughout the 1920s, it is perhaps not surprising that eventually a group of his comrades would turn against Péter. Early in 1929, the spokesman for the dissidents sent Jay Lovestone a long letter in which he complained of a leadership crisis in the Hungarian Bureau and outlined a "series of right[-wing] mistakes" committed by "the comrades associated with comrade Péter." The only solution, he asserted, was for Péter to be replaced as secretary.[72]

Lovestone was not inclined to turn against his staunchest ally in the Hungarian Bureau, but his own position as the national secretary of the Party had become increasingly parlous. By late 1928, Lovestone's faction was under increasing attack from the minority group led by William Foster, Earl Browder, and William Weinstone. Lovestone managed for a time to sustain his position, but when he traveled to Moscow in the spring of 1929 he discovered that a major ideological shift leftward was being orchestrated by the Soviet leadership. Lovestone and his closest followers now found themselves under attack for their alleged right-wing tendencies. When Lovestone tried to defend himself, he was personally and publicly denounced by Joseph Stalin. With full support now from the Comintern, the minority faction in the CPUSA gained the upper hand and, in June 1929, expelled the "Lovestonites" from the Party.[73]

For József Péter this turn of events was indeed threatening. Although he had always been careful in his ideological utterances, he was well known in the Party as a supporter of Lovestone. In the spring of 1929 Péter thus faced a bleak future, with the distinct possibility that he might also be expelled from the Party. How could he maneuver himself out of this predicament? A few Hungarian American Communists in similar circumstances chose simply to leave the Communist movement. They could contemplate a life outside the Party because they were American citizens. But Péter was an alien who was subject at any time to deportation, perhaps to Hungary, where he would likely be dealt with harshly because of his Communist activities in 1918–19.

It was probably this consideration that reminded Péter that he had not followed up on his initial application for naturalization. The five-year waiting period had nearly expired when, in mid-June 1929, he submitted his formal petition for citizenship. But his negligence in waiting until the very last moment doomed his application. In late June there was a flood of petitions from aliens who were anxious to begin the process of citizenship before a new naturalization law became effective on July 1. As a result, Péter's petition was not granted a certificate of arrival before the July 1 deadline. It was returned to him with the explanation that, according to the new regulations, he must begin the process again by submitting a "declaration of intent."[74]

One possibility open to Péter in 1929 was to join Lovestone and several hundred other Party members who defied the Comintern, separated (or were expelled) from the Party, and established an independent radical movement that would compete with the CPUSA. Once again Péter's status as an alien made this a problematic choice. The dangers of such a course were emphasized by Max Bedacht, who had been one of the leading Lovestonites but decided to suppress his personal opinions and abide fully with the Comintern decision. At a Party meeting in June 1929, he warned that those who chose to break from the Party on this issue, including such prominent veterans of the CPUSA as Lovestone and Benjamin Gitlow, were acting purely on the basis of "petty bourgeois individualism."[75]

In the circumstances, only one choice seemed available to Péter: he must emulate Bedacht and make a clean break from Lovestone and the other dissidents. Moreover, he would have to act in an open and decisive manner, so that the new, Moscow-sanctioned leadership of the CPUSA would not only overlook his past association with Lovestone but perhaps even reward him for his wise decision. Péter thus issued a public statement, published on the front page of the *Daily Worker,* in which he unreservedly accepted the decision of the Comintern and gave his "full support to the Central Committee fighting against all factionalism" and "for building the mass Communist Party in the United States."[76]

Quite quickly there were signs that Péter had indeed chosen the correct strategy. The new Party leadership was not inclined to discriminate against those from the Lovestone faction who chose to remain within the Party. In fact, the departure of hundreds of Lovestonites was creating a significant staffing problem throughout the Party's bureaucracy. It made sense to fill some of these positions with the most efficient of those former followers of Lovestone who pledged their loyalty to the new leadership. Péter was thus informed that he would remain an alternate candidate to the Central Committee,[77] and that he would in the near future be removed from the Hungarian Bureau and given a new, more important position in the national party. In March 1930, he was named organizational secretary in District 2, which covered the Greater New York City area.[78] From this point to the end of his career in the CPUSA, he was to have only occasional dealings with his former comrades in the Hungarian Bureau.

Nineteen thirty was in some ways a propitious time to take on a responsible post in the CPUSA. The stock market crash in October of the preceding year and the signs of a deepening economic recession suggested to many American Communists that the wheel of history was turning and the capitalist system was beginning its inevitable collapse. This growing conviction that in the near future American workers, led by the Communist Party, would triumph over their oppressors was reflected in numerous Party publications from the period, but particularly in William Z. Foster's *Toward Soviet America*, which posited an imminent civil war in the United States and the establishment of a Soviet dictatorship that would nationalize industry, collectivize agriculture, and eliminate religion and all political parties other than the CPUSA.

As organizational secretary, Joe Peter (as he would be known to his non-Hungarian comrades) was charged with the supervision of the fundamental tasks relating to membership and operation of the CPUSA in District 2, which was the largest by far of the eighteen districts, containing nearly one third of the national membership. This involved such things as recruitment of new members, cadre development, coordination of Party activities, establishing guidelines for the scheduling and running of meetings, drumming up support for rallies and solicitations, and in general exhorting members to become more active and zealous. These were tasks that many in the Party leadership probably preferred to avoid, regarding them as important but exceedingly tedious and generally unappreciated by the rank-and-file members. Yet Peter appeared to revel in organizational work. He did not seem to mind that much of his activity amounted to hectoring and admonishing Party members. It may be true, as Peter later admitted, that as organizational secretary, he was "working in a very bureaucratic way" and did not have "daily contact with the non party workers."[79] Nonetheless, he did participate openly in many mass demonstrations, sometimes leading them. He was known at times even to ride a motorcycle along the streets of Manhattan as part of a procession of the Red Front Fighters, a group based on the model of the German Rotfrontkämpfer that Peter had helped to organize.[80] His activities in this period brought him into contact with a broad range of Party members in New York, as well as the national leadership. This was to prove of great value to him when, in later years, his organizational skills were put to use at the national level.

The numerous organizational bulletins and newsletters that Peter composed in 1930–31 clearly reflected his enthusiasm and dedication to the cause. But in them one also detects some frustration with the shortcomings and apparent apathy of his comrades. CP members in District 2, it seems, were often negligent in their duties, lackadaisical in their attendance at Party-sponsored rallies, and unenthusiastic in their promotion of the *Daily Worker*. The lead article in one of Peter's bulletins nicely encapsulated his approach. With the hectoring title, "WHAT YOU DID NOT DO!" the article listed seven common failures and omissions of Party members. Pointing out that capitalism was collapsing and a Communist victory was imminent, Peter warned that those who refused to give a full commitment to the Party were traitors to the cause and would face "very severe disciplinary measures."[81] The historian is left to wonder whether the stern and pessimistic school master's tone adopted by Peter, combined with his insistence on a kind of "military discipline," was devised to drive already eager and committed Party members to a superhuman effort, or whether many of the workers were as indifferent and negligent as his words suggest.[82]

During his tenure as organizational secretary for District 2, Joe Peter was increasingly perplexed by the failure of the CPUSA to increase its membership substantially as the Depression deepened in the early 1930s. True, new members were being added at a rapid pace in 1930 and 1931, yet overall membership remained fairly static because so many quit or allowed their membership to lapse. Why were the Socialists, whom Peter held in the greatest contempt, able to outdraw the CPUSA at the polls in New York City by a 3-to-1 margin?[83] How could one account for the fact that the Communists seemed unable, for the most part, to take the lead in provoking strikes that won over the workers and proved to be successful? As Earl Browder, the emerging leader of the Party, put it in 1930, "Something must be wrong."[84] The task of devising a strategy for gaining and retaining members was one to which Peter was to devote himself over the coming years.

In 1930 and 1931 the Party had some successes and advances in District 2 for which Joe Peter deserved some credit, but these were infrequent and often proved illusory. It was Peter's conviction that the greatest emphasis should be on building up the "lower units" of the Party, since it was at that level that Party workers had the closest ties with the masses and were able "to become the leader of the workers in the factories, in the streets where they live and of course where they are organized."[85] One such area of success was in organizing unemployed workers who were being evicted from their apartments. One unit in Harlem, a "Negro section," was particularly creative and successful in supporting the unemployed who had been forced out of their apartments.[86] In contrast, attempts to organize factory workers and lead strikes in District 2 proved for the most part fruitless, despite the use of innovative tactics such as "shock troops."[87] In one of his first publications in English in a Party journal, Peter argued that success in shop and factory organization would not come about through "fantastic schemes" or "demonstrative activities." Rather, what was required was "daily plugging," which had to begin with the simple task of gaining the confidence of individual "contacts" in the targeted shop units. He claimed that such methods were bringing "very good results" in the New York District.[88]

Privately, however, Peter later admitted that the CP had not been successful in gaining control of strikes in factories in the New York City area. He attributed this failure in part to the reluctance of the national leadership to take forceful action. It appears that Peter in fact was frequently at odds with the CPUSA leadership's apparent tendency in 1930–31 to refrain from tactics that would thrust the Party too much into the public limelight and perhaps inflame anti-Communist attitudes. His preference was usually for radical measures. In January 1931, there were news reports of starving farmers in a town in Arkansas who had raided stores to procure food for their families. The three-person secretariat of District 2, of which Peter was a member, decided that conditions were ripe to stage a similar raid in New York. The target would be the fruit warehouses on the West Side, which would be stormed by unemployed workers. All the arrangements were made, a time and date were set, but at the last minute the operation was vetoed by the Party's PolBuro. This, in Peter's view, was just another example of how the Party failed to take the lead in a way that would fortify a "connection with the masses."[89]

Peter also did not shy away from the use of force or street violence when the interests of the Party demanded it, although he himself refrained from direct participation. Frustrated by the unimpressive results of efforts to organize factory workers in District 2, he became more and more obsessed with the notion that one of the chief obstacles to success was the enemy's use of provocateurs and spies, or "stool pigeons." Sometimes these "stools" managed to infiltrate the Party, and in one case one was clever enough to advance to the position of unit organizer in District 2. However, some comrades began to suspect him and an investigation revealed that he did not live at the address he had given the Party. Peter's solution to the problem was a blunt one: "Secretly we got two or three comrades together, and one fine evening they got him on the corner and beat the hell out of him, and that settled the spy."[90] On another occasion, when Peter was teaching a class at the National Training School, he came to the conclusion that one of the students was a spy for the New York Police Department. He thereupon gave one of the other students a blackjack and brass knuckles and instructed him to follow the "rat" and give him the "light works," which meant to "beat the hell out of him."[91]

Peter likewise favored a bellicose approach to political rivals, especially the Socialists. Like most Communists at the time, he believed that no purpose would be served by attempting to engage in debates or intellectual exchanges with the "social fascists." Instead, he sought to emulate the tactics of the Communists in Germany, who in the early 1930s engaged in frequent clashes in the streets with their political rivals. Members of the Red Front Fighters, or other Party members deemed suitable for operations involving intimidation or fisticuffs, were used to force confrontations with police or to disrupt meetings of rival political groups. Maurice Malkin, a veteran Communist who in 1928 had been expelled from the Party because of alleged Trotskyite tendencies, was able to rejoin the Party in 1931. He was told to report to Peter at the CPUSA headquarters. As his first assignment, Peter instructed him to mobilize "a sizable squad of labor goons" who were to disrupt a Socialist meeting to be addressed by Norman Thomas. The operation was successful, and Peter praised Malkin for his excellent work: "You have not lost your touch. You are better than ever."[92]

Overall, Peter's energetic organizational efforts in District 2 during his tenure led to few tangible results and many dashed hopes, although much the same can be said of the other districts of the CPUSA in this period. This created a good deal of soul-searching in the Party leadership and increasingly frequent rebukes from the Comintern in Moscow, which criticized the CPUSA for its weak leadership and the failure to build an effective organization to organize the unemployed.[93] In such circumstances, the usual response in Communist parties throughout the world was to engage in a round of intensive and, it was hoped, constructive Bolshevik self-criticism. Accordingly, in March 1931 the PolBuro formed a five-member committee to draw up a report on the strengths and weaknesses of District 2. Three of the five were the members of the secretariat of the New York District, Israel Amter, Rudy Baker, and Peter himself.

The Committee report, completed in late March, seemed to be a strongly worded indictment.[94] The report contained a long list of "grave and serious weaknesses" in District 2. The district's leadership had simply failed to "make the sharp turn to the new methods" that the Central Committee had been advocating. The few activities that had indeed achieved excellent results, such as a series of hunger marches in New York and New Jersey, did not offset or counter-balance "the bad work of the District," which was caused by a "lack of collective leadership" and "weak contact between the District leadership and lower units and fractions."

In the light of such devastating criticism one might imagine that those responsible for what seemed to amount to a crisis of leadership in District 2 would be demoted or shifted to other work. In particular, since many of the supposed failures and weaknesses in the New York District were linked to organizational methods and activities, it might seem that the intention was to make Peter, the organizational secretary, a scapegoat for the lack of success that the CPUSA was having. But apparently there were no further reprimands or recriminations against the leaders of the district and their status in the Party seemed unimpaired. All of this suggests that the severe tone of the "Resolution on the New York District" was designed in part simply to impress Comintern officials with the searching quality of the self-criticism. Of course, it was true that despite the opportunities created by the onset of the Depression, the Communist Party had made little progress in District 2. But this was true in all eighteen districts of the CPUSA, not just in New York. Peter himself seems not to have been too troubled by the stinging criticisms in the report. He did show proper contrition and admitted that he had succumbed to certain "bureaucratic tendencies." However, although he did not want to blame "higher committees" in the Party, he did think it was wrong to try to place the responsibility for the weaknesses of District 2 on just one individual.[95] In any case, Peter continued for the remainder of 1931 to carry out his duties as organizational secretary more or less as in the previous year.

2

The Making of J. Peters,
1931–32

In early 1931, Joe Peter was involved in one significant project that received no mention in the otherwise full committee report on the activity of District 2. In 1920 the Comintern had stipulated, as one of the twenty-one conditions for admission to that international body, that each Communist Party create and maintain a secret or underground apparatus, which was deemed necessary for two major reasons. The secret apparatus was responsible for a range of conspiratorial tasks that the legal Party could not easily perform, such as production of fraudulent passports and other documents, liaison with Soviet and Comintern intelligence agents, development of coded communications, establishment of secret printing presses, and educating Party members on the proper way to handle themselves if under police interrogation or in prison. Secondly, the secret apparatus was responsible for making necessary preparations so that the Party could survive if the government sought to suppress it. For this purpose, an "illegal apparatus" had to be created before any grave emergency so that Party work could continue using previously established clandestine methods. In the mid-1920s, the Commission on Illegal Work of the Comintern drew up an elaborate set of rules and principles for conspiratorial work, which were based primarily on the experiences of Russian and German comrades.[1] The key document, entitled "The Rules for Party Conspiratorial Work," was provided to each of the world's Communist parties. However, there is no trace in the CPUSA records of the arrival of this document, and in fact the American Party, distracted by the bitter factional struggles, gave little attention in the 1920s to the development of an underground apparatus.[2]

In 1929, however, with the factional struggle in the CPUSA ended, the Comintern began to insist once again on the need to create a functioning "illegal apparatus." After many months of procrastination, the Central Committee finally instructed the Organization Department, then headed by Rudy Baker, to work out a plan for the "illegal apparatus," which was to begin to function at once. The plan was to be tried out initially in the New York district, and then applied to the entire country.[3] As organizational secretary for the New York district, Peter was the obvious person to collaborate with Baker in drafting a plan of action.

Since neither Baker nor Peter had been involved in illegal or conspiratorial work before, they relied on the Comintern directive, "The Rules for Party Conspiratorial Work," a copy of which they apparently procured from Boris Mikhailov ("Williams"), who served as the chief Comintern representative in the United States in the early 1930s.[4] The result of their effort was a ten-page report containing a set of instructions that was sent to each CPUSA district on January 2, 1931,[5] with an accompanying letter signed by R.B. (Rudy Baker). In his letter, Baker made it clear that this document on what he called "conspirative work"[6] was highly confidential. District organizers were warned not to keep it in the Party office or at the homes of leading comrades. No copies were to be made, and instructions issued to members concerning the building of the apparatus were to be given verbally and not in written form. Since this involved the "most vital machinery of the Party," district organizers and organizational secretaries were to act with "military promptness and accuracy."

The document itself reflected the urgent tone of Comintern messages over the past several years and the prevailing view in Moscow that, as the economic crisis deepened, capitalist governments would in desperation seek to prevent a revolutionary outbreak by arresting leading Communists and disrupting the normal activity of the Party. District organizers were reminded that if the Party were forced underground, its efforts "must be intensified and no difficulties must be allowed to hinder the Party work." To insure this, however, there had to be a functioning "illegal apparatus" that existed not just on paper but had been tested and would not be foiled by "some act of stupidity or carelessness due to inexperience." The district leaders were instructed to take certain immediate steps that would make it possible for them to escape arrest and to continue to communicate securely and safely with the lower units and national headquarters. These included the establishment of a system of safe houses, creation of an illegal workshop with a mimeograph machine or printing press, and training in the use of coded messages.

The last section of the report dealt with general rules for conspiratorial work. Some of these were quite rudimentary and simplistic. Party members were warned not to gather in large groups in restaurants or other public places and to refrain from reading the *Daily Worker* while riding the bus or subway. Furthermore, they were to avoid wearing "bright neckwear" and "colored hats," as this could raise the suspicion of the police. Comrades were to carry as few documents as possible with them, and be prepared to destroy these documents if they were arrested. As a last resort, the documents were to be eaten, a task that would be made easier by "drinking a little water." Finally, instructions were given on how a Communist must conduct himself if arrested. No confession of any kind was to be made, and the best strategy was to "deny everything." The duty of an arrested Communist was to "put up a defiant aggressive Party attitude" and to "accuse the authorities, the bourgeois state, [and] the capitalist society."

One can imagine that district organizers, already confronting a constant stream of directives from the national headquarters of the CPUSA, were less than enthusiastic about this new plan, with its potentially heavy demands on time, personnel, and resources. Especially in the smaller districts it must have seemed a hopeless task. As a result, district leaders were lukewarm in their response to the call for the creation of an "illegal apparatus," despite Rudy Baker's warning that neglect, delay, or indifference in this matter "will be dealt with most severely by the C.C. [Central Committee]." By the end of 1931 little progress had been made, even in New York, which was to have been the model for other districts. Looking back a year later, Peter admitted that "the New York apparatus was not built properly. We entirely underestimated this face of our task."[7] In fact, when later in the 1930s Peter again took on the responsibility of creating an "illegal apparatus," he found that almost no foundation had been established at the district level. On the other hand, on the basis of the experience of working with Rudy Baker on this project, Peter gained the reputation in the Party as an emerging expert on conspiratorial activity and underground work.

Despite the mixed reviews and meager results of Peter's work as organizational secretary in District 2, he was considered by some in the leadership of the CPUSA, including Earl Browder, to be an energetic and promising cadre. One sign of this confidence in Peter was the opportunity he was given to teach in several Party schools in the early 1930s. In 1930 he was appointed by the Central Committee to teach a course on Political Economy in a training school for Party members of Hungarian descent. One student whom Peter met in these classes, John Lautner, was to become his protégé and in time his closest friend in the Hungarian American community.[8] Peter performed well in the classroom and made a good impression on the trainees. He was also appointed to a committee that was developing a plan for the revamping of the National Training School. On Peter's initiative the school introduced short-term courses for workers who could not spare more time from their jobs. In time he would become a regular teacher of classes on organization and other topics.[9]

In this period, Joe Peter had not only gained the confidence of certain CPUSA leaders but had also established a connection with the Comintern. How this came about remains unclear and undocumented, but most likely Peter came to know Boris Mikhailov while working on the plan for the illegal apparatus. By early 1931, Peter was sufficiently trusted by Comintern officials that he was asked to provide a confidential report on the leadership qualities of William Foster, one of several comrades who were jostling for power in the CPUSA after the ouster of the Lovestone faction in 1929. It was not clear why Peter should have been asked to offer an appraisal of Foster. Perhaps he was directed to comment on all the potential Party leaders, including Browder, Bedacht, Minor, and Weinstone as well, and only Peter's report on Foster has surfaced in the Comintern archives. Peter's only known direct contact with Foster occurred in 1928 when, by chance, they were fellow passengers on an ocean liner making the voyage from Hamburg to New York.[10] Peter nonetheless felt justified in providing a detailed, and generally negative, report. He suggested that Foster was a "poor Marxist," and in fact was really more a syndicalist than a Communist. Peter granted that he was a hard worker, a good speaker, and a "good, simple, modest" comrade who, if properly guided in the areas of theory and organization, could be useful to the Party, but not as the Party leader.[11]

The stage was now set for a development that was to have a major impact on Peter's career in the Party. Since early in 1931, Clarence Hathaway, who was in Moscow as the representative of the CPUSA to the Comintern, had been urging Party leaders to send several competent individuals to serve as trainees in the Anglo-American Secretariat of the Comintern. He pointed out in a letter in March that there was a special need for a trainee, known as a "practicant," who had experience in district work, could research and write reports on political and economic issues, and was a candidate for "leading work" in the future. After a delay of some months, the Central Committee, no doubt on the advice of Browder, selected Joe Peter to send to Moscow to assume the role of "practicant" in the organization area, that is, an "org practicant."[12]

Once he learned of his new assignment, Peter worked quickly to wrap up his work in District 2 and to make his travel plans. For his trip to Russia in 1928 Peter had used his real name, Alexander Goldberger, and had traveled under a legal passport. This time, however, there was a need for more conspiratorial methods. Using a certificate of nationalization obtained from some source within the CPUSA, Peter applied in early October for a passport under the name of Isadore Boorstein, a person who had been born in 1895 and whose physical features resembled those of Peter. The passport was quickly granted, and he was able to depart from New York on October 15 on the SS *Europa*, a new ocean liner that crossed the Atlantic Ocean in just five days. Peter's common-law wife, Lilly Szirtes, did not accompany him. In fact, she had recently left him to live with Rudy Baker, with whom Peter had worked closely over the past two years.[13] This was not particularly noteworthy, for, as a former Party official would later remark, "Party leaders changed their wives sometimes as often as one does an overcoat."[14] Nor, apparently, did Peter hold any sort of grudge against Baker, for jealousy in such a circumstance could easily be seen as clinging to a decadent bourgeois moral code.[15] Peter thus embarked on this new phase of his career unencumbered by personal attachments at home and primed for the new experiences he would have and the new contacts he would make in the U.S.S.R.

After a five-day ocean journey, Peter proceeded by train from Bremen to Berlin, where he obtained the necessary travel documents to enter the Soviet Union. He arrived in Moscow in late October and reported to Clarence Hathaway, the representative of the CPUSA to the ECCI (Executive Committee of the Communist International). Hathaway, who had served as district organizer in New York for a time in 1930, knew Peter well and apparently had a high estimation of his abilities. He gave Peter an introduction to the work he would be expected to perform as org practicant, and informed him that he would serve a three-month term.[16] In fact, Peter's stay in Moscow was later to be extended until June 1932, for reasons that neither Peter nor Hathaway could have anticipated.

Like other foreign Communists who journeyed to Moscow in connection with Comintern work, Peter was given a room in the Hotel Lux. Both at the Lux and at Comintern gatherings, his good speaking knowledge of German, the lingua franca of the Comintern, served him in good stead. During his stay in Moscow Peter was to meet many comrades from all across the globe who had chosen to reside in the Soviet Union and were active in the commissions and departments of the Comintern. There is evidence that while in Moscow Peter had a close personal relationship with, and perhaps for a time shared a room at the Lux, with an American Communist woman, Manya Reiss, whom he had come to know when they were both active in the Organization Department of District 2.[17]

All newly arrived Communists who were assigned to work in the schools or departments of the Comintern were required to fill out a detailed questionnaire and compose a brief autobiography. These documents were then kept in the individual's cadre file, which was carefully maintained by the Control Commission of the Comintern. Peter's questionnaire is notable in part because here, for the first time, he used the name "J. Peters."[18] Why he chose to do so at this point is not clear, and in fact during the remainder of his sojourn in Moscow he signed documents sometimes as "J. Peter" and other times as "J. Peters."

The wording of the autobiographical statement that Peter submitted on January 25, 1932, suggests that he feared that Comintern officials might look askance at some aspects of his life and career.[19] There was the matter of his fours years of service as an officer during the Great War, without any signs of disaffection or rebellion. Peter was careful to explain that he had become an officer not by choice, but because by law "high school graduates will be promoted to reserve officers." And he emphasized that when he was granted a furlough in September 1918, he made the decision not to return again to the front. On his role in the factional struggles of the CPUSA in the 1920s, Peter explained that he was initially inclined to support the Ruthenberg/Lovestone group because of its early attempt to woo American farmers. His experience working with peasants in Hungary and Czechoslovakia had convinced him that "the winning of the farmers" was the correct line. However, when the Comintern later condemned the Lovestone faction, he "did not hesitate for a moment to carry out the decision of the C.I. and carried it out with conviction." Finally, there was the question of his "bureaucratic tendencies," which in Communist rhetoric of the day implied an unwillingness to have direct contact with workers and which had featured as one of the main criticisms of Peter and his colleagues in the Central Committee report on District 2. Peter diligently listed all of the occasions when he did have contact with ordinary workers, including his numerous interactions with peasants in Hungary and Czechoslovakia, his job in a toy factory in New York in 1924, his work among Hungarian workers in the Midwest, and his frequent contact with workers at rallies and demonstrations in District 2.

As it turned out, Peter need not have been concerned that Comintern officials would find fault with his background or career as a Communist activist. In fact, as he would soon learn, officials of one branch of the Comintern were apparently very much interested in and impressed by his credentials. In the meantime, however, Peter set out to learn the routines and requirements of his position as org practicant in the Anglo-American Secretariat. He joined six other trainees, among them the British Communists Tom Bell and Peter Zinkin.[20] The major responsibility of the practicants was to prepare comprehensive papers on issues that were being studied and debated in the Anglo-American Secretariat. In conducting his research and formulating his ideas and proposals, Peter had at his disposal an archive of CPUSA materials, including back and current issues of the *Daily Worker* and other Party publications, as well as minutes of meetings of the Central Committee and PolCom. His first report, dated November 6, was a general overview of organizational problems in the CPUSA.[21] There followed, roughly once a month, studies on the fluctuations of Party membership, the development of cadres, and policies of the CPUSA concerning the war danger and imperialism.[22] From time to time Peter and other practicants presented their reports to Comintern and Soviet government officials. On February 20, 1932, for example, he and Tom Bell spoke before a large audience, which included Vyacheslav Molotov, chairman of the Council of People's Commissars, on "The War Danger and Struggle of American and British Parties against War and Intervention in the Far East."[23]

In the reports he composed as org practicant, which of course were not intended for publication, Peter showed an ability to present material in a clear and cogent manner. His English, though still marred by occasional errors, was certainly adequate to the task. Since his reports were designed to foster discussion and debate among Party leaders in the Anglo-American Secretariat, Peter could discuss certain difficult problems with a degree of realism and without the kind of obfuscation that was often deemed necessary in public Party forums. A recurring theme in these reports was "the immense fluctuation of the membership" of the CPUSA. Peter described the problem in stark terms: "In January 1930, the CP of the USA had over 10,000 registered paying members. Between then and the XIII Plenum of the Party in August 1931 about 12,000 workers joined the Party. However, by the XIII Plenum the number of paying members was less than 10,000 on an average. This means that . . . the Party actually recorded regress, having already lost more members than it had recruited."[24]

Peter was of course not the only member of the Party elite who was perplexed by this problem, which was widely discussed in the CPUSA in this period. In his reports he endeavored to identify the reasons for this dismaying situation. He cited the snobbish attitude of veteran Party members towards newcomers; ineffective and poorly run meetings; the bureaucratic attitude of district leaders; overburdening of new members with too many responsibilities, or, conversely, not trusting them with important tasks; and taxing members with "too many collections for various campaigns, organizations, affairs in their unit." Peter could not imagine, or at least was too prudent to suggest, that some new members might leave the movement because of their disillusionment over or disgust with the rigid conformism of Party life, the servile attitude to Moscow, the blind hostility to other reform movements like the Socialists, or the sterile intellectual atmosphere.

Peter's most important contribution to the discussions in the Anglo-American Secretariat came in a set of meetings in January 1932.[25] The purpose of these sessions was to discuss the general situation of the CPUSA, and in particular what was regarded in Moscow as the ineffective response to an ECCI resolution of October 1930, which had called for a "decisive turn to mass work." Comintern officials had also been unhappy over the failure of CPUSA leaders to cooperate and achieve unity since the ouster of the Lovestonites in 1929. In fact, there had ensued an often bitter struggle for power among the leading figures in the Party, including Earl Browder, William Foster, William Weinstone, and Max Bedacht. Although by early 1932 Browder was emerging as the strongest candidate to become national secretary of the Party, he had to contend with a constant stream of criticism not only from his rivals and opponents but from hostile Comintern officials as well, who were influenced by private communications from Weinstone and Bedacht that were sharply critical of what they regarded as Browder's ineffective and even inept leadership.[26]

To take part in the Moscow deliberations in January 1932, the Comintern summoned a CPUSA delegation comprised of Earl Browder, Robert Minor, and Jack Stachel. In the discussions at a session of the Anglo-American Secretariat that began on January 3, the members of the American delegation were duly deferential and readily submitted themselves to appropriate Bolshevik self-criticism. Peter, who was given an opportunity to address the Secretariat at length on January 7, joined in the exercise of self-criticism, but also gave examples of his attempts to strengthen the activities of the lower units of the Party in District 2.[27] In a speech lasting several hours, in which he buttressed his arguments with quotations from Lenin and Stalin, Peter identified a number of CPUSA practices that prevented the Party from taking advantage of the revolutionary situation created by massive unemployment and reduction of wages. Though he did not acknowledge that he had been one of the worst offenders, Peter criticized "excessive bureaucratic meddling" by Party leaders, who "put out decrees by the hundreds." As a result of these numerous directives from above, lower levels of the Party were loaded down with too much trivial work. At the same time, Party functionaries themselves were forced to take on too many responsibilities. Because they were busy with bureaucratic tasks and meetings virtually every night of the week, they were unable to "go out and do mass work."

Echoing comments that Clarence Hathaway had made earlier in the session on January 7, Peter lamented the proliferation of paid full-time functionaries. He gave Newark, New Jersey, as an example. In that section of 130 dues-paying members there were 18 or 20 full-time functionaries, including a section organizer, organizational secretary, trade union organizer, ILD (International Labor Defense) organizer, W.I.R. (Workers International Relief) organizer, *Daily Worker* agent, election campaign organizer, and others. Furthermore, each new Party campaign resulted in the creation of new full-time positions. It would be better, Peter suggested, to reduce the number of paid functionaries at the district level to just three who would have responsibilities in organization, agit-prop, and literature. This step, combined with an application of Lenin's rules of party discipline (which Peter quoted at length), would bring about the "very drastic changes" that were needed and would truly allow the CPUSA to "show its face" to the workers. At this point, Jack Stachel, who perhaps was finding Peter's presentation to be too long-winded and a bit pompous and cocksure for a mere org practicant, interjected sarcastically: "Did you know that in the U.S.?" Before Peter could respond, Hathaway defended him: "You sent him here to learn." Stachel's rejoinder bordered on the rancorous: "He did know, but he refused to carry this out." During this exchange Earl Browder, who was present, remained silent.

It soon became clear, however, that Stachel's criticism of Peter was not shared by those Comintern officials who made the key decisions about the policies and leadership of the CPUSA. In February the American delegation was given new Comintern "organizational directives," which, among other things, urged the reduction in the number of paid functionaries in the American Party that Peter had recommended.[28] Thus, Peter, whether by chance or by shrewd calculation, had correctly anticipated this new Comintern policy.[29] At the same time, the

Comintern also provided guidance on the leadership question in the CPUSA. Although Browder was still criticized for sowing discord among Party leaders, it was nonetheless decided that the troika of Browder, Foster, and Weinstone, which had been installed previously by Moscow, would continue. Moreover, Browder was designated to lead the "daily work of the Central Party apparatus."[30] Since Browder was instructed to remain in Moscow for several months of additional consultations, it was decided that Clarence Hathaway should return to the United States immediately to help with the implementation of the new "organizational directives."

With the departure of Hathaway, which occurred some time in early February, there was a need to appoint someone to serve as acting American representative to the ECCI. The choice, apparently made by Browder, fell on Peter, whose nomination was duly approved by the Political Secretariat of the ECCI.[31] From mid-February until his departure from Moscow in June, Peter thus served in two capacities: as org practicant and as the CPUSA representative to the ECCI. Neither job seems to have been particularly time consuming, for, as will be seen, he was soon to be drawn into a third activity. As the representative of the CPUSA, Peter was able to attend not only meetings of the Anglo-American Secretariat but of the Comintern PolCom as well. He thus had the opportunity to meet many of the most important Comintern officials. There were also material advantages to the position. Foreign Communists who visited the U.S.S.R. in the 1930s were often surprised, even shocked, by the low standard of living, the food shortages, and the public squalor. Peter Zinkin, the British Communist who served as an org practicant in this same period, later recalled the overcrowded conditions of the Hotel Lux, which "was far from living up to its name." Food was rationed and of poor quality and variety. Meat, eggs, and butter were "virtually nonexistent." Bread had "a greenish, black hue, its ingredients a mystery," although "hunger made it just palatable."[32] In later years Peter never spoke or wrote in this way about conditions in Moscow during his stay in 1931–32. Indeed, an American visitor who saw him at the time found him "looking well fed and well dressed."[33] The reason for this was that the CPUSA representative to the ECCI was entitled to a relatively generous ration book for use at the so-called Foreign Specialists Store, where one could obtain food items not otherwise available.[34] Like other committed Communists of his time, Peter viewed the world from a very narrow ideological perspective. Yet at times he could be a quite perceptive and reasonably honest observer of social and economic conditions. He certainly could not have overlooked the signs of poverty and deprivation that were so evident in Moscow and other parts of the U.S.S.R. that he visited. The ubiquitous block-long food queues were a constant reminder of the shortcomings of Soviet society. No doubt Peter, like another American Communist living at the time in Moscow, rationalized this as the sad but necessary prerequisite to "the new society emerging slowly out of czarist poverty and the devastation wrought by civil war and imperialist intervention."[35]

Peter's responsibility as the CPUSA representative to the ECCI was to solve a variety of problems relating to Comintern-CPUSA relations.[36] Much of his work seems to have been connected with CPUSA members who were visiting, studying, or working in the U.S.S.R. and were encountering difficulties of one sort or another. The most serious problem with which Peter had to contend occurred when a group of black American students at the International Lenin School, unhappy with what they found to be "remnants of white chauvinism" at the school, made a formal protest to Comintern officials. They presented a number of proposed reforms, including suggestions on how to eliminate the "disgusting atmosphere of the slave market" that they found among students and faculty. Peter, who was ultimately responsible for the discipline and conduct of Americans at the school, called a series of meetings with the entire group of about fifty students, at which "leading comrades of the Comintern" were present. Having listened to the complaints of the students, the Anglo-American Secretariat presented a resolution that demanded the "liquidation of all divergencies" among the students. The white students were warned to eliminate all traces of chauvinism, and the black students were told that there was no need for the proposals they had put forward. When several of the black students, including Charles H. White, George Hewitt, and William Odell Nowell, remained recalcitrant, Comintern officials criticized them for being "insufficiently armed against the influence of Negro bourgeois nationalism." Peter, whose responsibility it was to enforce the Comintern resolution, threatened the dissident black students with disciplinary action and expulsion. The students were forced to give in, but one long-term result was that Peter's reputation among black American Communists suffered. Significantly, at Peter's deportation trial in 1948, White, Hewitt, and Nowell appeared as witnesses against him. In recalling the incident many years later, the only explanation that Peter could think of was that the dissident black students had been "police spies."[37]

Another problem requiring Peter's intervention involved a Slovak American Communist, Andrew Smith, who had handed over his life savings in order to travel to the Soviet Union and contribute to the building of the "workers' paradise."[38] Before long, however, Smith became greatly disillusioned by the realities he encountered. He was unwise enough to write a letter to a friend in the United States warning him and others not to make the journey to Russia, since socialism there was "bankrupt," people were "starving in the streets," and the Soviet bureaucracy was callous and corrupt. Smith's letter was intercepted by the Soviet authorities and transmitted to Peter, who was instructed to take the appropriate action. Peter summoned Smith, whom he had briefly known a few years earlier when both men had leadership roles in CPUSA ethnic groups. At their meeting in Peter's office on the third floor of the Comintern administrative building, Smith readily admitted what he had done and asked if Peter could deny that he had told the truth. Peter's response was revealing: "Even if such things are true, as a Communist you have no right to write about them to the United States. You should have been more careful." Peter warned Smith that he would have to report this incident to the proper Comintern authorities, but he suggested that any punishment might be mitigated if Smith were to write a conciliatory article for a Slovak-American newspaper. Smith agreed to write the article, and not long after, to his surprise, he was offered a new, better-paying position in a Moscow factory. Peter, who clearly was aware of the conditions that had led to Smith's disillusionment, had chosen not to report the latter's infraction to the Comintern Control Commission.

As this incident shows, Peter was not a rigid apparatchik who felt that all deviations from the Party line must be immediately and severely punished. At times he successfully employed common sense and a human touch. Yet at the same time he felt a responsibility to take a firm stand on certain ideological issues. During his tenure as CPUSA representative in Moscow, Peter supervised the translation into Russian and publication of work by American Communists. In the case of four short stories written by Whittaker Chambers, whom Peter had met a few years earlier at the *Daily Worker* office, Peter had strong misgivings. The short stories, which described the experience of being a Communist in various settings, including the rural American Midwest and China, had been very well received not just in the United States but in Western Europe and Asia as well. But Peter tried, ultimately in vain, to forestall their publication in the U.S.S.R. because he concluded that the stories, with their implicit emphasis on the importance of individual struggle and the human experience, were fundamentally anti-Communist.[39]

As CPUSA representative to the Comintern, Peter met a number of people who would play important roles in his future career. Among them were the important Hungarian Communist émigrés who had settled in the Soviet Union and were active in the Comintern, including Béla Kun and Mátyás Rákosi. At this time he also met Jacob Golos, who was in Moscow ostensibly to study Soviet newspaper production.[40] Later, Golos was to be deeply involved in Soviet espionage activities in the United States. Peter also developed a particularly good relationship with Gerhardt Eisler, who participated in discussions of American problems at Comintern meetings and departed in 1933 to represent the Comintern in the United States and to help implement the latest Comintern directives. As Central European political refugees in the service of world Communism, Eisler (who went by the name of "Edwards" in the United States) and Peter shared many attributes. Later in the United States they became good friends and collaborated in a number of ways.

Peter continued to serve as the CPUSA representative to the Comintern until shortly before his departure in early July 1932. During his eight-month sojourn he gained much valuable experience and established important contacts. Furthermore, he had developed a good relationship with Earl Browder, to whom Peter largely owed his recent advancement in the Party. In turn, Peter offered his support to Browder in the ongoing power struggle among CPUSA leaders. Previously he had advised the Comintern that William Foster, one of Browder's chief rivals, did not possess the requisite leadership qualities to guide the CPUSA. At the last session of the Anglo-American Secretariat that Peter attended, he joined Robert Minor, who had just arrived to become the CPUSA's representative to the Comintern, in trying to deflect a renewed barrage of criticism directed at Browder.[41]

Joseph Peter's experiences in Moscow as org practicant and his cultivation of a good relationship with Earl Browder would, by themselves, no doubt have greatly enhanced his prestige and position in the CPUSA upon his return to the United States. But in fact he received certain additional training in the Soviet Union that was to have a profound impact on his future career. According to testimony Louis Rostovsky provided to various American governmental agencies in the early 1950s, during a visit he made to Moscow in 1932 he met a "talkative" female comrade named Manya whom he had known previously from Party work in Los Angeles. Manya, who was a student at the International Lenin School, allegedly told Rostovsky that her enrollment in the school was really a "cover for the espionage school" that both she and Joe Peter were attending.[42] The Manya to whom Rostovsky referred was almost certainly Manya Reiss (Maria Aerova), who had been a founding member of the American Communist Party, had been active with the Party in Los Angeles, and was considered one of the more promising female students at the Lenin School in 1931.[43] Later in the 1930s and during the war years she was a member of the Comintern apparatus and carried out various missions in France and Germany.[44] It is thus quite possible that Manya Reiss, as Rostovsky later claimed, had attended a Comintern school to obtain special training in conspiratorial work.

In his later public statements Peter always vehemently denied that he had ever been trained or involved in espionage or subversive activity of any kind. Indeed, he always claimed that there was no such thing as an "illegal apparatus" or underground in the CPUSA. Only in his unpublished memoir, written in the 1980s, did he finally reveal that in Moscow "part of my time was spent in the study of illegal work."[45] In his memoir Peter gave no details on exactly how he was recruited or on the nature and location of the school he attended. However, it is known that Comintern officials closely studied the autobiographical sketches and questionnaires of foreign Communists in Moscow to identify those who would be suitable candidates for work in the secret apparatus. Potential candidates were summoned before a committee for a personal evaluation.[46] One can understand why Peter's cadre file would likely draw the attention of such Comintern officials. In his autobiographical statement Peter mentioned that he had done some conspiratorial work for the Party in Slovakia and had worked, albeit without great success, to develop the "illegal apparatus" in the New York District of the CPUSA. Since apparently few members of the CPUSA had had any practical experience in conspiratorial work, Peter's record must have seemed especially promising to Comintern recruiters. Joseph Peter was also a likely recruit for work in the secret apparatus for other reasons. He had a good working knowledge of German, which was a prerequisite for those involved in the clandestine functions of the Comintern. Peter's profile also closely resembled that of many Comintern agents sent on missions abroad. There was a tendency to select as recruits those Communist émigrés from the successor states of the Habsburg Empire (especially Hungary) who were in effect stateless outlaws, since they could not return to their native lands because of their Communist activity, yet had not become citizens of another country.[47] Perhaps it was felt that such individuals would become reliable Comintern agents because, in times of trouble, they would never contemplate desertion of the Communist cause since they had no country, other than the Soviet Union, that would provide them a safe haven.

The nature of the illegal work Peter later performed strongly suggests that he attended the training school of the Comintern's most secret department, the International Liaison Section (Otdyel Mezhdunarodnoi Svyazi, or OMS). Best known by its acronym, the OMS was the Comintern's department for the coordination of subversive and conspiratorial activities.[48] Some of its functions overlapped with those of the main Soviet intelligence agencies, the OGPU and GRU, whose agents sometimes were assigned to the Comintern. But OMS maintained its own set of operations and had its own representative on the central committees of each Communist party abroad.[49] As a kind of "conspiratorial Intourist agency,"[50] OMS had a wide range of responsibilities and a global reach. It maintained communications between the center in Moscow and Communist parties throughout the world. This typically involved coded messages in letters and telegrams. To facilitate the movement of a large network of Comintern couriers and agents, as well as Communist functionaries who needed to travel abroad, OMS fabricated false passports and identity papers. It also guided and instructed Communist parties in the methods of conspiratorial work, including the important task of building an "illegal apparatus." OMS also at times engaged in espionage and intelligence operations independently of the main Soviet intelligence agencies (OGPU and GRU), although the latter came to usurp this role by the mid-1930s.[51]

The OMS ran its own training school in Kuntsevo, a suburb of Moscow,[52] and most likely this is where Joseph Peter received his initial training. Here carefully

selected foreign Communists were given instruction on the craft of conspiratorial work, including such subjects as secret codes, wiretapping, operation of
special cameras and radios, and passport forgery. One can gain a sense of the
meticulous attention to the details of the craft of spying, espionage, and conspiratorial work in general from the materials that the Comintern Commission
on Illegal Work had compiled in the 1920s.[53] The staff of the school consisted
mainly of OGPU and GRU agents, although OMS instructors seem to have
been responsible for much of the more practical training.[54]

There is no evidence available to determine how much time Peter spent in
the OMS school. However, when he departed from the Soviet Union at the
beginning of July 1932, arrangements were made for him to receive additional
training at the OMS center in Berlin, which coordinated the international work
of the Comintern apparatus.[55] There, Peter later recalled, he gained valuable
experience in "illegal work" as practiced by the German Communist Party and
acquired knowledge that "proved to be very useful in my subsequent party
work."[56] Almost surely it was in Berlin that Peter honed the skills in passport
forgery that he would put to effective use in the United States. The Comintern
apparatus in Berlin, known as the "Pass Apparat," was famous in the Communist world for the fabrication of the finest quality forged passports and other
personal documents.[57] Peter spent several weeks in Berlin, leaving at some
point in early August. Five months after Peter's departure, Hitler and his National Socialist Party came to power in Germany. Among the very first actions
undertaken by the Nazi government was a crackdown on the German Communist Party. Its leaders were arrested, its offices raided, and its records seized
or destroyed. Comintern activities in Berlin, including the vaunted production
of false passports, now came to an end. Those Comintern agents in Germany
who managed to escape arrest returned to Moscow or established themselves
in other key European cities, especially London and Paris. But some of the important work of the Comintern, most notably passport production, was now
shifted to New York, to which J. Peters, one of the last agents to be trained at
the Berlin center, now returned.

3

J. Peters in the 1930s

The Organization Man

When he arrived back in New York on August 3, 1932, Joe Peter jettisoned both of the names he had used while in Russia. He would never again make use of the name Isadore Boorstein, and instead of Joe Peter he rejoined his comrades as J. Peters. Why did he choose this particular variation of the names he had been using for nearly a decade? Of course, it was not uncommon for American Communists in this era, especially those who were aliens involved in clandestine activities or were traveling to and from the U.S.S.R., to change their names frequently.[1] Yet the choice of "J. Peters" as an alias is puzzling for several reasons. Although it was common for American Communists to be known by one word pseudonyms, very seldom was that one name preceded by just an initial. Perhaps this was simply an affectation on the part of Joe Peter. On the other hand, one wonders why he chose a new alias that was nearly identical to the names he had previously used. It would not require any great sleuthing to determine that the person known as J. Peters was probably identical with the one known earlier as József Péter or Joseph Peter.

There was, however, a compelling reason for Joe Peter to wish to identify himself now as "Peters." For some reason European Communists who were carrying on illegal or conspiratorial work in the United States on behalf of the Comintern or Soviet agencies often took one word names that were common Anglo-Saxon male first names, with an "S" added on. Joseph Peter certainly knew of this practice. He had probably worked with Boris Mikhailov (code-named "Williams"), who served as the chief Comintern representative in the United States in the early 1930s. When he was acting as a Comintern representative in the United States in the mid- and late 1930s, Gerhardt Eisler used the name "Edwards." Another example was Gregory Rabinowitz, known as "Roberts," a Soviet agent who arrived in the United States late in 1936 and with whom Peters was to have some contact. In following this practice Peters seems to have been suggesting that he was now a member of this fraternity of conspiratorial agents.

What exactly was the nature of Peters's new mission in the CPUSA? The available records of the Comintern and the CPUSA are almost completely silent on this issue. Only one document, a brief survey of the history of the secret apparatus of the CPUSA compiled in 1939 by Rudy Baker, throws some light on the subject. Here it is stated that "upon his return from Moscow the CC assigned him [Peters] to work in the secret apparatus."[2] It seems unlikely that the Central Committee would have taken this action unless word had come from Moscow that Peters's newly acquired training in conspiratorial work should be put to use. But, in light of subsequent developments, it also seems likely that Earl Browder was informed that Peters would henceforth be serving as a liaison between the CPUSA and the OMS. Hede Massing, an OGPU/NKVD operative in the United States during the 1930s, knew Peters as a member of the Comintern apparatus.[3] Peters himself apparently understood this to be intrinsic to his mission.[4] On the other hand, Comintern officials in Moscow were not always explicit in the instructions they gave to their agents or representatives abroad. For example, shortly after arriving in the United States in 1932, an unidentified agent wrote a letter to Comintern officials asking for a clarification of his mission, since he was "not entirely clear about all the tasks that are required in my role" in the United States.[5] In a similar way, Peters's mission may have been described somewhat ambiguously by Comintern officials, leaving him largely free to proceed on his own initiative.

Any discussion of Peters's work in the secret apparatus is also complicated by problems of nomenclature. One of the distinctive features of Communist parties throughout the world in the 1920s and 1930s was a preoccupation with conspiratorial language and practices. This was a legacy of the experiences of the Bolshevik Party in tsarist Russia. The Comintern assumed that all Communist parties faced the same problems that the Bolsheviks had encountered, and thus must adopt the tactics and strategy that had enabled their Russian comrades to survive government oppression and emerge victorious in 1917. Little or no thought was given to the possibility that a fixation on conspiratorial methods and underground operations might be counterproductive in democratic countries like the United States. As a result, CPUSA leaders in the interwar period, who were in no position to question the wisdom of Soviet leaders, employed the same conspiratorial jargon, institutions, and methods. It was taken for granted that every party had to appoint a trusted comrade to direct the underground or secret apparatus, which was designed to carry out a variety of both illegal and legal activities. In addition, all Communist parties had to create an "illegal apparatus," which was supervised by the director of the secret apparatus.

However Peters's new position was explained by Comintern officials, it quickly became clear to CPUSA functionaries that his status had been greatly enhanced. In the Party headquarters building on East Twelfth Street in New York, Peters was given an office on the ninth (and top) floor, a privilege granted only to the Party elite. He and Earl Browder were soon sharing the same administrative secretary, Grace Granich.[6] By the mid-1930s, even those Party leaders at the national headquarters who were not privy to the precise nature of Peters's assignment or his connection with the Comintern could see that he was responsible for overseeing a variety of underground activities and building the "illegal apparatus" (on this see chapter 4). There was to be an aura of mystery about J. Peters, highlighted by the fact that he began to use a bewildering variety of aliases. Peters would quickly correct a colleague who happened to address him by a name he was not currently using.[7] The great scope and conspiratorial nature of Peters's work was reflected in the numerous and diverse visitors who sought him out in his ninth-floor office. Although he was generally very tight-lipped about his underground projects, Peters was not above dropping hints to trusted comrades about the nature and significance of his work. He once told Louis Budenz, an editor for the *Daily Worker,* that the Party was like a submarine. The "open" Party, that seen by the public and most members, was the periscope, but the "most important part [of the Party] was the conspiratorial apparatus," which operated below the surface.[8]

It would be a mistake, however, to assume that Peters's role in the CPUSA after his return from Moscow was exclusively connected to the secret apparatus. In fact, much of his time in the period from 1932 to 1935 was devoted to the kinds of organizational problems that he had been grappling with and studying since 1929. As a sign that Peters would now be expected to participate in decision making at the highest levels of the Party, he was appointed a member-at-large of the three most significant Party committees: the Central Committee, the Secretariat, and the PolBuro.[9] Only the top three or four party leaders, and Gerhardt Eisler as a representative of the Comintern, regularly attended meetings of these three committees in the early and mid-1930s. Although Peters from time to time gave reports and speeches at these meetings, he rarely joined in debates and he generally refrained from taking sides in the Party power struggles. Mostly he preferred to sit back and play the role of the silent observer who offered his sage advice when it was solicited. When he later looked back on his career, he took the greatest pride in having been an effective "functionary" who was never "in the limelight."[10] However, CPUSA records for the period 1932–35 reveal that Peters was an active participant in a whole range of Party initiatives and activities. In recognition of the fact that he had emerged as an authority on organizational issues, Peters played a leading role in a reorganization of the Party structure in late 1932 and early 1933 and was chosen to write a manual on the principles of organization in the CPUSA.

In his memoirs, Peters was to boast that in the decade of the 1930s he was involved "in the organization of all of the more important actions" undertaken by the CPUSA.[11] Although this was an exaggeration, Peters in fact had a part in many Party activities that had nothing directly to do with the secret apparatus or underground operations. In May 1932, the Comintern PolCom had directed that members of the CPUSA Central Committee be sent regularly to industrial centers in order to provide direct and personal guidance.[12] In line with this directive, Peters spent much time in "the various centers of the automobile, steel, and rubber industries."[13] In 1932 the Party designated five industrial areas as places of special concentration: New York, Detroit, Chicago, Pittsburgh, and Cleveland. Peters made inspection tours at one time or another to each of these cities, but the best documented of his interventions occurred in Detroit. Less than a month after his return to the United States, he made a two-week visit to the auto center, where he had a series of talks with leaders of the Communist union, the Automobile Workers Union (AWU), the district leaders, and factory workers. When he returned to New York, Peters submitted to the PolCom a lengthy analysis of the situation and a plan of action.[14]

In his report Peters concluded that, despite the current low Party membership in Detroit and the financial constraints, there were reasons for optimism. It was his opinion that "if the comrades really carry out the plan that they worked out [under his direction] . . . and the center will give more direct guidance, the whole situation will be changed in no time." Peters's optimism proved to be justified. Although the number of professed Communists in the auto factories of Detroit remained small, and the Party's influence overall was, according to one historian, "superficial and fragile," the CPUSA nonetheless was to play a significant role in fomenting several of the key auto strikes of the 1930s, including the Briggs strike in 1933 and the General Motors sit-down strike of 1936–37.[15] To what extent the interventions of J. Peters, and of other CPUSA cadres from the central office who made visits to Detroit, contributed to this limited success is of course difficult to calibrate. No doubt some of the organizational advice that Peters provided in 1932 and during later visits in 1933 proved useful. On the other hand, there are hints that perhaps the Detroit district and AWU leaders in time became a bit weary of the pressure and constant flow of advice that emanated from the Party center. During 1932 and 1933, Peters sent frequent messages to Detroit-area Party functionaries, occasionally praising their efforts but most often pointing out where they were remiss in carrying out the program he had outlined.[16]

In his memoirs, Peters also wrote with pride about his accomplishments in the 1930s in what he termed "cadre affairs."[17] As an org practicant in Moscow, Peters had compiled several studies on the size and composition of the Party membership and the problems of recruitment. It was thus not surprising that Earl Browder would call on Peters to enlighten the party leadership on these subjects, which the latter did at length in a report to an expanded session of the Central Committee in late August 1932, several weeks after his return to the United States.[18] Peters first presented some statistics about membership fluctuation that, he suggested, should be cause for alarm. From mid-1931 to mid-1932 the Party recruited eighteen thousand new members. Unfortunately, during the same period fourteen thousand members dropped out, leaving a net gain of only four thousand. It was imperative that the PolCom thoroughly examine this "burning problem" and "take all the necessary steps to stop this fluctuation." Peters then provided a brief analysis of the Party cadre from the national headquarters down to the district level. His conclusion was that at all levels the Party had too many paid functionaries who had little "living contact with the workers in the large factories."

In his report, Peters proposed a number of changes to revitalize the Party cadre. Reprising an idea he had first put forward in 1929, he suggested that at least five new members should be added to the Central Committee. These should be American-born factory workers drawn from the concentration districts. In line with a recent Comintern directive, each member of the CC should be assigned to "responsible national tasks." Moreover, the members of the CC "must feel and act as Central Committee members not only at a Central Committee meeting, but every day in their work." As for the district-level cadre, here changes would have to be made gradually with the goal of creating district bureaus that contained a majority of factory workers. A major problem facing the Party, Peters asserted, was the insufficient number of cadres. One cause of this was the Party's inadequate system of training schools, which were "unsystematic and careless" in their selection and training of students. Citing the wise advice of Lenin, Peters concluded that the goal should be to fashion a party that was like a well-tuned orchestra in which "every comrade had his proper place" and played the instrument for which he had the greatest talent.

Shortly thereafter, the Secretariat set up two committees to study and implement the ideas Peters had proposed. One, consisting of Peters, "Brown" (Mario Alpi), and "Campbell" (Browder), was given supervision of all cadre affairs. The second, to which Peters was also appointed, was charged with the task of finding ways to improve the efficiency of the central apparatus so that it would function on the "basis of a definite calendar plan."[19] Peters embarked on this project for development of the Party cadre with great verve and determination. In a letter dated September 23 to the Anglo-American Secretariat in Moscow reporting on his activity since his return to the United States, he summarized his speech to the Central Committee and reported that he had been assigned the task of establishing a "cadre policy," which was "a very hard problem to tackle."[20] He intended to check up on the leadership of the concentration districts, "one by one," basing his work on the knowledge he had gained "over there" [in the Soviet Union]. Peters conceded that there were serious problems to be overcome. The financial situation of both the Party and the mass organizations was chaotic. The number of Party members who dropped out was much too large. Nonetheless, there were some hopeful signs, such as the rise in the number of native born ("splendid American elements") among the newly recruited members. Thus, he was confident that if he and his colleagues proceeded with "Bolshevik seriousness," much could be accomplished.

Over the next two years, Peters traveled extensively across the country and perhaps did in fact meet all district leaders in the concentration areas, "one by one." His message everywhere was the same. Recruitment must be made a high priority, with an emphasis on shop workers who were native born, especially African Americans. Better records had to be kept of new members and transfers.[21] In every strike, parade, and mass demonstration the "face of the Party" had to be shown by means of leaflets, chants, signs, and distribution of the *Daily Worker*. He also hammered away at these points in a variety of Party publications, but positive results were slow in coming.[22] In an interim report for the Central Committee at the CPUSA "emergency conference" in July 1933, Peters spoke bluntly.[23] Despite a series of recruitment campaigns, total membership in the Party remained stagnant, the Party remained "isolated from the main mass of the American industrial worker," and in general members were not being added at a pace that was commensurate "with the general revolutionary advance." After presenting the pertinent "dry facts and figures," he had to come to the same depressing conclusion: "we lose more members than we recruit." He expressed particular disappointment in the failure of the recent recruitment drive in the concentration centers. Even successful mass demonstrations, such as the one on May 1 in New York City, the "largest demonstration in the history of the Party," failed to aid recruitment. The only explanation that he could offer, other than the generic complaint that Party leaders, from the Central Committee down to the district level, were not "conscious enough of the necessity of daily recruiting," was his familiar theory that the "face of the Party" was not boldly projected during strikes and demonstrations.

J. Peters and other Party leaders must have been baffled and extremely frustrated by the persistence of membership turnover.[24] During 1934, Peters, perhaps concluding that recruitment problems were intractable, began to devote much of his time to other activities, particularly in the secret apparatus. Yet, when viewed in retrospect, it is clear that the groundwork for a major increase in Party membership had been laid by Peters in 1933. The number of new members began to spurt in the last half of that year, and the gain in 1934 would prove to be "the largest one-year increase in party history."[25] After stagnating or even declining in the first years of the Depression, Party membership rose from eighteen thousand in 1932 to thirty thousand in early 1935. Although there are a number of plausible explanations for this spurt in membership, much credit must be given to J. Peters, the Party official responsible in this period for recruitment and cadre development. It is true that Peters never found a solution to the problem of membership fluctuation, but other Party officials who would later be assigned to this problem were equally unsuccessful. In 1937, Jack Stachel was forced to admit that the annual membership turnover rate was still about 70 percent, and the Organization Department had run out of new ideas for dealing with this problem.[26]

Another area in which Peters played an important role was in the reorganization of the Party's governing structure. In his speech to the Central Committee in August 1932, Peters, responding in part to directives issued by the Comintern during his stay in Moscow, had made several proposals for improving the efficiency of the central apparatus. Over the next year he worked with Earl Browder and several colleagues from the Organization Department to develop these proposals, which were formally approved by the PolBuro in July 1933.[27] As Peters had suggested, PolBuro members were now to be assigned to specific concentration districts, in which they were required to spend at least one week a month working to guide the work of shop nuclei, the Youth Communist League (YCL), and other district and section activities. In the central apparatus, in addition to the Central Committee, PolBuro, and the Central Control Commission, there would be three standing committees: Org, Agitprop, and Language. The Org Department was to be run by a three-person steering committee of Peters, William Weiner, and "Brown" (Mario Alpi), with guidance from Jack Stachel.

As one of the triumvirate running the Org Department and a member of the Central Committee and PolBuro, J. Peters had his hand in a great variety of Party activities in the mid-1930s. Because he was an alien engaged in conspiratorial activity, he could not really aspire to a position of executive leadership that required interaction with the general public. Nor did he ever feel that he was entitled to contribute to the debates over fundamental questions of theory or strategy at Party conventions or in CC or PolBuro meetings. Indeed, he seldom spoke at all at such forums, except when reporting on issues related to his expertise in organizational or conspiratorial matters. Nonetheless, Peters built up an aura of authority in the Party based on his organizational work, connections with the Comintern, and service on various ad hoc committees. On the ninth floor of Party headquarters in New York he shared with Weiner and Brown, he had the formidable, and what must at times have been quite tedious, task of corresponding with the districts on the whole range of organizational issues, including recruitment, Party publications, disciplinary actions, strikes, and demonstrations of all kinds. He also had an important role in organizing and running national conventions and congresses, at which he served in various capacities.[28] At such meetings throughout the 1930s Peters was responsible for security, which meant above all taking measures to ensure that the police or political adversaries could not spy on the proceedings. A committee under Peters's supervision scrutinized admission cards to thwart any potential interlopers.[29] Apparent security breaches in any section of the Party were immediately reported to Peters, who made an investigation and sought to identify the guilty party.

Because of his involvement in cadre affairs, Peters was also responsible for many personnel decisions. To facilitate this work he sought to regularize the practice of requiring Party members to fill out personal questionnaires and submit brief autobiographies. This had been done sporadically in the CPUSA during the 1920s, but had fallen into neglect during the factional struggles at the end of that decade. Beginning in 1933, Peters arranged to have new members of the Party and each delegate at Party national conventions submit an autobiography to the Organization Department.[30] Since it was Peters's responsibility to review and safeguard these records, he in time became the Party leader who was most knowledgeable about the background and talents of Party functionaries. When Party members returned from training in Russia or graduated from Party schools, they were usually instructed to report to Peters "on the ninth floor" to get their next assignment.[31] Peters seems to have had a knack for making such personnel decisions in a smooth, tactful, and effective manner. Apparently he tried to take individual preferences into account, sometimes offering several possible assignments and allowing the individual to choose, although, as he would later emphasize, if "the class struggle demands it, he [a Party member] will leave his family for months, even years."[32] On the other hand, Peters was prepared to deal harshly with members who were seriously derelict in their duties or deviated from the Party's ideological positions. When the names of members guilty of such infractions were reported to Peters, he added this information to each member's personal file, reprimanded them, or, if the matter was serious enough, reported them to the Party's disciplinary body, the Central Control Commission.[33]

The Party autobiographies also proved useful in another activity that was considered to be in Peters's bailiwick because of its indirect connection to the "illegal apparatus": the discovery and punishment of spies and stool pigeons. In a political movement notorious for its obsession with the danger posed by spies and provocateurs, Peters was in the forefront. He insisted that the "bourgeoisie never sleeps" and was constantly seeking ways to infiltrate the Communist movement. Thus there was a need for the utmost vigilance. If suspicion fell on a Party member, Peters carefully studied that person's questionnaires and autobiographies for any inconsistencies or questionable activities. The usual practice in the Party had been that once a spy was discovered, he would simply be expelled, perhaps with a good deal of personal abuse from the workers who had been betrayed. In Peters's opinion, however, this was not enough. Too often spies, such as FBI informers, would simply be transferred to some other part of the country where they were not known and could carry on their insidious work. On Peters's instigation the Central Committee began in 1934 to print and circulate a "spy gallery," which contained photographs of exposed spies and descriptions of how they operated. These were distributed to each district and section committee. Peters insisted that once spies were discovered, they must be dealt with harshly. The spy's picture should be widely printed on flyers and, when possible, in the *Daily Worker*. He should be hounded, ridiculed, and even roughed up by fellow workers at the factory and jeered at by the children of workers in his neighborhood. A sign should be hung on his back stating "I am a spy." Workers should boycott any grocery store at which the spy's wife was permitted to shop.

By the mid-1930s, J. Peters was so ubiquitous in all activities relating to organization that he had become the Party's most authoritative and best-known specialist in that area. He wrote many articles for the *Party Organizer* and *The Communist* and frequently taught classes on organization at various Party schools, such as the Krumbein Training School.[34] Thus, when the idea arose that the CPUSA should publish a manual on organization that would be a handy reference guide for Party functionaries, Peters was the obvious choice as author. He may well have first contemplated such a project in 1932 in Moscow, where he made a systematic study of works on organization by Russian and German Communists.[35] In a letter to all district and section leaders in 1934, the Organization Commission stated that there was a "burning need" for a handbook on organization. The rapid growth of the Party in 1934 must have convinced Party leaders that previous Party publications that touched on organization were inadequate.[36] There was the need for quick publication of a new, thorough handbook, since the expansion and proliferation of sections and units would thrust into leadership roles many neophytes who were mostly unfamiliar with the Party's structure and procedures.

Having received this important assignment, Peters began to cull material from his speeches, articles, and reports and to shape the material into a coherent work. A short excerpt from the forthcoming pamphlet appeared in June 1935 in the *Party Organizer,* with the promise that the full handbook would soon be off the press.[37] In August the *Daily Worker* and other Party publications trumpeted the publication of the pamphlet, which, according to Jack Stachel "fills a long felt need" and "will be welcomed by many thousands of active Party members who have looked forward to its publication for a long time."[38] At a length of 127 pages and published in a three-by-five-inch pocket-size format by the Workers Library Publishers, J. Peters's pamphlet carried the full title of *The Communist*

Party: A Manual on Organization.[39] Although it was to have a relatively short shelf life, it became in time one of the most controversial publications ever sponsored by the American Communist Party. Many Americans during the Cold War would come to believe that it was the one document that most clearly revealed the diabolical, perverse, and threatening nature of Communism.

Peters's pamphlet was organized into five chapters, the largest of which was the third, "Structure and Functions of the Party Organizations." This section presented what the title of the pamphlet promised: a detailed description of the organizational structure of the Party and practical advice for lower-level functionaries on such matters as the length of meetings, amount of dues to be paid, transfers, and leaves of absence. Peters offered a guide to the labyrinth of Party units, from the shop nucleus at the bottom up to the national Central Committee and on to the Executive Committee of the Comintern. In much of chapter 3 Peters employed a question and answer format: What is the political task of the shop unit? How should a unit agenda be drawn up? What is the function of the financial secretary? (the *Daily Worker* agent? the unit organizer?) The wording throughout the pamphlet was serious, authoritative, didactic, and often hyperbolic. Peters seemed to take for granted that his readers would naturally be curious about such matters as the distinction between a shop unit, a town unit, and a farm unit. At times his explanations of some of the more arcane features of Party organization bordered on self parody. Perhaps even the most hardened apparatchik of that era might have smiled at Peters's attempt to describe the composition of a "leading fraction of a fraction."

When *A Manual on Organization* later became a controversial text in Cold War debates, it was not the section on organization but rather the shorter opening and closing chapters of Peters's pamphlet that were the focus of attention. In describing the nature and purpose of the Communist Party, Peters used the vocabulary, images, and analogies with which he and his comrades in the CPUSA leadership were familiar and to which they had given their full approval and affirmation. In its rigid Bolshevik orthodoxy, reverence for the Soviet Union and its leaders, call for iron discipline, and emphasis on the imminence of a workers' revolution, the *Manual* very much reflected the strategy propounded by the Comintern from the late 1920s until 1935 and formally adhered to by all Communist parties. According to this analysis, capitalism, which had entered the "third period" of its development, was moving rapidly and inexorably toward its final disintegration. In the resulting imminent crisis, Communists would ride a revolutionary wave to victory. This Communist line emphasized the idea of "class against class," which left no possibility for true cooperation with more moderate parties that were working for reform rather than revolution.[40]

The reader of *A Manual on Organization* was certainly left in little doubt about the author's understanding of the objectives of the CPUSA and the identity and nature of its enemies. The Communist Party, as the "trusted vanguard" of the working class, was leading the fight for "the revolutionary overthrow of capitalism, for the establishment of the dictatorship of the proletariat, for the establishment of a Socialist Soviet Republic in the Untied States, for the complete abolition of classes, for the establishment of socialism, the first stage of the class-less Communist society" (pp. 8–9). Without actually providing details on what violent methods the workers needed to employ in order to wage war against their oppressors, the *Manual* nonetheless bristled with military terminology: army of the proletariat, cadres, militant actions, mighty battles, ruthless combat. Because the enemies of the Party were so powerful and devious, Communists were required to adhere to a military-style discipline. "How can an army fight against the army of the enemy," Peters asked, "if every soldier in the army is allowed to question and even disobey orders of his superior officers?"(p. 28).

Lest prospective or new members fear that the CPUSA was an undemocratic movement, Peters insisted that there was "complete freedom of discussion in the Party until a majority decision has been made by the Unit or the leading committee" (p. 26). On the other hand, the principle of democratic centralism (which was illustrated by a handy pull-out section in the *Manual*) required that any decision by the Comintern, the Central Committee, or the National Convention "must be unreservedly carried out even if a minority of the Party membership or a minority of the local Party organizations is in disagreement with it" (p. 24). To allow a free discussion of such decisions would only allow "every under-cover agent of the bourgeoisie and every sympathizer of the ren-egades" to raise questions that were intended only to confuse the issues and disrupt the work of the Party, all disguised under a false call for "democracy" (p. 27). Moreover, there were certain basic principles and decisions that, by their very nature, could never be challenged: "We cannot imagine a discussion, for example, questioning the correctness of the leading role of the proletariat in the revolution, or the necessity for the proletarian dictatorship. We do not question the theory of the necessity for the forceful overthrow of capitalism. We do not question the correctness of the revolutionary theory of the class struggle laid down by Marx, Engels, Lenin and Stalin. We do not question the counter-revolutionary nature of Trotskyism" (pp. 26–27).

Voluntary submission to the rules of democratic centralism was, Peters argued, the highest duty of every Party member, for, as Stalin had written, "only conscious discipline can be truly iron discipline" (p. 28). To give the impression that large numbers of workers were willing to take on the solemn and admittedly difficult responsibility of joining the Communist Party, Peters noted that earlier in 1935 two thousand workers of the New York district had been initiated by Earl Browder, who read out a pledge that outlined the conditions of member-ship. According to this pledge, the new members were committing themselves to be firm defenders "of the Leninist line of the Party, the only line that insures the triumph of Soviet Power in the United States." In addition to devotion to the Soviet Union, each initiate also pledged to "take my place in the forefront of the struggle for Negro rights; against Jim-Crowism and lynching, against the chauvinistic lies of the ruling class" (pp. 102–3).[41]

Who were the enemies of the Communist Party, the "beloved organizer and leader of the struggle of the working class?" In Peters's reckoning they were numerous and ubiquitous. They were the capitalists, bourgeoisie, and "fascist demagogues" who "use all possible methods to disorganize, demoralize, and divide the ranks of the proletariat" (p. 119). A favorite tactic of these merciless enemies was to employ agents-provocateurs, stool pigeons, the Ku Klux Klan, and vigilantes, all of them "human rats" who attempted to infiltrate the Party and terrorize the workers. They were abetted by virtually every institution of "American democracy": the police "with their clubs and revolvers and gas bombs"; the militia "with their machine guns"; the churches; the press "with its poisonous anti-working class propaganda"; the judges "with their injunctions and vicious sentences against workers"; as well as mayors, governors, and the president, who always supported the capitalists. Although Peters conceded that there were occasions when limited cooperation with some other leftist groups in a "united front" was possible, he warned that the "reactionary leaders" of the AFL, aided by the Socialists, were "helping the bosses to crush the struggles of the workers for a decent living and against capitalism." Furthermore, Communists had to be constantly vigilant against the Lovestonites ("renegades from Communism") and the Trotskyites (the "advance guard of the counter-revolution") (p. 11).

Years later, CPUSA leaders and Party sympathizers were to be adamant in denying that Peters's *Manual* ever represented the true positions of the Party. Many would argue that the pamphlet was a "dead letter" practically from the moment it appeared, and that Peters's frank and open call for "Bolshevizing the Party" was never taken seriously. In his autobiography, John Abt, a close friend of Peters, remembered the *Manual* as "perhaps the most hidebound, imperious piece of Communist dogma we ever produced."[42] Yet in 1935, Party leaders had only praise for Peters and his pamphlet. In his preface to the book, Jack Stachel declared that the *Manual* embodied "the best that is available in the theory and practice of organization in our Party." J. Peters, with his thorough knowledge of "the fundamental principles of Leninist organization" and his many years of experience in organizational work, had produced a handbook that would be of "great benefit to every member of the Party in the daily work." In fact, Stachel suggested, once the *Manual* became widely available to Party members, "we will wonder how we could have gotten along without such a weapon for so long" (p. 3). Stachel's praise was echoed by Bill Lawrence in his review of the *Manual* in the *Party Organizer*. He lauded Peters for the "clear presentation of the principles of Party organization" and predicted that the pamphlet would become indispensable to CPUSA members.[43]

Although, viewed retrospectively, Peters's pamphlet might indeed be termed "hidebound" and "imperious," it should be noted that the rhetoric and arguments he employed were by no means simply a personal predilection. One can find similar language and themes in the *Daily Worker* and other Party newspapers in the first half of the 1930s.[44] Moreover, Peters's fawning attention to the wise advice of Joseph Stalin was just one example of how the "cult of Stalin" had begun to permeate the CPUSA by 1935. The mere mention of Stalin's name at Party conferences was likely to lead to the same kind of boisterous celebration to be found at similar meetings in the U.S.S.R. According to the minutes of the Eighth Convention of the CPUSA in April 1934, after Stalin was elected an honorary member of the Presidium, "the Convention rose and cheered for several minutes, after which the Internationale was sung."[45] The hostile attitude in Peters's manual towards reformist groups in general, and Socialists ("social fascists") in particular, was certainly shared by most CPUSA leaders at the time. Although there were a few signs in the early 1930s that some American Communists, particularly younger members and intellectuals, were open to a reevaluation of the Party's attitude to the Socialist Party,[46] the official Party position gained great public notoriety when in February 1934 several thousand Communists, led by Robert Minor and Clarence Hathaway, forcefully disrupted a Socialist Party rally at New York's Madison Square Garden. In the resulting pandemonium of brawls and violent encounters many were injured and hospitalized, and Hathaway and Minor were arrested. In the aftermath, Socialist leaders declared that in their psychology and conduct the Communists were no different from the fascists, and that "communism has become a pariah among the workers and all fighters for democracy and liberty."[47] J. Peters did not participate in this action, but his description in the *Manual* of the Socialists as an embittered enemy of the workers seemed to justify such violent confrontations.

Peters's pamphlet can likewise be regarded as in the ideological spirit of most CPUSA publications in the early 1930s. In a number of ways, *A Manual on Organization* resembled *Toward Soviet America,* which William Foster had written in 1932, the year in which he was the Party's nominee in the presidential campaign. Both books were characterized by extreme hyperbole that excoriated all other reform movements, lavishly praised the Soviet Union and its leaders, and assumed the eventual creation of a Soviet government in the United States. *Toward Soviet America* was followed by other booklets in the same vein, each imagining how a certain group (youth, Negroes, professionals, farmers, miners) would prosper when Communism triumphed in the United States. Several of these were published after the appearance of Peters's *Manual.* One biographer of Foster has called *Toward Soviet America* "an accurate reflection of the Communist line" at the time of its publication.[48] The same can be said of Peters's *Manual on Organization.*

When Peters's *Manual* first appeared, the CPUSA leadership envisioned that it would be widely distributed and used extensively in Party schools. Jack Stachel suggested that it was necessary to make sure that every Party member, and particularly those in positions of responsibility, get hold of the book and read it. Stachel added that "we must organize the collective study of the *Manual* in the units, among the various functionaries in the units, sections, and districts." Instructions along these lines were sent from the national Organizational Commission to all local districts. In the New York district, Israel Amter, a veteran Party leader, gave a one-and-a-half-hour speech extolling the virtues of Peters's pamphlet and insisted that every member must procure a copy.[49] There is also evidence that for a time the *Manual* was required reading in Party schools in Michigan, California, New York, and possibly elsewhere.[50] Orders for the book from the districts continued through the autumn of 1935.[51]

It is not clear whether ordinary Party members received free copies of Peters's pamphlet, or had to pay the relatively inexpensive cover price of five cents. In any case, despite the recommendations of Stachel, Amter, and other national leaders, there is reason to doubt that very many ordinary Party members read the book "cover to cover," unless they were required to do so at a Party school. Many would probably have shared the attitude of one Party member who, years later, remembered the *Manual* as being "so incredibly dull as to make the Army manuals seem melodramatic."[52] On the other hand, there may have been a few ambitious unit and section leaders who made sure to acquaint themselves with the pamphlet on the assumption that failing to do so would harm their chances for advancement in the Party. A few zealots may even have found Peters's prose to be compelling and exhilarating, although no Party member ever ventured to admit this publicly. In general, it seems most likely that the *Manual* was consulted only from time to time for practical advice on Party procedures. After all, any political party or movement needs to have certain rules and organizational principles, and *A Manual on Organization* was a handbook that did provide just such useful information for Communists who needed guidance.

Looking back on his career in the 1980s, Peters showed some pride in having authored the *Manual,* but admitted that the timing of its publication was somewhat inopportune and that it quickly became "outmoded."[53] In fact, the timing could not have been worse. Less than a month after the appearance of Peters's pamphlet, a major change in Comintern tactics was announced at the Seventh World Congress of the Communist International in Moscow. Abandoning the rigid "class against class" emphasis of the third period, Comintern officials now proclaimed the need to join other progressive, bourgeois groups, even the formerly reviled "social fascists," to create an effective anti-fascist coalition. Although it was implicitly understood that the ultimate goal of the creation of a dictatorship of the workers remained intact, the new "line" emphasized that all Communist parties must now cooperate in the building of a "Popular Front."[54]

The leaders of the CPUSA had for the most part not anticipated such a radical shift in the Communist line, and indeed some, like William Foster and William Dunne, were reluctant to fully embrace it. Nonetheless, by early 1936 the prescribed changes were well underway. The first initiatives were taken to draw Socialists and other moderate leftist groups into an anti-fascist coalition, and attacks on President Roosevelt were softened. Earl Browder emphasized the change in policy by declaring that "Communism is 20th Century Americanism." By 1938 the Party had agreed to accept what a historian has called "a junior and hidden role in the New Deal and labor movements."[55]

It did not take long for CPUSA leaders to realize that much of the Party literature in circulation was not in tune with the new Comintern line. As a result, in early 1936 the Literature Department issued a recall of numerous books and pamphlets, including the "In Soviet America" series.[56] Peters's *Manual* posed a special problem, in that the major part of the pamphlet, that dealing strictly with organization problems, remained useful, but the ideological framework was problematic. After all, Peters had vilified in the strongest language the very groups that the Party was now seeking to conciliate, and had insisted that the CPUSA was "the only Party that fights uncompromisingly for the interests of the workers" (p. 22). At a PolCom meeting in the fall of 1935, Peters was reproached for his failure to anticipate the new Comintern "line." His *Manual* contained "inflammable" material and a "too open advocacy of the use of force and violence to overthrow the government and deal with opponents." Having had much experience in the practice of Bolshevik self-criticism, Peters readily acknowledged his guilt and agreed to the proposal that he prepare a revised version of the pamphlet, shorn of the ideologically offensive language.[57] However, the revised work, which was to have been distributed by December 1935, did not appear and early in 1936 the Literature Department announced that "in view of changes in organization which will finally be passed upon by the forthcoming National Convention, the reprint of the revised edition must be held up until that time."[58]

In the end, the *Manual* was never revised. Despite an offer of assistance from an editorial specialist, Peters eventually refused to make the recommended changes.[59] Perhaps he privately regarded the new Comintern "line" as a mistake. The Popular Front that was proclaimed in August 1935 called on Communist parties to adopt the kind of effacing tactics that Peters had long excoriated. Of course, even if he was unenthusiastic about the idea of a Popular Front, he could hardly voice any objections, having declared in his *Manual* that decisions of the Comintern must be "unreservedly carried out." In refusing to revise his *Manual*,

Peters might have intended his inaction to be a kind of silent protest, but it is probably more likely that he simply did not have the time to spare for the revision, since by 1936 he was heavily involved in numerous projects connected to the secret apparatus. As a result, the *Manual* did not appear in a second edition and fairly quickly became irrelevant. It was not officially withdrawn, but district leaders were advised that it no longer had official approval. Those Communists at the local level, like George Charney, who had never found the pamphlet particularly useful or enlightening, were delighted to be able to literally throw it "out the window."[60] For the most part, however, copies of Peters's *Manual* were not discarded but just gathered dust in district file cabinets or on the shelves of left-wing bookstores. As late as 1940, copies were still available for sale for the cover price of five cents at the Communist book store in Chicago.[61] Peters could hardly have imagined the circumstances in which, less than a decade later, his pamphlet would become a scarce collectors' item and fetch prices as high as ten dollars a copy.

Given the hectic pace and heavy demands of his Party work in the 1930s, J. Peters had little time for recreation or a private life. His only hobby seems to have been reading American mystery novels of the hard-boiled genre, one sign of his growing Americanization. However, he retained an interest in and involvement with his Hungarian past. He kept in touch with his brothers and his mother, all of whom lived in the greater New York City area. At family gatherings he spoke Hungarian and ate his favorite Hungarian foods. He also enjoyed socializing with Hungarian American comrades at Hungarian restaurants in New York. On these occasions he met veterans from his Hungarian Federation days, like Sándor Vörös, newer Party members like John Lautner, and the occasional Hungarian Communist visiting from abroad, like Louis Gibarti (László Dobos). For the most part, Peters lived in straitened circumstances. Years later he would recall that "it wasn't easy to be a functionary of the Party in those days" on a weekly salary of $35.[62] Yet Peters managed in one way or another to dine out frequently and even to gain weight.[63] His closest friend in this period was Gerhardt Eisler, with whom he apparently shared an apartment for a time in 1933 and 1934.[64] Although Peters never actually took a vacation, he did spend an occasional weekend at a summer cottage that he and Eisler rented.

In 1935, however, J. Peters's personal life underwent a dramatic transformation. While teaching a class on Saturday afternoons at a Party Training School for section leaders, he met a woman who at the time was using the name Sophie Silver. She had been born in Galicia in 1906 as Sosse Sprechmann Frommer and arrived in the United States in 1914. As a young woman she worked in the silk mills of Paterson, New Jersey, and joined the Communist Party. In 1929 she married a Communist activist named Joe Silver and in 1934 she became an American citizen. In 1935, when she was selected to attend the weekend Training School, she was a section organizer of the United Office and Professional Workers of America on New York's Lower East Side. It is not clear whether she was still living with her husband, but quite quickly she and J. Peters developed a close relationship. By 1936 they were living together in a common-law marriage in Woodside, Long Island, and in 1943 they were legally married. Like her new partner, Sophie Silver would find it necessary to use a variety of aliases in the coming years. While living in Woodside she remained Sophie Silver, and Peters apparently sometimes used the name Joe Silver. Later, Sophie Silver became Sophie Stevens, then Ann Stevens, and finally Ann Peters. Their marriage proved to be a warm and enduring one, which ended only with Ann's death many decades later in Hungary.[65]

4

J. Peters and the
Secret Apparatus

On the agenda for the first Central Committee meeting scheduled after J. Peters's return from Moscow in 1932, there was an addendum (apparently inserted by Earl Browder) noting that "after the meeting for about a half hour, we shall, if possible, meet and discuss the illegal work of the Party."[1] There is no mention of this discussion in the meeting minutes, but it is likely that on this occasion Peters described to a small group of Party leaders (probably Browder and Weinstone, possibly also Stachel, Weiner, and Bedacht) the training he had received in Moscow and the role he was to play as liaison with the OMS. Soon thereafter Peters set about to create a functioning secret apparatus, but because he was so intensively involved in other organizational matters, particularly recruitment and cadre development, he was at first able to devote only a portion of his time to the task.

During 1933, Peters focused on two tasks: the safeguarding of the most sensitive Party records and the creation of a secure system for Party communications. In the former project Peters soon established procedures for storing the most important Party records in houses and apartments that the local police or FBI agents were unlikely to identify.[2] The second task proved more daunting. Peters and his colleagues were convinced that the FBI and local police forces were continuously seeking to intercept and read mail sent between CPUSA headquarters and the districts, since, as Peters frequently warned, "the enemy is alert, and diligently collects material which it can use against our organization."[3] To thwart "the enemy," Peters and his colleagues in the Organization Commission identified a number of houses and apartments in New York City occupied by Communist sympathizers who were not publicly identified with the Party. Local units were instructed to send what was termed "special mail" to these mail drops, which were frequently changed.[4] In the case of very sensitive and secret correspondence, couriers were to be used, or, alternatively, the messages were to be sent in code. The system favored by Peters, which he undoubtedly learned in Moscow and Berlin, was a book cipher in which numbers in the message referred to the page, line, word, and letter in a book or article that had previously been identified and distributed to district leaders.[5] Training in the cipher system was given to individuals by Peters either at national headquarters or in the districts, or in classes on the "illegal apparatus" at training schools that he taught regularly during the 1930s. At the National Training school, Peters's lecture on the underground apparatus was given at the end of the term and was regarded by some students as the capstone of the course.[6]

To maintain Party communications if the Party were driven underground, it was also essential that each district have the capacity to print material rapidly and secretly for distribution to members and workers in the factories.[7] When, for example, numerous leaflets were needed to promote strikes or advertise rallies, at least one comrade in the district should be able to operate a "brass plate, drying cloth, and stencil apparatus."[8] An extra mimeograph machine was to be cached in a secret location and used only when an emergency arose. It was also highly desirable that the lower levels of the Party have access to a printing press. If the government suppressed the Party, it was likely that any printing presses in normal use by the Party would be confiscated or destroyed. Thus the alternate printing press would have to be cached in a secure place or placed in the home or business of a Party sympathizer who would not be suspected by the police. Of course, since printing presses were an expensive item that few Party districts could afford, Peters had to be creative in finding sources of support among well-to-do Party sympathizers.

By early 1934, this initial phase in the creation of the "illegal apparatus" had been completed, and Peters was able to report to a plenum of the Central Committee that "we have established a fairly well functioning apparatus for communications from the Districts to the Center and vice-versa."[9] But, Peters added, this was only the beginning, and recent events had created a much greater sense of urgency. In his speech, and in an article in the *Party Organizer* a few months later, Peters reminded his comrades of the "fascist terror" that had been unleashed once Hitler came to power. Communist Party leaders were arrested and sent to concentration camps, where they were tortured and killed. The Party offices, printing plant, and publishing house were raided and confiscated. It would be foolhardy, Peters warned, to think that American capitalists would shrink from similar measures, especially in time of war or civil strife.[10] In fact, the "extra-legal fascist forces financed by the bankers and sponsored by the Local, State, and Federal government" were, like Mussolini's black guard, already unleashing "the most vicious fascist terror."[11] Perhaps concerned that district leaders might show the same reluctance and indifference that had thwarted his and Rudy Baker's efforts in 1930–31, Peters warned that any American Communist who thought that the building of the "illegal apparatus" was not a high priority was guilty of "social-democratic legalism" and "must be eliminated from our ranks."[12]

In the course of 1933, Peters began to work with individual districts to prepare them to survive in the case of suppression of the Party by the government. No records that directly document this process have survived, but Peters's methods and directives can be reconstructed from scattered references in the CPUSA archive, material supplied to the FBI by informers, and the recollections of former Communists who had served as district organizers. For the most part, Peters's guidelines and recommendations were based on various Comintern documents and were similar to those contained in the directive that he and Rudy Baker had sent out to the districts in January 1931. Peters insisted that various precautions had to be taken immediately since "the present wave of terror is only the beginning of bloody suppression against the struggles of the workers," and the police might raid Party offices at any time.[13] Local leaders were advised to shift their meeting places frequently, to use passwords to prevent the infiltration of meetings by outsiders, and to leave meetings one or two at a time at various intervals. Each Party member was advised to identify beforehand a place that could serve as a haven or temporary residence in the event he or she needed to hide from the police.[14]

Peters insisted that strict rules be observed in communications at the local level. As much business as possible was to be conducted orally. When written materials were necessary, care should be taken to avoid revealing names and addresses. Thus, in the minutes of meetings or in correspondence only pseudonyms and coded addresses were to be used. There was no need to place names and addresses in the heading of a letter: this practice was a trick used by the bourgeoisie to force their enemies to reveal important information.[15] Only rarely should members carry Party documents on their person, and district or section leaders were never to take with them full membership lists or groups of membership cards. Party records and correspondence should be on onionskin paper, so that they could be more easily concealed or destroyed in a sudden police raid.[16]

In 1931, CPUSA leaders at the lower levels had been extremely reluctant to expend time and resources on the building of the illegal apparatus. But domestic and international conditions had greatly changed by 1933, and the response to Peters's call for action was more favorable.[17] The best documented and probably most extensive of the efforts to build the "illegal apparatus" at the local level occurred in District 16 (the mid-South states). Paul Crouch, the district organizer from 1934 to 1937, was eager to work with Peters and traveled several times a year to New York City to consult with him. Crouch diligently followed all the guidelines. He created, at least on paper, numerous five-member units that would operate independently in a time of illegality. Two individuals, one a professor at the University of North Carolina, were designated to serve as district leaders should Crouch and the org specialist be arrested. With Peters's financial assistance, Crouch was able to purchase an underground printing press that was stored at the back of the Intimate Bookshop in Chapel Hill. Several mimeograph machines and supplies were kept in private homes. A reserve fund of $100 was established, to be used only if the Party were forced to operate underground. Later in the 1930s, Crouch was sent by the Party to Alabama, Tennessee, and California, where he took similar steps to build an illegal apparatus.[18]

Paul Crouch's thorough commitment to Peters's project was probably the exception, but on the basis of the available evidence one can conclude that most of the CPUSA districts made at least some effort to create plans to operate during a period of illegality.[19] Compliance with the guidelines that Peters had established was probably greatest in the first year or two. In time a degree of laxness set in. In late 1934, for example, the Organization Commission lamented that "there has been a decided loosening up by the districts in the matter of sending letters and other materials to the Center."[20] No doubt in the smaller districts, where one or two overworked leaders could hardly keep up with essential tasks like recruitment and organizing the workers, very little was done. District organizers were bombarded with demands and requests from national headquarters. Who can blame them for placing a low priority on such tasks as securing a reserve hideout, creating a set of mail drops and safe houses, or following each and every one of Peters's suggested procedures for safeguarding records? Most districts operated on miniscule budgets and often could not afford a mimeograph machine, let alone a reserve one not to be used except in an emergency. Thus the poorer and smaller CP districts, often located in the South or Southwest, frequently disregarded the safeguards Peters advocated. Ironically, they were often at the greatest risk from local police and governmental authorities determined to harass and intimidate the Communist movement. The results were often disastrous for the local Party organization, as when in 1935 the CP organizer in Birmingham was arrested while carrying new membership books for every district member.[21]

Peters apparently gave personal instructions to each district organizer in the use of the book cipher code. In the available CPUSA records, however, one finds only an occasional use of the code for messages between the center and the districts.[22] It is possible that coded messages were more frequent, but since they by definition were used only for the most sensitive material, they would likely have been kept in the secret Party archives that have not survived or become available to researchers. However, there is evidence that some local leaders, though diligent in sending and receiving mail at appropriate mail drops, preferred not to go to the trouble of encoding messages. This was true even of John Lautner, one of Peters's best friends, who became district organizer in West Virginia in 1936. When Peters gave Lautner a briefing on his duties, explaining how the code worked and giving him a copy of the book to be used, Lautner asked, "Why do I need this?" To which Peters responded, "Well, the other districts have it, so you might as well have it too." But Lautner never used the code, preferring instead to discuss sensitive matters personally during his frequent visits to New York City.[23] No doubt there were other district leaders who regarded the cipher code as unnecessary or too cumbersome.

Overall, the "illegal apparatus" implemented by J. Peters was thus a haphazard affair, leaving few districts truly prepared for a dire emergency. Had the American government decided at some point in the 1930s to suppress the Communist Party, it would likely have been successful, with only scattered CPUSA units maintaining a foothold in factories. But in fact the fears of Peters and other CPUSA leaders that the government was intent on suppressing the Party were greatly exaggerated. Through most of the 1930s, federal agencies, including the FBI, lacked the manpower, legal authorization, public backing, and even the inclination for intensive surveillance, let alone outright suppression, of the Communist movement.[24] During the Popular Front era, when CPUSA leaders were eager to emphasize the American character of their movement, many Americans no doubt regarded a Nazi German fifth column as the greater potential danger to national security. In the middle and late 1930s many Communists at the local level may instinctively have sensed this and become increasingly disinclined to heed the apocalyptic warnings of J. Peters and the Organization Commission.

Despite the ominous words Peters employed and the clandestine and conspiratorial activities he advocated, nothing about the "illegal apparatus" was in fact unlawful or criminal. There were no laws preventing a political party, should it deem it necessary because of perceived threats of government repression, from holding clandestine meetings, establishing mail drops and safe houses, communicating through secret codes, using pseudonyms, establishing secret printing presses, and caching mimeograph machines.[25] At no time did J. Peters call for such truly illegal measures as the caching of weapons to be used against the authorities, terrorist acts, or explicit plans for sparking civil disorder.[26]

On the other hand, Peters found that some of the methods used and personnel employed in the "illegal apparatus" could be put to use in other operations in the secret apparatus as a whole that were clearly unlawful. Safe houses, mail drops, and business fronts could, and sometimes were, placed at the disposal of Soviet intelligence agents. Individuals who proved proficient in clandestine operations in the "illegal apparatus" were recruited by Peters for projects involving courier service, money laundering, the production of false passports, espionage, and various conspiratorial projects sponsored by the OMS, GRU, or

GPU. By the mid-1930s, Peters had assembled a sizable group of such skilled operatives whose talents he could employ as the need arose.

At times the overlap between the "illegal apparatus" and Peters's other conspiratorial projects caused friction. In 1933, his initial efforts to establish the "illegal apparatus" in Baltimore met with resistance from the leader of the movement there, who apparently resented the amount of time and resources devoted to that effort and the fact that Peters was monopolizing the time of the organization specialist in Baltimore, Ed Williams. In a letter to the district organizer, Peters complained about "the impermissible situation which exists in Baltimore" in connection with "this important work." He warned that the "smallest negligence in this phase of work becomes a political crime against the movement." Significantly, Peters added that Baltimore is "one of the most important place[s] because of its location," a hint that he hoped to expand his conspiratorial work in Washington, D.C.[27]

In speaking before Party members on the subject of the "illegal apparatus," Peters was generally careful to refrain from revealing other conspiratorial operations of his secret apparatus. However, in some cases such operations depended on cooperation from district leaders. On only one documented occasion, to be described more fully below, did Peters speak openly at a Party meeting about such a highly secret project. But so close and frequent were his contacts with district leaders in the building of the "illegal apparatus" that all higher-level and most middle-level CPUSA leaders came to know that J. Peters was director of the Party underground, even if they were not quite sure exactly what sort of projects, other than the "illegal apparatus," he was engaged in. By the same token, many Party functionaries learned in time that Peters frequently traveled to Washington, D.C., in order to supervise Communist activity among government workers.[28] On the other hand, only a handful of the Party elite (in some instances only Earl Browder) had knowledge of Peters's most secret activities, such as the true nature of his work in Washington and his collaboration with Soviet intelligence agencies.

From the earliest days of the world Communist movement it was understood that the secret apparatus in each Communist Party would cooperate with Soviet intelligence agents and abet them in their clandestine activities.[29] During the 1920s, when Soviet intelligence operations in the United States were minimal and the CPUSA secret apparatus was in an embryonic stage, it appears that the head of the CPUSA served as liaison with Soviet agents. Jay Lovestone, national secretary in the second half of the 1920s, is known to have cooperated with both the OGPU and GRU in matters such as recruiting Party members for work in Soviet intelligence and production of fraudulent passports. It appears that Max Bedacht also gave assistance to Soviet agents in that period, especially in procuring documents to be used in the manufacture of fraudulent passports.[30] After the expulsion of Lovestone and his supporters in 1929, Bedacht was appointed interim head of the Party and assumed Lovestone's role as the main liaison between the CPUSA and the Soviet intelligence agencies. In the early 1930s, Bedacht worked closely with two GRU agents, the husband and wife team of Alexander and Nadezhda Ulanovsky. In response to their request, Bedacht in the summer of 1932 assigned a suitable CPUSA member, Whittaker Chambers, to go underground and work with the GRU.[31]

When J. Peters returned to the United States in August 1932 and began his work in the secret apparatus, he did not at first supplant Bedacht as liaison with Soviet intelligence agencies. Initially he worked closely only with the OMS station chief in the United States, Solomon Vladimirovich Mikhelson-Manuilov.[32] In late 1932 and early 1933, Bedacht maintained his contacts with Soviet agents, but there are indications that he was eager to jettison this work. In the late spring of 1933 Bedacht departed for Moscow to join in discussions about the leadership crisis in the CPUSA.[33] He apparently arranged for Peters to take his place as liaison with Soviet agents and informed Whittaker Chambers that he was leaving for a mission out of town and that during his absence Chambers should report to J. Peters.[34] Three months later, Bedacht returned in a dejected mood, for his rival Earl Browder had received support from the Soviet leadership and was soon to assume the title of national secretary of the CPUSA. Bedacht seems to have resumed some of his duties in the secret apparatus, and for a brief time Chambers found himself reporting to both Bedacht and Peters. But the former was increasingly indifferent to such matters and the latter "very friendly and helpful."[35] By June the change of guard was complete: Bedacht now focused his attention on the IWO (International Workers Order), of which he had recently been named national secretary, and Peters assumed responsibility for contacts with the GRU.

Between 1933 and 1938, J. Peters was involved in a variety of clandestine operations that brought him into contact with many Soviet intelligence agents. He came to know most of the OMS and GRU operatives, and at least some of those attached to the OGPU (from 1934 the NKVD). In his capacity as director of the secret apparatus, Peters answered only to Earl Browder, who himself collaborated closely with the NKVD and became the "pivotal figure" in Soviet espionage in the United States.[36] For the financing of his "special work," Peters was able to draw on a secret fund administered by William Weiner.[37] However, Peters was to prove quite creative and entrepreneurial in finding other sources of financial support for his underground work, primarily from "people who are entirely without party affiliation, and hence undercover."[38]

Because he remained a functionary of the CPUSA and was never formally attached to any of the Soviet intelligence agencies, J. Peters retained a degree of independence in supervising the work of the secret apparatus. Although he did his best to comply with requests from Soviet agents, many of his projects were launched on his own initiative. He did, however, have a special relationship with the OMS and felt an obligation to facilitate its work. The OMS station chief, based in New York, directed the movement of couriers, handled the distribution of Comintern funds, supervised the flow of coded telegrams to and from Moscow, obtained travel documents for Soviet agents, and answered the queries of CPUSA officials or passed them on to the Comintern leadership. Peters was able to assist the station chief, Mikhelson-Manuilov, in many of these activities, including serving as liaison with OMS operatives newly arrived in the country.[39] Under Peters, the secret apparatus helped to set up and maintain radio links with the Soviet Union. Experiments were conducted to develop equipment for sound and signal reproduction and "an electrical device for detecting enemies."[40]

Peters also provided invaluable support to Comintern agents when they ran into difficulties. For example, in the spring of 1933 Albert Feierabend, a Latvian American serving as a Comintern courier, was arrested by immigration authorities upon his arrival in New York. He was found to be using a false passport and illegally bringing into the country $28,700 in cash and gold certificates. With the assistance of J. Peters and the CPUSA, Feierabend was able to make his very sizable bail of $10,000. He then reported to CPUSA headquarters and handed over to Peters the sum of $7,000, which had been so cleverly hidden on his person that the INS authorities had not detected it. Despite strong suspicions by the prosecution that Feierabend was working for Soviet intelligence, the inadequacy of existing legislation resulted in his being charged and convicted only of traveling on an illegal passport. He was fined $1000 and placed under a two-year probation. However, he quickly jumped probation and returned to conspiratorial work.[41]

One mission of the OMS, based on its experiences in Germany during the 1920s, was to obtain information that would be useful in future revolutionary activity or civil war. Along these lines the Comintern in 1932 had instructed local parties to "form strictly secret nuclei in military units and the militarized organizations of the bourgeoisie." It was hoped that a successful infiltration of the armed forces would yield important intelligence on supply depots, military installations, troop personnel, and weaponry. In addition, Party members who were in the military or National Guard would be in the position to spread propaganda, undermine morale, pass on secret information, and, if the situation required it, commit acts of sabotage.[42]

In 1933, Peters began to plan how the CPUSA could implement this Comintern strategy, which dovetailed with ongoing interests of the GRU as well.[43] Since the success of this sensitive and, for the most part, highly illegal operation would depend on cooperation from district organizers, he had to deviate from his normal practice of keeping to an absolute minimum the number of people who would be informed. At the Central Committee plenum of January 16–17, 1934, which has previously been discussed, Peters began his speech with the following words: "There will be certain questions touched on in this report which shall not go out of this room because of the character of these questions."[44] The sensitive matter to which Peters referred was "work in the armed forces," that is, propaganda work directed at, and infiltration of, units of the National Guard, Army, and Navy. This work, he warned, "is absolutely illegal and cannot be connected up with the Party." But in view of the growing danger of war, it was imperative that the districts devote more effort to the task of "systematically building up the Party inside the armed forces." Despite all promises, some districts were not taking this seriously and had not done "a god-damned thing about this work." Yet he remained hopeful that with very little effort "splendid results" could be achieved: "These soldiers are ready to struggle and to follow us if we give them leadership and we must give them this leadership."

Peters repeated this message about the need to infiltrate the armed forces at subsequent meetings of district organizers that were sometimes held at Camp Unity, a Communist Party summer retreat about sixty miles north of New York City. At one such meeting for District 2 section organizers, Peters emphasized the need to expand Communist influence in the National Guard and in the Brooklyn Navy Yard. Party organizers were urged to determine the schedule of training sessions and be on hand to distribute leaflets and socialize with the Guardsmen.[45] On one occasion in 1934 Peters alluded to this "work in the armed forces" in a CP publication, the *Party Organizer*.[46] There he called for the infiltration of National Guard units and the creation of organized defense groups that "can fight back the attacks of the armed forces either legal or extra-legal." Later the FBI and INS would cite this article as evidence that Peters had advocated sedition.

Before 1934, some work on recruiting servicemen had been conducted by the Anti-Militarist Department of the CPUSA, which was attached to the Young Communist League.[47] Building on this foundation, Peters revised the questionnaire that Party members filled out by adding a question asking for the name, rank, and unit of any relatives in the armed forces. On the basis of these questionnaires, and information obtained from local Party leaders, he began the process of "colonizing" National Guard armories in and around New York City.[48] According to one source, by the end of 1934 there was a Party sympathizer or member in each of these armories, and small Communist cells in military units in Hawaii, Maryland, and the Panama Canal Zone.[49] Peters also organized a special course in the Workers School that focused on work within the armed forces. He contributed a lecture on ciphers and the clandestine methods of communication servicemen could use when they needed to communicate with national headquarters. Efforts were made to entice soldiers or sailors on leave to take this course.[50]

Given the paucity of relevant sources, it is difficult to determine how extensive and successful Peters's efforts to infiltrate the armed forces were. Only two individuals who participated in this operation later told their stories. The most important was Robert Gladnick, who joined the Party as a young man in 1930 and became involved in anti-militarist work as a member of the Young Communist League. After taking Peters's course on work within the armed forces, Gladnick was summoned to his office on the ninth floor of the party headquarters. Joining them was Irving Charles Velson, a civilian machinist at the Brooklyn Navy Shipyard who, Gladnick soon concluded, was "Peters's lieutenant in that he supervised all the agents and received their reports through mail drops."[51] At this meeting Peters instructed Gladnick to proceed to San Antonio and to contact an Army pharmacist at Kelly Field who was sympathetic to the Communist movement. He was to attempt to persuade the pharmacist to join the Party and to organize a Communist unit at Kelly Field. Peters further assigned Gladnick the task of gathering information about troop movements, number and types of planes, plane armament, troop morale, and the training and equipment of the troops at Kelly Field, Fort Sam Houston, and Randolph Field. His reports were to be sent to mail drops in Brooklyn that had been provided by Velson.[52] After completing his assignment in Texas, Gladnick was sent by Velson to do agitational work among sailors on ships based in California.

Another Party member who was recruited by Peters for "work in the armed forces" was Franklin Victor Reno, a mathematician whom Peters learned of from David Carpenter, the organizational secretary in Baltimore. Reno joined the Party in 1933 while a graduate student at the University of Virginia. In 1935 he moved to Baltimore, where Peters gave him the "confidential and important assignment" of recruiting members and organizing Party cells at military bases in the Washington/Baltimore area, including Fort Meyer, Fort Belvoir, Quantico, and Bolling Field.[53]

Whether Peters, Velson, and their agents had any significant successes in their "work in the armed forces" is difficult to judge. They may have facilitated the work of Cpl. Robert Osman, who is known to have engaged in espionage in the Panama Canal Zone on behalf of the GRU.[54] Reno later went on to engage in military espionage in collaboration with Whittaker Chambers. Peters no doubt passed on to the OMS or GRU any reports sent by his agents, such as those submitted by Robert Gladnick on military installations in Texas. However, the attempt to attract members of the armed forces to the Communist cause was, as Robert Gladnick later recalled, a "most difficult" one, since he discovered that the servicemen he approached were "fully content with life in the Navy."[55] One sign that the project had not brought the desired results was the decision of the Party in 1937 to abandon such work as "too risky."

If the results of Peters's project on "work in the armed forces" perhaps did not meet his expectations, the same cannot be said of his fraudulent passport operation, which was a spectacular success. False passports, known to Soviet operatives as "boots," were a highly prized commodity in the Communist world during the interwar period. They were needed in large quantities for use by Soviet and Comintern intelligence agents and political operatives, as well as by Party members from all across the globe who traveled in large numbers to the Soviet Union for meetings, training, or consultations. Lower level Communists might be able to travel on authentic passports under their true name, as Peters did when he attended the Sixth World Congress of the Communist International in 1928. But CPUSA leaders, motivated by an instinctive reluctance to use their true names in dealings with governmental agencies, usually opted for false passports, even in those cases when they probably could have traveled on authentic passports.[56] The chief centers for the fabrication of fraudulent passports in the period before 1933 were Moscow and Berlin. The favored technique was to obtain authentic passports that could be used by Communists who resembled the individual in the passport photo. Alternatively, the original photograph would be removed and a new one skillfully added. A second, more difficult, approach was to manufacture entirely new passports. This required very high levels of craftsmanship and counterfeiting skills, but by the late 1920s the Comintern "Pass Apparat" in Berlin was producing such false passports in large numbers.[57]

For several reasons, European Communists regarded passports issued by the United States as the most desirable. Bearers of American passports were usually treated with a certain amount of respect and cordiality by border officials throughout the world. Given the great diversity of American society and the presence of large numbers of recently arrived immigrants, almost any individual, regardless of his or her racial or ethnic background, could plausibly pose as an American citizen. Likewise, the fact that a bearer of an American passport spoke with an accent or lacked fluency in English did not normally raise undue suspicions of border agents.[58] Finally, American officials were extremely lax in their procedures for issuing passports and supervising their use. Only rarely, and often only by accident, did they apprehend individuals who were using false American passports. As a result, during the interwar period thousands of foreign and American Communists were able to travel across the globe with relative impunity using false passports, often posing as the very American businessmen they regarded as their mortal enemy.

During the 1920s the primary responsibility of the CPUSA in the production of false passports was the procurement of birth certificates, naturalization papers, and old passports. These were provided to Soviet agents for shipment to Berlin or Moscow. Several Party leaders, including Jay Lovestone, Benjamin Gitlow, and Max Bedacht contributed to the success of this operation.[59] American Communists needing fraudulent travel documents had several options. Leon Josephson, a Communist lawyer, appears to have pioneered the practice of applying for passports using the birth certificates of individuals who had died in infancy.[60] George Mink, a Communist Party maritime union organizer, also dabbled in passport fraud.[61] In 1929, Jacob Golos, a GPU operative in New York, was placed in charge of the fraudulent passport operation that served the CPUSA, the Comintern, and the GPU. However, until the early 1930s, false passports were generally not fabricated in the United States, since, according to Whittaker Chambers, "there was nobody in the Soviet intelligence in the United States who could be trusted safely to change the picture on a pass."[62]

Soon after his return from the Soviet Union in 1932, Peters, recently trained by the experts at the Pass Apparat in Berlin, took the initiative in reorganizing and centralizing the CPUSA passport operation. Soon he had largely supplanted Jacob Golos, who had other pressing responsibilities as manager of the Comintern-owned travel agency, World Tourist. Several factors explain the success Peters was to have. Because of his years of work with the Hungarian Federation and with members of other CPUSA language groups, as well as the relationships he was developing with district leaders as he created the "illegal apparatus," Peters had many contacts who could supply the naturalization papers and other personal documents that Party members could use to document their passport applications.[63] His work was also facilitated by his role as liaison between the CPUSA and the OMS, which enhanced his status in the Party, streamlined the process of distributing the fraudulent passports, and brought him into contact with other Soviet agents who could offer financial support. Finally, Peters brought to this task a blend of creativity, managerial efficiency, and entrepreneurship that his contemporaries in the American business world would surely have admired.

Although he was familiar with and applied the traditional methods of passport fraud, Peters introduced and perfected a new system of "ingenious simplicity."[64] CPUSA officials who worked in the false passport operation had known for some time that passports could be obtained by individuals submitting to the passport agency an authentic birth certificate of a person who had died as a child. But the problem of obtaining such birth certificates and matching them to the approximate age of the applicant had proved formidable, and there was always the danger that the parents or other relatives of the deceased child would somehow discover what had been done. The method had thus been used only sporadically in the 1920s. Peters was able to develop this idea in a systematic way. He managed to recruit "several quiet-looking women" who worked in the

Genealogical Department of the New York Public Library. In their spare time these women diligently read the obituary columns of various newspapers for the period of the late nineteenth to early twentieth centuries. Having identified the names of infants or children who had died at a young age, they then searched through other records to verify such vital statistics as date and place of birth and the parents' names. This information was forwarded to Peters, who in time had an extensive list at his disposal. When an American or foreign Communist in the United States needed a passport, Peters searched the list for an appropriate name that would be a good match in terms of age and ethnicity. Thus, if in 1934 a forty-year-old male who had been born in Poland needed a passport, Peters sought to identify a child with a Polish-sounding name who had been born in or around 1894. With Peters's assistance the Party member, using the deceased child's name, would then write to the appropriate records office and request a duplicate copy of the birth certificate, claiming that the original had been lost. Upon payment of the appropriate fee, such requests were routinely granted without any further investigation. At a time when there was no such thing as a social security card and few people had a driver's license, it was difficult to verify the identity of individuals.

The applicant would then proceed to the passport office in Manhattan, submit the birth certificate as proof of citizenship, fill out the application forms, and pay the required fee. Peters supplied the required two witnesses, Party members, who swore under oath that they had known the applicant under the claimed name for at least five years. No case is known of the passport agency questioning the bona fides of any of the applicants who used the birth certificates that Peters had illegally obtained. During the time Peters oversaw this operation, from 1932 to 1938, he arranged for thousands of illegal passports, and could confidently boast that "it was easy to obtain American passports on the basis of such papers."[65]

In time, Peters added certain refinements to his passport operation. He managed to gain the cooperation of several officials in the New York County Clerk office, which had the authority, though one rarely exercised, of issuing passports. In an emergency or when very high-level individuals were involved, Peters was able to secure a passport through this channel.[66] He also had a contact in the city hall at Atlantic City, New Jersey, who, for a fee, would enter a name in the official register of births and issue a birth certificate in that name. This procedure was particularly useful in those situations requiring a passport for a child, or children, of a couple who already had false passports.[67] Peters successfully tackled other difficult problems, such as passports for departing Russian families in which the parents had entered the country illegally but the child, or children, had been born in the United States and were thus entitled to American citizenship. In risky or particularly sensitive cases, Peters made sure that the passports passed through a chain of individuals, preferably innocent non-Party members, before reaching him or the recipient. The intention was to obfuscate the process and confuse the police should any of Peters's clients be arrested while carrying the fraudulent passport.

Peters's passport operation had originally been designed to serve mainly the needs of CPUSA members and the many Comintern operatives, couriers, and instructors who were sent to the United States during the 1930s.[68] However, the need for fraudulent passports increased dramatically when Peters began to collaborate with a GRU agent named Arnold Ikal, who was known to American comrades as "Richard" and to Europeans as "Ewald." Ikal, who had received special training in engraving and other skills of document forgery, was sent to establish a passport operation in the United States.[69] Some time after his arrival in May 1932, Ikal applied for assistance to Max Bedacht, who apparently suggested Peters, recently returned from Soviet Russia, as the logical CPUSA contact for the GRU operation.

Once he learned what Ikal had in mind, Peters enthusiastically accepted the proposed partnership, which in effect "annexed the underground Communist Party to the Soviet secret service." Because the budget over which Ikal presided was quite sizable, he was in a position to offer Peters generous payment for his assistance.[70] In the Communist movement the going price for an uncomplicated American passport in the early 1930s was two hundred dollars.[71] But it seems that Peters was able to charge more than the standard rate. In this way he succeeded in acquiring substantial funding for his secret apparatus while at the same time making an important contribution to the success of the GRU passport operation. He supplied innumerable sets of nationalization papers, birth certificates, and passports, as well as cover addresses and "reliable contacts of various kinds."[72] He arranged for Ikal's new American wife, Ruth Braman, to join his team of genealogists at the New York Public Library. When Ikal expressed the need for some sort of business cover for his operation, Peters set him up as a silent partner in a small publishing company. By 1934 the joint CPUSA/GRU operation was in full swing and each month Ikal was dispatching to Moscow over one hundred "good safe useable 'boots.'" Beginning in 1936, when the Spanish Civil War was intensifying, Peters worked closely with Ossip Garber, Ikal's technical assistant, to supply fraudulent travel documents for those volunteers in the Abraham Lincoln Brigade who were unable to obtain legal American passports.[73] Peters's cooperation with the GRU was amply rewarded. The money he received helped to fund many of his other underground operations. And he benefited personally as well. Most Soviet operatives in the United States preferred a modest, unobtrusive lifestyle. Ikal, who padded the expense reports he sent to Moscow, lived quite lavishly, with two apartments, two cars, a motor boat, and membership in a tennis club.[74] He was happy to share some of his largesse with Peters, whom he dubbed his "poor cousin," by treating him to frequent meals at Zimmerman's Budapest and other New York restaurants.

Having successfully tapped into the GRU budget for its American operations, Peters was eager to comply when the NKVD came calling in 1935. Early that year Hede Massing (Hede Gomperz), an NKVD operative, was told by her superior, Iskhak Akhmerov, that there was an urgent need for a large number of fraudulent American passports, or at least birth certificates that could be used to apply for passports.[75] Apparently Jacob Golos, who was in charge of procuring false passports for the NKVD, was on this occasion unable to supply the large number of documents, some of a highly specialized kind, that were needed. So Akhmerov had to look elsewhere. Since Soviet intelligence services in the field were, by design, highly compartmentalized, neither Massing nor Akhmerov was aware of Peters's thriving passport mill and the mutually beneficial relationship he had established with the GRU. Because Massing had previously never given any thought to false passports or where they came from, she suggested that she could consult with Gerhardt Eisler, a former lover with whom she had remained on close terms. It seemed likely to her that Eisler, having served in the United States since 1933 as a representative of the Comintern, would have good connections with both the OMS and the CPUSA underground. Akhmerov had misgivings about this idea, which violated the rule that the various Soviet intelligence organizations should avoid any overlap in their operations. But his need for the passports was urgent, and he instructed Massing to proceed as she proposed.

Eisler was happy to be of assistance and told Massing that he knew exactly the person she needed to see. A few days later at a Childs Restaurant in New York he introduced her to Peters, whom Massing had previously known only by reputation. She found Peters, "a dark, heavy-set Hungarian with a clipped mustache," to be "amiable and soft-spoken." After Massing explained what she needed, Peters casually asked what organization would be using the passports. "You know I can't tell you," was Massing's reply, which was literally true because in fact she did not know which apparatus she worked for. In any case, Peters probably suspected that he was dealing with the NKVD, which he hoped was as free-spending as the GRU. He indicated to Massing that he could indeed supply passports, naturalization papers, and birth certificates, but "such things cost real money." Massing's reply was that "price, within reason, was no consideration."[76]

Akhmerov had heard of the "fraternal operative" (that is, someone attached to the CPUSA) known as "Peter" and had mentioned his name during a recent visit to the NKVD headquarters in Moscow. Confident that there would be no harmful consequences, he therefore quickly approved the arrangement Massing had made.[77] Over the next year Peters and Massing met roughly once a month, at which time she handed over an envelope containing the personal facts (sex, age, national origin) about the individuals for whom passports were needed. Peters in turn would give her an envelope containing the passports or other documents that had been requested the previous month. According to Massing's later testimony, in each transaction she made payments in cash to Peters that amounted to "several hundred dollars," which, apparently, was "not as much as Peters had requested."[78] However, for difficult or complicated cases Massing was authorized to pay above the usual rate. On one occasion she stated the need for a group passport to fit a whole family, including children of various ages. Peters "threw up his hands at this," but promised to do his best and try to "perform the miracle." At their next meeting Peters appeared with a broad smile on his face and handed over a thicker than normal envelope of documents, and Massing in turn gave him "a money envelope to match."[79]

As members of a cohort of Central European Communists who had spent a considerable part of their lives in the United States, Massing and Peters had a good deal in common. Their meetings were friendly and their conversations were not confined simply to the business at hand. On one occasion Peters even ventured to ask, "What sort of guy is it that you're working with?" Massing, who considered Akhmerov to be "dumb, arrogant, [and] conceited," replied, "The kind you wish on your enemy!" Toward the end of 1935 Akhmerov requested a personal meeting with Peters, perhaps to discuss some matter that could not be entrusted to Massing. Later Peters told Massing that he too found her boss to be "insufferable." This led to further banter between them about the "idiocy of Soviet bureaucrats as a breed."[80]

Peters may indeed have found Iskhat Akhmerov insufferable, but this did not prevent him from developing a good working relationship with him, as he had with other Soviet intelligence agents. Indeed, what is perhaps most striking about Peters's whirlwind of Party activities in the mid-1930s was the ease with which he gained the confidence and support of individuals who differed widely in their social origin, education, ethnicity, and Party status. His easygoing manner, wit, intelligence, and a certain kind of Old World charm proved effective in a variety of settings. Peters was able to gain support for his projects from many district organizers and other local CPUSA leaders, most of whom came from a working-class background. Yet, having received an excellent classical training in Hungarian schools, he was equally at home with Party members and sympathizers who were college educated. And he also proved surprisingly successful in persuading wealthy and highly educated Americans not only to support the Communist Party, but also to take assignments from the CPUSA secret apparatus and, in some cases, from Soviet intelligence agencies.

Peters's abilities as a recruiter, mentor, and handler can be seen in the rapport he was able to establish with a diverse group of individuals in New York City in the mid- to late 1930s. Edward (Ted) Fitzgerald, who came from a working-class family, joined the Communist Party around 1935, along with his wife, mother, sister, and two cousins. It is not known whether Peters recruited the Fitzgerald family, but soon after joining, Ted Fitzgerald became a member of what he called a "closed group" (underground party unit) under Peters's direction in New York, Philadelphia, and Washington. He maintained his relationship with Peters for nearly ten years, during which he worked in a series of wartime agencies and passed information to Soviet intelligence.[81]

At the other end of the social spectrum was Frederick Vanderbilt Field, scion of one of the wealthiest American families, the Vanderbilts. Educated at Harvard and the London School of Economics, Field as a young man gravitated toward radical left-wing politics. In the early 1930s he told a friend, Sylvia Castleton (later Sylvia Weyl), that he wanted to associate with the Party and contribute to its success. Castleton moved in the highest Party circles and was able to arrange for him to meet Earl Browder, who passed Field along to Peters. Some time later when Castleton encountered Peters and asked if things had worked out well, he replied, "Oh yes. Field has entered my organization and is a good asset, and is going to do some good work."[82] In fact, Field quickly embarked on a Party career that would include extensive financial support, contributions to Party publications, and participation in numerous front organizations. From time to time Peters enlisted Field's support to promote some of his projects in the secret apparatus.[83]

Although he had no special training or interest in cultural affairs, Peters also found fertile ground for his recruiting in the community of left-leaning artists and literati in New York City. In his memoir, Peters recalled that one of his Party assignments was to work with sympathizers in the cultural field, and as a result he came into contact "with both Hollywood and Broadway."[84] Peters came to know some established writers, like Agnes Smedley,[85] but his contacts were for the most part with younger, aspiring talents whom he perhaps found to be more open to making a deep commitment to the Party and serving in the secret apparatus. Hideo Noda, a Japanese-American painter and protégé of the renowned muralist Diego Rivera, was recruited by Peters in 1933 and a few years later agreed to cooperate in establishing a GRU espionage operation in Japan.[86] Joseph Losey and James Proctor, then just embarking on careers that would lead some years later to considerable success in Hollywood and Broadway, were members of a small organization that Peters dubbed the "Arts Project." Proctor was a Party member from the early 1930s, but Losey did not join until after World War II, perhaps because Peters decided he could be more useful if he were not formally connected with the CPUSA. Under the tutelage of Peters (whom a mutual friend called "Joe's mentor"), Losey developed such strong sympathies for and commitment to the Communist movement that he was willing to serve from time to time in the 1930s as a transatlantic courier for Peters in communications with Soviet agents in Europe. He became a lifetime friend of Peters and was one of only a few of his American comrades who was able to visit him in Budapest after his return to his native land.[87] Another of Peters's important contacts in the cultural world was Maxim Lieber, a Party member who headed a small but growing New York literary agency with such clients as Erskine Caldwell and Langston Hughes. Lieber was not active in the everyday affairs of the Party, but, at Peters's prompting, he was willing from time to time to demonstrate his Party loyalty and anti-fascist convictions by lending his support to various projects in the secret apparatus. Lieber would later describe Peters as a "short, stocky, mysterious figure" who was the "head of the whole Communist espionage operation in the country."[88]

Ted Fitzgerald, Frederick Vanderbilt Field, Joseph Losey—these were just some of the individuals whom Peters was able to draw into what he called "my organization" in the New York area. Doubtless there were others whose participation is not recorded in the surviving sources. Only one case is known in which Peters asked a Party member for cooperation in a clandestine operation and was rebuffed. At some point in 1933 or 1934 he approached Sylvia Castleton (later Sylvia Weyl) and told her he was thinking of opening a travel bureau that, like Intourist, would operate in the normal way but would also serve the purposes of the secret apparatus. If she would be willing to run the travel bureau, he "would send her customers; and the business would be used for his ends also." But, wary of becoming involved in "underground work," she declined and it is not known whether Peters ever carried through on his plan.[89] On the other hand, Peters was apparently successful in creating a number of other business fronts, which required the collaboration of individuals who sympathized with the Party. One such establishment took the form of an architect's office located near Columbus Circle in New York City. This office had the complete appearance of an architect's place of work, and perhaps even functioned as such, but also served the secret apparatus as a mail drop, a meeting place, and a business at which underground workers could claim they were employed.[90] It is also likely that Peters created other organizations akin to the "Arts Project." He would later quietly boast in his memoir that he supervised a number of such "semi-legal" groups of artists and intellectuals, which had great influence in their fields and provided "significant material support" to the Party.[91] New York during the Depression era, with its large concentration of intellectuals and artists who were radicalized by the apparent failures of capitalism and the growing threat posed by the fascist powers, was fertile ground for Peters's recruitment efforts. However, his greatest success came not in New York but in the nation's capital, Washington, D.C.

5

Whittaker Chambers and the
"Washington Set-up"

On a number of occasions in the late 1940s, J. Peters, in response to questions from government investigators, prosecutors, and reporters, adamantly denied that he had ever had anything to do with a Communist underground operation in Washington, D.C.[1] Even in his unpublished memoir, where he finally alluded to "my secret work in the Party" (különleges pártmunkám), he remained silent about his conspiratorial activity in Washington. Indeed, aside from the actual participants in what Peters liked to call his "Washington set-up," only a few Party members ever learned about this highly secret project. One of them was his closest friend, John Lautner, to whom he admitted in 1948 that he had indeed been in charge of an underground operation in Washington that functioned separately from the legal, open Party in that city.[2]

J. Peters's "Washington set-up" was initially built in collaboration with a remarkable political activist, Harold (Hal) Ware, a veteran Party member who took a keen interest in agricultural problems. In 1933 Ware decided to accept an offer to work in the newly created Agricultural Adjustment Agency (AAA).[3] There is no evidence to suggest that in joining Roosevelt's New Deal administration Ware had the ulterior motive of burrowing from within by creating a secret Communist unit in the AAA. Ware apparently had no experience or expertise in clandestine work, but soon after he arrived in Washington he must have been struck by the relatively large number of lawyers and economists in the AAA who were inclined to support radical measures to solve the country's agricultural problems. This was a new kind of recruit to government service, aptly described by one historian as "the bright young person with a social conscience."[4] He soon discovered that a few of his new colleagues, such as Nathaniel Weyl and Charles Kramer, were already Communist Party members. Others, like Alger Hiss, Nat Witt, John Abt, and Lee Pressman, were being pushed towards political radicalism by the impact of the Depression, the threat posed by Fascist Italy and Nazi Germany, their growing admiration for the apparent economic successes of the Soviet Union, and, eventually, by their frustration over what they perceived to be the slow progress toward reform in Roosevelt's administration.

Hal Ware had about him a certain mystique that must have been fascinating to contemporary American Communists: he had spent many years in the Soviet Union, where he had been warmly praised by Lenin, had worked side-by-side with farmers on their collectives, and in general had been an eyewitness to the first years in the construction of what was proclaimed to be a true workers' state. He thus proved very adept at converting some of the "radical New Dealers" he met into committed Communist Party members. He was shrewd in focusing his recruiting efforts on those individuals he concluded would be most susceptible to the lure of what has come to be called "romantic anti-fascism" and to the notion that the world was confronted by only two ideological choices—fascism or communism.[5]

By the summer of 1933, Ware seems to have identified a group of perhaps four or five colleagues who would represent the nucleus of the Communist Party unit that historians would later call the Ware group. Ware may have had some ideas about how this group should function and what contributions it could make to the Party, but it must have been clear to him that he needed the approval and advice of Party leaders before he proceeded any further. He may well have first broached the idea during a trip to New York in May, at which time he gave a report on agrarian work to a PolBuro meeting that J. Peters attended. It seems likely that it was during this visit that Ware privately informed Browder about the Communist group he was forming and asked for guidance.[6] Since such an operation fell under the rubric of "special work," Browder, who in this period was beginning to cooperate closely with the OGPU, charged Peters with responsibility for supervising the nascent Ware group and maintaining an "illegal connection" with Soviet intelligence agencies.[7] As events would later demonstrate, Browder gave Peters almost complete autonomy in creating and supervising the clandestine Party unit in Washington.[8]

Once he had been given the go-ahead by Browder and Peters, Ware was able to inform prospective members of the group that he had been authorized by the Political Bureau of the Communist Party to proceed with the formation of a secret Communist unit. One new member, however, was made uneasy by this news. Nathaniel Weyl, who had joined the Party late in 1932 while a student at Columbia University, told Ware that the existence of the group, and thus the security of his job, would be in jeopardy since the leaders of the CPUSA "were unable to keep anything secret." Weyl found Ware's response reassuring: the leaders of the Party in New York would be kept in complete ignorance of the secret cell in Washington, and it would be "under the direct control of the Communist International." Ware could hardly have believed this, although Peters may well have told him of his Comintern connections. In any case, Weyl was flattered by the idea that he now had a direct connection to the Comintern, "the general staff of the coming socialist revolution."[9]

Most likely Ware used a somewhat different approach with other potential members who felt more comfortable with the notion that they would be providing assistance to an American political party (the CPUSA) rather than a foreign regime. Some of the members of the group seem to have rationalized their participation in a secret Communist unit as a way of combating malevolent, reactionary forces in Washington. Looking back on these events many years later in his autobiography, John Abt, one of the original members of the Ware group, argued along these lines: "Our purpose was not to help foreign governments but to help our own, to defeat those who wanted to obstruct the progressive tendencies within the administration."[10] Whatever their individual motivations, all members of the Ware group must have been gratified by Ware's assurance that they had been selected because the Party anticipated they "might rise high in the echelons of political power." Many members must have felt, as did Nathaniel Weyl, that they "were acquiring the training in the complex business of running a state that would be in high demand and short supply when the United States chose socialism." In a Communist regime they would be poised to "move to the head of the table."[11]

At the first known formal meeting of the Ware group, probably late in the fall of 1933, about eight members were present.[12] Among them were four lawyers (John Abt, Alger Hiss, Lee Pressman, and Nat Witt); and three economists (Henry Collins, Victor Perlo, and Nathaniel Weyl).[13] Most of these original members were employed by the AAA, but two of them, Collins and Perlo, worked for the National Recovery Administration (NRA). Over the next year there would be several additions to this nucleus, including Charles Kramer (Charles Krivitsky), the husband of the novelist Josephine Herbst, Marion Bachrach (the sister of John Abt), George Silverman, an economist with the Railroad Retirement Board, and possibly Donald Hiss, Alger's brother.[14] Ware group members were quite young (all were in their twenties, except for Ware himself) and possessed dazzling academic credentials. A few came from wealthy families, and as middle- and upper-level civil servants all earned salaries that, especially in Depression-era America, placed them solidly in the upper middle class of society.

It was J. Peters's responsibility to determine how the Ware group, this "new breed" of Communists, could best be employed to further the interests of the Party. At the outset he established certain firm guidelines. Because they were intellectuals without open Party experience, it was extremely important to their feeling of Communist solidarity that they make exceptional money sacrifices for the Communist Party. As Lenin himself had emphasized, dues were "a test and a binder of party loyalty." From the beginning Ware group members were thus expected to tithe, that is pay dues amounting to 10 percent of their annual salaries.[15] Peters also played up the conspiratorial nature of the Washington unit, perhaps sensing that these otherwise staid American bureaucrats would regard clandestine work as an exciting adventure.[16] As with similar Communist cells in European governments, members were to observe the strictest secrecy so that no one would "suspect the existence of the Washington underground."[17] Members were warned to use utmost caution in communicating with each other by telephone and in traveling to meetings. They were to have plans in place to deal with an emergency, such as a sudden police crackdown. Of course, members were expected to study Marxist theory and read Party publications, but such material was never to be purchased openly or left lying about in their residences. Instead, the *Daily Worker, the Communist International, New Masses,* and other Party literature would be delivered by a courier each week to Ware or another unit member, who would distribute the material at the next meeting. Group members (and even their spouses, if they were deemed politically reliable) could expect that on occasion Peters would ask them to serve as couriers or to offer their homes or apartments to be used temporarily for storage of records or photographing of documents.[18]

Peters must have also made it clear to Ware that the Party would welcome reports on policy issues, insider information on developments in the AAA and other federal agencies, and in general any government documents group members could lay their hands on. Peters might not have expected to receive much of significance from such reports or documents, which, given their provenance, would deal mostly with agrarian issues. But it was important to foster these kinds of covert activity and habits, which would be useful if and when members moved on to work in agencies of greater interest to the Communist movement. Ware group members were thus encouraged to take small initial steps that might lead later to larger and more important operations. It was, as one historian has aptly put it, a kind of "incremental cultivation of sources" that represented a "dress rehearsal" for espionage.[19] Only one of the original Ware group members, Nathaniel Weyl, is known to have expressed uneasiness about some of these clandestine practices. The others apparently went along with whatever Peters or Ware proposed.

In the first year of the existence of the Ware group, Peters apparently traveled to Washington from time to time to resolve any problems that had arisen and to assess the potential of any new members.[20] It is not clear whether in this period Peters met with the group as a whole, but it is certain that he met frequently in New York and Washington with Ware to coordinate activities.[21] Peters also had occasional private meetings with individual group members, with whom he quickly developed an excellent rapport. Perhaps some of them had feared that their Party supervisor would be a humorless and coarse Russian apparatchik, or his American equivalent. Instead they found Peters, whom they were soon calling "Pete" or "Steve,"[22] to be an affable and effective leader with a good sense of humor and a ready smile.[23] He gave the appearance of being a mysterious European Communist, perhaps a Comintern representative, yet he spoke good colloquial American English, albeit with a charming accent. True, he could be quite stern and even rigid in his ideological pronouncements, but in practical matters he used common sense and a human touch. Several members of the Ware group, notably John Abt, Nat Witt, and Charles Kramer, established a close friendship with Peters that continued long after they had left the Washington underground.[24] Even those group members who in later years left the Communist Party retained favorable impressions of Peters as a "highly intelligent" leader and a tactful and "shrewd organizer."[25]

In the first year of its existence, the Washington underground unit functioned mainly as what Lee Pressman would later call a "Marxist discussion group."[26] At the weekly meetings the collection of dues would be followed by "reverential discussion of Marxism-Leninism and of the world situation as perceived by the Comintern."[27] Members might also present reports they had drawn up based on their "positions as insiders in federal agencies." These reports, along with any documents or other materials members had obtained at their offices, were turned over to Ware, who, according to John Abt, passed them on to "the national leadership in New York for its consideration in estimating the direction of the New Deal and what might be done to influence it."[28] Since documents clearly emanating from the Ware group have not been identified in surviving CPUSA records, it is difficult to determine the quantity and significance of any material the Washington unit provided to the Party in this period. Josephine Herbst, who examined some of the documents her husband and other members had obtained from their offices, found the material "thoroughly innocent and innocuous." On the other hand, Hope Hale Davis, who joined one of the subunits in late 1934, later recalled that already at that time "a great deal of highly confidential and valuable (to the Party) material was being turned over systematically."[29] Whittaker Chambers, who saw some of this material, characterized it as "usually not privileged or confidential, but still useful."[30]

There was also a general understanding among Ware group members that, without calling undue attention to their ideological views, they would attempt to influence policy formation in the agencies in which they were employed. In addition, whenever possible they would try to facilitate the hiring of Party members or sympathizers and the promotion of fellow members. All this had to be done with the utmost caution, since already in 1933 the alarm was being sounded by conservative groups and politicians about the alleged "Bolshevistic" tendencies of New Deal legislation.[31] The original group members were also encouraged to be on the lookout for federal employees who might be suitable recruits for their secret unit.

In 1933, J. Peters could spare only a limited amount of time to the organization of the Washington underground, since he was very busy with his previously described activities as the Party's specialist in cadre development, recruitment, and creation of the "illegal apparatus."[32] But by early 1934 Peters's relationship with Soviet intelligence agencies had developed in ways that suggested new possibilities for the Ware group. When in the early summer of 1933 Peters began to serve as the Party's liaison with the chief GRU illegal resident, Ulrich (Alexander Ulanovsky), he was not inclined to assume the passive role that had been preferred by his predecessor, Max Bedacht. The latter had for the most part limited his activity to supervising Whittaker Chambers as the courier between GRU agents and the CPUSA and as the recipient of Comintern subsidies. But Peters, with his many contacts at all levels of the Party and his creative approach to conspiratorial work, was apparently eager to cooperate with Ulrich in his underground operations. He quickly established a good working relationship with Chambers, whom he had first met in the late 1920s in the offices of the *Daily Worker*. Peters apparently concluded that Chambers's organizational abilities and developing skills as a worker in Soviet intelligence could be of great use to him in the CPUSA secret apparatus should the opportunity arise. Chambers at first found his new handler to be "reserved, innately distrustful, [and] secretive," but he was soon impressed by his friendliness, tact, and sense of humor.[33] Over the next five years they would work together closely and harmoniously on many clandestine projects. Later, after he had left the Party and was beginning to disclose what he knew about the Communist underground, Chambers admitted that it was an unpleasant task to testify against Peters, whom he regarded as "one of the few American Communists who is at once decent and intelligent."[34]

In the summer of 1933, Chambers acquainted Peters with the GRU operation and the methods of his handler, Ulrich. Peters, who probably also met Ulrich from time to time, no doubt quickly realized that the GRU illegal resident was not a very ambitious or creative operative. In fact, he was regarded by some of his fellow Soviet agents as a "confused and inept man."[35] In these circumstances, Peters seized the initiative and sought to identify opportunities for espionage that he could bring to Ulrich's attention, using Chambers as his intermediary and providing his own expertise in conspiratorial work. The best documented of these occurred late in 1933, when Peters learned from Isadore Wofsy, the Party organizer for New England, that two Communists employed at the New London, Connecticut, plant of the Electric Boat Company, the leading American manufacturer of submarines, were able and willing to procure highly secret blueprints.[36] At the urging of Peters, Chambers passed on this information to Ulrich, who agreed that this was worth exploring. Accordingly, Peters and Chambers traveled to New Haven and met Wofsy at a restaurant near the Yale University campus. Arrangements were made for the two workers to supply blueprints to Chambers, who would photograph the material and promptly return the originals. The photographs would then be turned over to Ulrich.[37]

In the end, however, J. Peters's first foray into espionage proved, through no fault of his own, to be a fiasco. Ulrich insisted on taking an active role in the operation, and a meeting was set up with Wofsy and one of the workers. Chambers introduced his Soviet handler as an engineer with expertise in submarines, but Ulrich's obvious ignorance on that subject soon became clear to those present. As a result, the Electric Boat Company worker, no doubt made uneasy by his meeting with a seemingly incompetent foreign agent, had second thoughts about the operation and decided to report what was afoot to a local American Legion chapter and, in turn, to the FBI. Before the operation collapsed, Chambers did manage to obtain some submarine blueprints, but the photographs he took turned out to be blurred and unreliable.[38] By this time the FBI had begun its investigation, but they were unable to follow up on the information they obtained and the involvement of Ulrich, Peters, Chambers, and Wofsy was not detected at the time.

Although this attempt at naval espionage proved unproductive, Peters was by no means deterred. He remained alert to other opportunities,[39] and continued to groom members of the Ware group, as well as other smaller units in Washington and Baltimore, for possible espionage work in the future. To be sure, in normal circumstances the head of the CPUSA's secret apparatus would not have been expected to develop and oversee a major espionage operation in Washington, D.C. Such an enterprise would clearly be in the bailiwick of Soviet intelligence agencies. But for a period of several years beginning in late 1933, Soviet intelligence work in the United States was stymied by interagency rivalries, bureaucratic difficulties, and the repercussions stemming from the resumption of formal diplomatic relations between the United States and the U.S.S.R.[40] J. Peters took advantage of these unusual circumstances and was responsible for the creation of a Washington underground organization that an NKVD document composed in 1946 referred to as a "group of agents comprised of illegal fellow-countrymen working in various government agencies" that supplied information to the CPUSA and the GRU.[41]

In 1934, Valentin Markin, supervisor of the NKVD's illegal station in New York, had to take into account the new situation created by the decision of the American government in November 1933 to grant diplomatic recognition to the Soviet Union. Soviet intelligence agents in the United States, both legal and illegal, were now warned by their superiors in Moscow to avoid "mass recruitment" of new operatives and to avoid risky operations that might be discovered and cause adverse publicity that could endanger the newly established diplomatic ties between Moscow and Washington. Accordingly, Markin was advised to proceed cautiously, since with his "small apparatus" it might be difficult to operate effectively and in accordance with the "principles of our profession."[42] In response to these developments, several GRU residents were ordered to cease operations or to remain dormant for a period of time.[43] Accordingly, Ulrich began early in 1934 to sever his ties with his American agents and to dismantle his apparatus. Since Whittaker Chambers had worked briefly under Markin earlier in 1933 and the relationship had been a tense and unproductive one,[44] Ulrich proposed that Chambers instead return to the CPUSA and work exclusively in Peters's secret apparatus. Markin apparently raised no objections, and Peters for his part was "very pleased with the arrangement."[45]

Because of his myriad activities at this time in New York and elsewhere, Peters no doubt found it difficult to spare time for regular visits to Washington to supervise the Ware group. Chambers, who had served for more than a year as the courier between the GRU and the CPUSA and had received training in conspiratorial work, must have seemed to Peters a good choice to become his representative to the Ware group. It is even possible that Peters had approached Markin and requested that Chambers (whom Markin knew as "Bob") be attached to his apparatus in order to assist in the development of a very promising underground operation in Washington. This would explain certain cryptic remarks Markin apparently made to Chambers at some point late in 1933. On that occasion the normally cold and contemptuous Soviet agent was in a friendly mood. Chambers later recalled that "he took my arm cozily" and asked, "What's doing in Washington?" When Chambers expressed ignorance of developments in the nation's capital, Markin continued, "Bob, you have a great career ahead of you." He explained that there were "colossal opportunities" in Washington and that Chambers should go there and "build the apparatus."

In light of Markin's advice, Chambers perhaps was not completely surprised when, soon after being permanently attached to Peters's secret apparatus, his new handler began to drop hints that "he had something extremely interesting operating in Washington, D.C." Over the course of several months in early 1934, Peters gave Chambers an orientation on the background and workings of the Washington underground unit. Chambers learned that Harold Ware, whose name he had never before heard, was the "spark plug" of a group of Party members employed by the AAA and other New Deal agencies. Peters explained, however, that this was just the beginning, for his ultimate objective, his "dream," was to penetrate "old-line agencies" like the Navy, State, and Interior Departments.[46]

At some time in the late spring of 1934, Peters took Chambers to an automat in New York City and introduced him, under the name "Carl," to Hal Ware.

Despite their quite different personal backgrounds and experiences in the Party, Chambers and Ware got on well. Chambers discovered that "we had the same unromantic approach to conspiracy, the same appreciation of the difficulties in organizing intellectuals, and a common interest in farm problems." The three men discussed the personnel and activities of the underground Washington operation and the nature of Chambers's assignment as courier and Peters's representative to the Ware group. It was agreed that Chambers's duties as Peters's representative to the secret unit in Washington would include the carrying back and forth between New York and Washington of messages, literature, and dues. In addition, he was to provide general assistance to Ware in what Chambers would later call, in typically melodramatic terms, his "heavy load of conspiracy."[47]

Early in the summer of 1934 there was an important new development in the Ware group. Peters had at some point begun to encourage the group members to explore employment opportunities in other government agencies or congressional committees. Along these lines, Ware suggested to Nathaniel Weyl that he try to get into the State Department and work on the staff of William Bullitt, the first American Ambassador to the Soviet Union. But Weyl, believing that this would put him in a "morally difficult position," declined. Feeling increasingly uneasy about the "duplicitous" nature of the secret Communist unit, Weyl soon thereafter informed Ware that he had decided to withdraw entirely from participation in the group and in fact to resign his government position.[48] On the other hand, Henry Collins was apparently eager to comply with Peters's request and urged Ware to help him find a position in the State Department. However, it was not Collins but Alger Hiss who had the first opportunity to move on to a position of greater interest to Peters and the CPUSA. In the early summer of 1934 he was asked to become general counsel for the Senate's Special Committee on Investigation of the Munitions Industries, chaired by Gerald Nye. With the strong encouragement of both Peters and Ware, Hiss accepted this assignment, which was regarded as temporary, since he was technically only "on loan" from the AAA to the Nye Committee.

J. Peters was elated by this news, for he envisioned that Hiss, whom he considered one of the brightest and most promising of the Ware group members, would not only be able to exert influence on the activities and decisions of the committee but would also gain access to important and confidential government documents. This development prompted Peters to implement a decision that he had perhaps been contemplating for some months. In the Soviet intelligence world of the early 1930s, one of the concepts much in vogue was that of the "parallel apparatus." In order to maintain the secrecy and efficiency of expanding clandestine units, it was deemed best to limit their size by removing some members to form the nucleus of a new, parallel apparatus that would be rigidly segregated from the original group. Along these lines, Peters decided that Hiss's new assignment, with the potential it represented for espionage, necessitated the creation of a new apparatus that would have as its objective the "gradual infiltration of the old-line departments, with the State Department as the first objective." Shortly before Chambers's departure for Washington, Peters thus informed him that, in addition to the duties previously agreed on, he would be responsible for establishing and supervising what Chambers would call Apparatus B, the initial member of which would be Alger Hiss.[49]

Peters was in an ebullient mood when, some time in early or mid-July 1934, he traveled by train from New York to Washington. Chambers, who had made the trip earlier in the day and had already received an on-the-spot orientation from Ware, met Peters at Union Station. In order "to kill time and to make sure that we were not followed," they walked downtown, where they were scheduled to rendezvous with Ware. Chambers was surprised to find the normally reserved Peters acting like a "king returned to his kingdom—suddenly gay and expansive." He spoke with pride of the organization he was constructing in Washington, and had particular praise for Alger Hiss, whose first name he pronounced, "with a drawling pleasure," as "Awl-jur." Then, with "a little inclusive wave of his pudgy hand," he summed it all up: "Even in Germany under the Weimar Republic, the party did not have what we have here." Once they met up with Ware and had a preliminary discussion, they proceeded in Ware's car to a downtown cafeteria, where Chambers was introduced for the first time to Hiss. This meeting was brief; Peters and Hiss left together, and Ware took Chambers on a tour of the capital and to an apartment where he would spend the night.[50]

Once back on the ninth floor of the CPUSA headquarters in New York, Peters no doubt felt confident that his Washington operation, both Apparatus A (the Ware group) and Apparatus B, were in good hands and would, in time, provide intelligence useful both to the CPUSA and to the Soviet Union. However, quite quickly there were new developments in the Soviet intelligence world that forced Peters to make important adjustments. In August, Valentin Markin, who since early in 1934 had been in charge of both GRU and NKVD illegal operatives in the United States, died suddenly in an auto accident. Fearing that an investigation of Markin's death might lead American counter-intelligence agencies to clues about Soviet intelligence activity, the Moscow Center ordered all "illegals" in the United States to cease their activity and destroy all incriminating documents.[51] At first Peters probably did not suspect that this would have any impact on his own operations. However, a few weeks after Markin's death Whittaker Chambers, who was in New York on one of his periodic visits, was summoned by one of his former associates in the GRU apparatus and introduced to a new handler. Unlike Markin, this new Soviet agent, who used the cover name "Bill," had definite plans for Chambers, which he expounded on in their initial conversations in late August 1934.

Bill, according to Chambers, "quickly took me away from Peters" and "put me in his own Soviet underground apparatus."[52] But Bill made it clear that he did not wish to get involved with Chambers's conspiratorial work in the United States. His "chief project," in fact, was to set up a Soviet apparatus in England, and he wanted Chambers to accompany him to London as his assistant. Bill instructed Chambers to secure a business cover for himself, such as a "representative of a legitimate American firm," and fraudulent passports for himself and his family, since they would travel with him. Furthermore, Chambers was to establish a courier system that would operate between New York and the new Soviet apparatus in London and various English port cities.[53]

Chambers was given this new assignment by Bill some time in late August or early September. Since Bill indicated that there was need for immediate action and that they would both leave for England just as soon as their "covers and other practical matters were taken care of," Chambers immediately went to his resourceful CPUSA handler to explain the new situation and to request assistance in procuring the required passports and business covers.[54] Although he must have felt some disappointment in apparently losing the services of Chambers precisely at a time when the Washington operation was developing in such a promising way, Peters indicated that he would help in any way he could with Chambers's "complicated problem." He "foresaw certain difficulties, but none that were insuperable." In fact it took only a few days for Peters to find what he described as the "perfect cover" for Chambers. He introduced him to Maxim Lieber and explained to the two comrades what he had in mind: Lieber would open a branch of his literary agency in London and Chambers, who had experience in editorial work, would be the office manager. Chambers would in fact spend some time in legitimate editorial work, but mostly he would assist Bill in his "project." All expenses in setting up the operation, as well as Chambers's salary, would be paid by the Soviet apparatus. Lieber was pleased with this proposal, since he would be able "to combine business and party duty" at no cost to himself.[55] Chambers found Lieber to be a congenial collaborator; in fact, they became good friends and soon Chambers was using Lieber's apartment on West Forty-seventh Street as his "unofficial headquarters" whenever he visited New York.

Although Bill quickly gave his approval to Peters's scheme, his sense of urgency about the London apparatus seemed to diminish rapidly and within a few days he informed Chambers about another new project that had an even greater priority. This involved an American, John Sherman (who was using the cover name "Don"), whom Chambers had first met in the late 1920s in the *Daily Worker* office and with whom he had had dealings when he was first selected for work in the GRU apparatus in 1932. Bill instructed Chambers to provide assistance to Sherman, who had been given the assignment of establishing an espionage apparatus in Japan. Sherman's problem was "simple and formidable": he needed an appropriate business cover, passport, and an assistant who spoke Japanese, was an American citizen and a Communist Party member, and also had good connections with governing circles in Japan.[56] For the business cover, Bill, Sherman, and Chambers conferred and decided to establish a news syndicate, under the direction of Maxim Lieber. When apprised of this new scheme, Lieber was not enthusiastic, since he regarded the English project as a much better fit with the activities of his literary agency. But he was soon persuaded, probably by J. Peters, who was quickly drawn into the planning and perhaps clinched the deal by offering $5,000 or more to finance the operation.[57] Over the course of just a few weeks in September 1934, all the necessary steps were taken to ensure a successful launching of the project. The news agency, called the American Feature Writers Syndicate, was duly incorporated on September 4, and Peters came up with the requisite documentation to allow Sherman to obtain, on September 24, a fraudulent passport. As for Sherman's Japanese-speaking assistant, here too Peters worked his magic. He proposed that Chambers seek out Hideo Noda, one of the Communist artists in New York who had become loosely attached to his secret apparatus. Chambers proceeded to get in touch with Noda through a mutual friend and non-Party member. Noda, who claimed to be related to the imperial family in Japan, was willing to cooperate, and soon he and Sherman had departed for Japan.[58]

The new espionage apparatus in Japan had thus been swiftly and successfully launched, although ultimately the operation proved to be quite unproductive. Chambers no doubt now expected that Bill would insist that planning continue at a brisk pace for the London project. But in fact Bill's interest in the matter seemed greatly diminished, and before long Chambers concluded that the project "had lost its urgency." Furthermore, Bill did not seem to have any other pressing assignments for Chambers and he even suggested he stay away from New York while the English project gestated. Chambers and his family had earlier moved to an apartment in Baltimore, from which he could easily commute to Washington to carry out his work in Peters's underground operations. When Chambers now proposed to resume his work for the CPUSA secret apparatus, Bill voiced no objections. He thought Chambers should "pull together the rudiments of an apparatus" in Washington, which later could be turned over to someone else or perhaps even be of use to the "English venture." As a result, for about a year and a half, beginning in the fall of 1934, Chambers was in theory working simultaneously for two handlers, Bill and J. Peters.[59] Most of his activity, however, was concentrated in Washington, where he helped coordinate the Ware group and began to develop what he and Peters called Apparatus B.

In late 1934 and early 1935, the Ware group continued its usual schedule of meetings and activities. Members continued to submit reports in their areas of expertise, and these were forwarded, usually by Henry Collins, to Chambers, who delivered them to Peters.[60] Two of the original members had left (Weyl and Hiss), but new members had been drawn in, and all had been diligent in recruiting fellow government employees who showed radical inclinations. By 1935, enough new members had been added that four or five sub-units had been established, each headed by one of the original group members.[61] For the most part, Peters continued to leave the day-to-day running of the underground operation to Ware, but beginning in the summer of 1934 he began to give occasional talks to the central group on such topics as "The Theory of Underground Organizations and the Nature of Parallel Apparatuses."[62] Occasionally Peters's personal intervention was required to resolve a personnel problem or to smooth over personal differences among group members.

In August 1935, the operations of the Washington underground were suddenly disrupted by the news that the group's leader, Hal Ware, had died in an auto accident in Pennsylvania. Fearing that Ware's death might in some way compromise the group, members dutifully adhered to the "conspiratorial techniques" that Peters had set forth in one of his lectures. Unit meetings were suspended for a time, members avoided unnecessary contact with each other, and absolutely essential communication was conducted only through "pay phones at preplanned hours and intervals."[63] Once things had calmed down and no dire consequences had resulted, the members began to ponder the key question of who would take over Ware's role as leader of the Washington underground units. To resolve this matter, Peters traveled to Washington and called a meeting of the central Ware group, which was held in Henry Collins's apartment. Peters's personal choice as Ware's successor was Nathan Witt, and this seemed to be the consensus of the members in attendance. Witt was duly elected and became the nominal leader of the group, although later he may have shared the responsibilities with John Abt.[64] However, the group leader's authority was now greatly diminished. Perhaps no one could have fully replaced the charismatic Ware, but in any case Peters now decided to take a more active personal role in supervising the Washington underground units. Years later both Lee Pressman and John Abt claimed that after Ware's death it was Peters who in effect took over leadership of the group.[65]

Beginning in the summer of 1935, Peters began to travel to Washington at least once a month.[66] Perhaps sensing that Nathan Witt and John Abt, both of whom had been in the Party only since 1933, would not be able to provide reliable guidance to Ware group members on ideological problems, Peters made himself more frequently available to give "authoritative answers" to the questions they seemed eager to pose. Peters would suddenly appear in Washington, Hope Hale Davis later recalled, "like a god in a Greek play, to give the word from on high."[67] In his dealings with group members, Peters seemed to have an intuitive sense of how to handle these highly educated but often politically naïve professionals who were eager to throw off their previous liberal or "bourgeois" sentiments. At times he could be quite stern and reproving. Once at a meeting of unit heads and their spouses held in Lee Pressman's house, Peters opened the floor to questions. Hermann Brunck, who worked for the National Recovery Administration, innocently remarked that he was puzzled by the way a recent book by the philosopher Sidney Hook had been reviewed in Party publications. "Wouldn't Party critics have a more convincing effect," he asked, "by analyzing and demolishing the book's arguments on philosophical grounds rather than using the space for invective?" Peters, his heavy brows "knotted furiously," responded with histrionic fury: "This kind of stupid talk I never expected tonight! To call by the name philosophy the filth that renegade spews out!" Peters managed to calm down only after a gentle reminder from John Abt that Brunck was a new comrade who had faithfully followed Party directives and had done a good job handling a difficult unit. But Peters's point had been made: anyone who, like Hook, had once supported the Party but then turned against it was a despicable "renegade." Peters's outburst had its intended impact; from then on "the comrades asked only cautious questions."[68]

On certain issues, however, Peters could be relatively tolerant and open-minded. When in 1937 the underground Communists in Washington struggled over the question of how to convince "confused liberals" that the purge trials in Moscow, at which many prominent Bolsheviks had confessed to treason, were legitimate and necessary, Peters urged a cautious approach. He informed the Washington units that to ensure the success of the Popular Front, Party members needed to be skillful in "correcting the widespread misunderstanding of the Moscow Trials." He warned against criticizing the position of the liberals, which would only alienate them. It would be better to try to understand their point of view and, as Lenin advised, "patiently to explain."[69]

In his personal dealings with the Washington underground Peters struck most members as a reasonable, tactful, and even compassionate manager. Whenever possible he seemed to seek a common-sense solution to a problem. Peters's tactfulness in dealing with delicate personal problems made a particularly strong impression on Hope Hale Davis, one of the few women active in the Washington underground. In 1936, Davis had arranged for her husband, who had begun to suffer from bouts of paranoia, to enter a psychiatric clinic. In her desperation to ensure that the staff would make a proper diagnosis, she decided to inform the clinic director that her husband was a Communist. Only later did it dawn on her that she had committed a "sin of the highest magnitude," since there was the possibility that the clinic director or staff might divulge this information to the police or FBI. When she confessed her transgression to members of her unit, they reacted with alarm and found her action "too heinous to believe." The unit leader, Charles Kramer, looked stricken, and Victor Perlo declared that she "might have wrecked our whole organization," and just at a time when "it was beginning to affect key areas of government." Davis was ordered to avoid all Party contacts until further notice, and she took it for granted that she would now be denied the chance to become the head of her own sub-unit. Not long afterward, however, her friend Marion Bachrach informed her that not only was she being reinstated as an active member but also that she would lead her own unit after all. "Whatever they [Kramer and Perlo] may have thought before," she said, "they now agree with Steve." Clearly Peters had decided that Davis's transgression was minor and did not warrant drastic action.[70]

In the autumn of 1937 Peters was similarly understanding when Davis once again committed an apparent blunder. Living at the time in New York, Davis met Joe Freeman, the literary editor of *New Masses* and a friend of Peters. In the course of their conversation Freeman asked her about her activities in Washington, and without thinking she proceeded to tell him about her role in the underground. Almost immediately she realized that she had broken another "inviolable rule" of clandestine operations. Feeling intense guilt and shame, she rushed to the CPUSA headquarters and made her way to Peters's "dread ninth floor office." Peters listened calmly to her confession, and then, to her amazement, leaned forward "with a gentle smile" and let his hand rest softly on her hair. The Washington secret, he said, was safe with Joe Freeman. From that moment, she later wrote, Peters's "authority, accepted technically before," became "emotionally real."[71] Of course, Peters must have calculated that a pardoned sinner is likely to be an even more willing collaborator in the future. Not long after this incident he prevailed on Davis to make one room of her apartment available to the Party for the storage of highly confidential files. For six months starting in September 1937, an agent using the name "Young" made almost daily visits to study these records and from time to time fulminated against the Trotskyites. This led Davis to suspect that the records stored in her apartment dealt with the campaign against the Trotskyites and perhaps even the plans for the assassination of Trotsky.[72]

Although the members of secret American Communist units, such as Peters's Washington underground, were in general very dedicated and disciplined, as in any organization there were a few eccentrics and malcontents. One, George Silverman, annoyed Peters by balking at paying his Party dues. This outraged Peters, who complained to Whittaker Chambers that Silverman was a "whiner."[73] Two other original members of the central Ware group, Victor Perlo and Lee Pressman, also proved troublesome at times. Peters once told Chambers that he did not think highly of Victor Perlo, who had an exaggerated estimate of his own abilities and great ambitions to rise in the Party ranks.[74] Peters also did not have complete confidence in Lee Pressman and seemed to have shared the opinion of some Ware group members that he was "quite a climber" and had "a bad case of big-shotitis."[75] In 1935, Pressman decided to leave government work and return to private practice in New York. At his final Ware group meeting he indicated that he would be severing his ties to the Washington underground, although he apparently promised that he would remain committed to the Communist movement. One year later Pressman was offered the job of general counsel for the CIO (Congress of Industrial Organizations).When apprised of this development the Central Committee of the CPUSA discussed the situation and, no doubt acting on a recommendation from Peters, who was the only leading Party official who had worked closely with Pressman, informed him that he should not accept the offer. Peters explained to Whittaker Chambers the reason for this decision: "The party felt that Pressman was a lone operator and impulsive and the Party was afraid that if he took this job, that they could not control him." Nonetheless, Pressman showed his independent streak and ignored the decision of the Central Committee.[76] He remained general counsel for the CIO until 1948.

It is noteworthy that despite their less than harmonious relations with J. Peters, Perlo and Silverman both remained active and dedicated members of the Washington underground. Both of them, and even Pressman on one occasion, provided important assistance to Soviet intelligence agents.[77] By the mid- to late 1930s other members of the original Ware group had moved on to important government posts. John Abt served for a time as chief counsel for the influential Civil Liberties Subcommittee of the Senate Committee on Education and Labor, and later in the Department of Justice as a special assistant to the attorney general. Nathan Witt became Secretary of the National Labor Relations Board. Both Abt and Witt were successful in hiring a number of secret Communists who attempted, though not always successfully, to shape policy along lines preferred by the CPUSA.[78] By 1938, perhaps as many as one hundred secret Party members were scattered in numerous government agencies and congressional committees. Some of them continued to send reports on their activities that reached Peters through various channels. Peters could feel proud of the underground organization he and Ware had launched in 1933. The reports these secret Communists sent may not have been of great significance and they may not always have been successful in their attempts to influence policy in their sphere, but, in Peters's eyes, they constituted a valuable sleeper apparatus. In that future time when conditions became ripe for revolutionary change, the members of the Washington apparatus would constitute a nucleus of experienced and ideologically sound bureaucrats and administrators ready to serve a new Communist regime in the United States.

Those NKVD/KGB operatives who came to know of Peters's apparatus in Washington were often impressed by what he had accomplished. They understood that he had his own "group of agents comprised of illegal fellowcountrymen working at various govt. agencies" who provided confidential material to both the GRU and to Earl Browder and the CPUSA.[79] At the same time, they often expressed consternation at the haphazard way in which the principles of "konspiratsiya" were being adhered to.[80] Peters had discovered early on that his "Washington set-up" could not in fact operate in all ways like a Communist underground unit in Europe. In theory, the members of the different units of the Ware group should not have known each other's real names and should have avoided any social contact with each other. But this was highly impractical, since not only had many Ware group members known other group members in college and become good friends or colleagues, but their spouses (only some of whom were Party members) also tended to know each other and invariably gained some knowledge of the underground operation. Peters accommodated himself to this reality, but he sometimes found himself frustrated by these neo-phyte American Communists, whose pragmatic or humanitarian impulses at times led them to act in ways that flouted the rules of conspiratorial work.

An important example of this occurred in 1936. Having bought a new car that year, and having no use for his old 1929 Ford sedan, Alger Hiss proposed to Whittaker Chambers that the Ford be turned over to the Communist Party so it could be used by "some poor Party organizer in the South or the West."[81] Cham-bers opposed the idea, as did Peters when he was informed of it, since it would represent a direct connection between the open Party and the underground. That would violate "all the rules of underground organization" and might some day prove incriminating. But Hiss was adamant and Peters, against his better judgment, finally relented. He arranged with Hiss for the car to be delivered to an auto dealership in Washington, from which, through a complicated process, it presumably was passed on to the Communist Party. In 1948, however, the concerns expressed by Chambers and Peters proved justified. Chambers related the story of the sale of the Ford sedan to government investigators, and Alger Hiss could give no satisfactory explanation of his role in the incident.[82]

Despite the fact that "rules of underground organization" were not always scrupulously followed in Peters's Washington underground operation, the Ware group and related information-gathering units were never discovered at the time by American authorities. Furthermore, by 1935 the groundwork had been completed and Peters was prepared to expand his "Washington set-up" by es-tablishing an espionage ring in the "old line" government agencies that he had long hoped to infiltrate.

J. Peters and his famous smile. Courtesy of the Library of Congress, *New York World-Telegram and Sun* Collection.

J. Peters's passport photo of 1931 under the name Isadore Boorstein, from Peters's FBI FOIA file. This is the earliest known photo of Peters.

J. Peters with his attorney, Carol Weiss King, in 1948. Courtesy of Associated Press Images.

J. Peters being sworn in at the HUAC hearing, August 31, 1948. Courtesy of the Library of Congress, *New York World-Telegram and Sun* Collection.

Whittaker Chambers (*left*) confronts J. Peters (*right*) at HUAC hearing. Courtesy of Associated Press Images.

Ann Peters as she departed for Hungary in June 1949. Courtesy of the Library of Congress, *New York World-Telegram and Sun* Collection.

The front cover of Peters's most controversial publication.

The front cover of a reprint of Peters's *Manual* by an anti-Communist organization in 1948.

6

J. Peters's Espionage Ring, 1934–38

By 1934 it was becoming clear to the Soviet leadership that the rise of Nazi Germany and an expansionist Japan posed a substantial threat to the national security interests of the U.S.S.R. Soviet intelligence agencies were thus instructed to place a special emphasis on information gathering that related to these two potential enemies. In this effort, intelligence obtained in the United States now took on a new importance, for it was believed that there were "no problems, not even 'purely' European ones, that America doesn't take part in resolving by virtue of its economic and financial might."[1]

The main focus of this new Soviet intelligence initiative was the State Department, because it was felt that reports by American diplomats and military attachés in Europe and the Far East would be of particular value. However, Soviet operatives in the United States were not sanguine about the prospects for immediate successes in Washington and specifically in the State Department, since they had few reliable agents there and had to "begin this work from scratch."[2]

It was in this period that some Soviet agents were beginning to realize that among the sizable number of well-educated, idealistic Americans who had been attracted to Washington to staff President Roosevelt's New Deal administration, there were some who harbored left-wing sympathies, a strong aversion to the fascist regimes, and an admiration for the Soviet Union. If properly approached, some of these "romantic anti-fascists" might be persuaded to engage in espionage. One Soviet agent who in time proved successful in cultivating these new sources was Hede Massing, who, unlike many Soviet operatives in the United States at the time, spoke good English and was able, with her husband Paul, to move easily in left-wing American social circles. But it was J. Peters, with his ability to draw on the rich resources of the secret apparatus of the CPUSA and the personnel of the expanding Ware group, who was the best positioned to take advantage of the favorable situation and "to establish an agent beachhead within the Roosevelt Administration."[3]

By late 1934, it was becoming clear to Peters that Whittaker Chambers's GRU handler, Bill, did not intend to proceed very quickly with the plan to establish a new espionage apparatus in England. Chambers was thus free to resume his work in Peters's Washington operation. In this period, Chambers was on the move frequently between Baltimore, Washington, and New York. To save on commuting time and railway tickets, at the beginning of 1935 Chambers bought a Ford Sedan with money provided by Peters. From time to time Peters would hitch a ride with Chambers to or from Washington, since in this period Peters did not have a driver's license.[4]

Alger Hiss was the first, and for more than a year, the only member of the parallel apparatus (Apparatus B) that J. Peters established in the summer of 1934. Peters hoped that in his capacity as general counsel for the Nye Committee, which was investigating the role of the munitions industry in World War I, Hiss would have access to such materials as the files of arms manufacturers and State Department documents. For his part Hiss seemed to understand what was expected of him, and he apparently expressed no reservations to Chambers or Peters about getting involved in espionage.[5] A further impetus to this operation came in September, when the Comintern evinced great interest in the Nye Committee and confidentially advised the Swiss Communist Party (and presumably the CP of other countries) that it regarded information coming out of this congressional investigation as of "great importance" for its propaganda campaigns.[6] In due course, Chambers was able to report to Peters that Hiss had been successful, though not without some difficulty, in procuring copies of confidential State Department records.[7]

At this point Peters and Chambers needed to work out a procedure for the handling and photographing of the stolen documents. Clearly, they wanted to avoid the mistakes committed in the failed attempt to obtain submarine blueprints from the Electric Boat Company in 1933. Peters now provided Chambers with a Leica camera and a stand for photographing documents, all contained in a suitcase. On a prearranged day in late 1934 or early 1935, Hiss brought home a small group of documents and passed them to Chambers, who quickly photographed them and handed them back so that Hiss could return them the following morning. This time Chambers's photography proved proficient and he made the journey to New York to deliver the photos (which numbered "not more than ten") to Peters, whose plan was to present them to Soviet military intelligence. The GRU agent he knew best was Arnold Ikal, but his specialty was forged passports. So instead Peters got in touch with Bill and offered him the State Department documents as an indication of what his Washington apparatus could produce. But Bill, Chambers later recalled, "showed a complete lack of interest in the documents."[8]

This response no doubt puzzled Peters, as it has historians: why would a GRU agent show no interest in stolen State Department documents, especially at a time when Soviet intelligence leaders were emphasizing the need to obtain precisely those kinds of records? One possibility is that the documents in fact did not contain particularly secret or valuable information. Even so, it would seem that an astute intelligence agent would not have simply refused the offer, but would have urged Peters to go back to his source and try to get documents more relevant to current Soviet interests. More likely, Bill's indifference to Peters's offer was a reflection of the current disarray of Soviet intelligence work in the United States. With the arrival of Valentin Markin early in 1934, the NKVD had assumed the leading role in promoting espionage, while at the same time GRU activity in the United States had been greatly curtailed. The death of Markin in August had caused a minor panic in Soviet intelligence circles. So in these circumstances Bill would probably have been very cautious about getting involved in espionage activity centered in Washington. Furthermore, he himself had been given an assignment that would presumably soon take him (and Chambers) to England.

Whatever the reasons for Bill's apparent indifference, Peters now seemed all the more determined to recruit new members for Apparatus B who were actually employed in the "old-line agencies," particularly the State Department, and would thus have ready and ongoing access to important documents. Since his arrival in Washington, Chambers had been on the lookout for possible recruits for the spy apparatus, but it was Alger Hiss who was the first to identify a likely prospect, Noel Field, who worked in the European Division of the State Department. Soon after arriving in Washington, Field, who joined the Communist Party in late 1933, met Alger Hiss. "During our discussions," Field later recalled, "we discovered that we were both Communists."[9] Over the next year Hiss and Field, along with their wives, became close friends. In August 1935 Hiss moved to the Department of Justice, where he took a position as an assistant to the Solicitor General. By the end of 1935, Hiss felt close enough to Field to sound him out on his willingness to work for Peters's apparatus. He pointed out that since Field would soon be out of the country for an extended period (as a State Department participant in the London Naval Conference), it would be a good idea to establish a closer connection between them. Field responded that Hiss was "too late," because he already worked for another Soviet agency. Greatly surprised by this revelation, Hiss suggested that Field's connection to the Soviets might not be solid enough and that probably "his knowledge is being misused."[10] Hiss then proposed that when Field returned from London, he give him a detailed account of the conference. Flustered by Hiss's persistence and a vague sense that he had revealed too much to his friend, Field ended the conversation by insisting that he needed to consult his "connections."[11]

In reporting on this conversation to Chambers, Hiss expressed his astonishment: "Is it possible? Can there be another apparatus working in Washington?" Chambers thought it quite possible, and when he apprised Peters of what had happened, the latter suggested that it was probably "the apparatus of Hede Gumperz [Hede Massing]." Peters of course knew one of the fundamental principles governing Soviet intelligence work: the GRU and NKVD were to operate as distinct, independent agencies. Accordingly, Soviet agents must not know the identity of, and must not interact with, their counterparts in the other branch of Soviet intelligence. Peters thus instructed Hiss, through Chambers, to refrain from any further recruitment of Noel Field.[12] As a result, when Hiss met Field several days later he did not bring up the subject again, and withdrew his request that Field give him a briefing on the London Conference. However, Peters apparently encouraged Hiss to push on in another direction, the recruitment of Larry Duggan, a State Department employee who was a good friend of Field. For some time Peters and Chambers had been targeting Duggan as a possible recruit. On his first day in Washington, Chambers had learned from an associate of Hal Ware (probably Henry Collins) that Duggan was "very sympathetic" to the Communist movement. Peters and Ware at that time had authorized Collins, who had known Duggan in their university days, to approach him about joining the Ware group or Apparatus B. But Collins was unsuccessful.[13]

Some time in the late winter or early spring of 1936, after Noel Field had returned from the London Conference, Hiss followed up on Peters's suggestion. Knowing that Field and Duggan lived in the same apartment house, Hiss began to quiz Field about his friend. What was he like? Would Field contact Duggan and his wife Helen and "tell them who he is and give him [Hiss] access to them?" Field, unaware that the NKVD had also been for some time trying to recruit Duggan, grudgingly agreed to make an effort along these lines. As a result, Field entertained the Hisses and Duggans in his home several times. On these occasions, Hiss tried to sound out Duggan about his willingness to join Apparatus B.[14] When Duggan remained noncommittal, J. Peters tried another approach. He asked Frederick Vanderbilt Field, who had been a classmate of Duggan's at Harvard, to visit Duggan and see if he could persuade him to cooperate. Fred Field, who was not related to Noel Field, proceeded to travel to Washington in mid-May and had a long conversation with Duggan. Several days later he reported to Peters that his mission had been a failure, since Duggan was already connected with another apparatus. In fact, Duggan, who had been pondering the matter for some time, informed Hede Massing of his decision to work for the NKVD only in late May, a week after his meeting with Fred Field. He preferred to work for Massing's organization, he said, rather than the one to which Hiss and Fred Field belonged, because the former seemed to him a safer and a more direct connection to the U.S.S.R.[15]

In the NKVD organization, Hiss's approaches to Field and Duggan caused a good deal of consternation. Hede Massing, Field's handler, berated him for his "terrible discipline" and for having committed an "unpardonable indiscretion" by revealing to Hiss that he worked for Soviet intelligence and by abetting Hiss in his effort to recruit Duggan.[16] But Massing's attempt to repair the damage merely exacerbated the problem. At some point in the late winter of 1936 she agreed to a personal meeting with Hiss at the home of Noel Field to talk things out. News of these events greatly alarmed Massing's superiors, who reported back to Moscow and asked for instructions. From the NKVD leadership they had learned that Hiss was "the neighbor's man" (that is, he worked for the GRU) and that NKVD agents were not to have any contact with him, since "experiments of this sort could have undesirable consequences." Hede Massing was thus instructed to break off contact with Hiss.[17] Certain steps were now taken to defuse the situation. In the spring of 1936, Noel Field resigned from the State Department and accepted a position at the League of Nations in Geneva, where he maintained his connection with Soviet intelligence. Hede Massing was given a new assignment that took her back to Europe in the summer of 1936.

When J. Peters learned that Hede Massing had met with Alger Hiss and Noel Field, he too was alarmed, for he suspected that Massing was trying to draw Hiss into her own organization. When they next met in New York in one of their false passport transactions, he expressed his concern to Massing: "In Washington you stumbled across my buddy [Hiss], you had better keep your hands off him."[18] Massing may have been somewhat puzzled by Peters's reference to Hiss as "my buddy," which implied that he was Hiss's handler. The NKVD Center, presumably on the basis of information obtained from the GRU leadership in Moscow, had informed NKVD agents in the United States that Hiss was "the neighbor's man." This suggests that Bill, Chambers's GRU handler, had at some point in 1934 or 1935 informed his superiors in Moscow about Chambers, Peters, and Apparatus B, which at that time consisted only of Alger Hiss. Yet Peters was perhaps justified in his possessive attitude toward Hiss, since Bill had shown little interest in Apparatus B or the documents that Hiss had obtained while working for the Nye Committee. Several years later, NKVD operatives were still trying to figure out Hiss's past and current status. To clarify the matter, Iskhak Akhmerov consulted with Peters, who gave the following explanation: "Hiss was a member of the fraternal organization [the CPUSA] who had infiltrated the State Department and was then transferred to the Neighbors [GRU]." Peters was suggesting that in the mid-1930s Hiss was a member of his secret apparatus and thus under his jurisdiction.[19]

Although Noel Field and Larry Duggan were no longer potential recruits for Apparatus B, J. Peters had a number of other possibilities to work with. One was Harry Dexter White, an economist with impeccable educational credentials (Columbia, Stanford, and Harvard) who began work in the Treasury Department in 1934. Word quickly spread among Ware group members that White was sympathetic to the Communist Party, though he was not a member. One of White's friends was Robert Coe, who was a close collaborator with Hal Ware on various farm-related projects. At some point in early 1935, Coe apparently told Ware, who passed it on to Peters, that White would be willing to turn over to him "certain official Treasury documents which could then be photographed."[20] Peters seized the opportunity. He introduced Chambers to Coe and suggested they work out a procedure for transferring and photographing any documents provided by White. Before long, White was able to hand over to Coe some documents he had obtained in the Treasury Department. The content of these documents is unknown, but, in light of later developments, it is probable that they were mundane monetary and fiscal reports.[21] Coe delivered the documents immediately to Chambers, who that evening photographed them with his Leica. The next morning he was ready on a designated street corner to return the documents, but Coe was one hour late for the appointment. This infuriated Chambers, for the delay in returning the documents might well have placed White in a compromising position. As a result, Chambers concluded that Coe was "unfit for underground work" and resolved to have nothing to do with him in the future. Peters took the photographic copies to Bill, but he had no more luck than he had had with the Nye Committee documents. Bill examined the documents "at his leisure," but finally told Peters that they did not interest him. Furthermore, he did not want Chambers "to continue with such work."[22]

No doubt Peters was disheartened and perplexed by the indifference that Chambers's GRU handler was showing towards the work of the Washington apparatus. This first batch of records that White had been able to obtain might not have been of much importance, but he seemed to be a rising star in the Treasury Department and in the future could be useful to the Party in a number of ways. Thus it would be wise to find someone to replace Coe who could serve as the liaison between White and the secret apparatus. Before long, Peters suggested to Chambers that George Silverman could play that role. Peters considered Silverman, who was the research director at the Railroad Retirement Board, to be a "whiner," but he seems otherwise to have been a dependable underground worker. Furthermore, he was on very friendly terms with White. Chambers fairly quickly ingratiated himself with Silverman, who in time agreed to introduce him to White. For the duration of 1935 and into 1936, Chambers met on an irregular basis with White, the objective being, as Peters had put it, to keep him in "a productive frame of mind." In Chambers's estimation, White seemed to revel in the secrecy and enjoy "the sense of being in touch with the Party, but not in it."[23] White could thus be considered a dormant member of Apparatus B, ready to be called on if and when the necessity arose.

This is how matters stood until April or May of 1936, when Whittaker Chambers was surprised to learn from Peters that he presided over another espionage ring of government employees that he now proposed to transfer to Apparatus B.[24] Chambers had previously known nothing of this other apparatus, which has long remained an obscure part of the story of Communist-sponsored espionage in the 1930s. However, on the basis of the widely scattered evidence now available, it is possible to throw some light on the origins of this espionage operation. This second spy apparatus was formed by Peters in collaboration with Eleanor Nelson and David Carpenter (Zimmerman), two Communists who were active in the Washington area. Nelson, a graduate of Wellesley College, in the mid-1930s held an important position in the government employees union, which brought her into contact with a wide range of friends and associates among government workers. A sincere person with a strong commitment to the Communist movement, she proved to be a very successful recruiter for the Party.[25] Nelson concentrated her work on what Chambers later called "somewhat less-exalted government employees," but from time to time she had dealings with Hal Ware and other upper-level government workers.[26] Her most important recruit, Henry Julian Wadleigh, had a career profile that resembled that of such Ware group members as Nathaniel Weyl and Victor Perlo. He was an economist who had trained at the University of Oxford, the London School of Economics, and the University of Chicago. In 1934, while working in the Department of Agriculture, he had become deeply alarmed by the rise of Fascist Italy and Nazi Germany. Wadleigh thought of himself as a "Fabian Socialist," but he was increasingly attracted to Communism, in part as a result of conversations with Eleanor Nelson, a friend he greatly admired. Finally, in 1935 he decided that he would have to "come out of my cocoon and work with the Communists." He informed Nelson that he was interested in assisting the Party and asked "if there was anything useful I can do?"[27]

It was at this point, or not long after, that J. Peters learned about Wadleigh, who clearly could be useful to the work of the secret apparatus. The contact person between Peters and Nelson was David Carpenter, who lived with Nelson in Washington from late 1934 to 1938.[28] Fiercely dedicated to the Communist movement, Carpenter prided himself on being a "professional revolutionary," who would rise high in the Party. In 1933 he had been selected organizational secretary for the Party district comprising Baltimore and the District of Columbia, and in this capacity had worked with Peters on organizational matters and the creation of the "illegal apparatus" in Baltimore.[29] So it was only natural that Carpenter would alert Peters to this promising development and seek his advice on the best way to approach Wadleigh. After some delay, and with guidance from Carpenter and Peters, Nelson got back in touch with Wadleigh and asked him to procure documents and reports dealing with foreign countries, particularly Germany and Japan. Wadleigh, who initially did not suspect that he was being groomed for espionage work, was "pleased and proud" to accept the assignment and to have the opportunity "to do something practical in checking the great menace of Fascism in the world." In time he realized that he was actually being asked to supply "some of the secrets of my own government to agents of a foreign country." He agreed to do this and justified his willingness to engage in espionage with an idealistic argument that might well have been shared by Alger Hiss and other Americans who chose the same path: "I did not regard my action as contrary to the interests of the United States, but definitely the opposite. Anything that would help the Russians, or anyone else, to resist German or Japanese aggression would not only foster U.S. interests, but benefit the whole of mankind on the purely nationalistic level."[30] Wadleigh also believed that the Communist Party had become the only reliable opponent of Fascism, since "the Social Democrats had shown a remarkable lack of vitality and ability to resist the Nazis."[31]

The recruitment of Henry Wadleigh occurred in the spring and summer of 1935. Peters now had to decide the best place for Wadleigh in his Washington underground operation. The obvious choice would have been simply to integrate him into Chambers's Apparatus B. But Peters decided instead to create another parallel apparatus to be directed by David Carpenter. Several factors must have influenced this decision. Bill's London project now seemed about to be launched. Some time in the spring of 1935 Bill suddenly told Chambers to prepare "to go to England at once."[32] In May, Peters had accordingly procured passports for Chambers, his wife, and his daughter, and Chambers had found a person willing to serve as his transatlantic courier. Then in July Bill left the country, and it seemed possible that at any time Chambers might be summoned to join his handler in London.[33] Should that happen, it would be helpful to have on hand an experienced person like Carpenter to take over Apparatus B. Peters apparently had confidence in his ability to do clandestine work, although he may have had some doubts whether he had the personal skills needed to supervise agents. In any case, Carpenter probably expected that he would be designated to be Wadleigh's handler, since he had been so closely involved in his recruitment. Accordingly, early in 1936 Nelson introduced Carpenter to Wadleigh as his new "contact."[34]

Peters probably did not harbor any great hopes that Wadleigh could provide information or documents from the Agriculture Department that would be of interest to Soviet intelligence. But in March 1936, Carpenter brought Peters some unexpectedly good news: Wadleigh had been transferred to the State Department, where he was assigned to work as an economist in the Trade Agreements Division. Peters's dream of placing an agent in one of the "old-line agencies" had finally been fulfilled. Wadleigh quickly discovered that purloining documents was not really difficult: "I would go through the papers on my desk, pick out the ones that I judged would be of interest to the espionage apparatus, put them in a leather envelope, and walk out of the office." Wadleigh then handed the documents over to Carpenter, who photographed them and returned them the next morning. The system they had worked out, Wadleigh later recalled, "was so methodic, so detection-proof, that no document going to the spy ring ever was out of its proper place in the State Dept. during working hours."[35]

Surprised and excited by the initial flow of documents from Wadleigh, and also from another source, William Ward Pigman, a chemist employed by the Bureau of Standards, Peters now had second thoughts about leaving this second apparatus under the direction of David Carpenter. There are hints that Peters came to suspect that Carpenter possessed certain foibles that might cause problems with agents in the apparatus.[36] Furthermore, Bill's on-again, off-again London operation had by this time again stalled, thus freeing Chambers to devote much of his time to Apparatus B. So Peters decided to merge the Nelson/Carpenter apparatus into Apparatus B. He arranged for Chambers and Carpenter to meet him at a hotel in Washington and announced his plans: Chambers would be in charge, and Carpenter would be his assistant. Despite the fact that Carpenter resented his apparent demotion, the newly expanded apparatus began to function smoothly and at a very productive rate. Chambers and Carpenter shared the duties of collecting and photographing documents, and Chambers remained the chief contact person with Peters. Chambers also was responsible for maintaining contact with a few individuals who did occasional work for the apparatus, such as offering their homes as mail drops or serving as couriers.[37]

The quantity and quality of stolen government documents that Wadleigh and Pigman were providing by the late spring of 1936 led Peters to consider making yet another attempt to interest Bill, who was now back in New York again, in the operation.[38] With considerable excitement, Peters now told Chambers that he had "an interesting suggestion." Now that Apparatus B was obtaining government documents that surely would be of interest to Soviet intelligence, Peters urged Chambers to take a sample to Bill and see if he would be interested in purchasing such material. The payments made by Bill would be used to help finance the CPUSA secret apparatus.[39] In retrospect, Peters's proposal might sound a bit fanciful or even arrogant. After all, on two previous occasions the GRU resident had reacted with apparent indifference when shown confidential U.S. government documents obtained by Peters's agents. Bill had even suggested that Chambers discontinue his espionage work in Washington. On the other hand, Peters had probably convinced himself that the GRU would surely realize that the materials Wadleigh and Pigman had access to were of the highest importance. Furthermore, from his relationship with the GRU in his fraudulent passport operation, Peters had gained the impression that the Soviet military intelligence agency had a sizable budget and that its agents were willing to make lavish payments to collaborators in the CPUSA. If Richard Ikal could pay handsomely for passports and naturalization papers, surely Bill could do likewise for stolen government documents.

Chambers made his approach to Bill some time in April or May of 1936. Once again, however, Bill seemed unenthusiastic, although he did agree to take a look at the documents. Over the course of about two months ("four or five transmissions") Chambers dutifully made his way from Washington to New York with photographs he had made with his Leica camera. Presumably Bill showed the documents to his superior in New York, and they must also have been forwarded to Moscow. But, as on the previous two occasions, Bill in the end told Chambers that "this material was of no interest to him."[40] Once again, Peters and Chambers were left to puzzle over Bill's inexplicable attitude. Only later did Chambers hit upon what he believed to be the likeliest explanation. The GRU must have intended for Peters's Washington operation to be a "sleeper apparatus" that would be allowed to develop but would not be activated until it matured and the situation was opportune. Thus, Bill had allowed and even encouraged Chambers to spend most of his time building the apparatus in Washington and had listened to his periodic reports on this activity "like a somnolent (but vigilant) cat." But he had summarily rejected "Peters's premature attempts at photography," since the time for the activation of the sleeper apparatus had not yet come.[41]

Chambers's idea of a sleeper apparatus is plausible, but there is another, and perhaps more convincing, explanation for Bill's bizarre behavior. In 1936 the Soviet leadership, guided by Stalin, began a systematic, and largely indiscriminate, purge of the Soviet officer corps and intelligence services. By 1937, hundreds of GRU and NKVD agents had been recalled from their foreign posts, arrested, and in many cases executed.[42] Most likely Bill, who was summoned to Moscow in the summer of 1936, was one of the early victims of this purge. If so, he must have come under suspicion earlier in 1936, and GRU officials would not have wanted an agent soon to be accused of some serious crime to become too involved in an important American operation like Peters's Washington apparatus. Thus, when Bill showed a lack of interest in the documents Chambers presented to him, he did so most probably on orders from Moscow rather than on his own initiative. That the GRU leadership was in fact very interested in receiving the fruits of the espionage apparatus that Peters and Chambers had established is demonstrated by the actions of Bill's successor, to be described below.

Bill left New York some time early in the summer of 1936. His final instructions to Chambers were "to hold together the Washington group and wait for orders to proceed to England."[43] For the next six months, Chambers had no GRU handler and he reported exclusively to Peters. Since Wadleigh and Pigman continued to supply documents on a more or less regular basis, it now seemed expedient to find a reliable photographer who could relieve Chambers and Carpenter of that duty. The person Peters selected was Felix Inslerman, an Estonian American who had been recruited by Bill and sent, in the latter half of 1935, to Moscow for training in photography and the use of international codes. When he returned to the United States in December 1935, Inslerman, following Bill's instructions, took a course on short wave radio operation that was arranged by Peters, whom he knew as "Ben." After Bill's departure, Peters became Inslerman's handler. As Peters had no pressing need for Inslerman as a radio operator, he sent him instead to Baltimore, where Chambers and Carpenter established a photographic workshop in an apartment they rented part-time. Inslerman now became the main photographer for Apparatus B.[44] The flow of documents to be photographed increased after September 1936, when Alger Hiss joined the Trade Agreements Division in the State Department as assistant to Francis B. Sayre, the assistant secretary of state. Both Hiss and Peters had long hoped for this development. With two of his agents now ensconced in the State Department, Peters could foresee a steady flow of valuable documents. Hiss's new position in the office of the assistant secretary of state was particularly well suited to the needs of Apparatus B. As Hiss's predecessor on the job would later remark, it was "the best possible place to work" for someone engaged in espionage.[45]

From the spring of 1936 until the end of that year, J. Peters was thus the recipient of a steady flow of documents stolen from the State Department and Bureau of Standards. What use he made of these documents remains a mystery. Having failed to interest Bill in a selection of this material, it is possible that Peters showed them to his other GRU contact, Richard Ikal, in the hope that he might purchase them and pass them on to GRU headquarters in Moscow. Alternatively, Peters might have offered the documents to one of his NKVD contacts, although available NKVD records mention no such transaction. There is evidence, however, that in this period at least some of the documents obtained by Peters's espionage ring found their way into the hands of CPUSA leaders. In the CPUSA records preserved in the Comintern archive, one folder from 1937 contains, in addition to miscellaneous items relating to churches and congressional legislation, two items with a State Department provenance. One is a typed copy of a letter dated October 19, 1936, from William Dodd, the U.S. ambassador to Germany, to President Franklin Roosevelt. The second consists of an excerpt from a letter (undated, but likely October or November 1936) written by William Bullitt, then ambassador to France, to Assistant Secretary of State R. Walton Moore, and Moore's comments on Bullitt's remarks. The document also contains explanatory annotations presumably made by the person who had copied the material.[46] Both documents offered important insights into how several key American diplomats viewed the situation in Europe, particularly in Nazi Germany.

How did these documents, which almost surely were supplied by a member of Peters's Washington apparatus, end up in a file of miscellaneous material in the Party archive?[47] Peters would no doubt have been careful to keep the photographs (or perhaps just the negatives) of stolen government documents in one of the secure archives in his secret apparatus. However, the documents in question were not originals but copies that either he, Chambers, or one of the members of Apparatus B had made.[48] Perhaps Peters wanted to show Earl Browder or other high-level Party officials some samples of what his spy apparatus was obtaining. If so, he may have reasoned that it would be somewhat less risky to pass along typed copies of such material, rather than the original photographs. For some reason, however, the material was never returned to Peters and instead was filed away with other miscellaneous material in a folder that future historians would eventually stumble upon.

J. Peters's tenure as a more or less independent spymaster proved to be fleeting. In late November or early December 1936, Peters turned over to Whittaker Chambers a note that Bill, facing an uncertain future in the U.S.S.R., had managed to send to Richard Ikal. In the message, which was addressed to Chambers, Bill advised that a new GRU chief would soon be arriving and would be Chambers's new handler. But the note was worded in such a strange and cryptic fashion that Chambers took it be a warning that Bill's successor was a dangerous man who was not to be fully trusted.[49] The new GRU illegal resident was Col. Boris Bykov, a veteran of fifteen years of military intelligence work in Europe. Soon after his arrival he summoned Peters to a meeting. Speaking in a "foul Yiddish German," since his English was very poor, Bykov showed a great interest in Peters's espionage apparatus.[50] He was eager to learn all about his "Quellen" (sources) in Washington, and wanted to meet with Chambers as soon as possible. The two men thereupon arranged a time and place for that meeting.

Shortly thereafter, Peters met with Chambers and informed him that he was going to introduce him to a person who would be "more or less" his boss from that time on, and that Chambers was "to take and execute any orders that would be given by this person."[51] Then Peters took Chambers for a walk up Fifth Avenue during the evening rush hour. When they reached Forty-ninth Street they halted and Peters peered across the street at the crowd of pedestrians in front of St. Patrick's Cathedral. Soon he spotted Bykov, no doubt recognizing him by his distinctive red hair: "There's our man!" Once they had come up to

Bykov, a few words were exchanged and Peters quickly left them and melted into the crowd.[52] In his dealings with Bykov that day and in the following weeks, Chambers found his new handler to be harsh and impetuous, subject to fits of "rage, fear, and suspicion." Constantly fearful that he was being trailed by U.S. government agents, Bykov seemed to be distrustful even of Chambers. When the latter asked what name he should call him, Bykov responded, "Peter." When Chambers pointed out that this would be confusing, since his CPUSA supervisor was called Peter or Peters, Bykov's only response was an angry glare.[53] On only one topic was Bykov direct and forthcoming. Unlike Bill, he was very interested in fostering and even expanding the Washington spy apparatus. He subjected Chambers to frequent cross-examinations about Hiss, Wadleigh, Pigman, and others who contributed to the work of the apparatus. Towards the end of 1936, Bykov proposed that the important "sources" in the apparatus be given "a big sum of money" as a Christmas gift. This would reinforce the principle that "Who pays is boss, and who takes money must also give something." When Chambers argued strenuously against this idea, pointing out that such a gift would be an insult to principled Communists, Bykov relented but insisted that "some costly present" was still in order. As a result, four of the "romantic anti-fascists" whom J. Peters had recruited for his apparatus were recipients of an expensive Bokhara rug, "a gift from the Soviet people, in gratitude for their help."[54]

When Peters and Chambers next met to evaluate the new situation, they no doubt agreed that Chambers's new handler was a disagreeable character. But it was actually Peters who was most apprehensive about the new situation. He expressed his concern that Bykov wanted to take complete control of the "Washington set-up," in which he, Peters, had "a vested personal interest." He strongly hinted that, if possible, Chambers should obstruct Bykov in his effort, for example by not telling "everything" about the Washington apparatus.[55] Chambers might have wanted to comply with Peters's request, but this seemed impossible. It had become clear to him that Bykov was not only his superior but Peters's as well. Any attempt on his part to deceive Bykov, if discovered, would be viewed by the Soviets as a serious breach of Communist discipline. Peters soon realized this as well, and he did not put any further pressure on Chambers.

By early 1937, Apparatus B was operating at a stepped-up basis. Bykov even met with several of the "sources" in order to spur them on to greater productivity. Three photographers were now being used, and, with Peters's help, a new source was added to the operation. Vincent Reno, who had worked for Peters as a recruiter on military bases, began to supply Chambers with documents related to his work at the Aberdeen Proving Ground, an important testing site for the U.S. Army.[56] Although Peters continued to confer occasionally with Bykov and frequently with Chambers, his role in Apparatus B was now peripheral, and, although he often traveled to Baltimore and Washington, copies of stolen government documents no longer passed through his hands. However, on occasion his specialized knowledge or experience was drawn on to help solve a problem relating to personnel or procedures. On one occasion in 1937, Chambers reported to him that Bykov was furious because he believed that Harry Dexter White, who turned over documents regularly but only in small quantities, was "holding back material." Bykov wanted someone to investigate the matter and to spur White to a greater productiveness. Peters proposed that he arrange for Harold Glasser, who like White was employed by the Treasury Department, to check up on his colleague. Peters had apparently come to know Glasser in 1936 when he had entered government employment and had presumably become a member of one of the sub-units of the Ware group. Glasser undertook the assignment and soon reported to Chambers that in fact White "was turning over everything of importance that came into his hands."[57]

The fact that J. Peters had lost his authority over Apparatus B did not mean that he no longer had sources of his own in Washington. Through his contacts with CP organizers in Baltimore and Washington, he still had at his disposal a network of Party members and sympathizers in the government who were willing, when possible, to provide him with documents or confidential information. Those who did not have access to such material would often be asked to serve as couriers, to provide mail drops, or to assist him in other ways in his various projects. Peters had particular success in penetrating the Treasury Department. Another economist recruited by Peters was Solomon Adler, who, like Harold Glasser, entered government service late in 1936. Soon Adler began to send Peters weekly reports on financial topics.[58] Also available to Peters were members of the sub-units of the Ware group. Of the original Ware group members, some (Hiss, Silverman) were active in Apparatus B; others (Abt, Pressman, Collins) had moved away from Washington to take other jobs, but were willing to assist Peters when he called on them. Victor Perlo was the only Ware group "veteran" who in the late 1930s remained in Washington. Almost by default, leadership of the Ware sub-units thus fell to Perlo, who had long coveted that position. In 1937 and 1938, members of these sub-units continued to provide Peters with information obtained in the government offices in which they were employed.

Now that he no longer needed to devote so much of his time to the supervision of Apparatus B, Peters was free to work more intensively on other projects. For a time he apparently contemplated setting up a new spy operation in Washington that would focus on obtaining information on U.S. policy in the Far East.[59] Peters also found time in 1937–38 to contribute his services to some of the Party districts with which he had developed close ties. For example, from time to time he attended meetings of the Baltimore district and supervised the activities of that district's delegation when it attended national meetings in New York.[60]

Peters was also kept busy with various responsibilities relating to CPUSA involvement in the Spanish Civil War. He apparently had a major role in the recruiting and dispatching of American volunteers for the Abraham Lincoln Brigade, which, Peters later asserted, was "not as easy as organizing a strike picket line."[61] Peters paid CP organizers a "bounty" for each volunteer from their district. The volunteers were sent to a private address in Brooklyn, where Peters provided them with false passports (if needed) and travel funds for the trip to Spain.[62] Peters also seems to have had a role in selecting commanders for the American forces sent to Spain. In the period 1936–38 he several times tried to persuade Louis Gibarti, the peripatetic Comintern agent who spent several years in the mid-1930s in the United States and spoke Spanish well, to become commander of the Abraham Lincoln and the George Washington Brigades.[63] Peters also helped facilitate the work of a shadowy Soviet agent named Mark Moren, who was buying arms for the Loyalist government in Spain. He arranged for a woman fluent in Spanish to interpret for Moren in his dealings with a representative of the Spanish government, and he helped arrange for Lee Pressman to provide legal and other assistance for Moren.[64]

Probably Peters's most important new activity in this period was the assistance he provided to the NKVD. Perhaps because he did not see in Boris Bykov a congenial collaborator in intelligence work, Peters began to collaborate more frequently with the NKVD illegal resident in New York, Iskhak Akhmerov. A decade later a KGB official, summarizing the connection that his agency had had with Earl Browder ("Helmsman") and J. Peters ("Steve" or "Storm"), stated that they had proved useful for various intelligence purposes. In particular, they had provided leads to "so-called illegal fellowcountrymen [CPUSA members] working at various govt. agencies, private companies and defense plants and laboratories." Those recruited were used for "infiltration into local Trotskyite organizations, as illegal couriers, owners of apartments for konspiratsia and secret meetings, group leaders for obtaining passports and other citizenship papers, for direct use as agents and, finally, to carry out various special assignments." In addition, those in relevant government departments sometimes provided "information, various documents and other intel. materials."[65] In fact, J. Peters had assisted Soviet Intelligence in all the areas mentioned in this report.

For example, in 1937 Peters lent his support to Gregory Rabinowitz ("Roberts"), who was in charge of the NKVD's anti-Trotsky campaign. Peters supervised the work of Louis Budenz, a Party official who had been recruited by Roberts to infiltrate Trotskyite organizations in the United States. When he was successful in obtaining a collection of confidential documents, including the proceedings of the national committee and other organizations loyal to Trotsky, Budenz passed the material on to Peters, who safeguarded the documents. Budenz would later claim that he put Soviet agents in touch with American Communists willing to cooperate in the campaign against the Trotskyites, including Frank Jackson, who in 1940 assassinated Trotsky.[66]

It was also in 1937 that Iskhak Akhmerov asked Peters to help him find "one or two decent chaps" in Washington who would be willing to assist him in information gathering and perhaps serve as talent spotters. Peters checked with Victor Perlo, who recommended a member of his unit, Gerald Graze, who worked for the Civil Service Commission and had access to lists of names and addresses of all government workers. Peters, who in fact had met Graze once or twice before, had no difficulty in persuading him to "render every kind of help" to Akhmerov, although Peters thought it wise to tell Graze that Akhmerov was a local Communist and that this was an assignment from the CPUSA.[67] In turn, Graze (referred to in NKVD records by the code name "Arena") introduced Akhmerov to his friend Victor Perlo. Peters had at one time also mentioned Perlo to Akhmerov as a "good worker." The NKVD agent now asked him again for an evaluation, and Peters assured him that Perlo was a "good, loyal, and developed Marxist." Peters warned, however, that Perlo's wife, though nominally a Party member, was "deep down . . . a typical petty bourgeois, who has nothing in common with the fraternal's ideology."[68] J. Peters's judgment proved shrewd on all counts. During World War II, Graze and Perlo provided important service to Soviet intelligence. However, in 1944, having broken with the Communist movement and gone through a bitter divorce with her husband, Katherine Wills Perlo wrote a letter to President Roosevelt in which she claimed that Soviet espionage agents had penetrated several government agencies and that numerous Americans, including her former husband, were involved in the conspiracy.[69]

Between 1933 and 1938, J Peters worked with hundreds of Communist Party members and sympathizers to promote the various projects of his secret apparatus. But his closest collaborator was Whittaker Chambers. No one, not even Earl Browder, knew as much as Chambers did about the people involved in Peters's underground work, his fraudulent passport operation, and his relationship to Soviet intelligence agencies. Peters and Chambers spent countless hours together, particularly during their numerous trips by car or train between New York and Washington. In time their relationship became a kind of friendship, at least to the extent that two Communists involved in conspiratorial work could become friends. At first the highly secretive Peters was no doubt wary of opening up to Chambers. Eventually he gained sufficient confidence in his collaborator that he revealed things about his personal life that only a handful of other American Communists knew. Chambers learned that his birth name was Sándor Goldberger, that he had studied law at a Hungarian university, and that he lived with a woman named Silver in the New York borough of Queens. Peters regaled him with stories about his experiences as an officer in the Great War and a participant in the brief Communist regime in Hungary. Peters never wrote about his relationship with Chambers; indeed, later he would claim that if he had met him at all, it was just for a brief time in the late 1920s. But from his actions one can deduce that he regarded Chambers as trustworthy, intelligent, and efficient. One particular incident related by Chambers in his memoirs suggests that Peters even developed an affection for his reliable but quirky American comrade. Once when buying their tickets at Union Station for a return to New York, Chambers noticed that a man was watching them closely. After Chambers and Peters had purchased their tickets, the man approached them and Peters instinctively walked quickly away, no doubt fearing that he was a policeman or government agent. But Chambers talked to the man, who said he had a ticket to New York that could be used only that day, Sunday, and he had to stay in Washington until the following day. Would Chambers exchange tickets with him? Chambers agreed to do so. Once he had caught up with Peters and explained what had happened, Peters admonished him: "Bob, you're a fool." But as they walked towards their train, Peters put his hand on Chambers's arm and said gently, "The Party needs more fools."[70]

In his publications, lectures, and communications about conspiratorial activity, J. Peters had always placed an emphasis on the need for strong safeguards to thwart counter-intelligence activity by the police or government agencies. Through a combination of his own diligence and the FBI's relative lack of interest in the Communist movement at the time, Peters's Washington underground operation ran smoothly and remained undetected by the police or by the government agencies that were being infiltrated. There was always the danger, of course, that one of the "romantic anti-fascists" in the apparatus would become disillusioned and withdraw from the operation and leave the Communist Party. But the ardor and idealism of the individuals Peters had recruited was so strong that such a development seemed only a remote possibility. In 1936, however, there began a series of events in Soviet Russia that created a kind of crisis of conscience for some American Communists, among them Whittaker Chambers.

In August 1936, Chambers happened to read a newspaper article that made him uneasy: in what would later be known as the first of the Moscow Show Trials, a number of veteran Bolshevik leaders and an army general confessed to having planned, with the aid of Leon Trotsky, to assassinate Stalin and overthrow the Soviet regime.[71] From that point on there were a series of equally incredible reports of arrests, trials, and executions of alleged traitors in Soviet Russia. In 1937 the Stalinist terror spread rapidly and claimed numerous victims among high-level Red Army officers and Soviet intelligence officials and agents. Deeply troubled by this and unable to suppress the feeling that "something terrible is happening," Chambers asked Peters for an explanation. The response he received was not helpful: "A comrade who has just come back from Moscow is going around saying that there is terror going on there and that they are arresting and shooting everybody. He should be taken care of."[72]

Peters's response to Chambers's inquiry about the puzzling events in Soviet Russia was the knee-jerk reaction of an orthodox Communist, but soon Peters also began to have misgivings. In the summer of 1937, at the height of the purges, Richard Ikal was ordered by his superiors in Moscow to return to the Soviet Union. In discussing the matter with Peters, Ikal expressed his fear that he, like so many other GRU agents who were recently ordered home, would be arrested.[73] Nonetheless, Ikal decided that he had no alternative but to return to the Soviet Union. Peters, of course, was willing to provide false passports for Ikal, his wife, and their daughter. However, he urged Ikal not to take his wife and child into what he delicately called an "unstable situation."[74] Ikal agreed to leave his daughter with relatives in Philadelphia, but insisted that his wife would accompany him. They departed New York in mid-October with two sets of passports (one in the name of Rubens, the other Robinson) that Peters had obtained through his contacts in the New York County Clerk's office.[75] But the worst forebodings of Peters and Chambers were soon realized: soon after his arrival in Moscow in November, Richard Ikal was arrested. His frightened wife, an American citizen, sought the help of American journalists in Moscow, who quickly alerted the American Embassy. Soon thereafter Ikal's wife was also arrested.[76] By late December, American newspapers were carrying detailed accounts of the sensational and mysterious story.

J. Peters must have been greatly alarmed to learn from these newspaper articles that "the Robinson/Rubens affair" had sparked a federal investigation into a possible fraudulent passport mill in New York, and that several of the people with whom he had collaborated were being interviewed.[77] For the first time, Peters's passport operation, which had functioned for years without raising the slightest suspicions of officials in the Passport Division of the State Department, was now under scrutiny. Equally disturbing was the fact that the GRU resident with whom Peters had worked so closely had been, to all appearances, arbitrarily arrested by his own government. Perhaps Peters also felt the same twinge of human sympathy that Chambers later recorded in his autobiography when describing his reaction to the news about Ikal's arrest: "It is all but impossible to have any man whom you have talked to, walked with, lunched with, shot down beside you, without feeling a small, very definite jolt."[78] One lesson that Communists worldwide could draw from the show trials in 1937 was the danger of "guilt by association." People known to have associated with those who had been arrested and subsequently confessed publicly to hideous crimes were almost invariably in grave danger themselves. What made the situation all the more disquieting was the fact that Boris Bykov had since his arrival been making sinister remarks about the dangers of consorting with people like Ikal.[79]

Of course, J. Peters and other American Communists could still cling to the hope that the reports about Stalinist terror were, as Party propagandists were asserting, distortions of the bourgeois press or vile propaganda spread by the Trotskyites. But even that hope was quashed by a report made to a PolCom meeting in January 1938 by Jacob Golos, who had recently returned from a trip to Russia.[80] Golos, a major figure in the CPUSA who worked intimately with the NKVD in the 1930s, had shattering news. There was indeed a wave of terror underway in Moscow and many people very well known to American Communists were among the victims, such as I. G. Mingulin, former head of the Comintern's Anglo-American Secretariat, and Béla Kun, the Hungarian revolutionary. It is not known whether J. Peters attended this PolCom meeting, but even if he had been absent, he surely would soon have learned about such an alarming report from a highly credible source like Golos. What did Peters make of all this? He had worked with Mingulin in Moscow; had met and admired Béla Kun. Despite his reputation as a quintessentially loyal Communist who conformed readily to shifting winds from Moscow, Peters was also capable of making a shrewd analysis of events. Surely he could not believe that Mingulin, Kun, Ikal, Bill, and all the others had actually been spies, counter-revolutionaries, or Trotskyites. But Peters also knew that no good could come from revealing his doubts to even trusted comrades or seeking further explanations of what was happening in Russia. The best strategy was to remain silent, await further developments, and hope that the terror would be a temporary phenomenon and that in the meantime he would not be called on to undertake a mission that would require a return to the Soviet Union.

Unlike J. Peters, for whom a complete break from Communism was unthinkable, Whittaker Chambers had other options. During 1937 he became increasingly frightened and despondent. Late in the year, at about the same time as the Robinson/Rubens affair, newspapers reported on the mysterious disappearance of Juliet Stuart Poyntz, a highly visible CP member since the early 1920s. Poyntz had been a speaker at the first Party meeting Chambers had ever attended, and since 1934 had been involved in underground work for the NKVD. Rumors quickly circulated, fed to Chambers in part by a handful of anti-Stalinist left-wingers with whom he remained in contact, that Poyntz had become disillusioned with the Soviet Union during a trip there in 1936 and had returned to the United States determined to sever her ties with the Party, openly denounce the Communist movement, and reveal what she knew about the work of Soviet intelligence agencies in the United States. To prevent this, the NKVD had allegedly seized her and either killed her or spirited her away on a Soviet ship. Bykov only heightened Chambers's suspicions by his chilling commentary on this: "Where is Juliet Poyntz? Gone with the wind."[81] Perhaps the decisive factor in pushing Chambers to a break from the Party and his espionage work were the sinister tactics of his handler. Not only did Bykov regularly grill Chambers in a hostile manner about his possible ties to the Trotskyites or insufficient loyalty to Stalin, but, learning that Chambers had never been to Russia, he urged him on several occasions to go to Moscow as soon as possible.[82]

By late 1937, J. Peters may have noticed Chambers's increasing anxiety and pensiveness.[83] Perhaps he even tried to calm him by suggesting he simply continue his valuable work along the old lines and ignore his erratic handler and the inexplicable developments in the Soviet Union. Of course, Chambers was not about to drop any hints to Peters about his plans to defect, but he did call on him for assistance in one of the steps he felt he must take. In order to earn some extra money and to be able later to demonstrate that he had procured a government job under his true name with the assistance of the CPUSA, he asked Peters to find him a government position that would provide him a further "cover" for his underground work. Peters, who had been able to arrange such jobs for Party members on numerous occasions, passed on this information to George Silverman and soon J. V. David Chambers was hired as a "Report Editor" on the National Research Project, with Silverman himself as his boss.[84] In late 1937 and early 1938, Chambers, even while continuing his normal routine as supervisor of Apparatus B, carried out his preparations for a break from the Party. He persuaded Bykov that he needed a new, more reliable car. He explored ways to forge a new career as a writer or translator. And, most significantly, he began to hold back some of the stolen documents and microfilms from the batches he forwarded to Col. Bykov. These he regarded as possible "life preservers" to enable him to be able to survive the fury of the storm that he anticipated his defection would unleash. Chambers proceeded on his plan for defection methodically and with grim determination, for, as he later told the FBI, "I considered that I was at war with the Communist Party."[85] Finally in mid-April 1938, he was ready to put his plan into action. He packed his family and belongings in the new car purchased with apparatus funds and headed for a hideout in Florida.

J. Peters first learned what was afoot when he was summoned by Bykov, who was greatly agitated by the fact that the normally reliable and punctual Chambers had failed to show up for a planned rendezvous. They immediately sought out Maxim Lieber in his office and instructed him to search for Chambers in Baltimore. When he returned a few days later, Lieber reported that Chambers and his family had disappeared. Bykov, realizing that his own career as a GRU operative might be at stake, suggested an explanation that would be for him the least damaging: Chambers might have been injured or killed in a car accident. But Peters, no doubt reflecting on the events of the past year, shook his head and said quietly: "He has deserted."[86]

7

From Peters to Stevens

Life in the Underground

J. Peters realized that if Whittaker Chambers went straight to the FBI or attorney general and told all he knew, his "Washington set-up" would be in grave jeopardy and immense damage might be done to the CPUSA and to Soviet-American relations. Yet his actions in the immediate aftermath of Chambers's defection suggest that he held some hope that Chambers would not take such a drastic step. It seems that Peters urged restraint on the part of Col. Bykov and his superiors in Moscow, whose inclination might have been to send agents to find Chambers, with the idea of abducting or even assassinating him. In any case, the Soviet response was relatively subdued. GRU leaders soon concluded that Chambers had been a German spy all along,[1] which would make it unlikely that he would turn himself in to the American authorities. Peters certainly did not believe that Chambers was a German spy, and he may have felt that if he could just have a personal meeting with Chambers, he could persuade him to return to the fold or at least to promise to remain silent about his underground activities.

In mid-May 1938, a month after Chambers's disappearance, Peters made his first move. He arranged for Grace Hutchins, a loyal Party member who knew both Whittaker and Esther Chambers and had been a witness at their wedding ceremony, to take a message to Esther's brother, Reuben Shemitz, who was an attorney in Manhattan. Hutchins informed Shemitz that she had a "very important" message for Esther: either she or her husband should call her or "Steve" (Peters), because they had some "important memos" for them. However, Shemitz at that time did not know where the Chambers were, and even if he had known he would not have informed Hutchins, since Chambers had earlier told him of his plan to defect and the possibility that his life would be in danger.[2]

Peters undoubtedly kept Earl Browder informed of the developments surrounding the defection of Whittaker Chambers. His initial effort to locate Chambers having failed, he had to admit the possibility that Chambers would remain in hiding for an indefinite period, even if he did not become a government informer. Since Peters clearly was in a perilous position and his underground operations were endangered, Browder took decisive action. On June 13 Peters was formally removed from his position as head of the secret apparatus and replaced by Rudy Baker, with whom he had collaborated early in the 1930s in the initial attempt to establish the "illegal apparatus." Browder apparently thought it best that as few people as possible should know the real reason why Peters had to be removed. In addition to Baker only three other CPUSA officials were informed of this change, and perhaps not all of them were given specific information about Peters's espionage apparatus and the defection of Chambers.[3]

It is possible that even Rudy Baker was kept in the dark about the true reason for Peters's removal. In a report on the CPUSA secret apparatus that he composed for the Comintern in early 1939, he explained that Peters had been relieved of his position because "it became generally known that this work [in the secret apparatus] was being directed by Peters."[4] Yet this is hardly a credible explanation. It is certainly true that by 1938 most middle- and upper-level Party officials had concluded that Peters directed the CP underground, since it was he who had worked with district leaders in making preparations to create the "illegal apparatus." If the director of the Party's secret apparatus was also to be responsible for coordinating the "illegal apparatus," there was no way that his identity could be kept secret from a broad range of Party officials. On the other hand, only a few high Party officials knew about the conspiratorial operations with which Peters was involved, and apparently even Browder had only a general idea of the precise nature of Peters's "Washington set-up."[5] Neither in his survey of the work that Peters had accomplished in the secret apparatus nor in his outline of the projects he himself would emphasize, did Baker make any mention of Peters's most sensitive underground projects, such as his "Washington set-up" or the production of fraudulent passports.[6]

Although after June 1938 J. Peters was no longer officially connected with the secret apparatus, he did continue to contribute, as will be seen, to certain operations in the CP underground. Moreover, he did not completely sever all ties with his agents in Washington. His main duties, however, were now once again in the open Party. In May 1938 at the Party's Tenth annual convention, Peters to all appearances regained the high standing in the Party that he had enjoyed in 1932–35, before he became fully immersed in the work of the secret apparatus. At the convention Peters served, with six other prominent Party leaders, on the committee that was revising the CPUSA constitution.[7] At a meeting of the National Committee (formerly the Central Committee) shortly after the convention, Peters was elected to the Central Control Committee (CCC), which was responsible for Party discipline. Through 1938 and early 1939, Peters also attended meetings of the National Committee as an "invited member of the Org. Committee." On several occasions in this period he gave public speeches, under the name J. Peters, as a representative of the National Committee at various district meetings and conventions.[8]

With each passing month in 1938, Peters seems to have become more confident that Whittaker Chambers had not passed on information to any government agency and had no immediate plans to do so. In fact, Chambers had decided to try to regain for himself a public identity so that the Party would find it more difficult to take any drastic action against him. As early as May he and his family were once again living in Baltimore, and by August he was traveling from time to time to New York, where he even took the risk of meeting Max Lieber and walking openly with him on the streets of Manhattan. At this time Chambers was being strongly encouraged by his anti-Stalinist associates to issue a strong public statement about the reasons for his defection. But in fact he shrank from such a bold step, and was interested mainly in "getting clear of the CP, living out his life with his family, retiring to some remote neighborhood, and getting back to literary work." At this point, and for many years to come, Chambers feared that if he confessed his espionage activity to the United States government, he might well end up with a long prison term.[9] One important reflection of his ambivalence about the idea of becoming a government informant was an article manuscript he composed in the fall of 1938. In this proposed article, entitled "The Faking of Americans," Chambers offered a detailed description of the cooperation between the CPUSA and Soviet intelligence agencies in the production of fraudulent passports. Yet Chambers remained averse to providing specific details. He signed the article with the name "Karl," and referred to Peters as "Sandor" and Max Bedacht as "Barber." However, he prefaced the article, which was never published, with a warning that "if the usual campaign of slander and denial begins," he would publish material he had purposely omitted and would give the true names of "Barber" and "Sandor."

J. Peters must have been relieved by the intelligence he had gathered in this period concerning Chambers's actions and plans. He knew nothing, of course, of the article Chambers had written about his passport operation. However, from George Silverman and Alger Hiss, and perhaps even Max Lieber, he may have learned that Chambers was urging others to join him in abandoning the Party, but also that he had no plan of becoming an informant so long as the Party did not try to retaliate against him.[10] For several months in the late summer and early fall, Peters accordingly took no further steps to locate and meet with Chambers. But in November a crisis erupted. Chambers learned from his literary agent, Paul Willert, that a Comintern agent had asked for his assistance in locating his client.[11] Willert had not obliged, but Chambers imagined the worst: a Soviet agent had apparently been dispatched from Europe to track him down and mete out the same punishment that Juliet Poyntz had received. In fact, the Comintern agent, Otto Katz, almost surely had not been given the task of eliminating Chambers, although he may well have been asked by Peters, who still served as the liaison between Comintern agents and the CPUSA, to assist in locating the exact whereabouts of Whittaker Chambers.[12]

Fearing that the Comintern agent asking about him was a "hit man," Chambers now resolved to launch a counterattack. In December he arranged to have a letter delivered to Peters and Bykov in which he warned that "at the first sign of monkey business on their part" he would seek "protection in an American prison." He enclosed in the package a copy of one of the State Department documents he had retained, part of his collection of "life preservers."[13] To reinforce his point, he dispatched a second letter to his former handlers in January 1939, using Felix Inslerman as his intermediary. In it he warned that if his adversaries continued "violent projects against me and my family," they would be courting a "major disaster." Chambers hinted that the State Department was about to launch an investigation, perhaps on the basis of information he had supplied. "There is something brewing now [in the State Department]," Chambers warned, "but from the calm way in which you are running around, you do not seem to know it."[14] This jab was surely directed at Peters, whose comings and goings on Party business were still being reported on a regular basis in the *Daily Worker*.

In his suggestion that some sort of investigation into a possible espionage ring had been launched by the State Department, Chambers was bluffing, but Peters could not know this. So as not to provoke Chambers to the retaliation he was threatening, Otto Katz was apparently told to cease his investigations. Col. Bykov was soon recalled to Moscow and no further attempts were made by Soviet Intelligence agencies or by Peters to locate or intimidate Chambers. But if the threat posed to J. Peters by Chambers's defection no longer seemed imminent, there were alarming developments on another front. As a result of the sensational press coverage of the "Robinson/Rubens affair," the Department of Justice had launched an investigation that soon brought to light a fraudulent passport operation that had been active in New York City for some years. In March 1939, a number of individuals were indicted by a federal grand jury. Among them were Ossip Garber, who in fact had been a collaborator of Peters and Richard Ikal in the false passport ring, and Mark Moren (Phillopovich), a Soviet agent whose work Peters had facilitated. But in addition, the grand jury issued indictments for several unknown individuals, including one identified as "John Blank," thought to be the leader of the passport operation, and several Russian agents referred to as Ivan, Dmitri, and Alexis Doe.[15]

The subsequent press reports of the trial in the spring of 1939 must have made Peters increasingly nervous, especially since he no doubt feared that he in fact was the "John Blank" the authorities were seeking. As the trial progressed it was disclosed that the prosecutors had concluded that the fraudulent passport ring was connected to the Communist Party and that it had been in existence at least since 1934. Furthermore, there was evidence that some of the false passports had been provided to individuals recruited by the Communist Party to fight in the Spanish Civil War on the Loyalist side. Finally, and most ominously, one witness, the sister-in-law of Ossip Garber, made a cryptic remark during court testimony: at one time her home had been proposed as a mail drop for someone named "Peter."[16]

These developments in the fraudulent passport case, combined with lingering concern over Whittaker Chambers's intentions, convinced J. Peters that the time had come for him to assume a new identity and retreat into the underground, at precisely the same time that Chambers was finally emerging and assuming a public identity. In May 1939 he took the first steps to establish himself as "Alexander Stevens." It is not difficult to determine the process by which he chose this particular pseudonym. Alexander is the English rendering of his Magyar name, Sándor. "Steve" was one of the names he had used for much of the 1930s, and by adding an "s" to Steven he came up with Stevens, the kind of name that Communists involved in conspiratorial work had traditionally chosen.

In New York State at the time a person desiring to use a new name did not have to go through any legal procedure. All an individual needed to do was to begin using the new name in official documents. On June 30, 1939, Alexander Stevens opened up a bank account and described himself as the owner of European Motors, a fictitious company.[17] A further step in establishing his new identity occurred the next day when Stevens submitted his "Declaration of Intention" forms to the INS to begin once again the process of applying for citizenship. There were several reasons why Peters decided on this step. If his application were approved, he would have legal sanction for his new identity as Alexander Stevens. Furthermore, the CPUSA, in the spirit of the Popular Front, had recently declared that all Party members must be American citizens or must be in the process of applying for citizenship. Still there were certain risks for Stevens in submitting the necessary forms to the INS. He was required to enclose a recent photograph with his application, which would prove useful to government investigators should they ever come to suspect that Stevens was in fact J. Peters. There was also the problem posed by the necessity of providing an address to which mail should be sent. Since Stevens did not wish to reveal his true home address in Kew Gardens, he entered instead a CP mail-drop address on Eleventh Avenue in Manhattan. Finally, how was he to respond to the section asking for his name and any aliases he had used? It would hardly do to list all the names he had used, especially J. Peters. So he identified himself simply as "Alexander Goldberger known as Alexander Stevens."[18]

In moving to the underground, Alexander Stevens had to sever most ties with the open Communist Party; he could no longer serve on most Party committees and was able to visit Party headquarters only rarely and surreptitiously. He kept in communication with Party leaders using a member of the PolCom as his intermediary.[19] The last Party meeting he is known to have attended was that of the Central Control Commission on June 6, 1939, although it is possible that he continued for some years to remain a nominal member of that committee. Stevens nonetheless remained a full-time paid apparatchik who now was given special assignments by the Central Committee.[20] Precisely what tasks he performed in the summer of 1939 is not known. However, as the threat of a renewed war in Europe loomed he was called on once again to serve the Party as its acknowledged expert on the "illegal apparatus." When, after a few weeks of initial confusion, the CPUSA fully endorsed the Nazi-Soviet Non-Aggression Pact signed on August 23, most of the liberal and left-wing groups who had participated with the Communists in Popular Front organizations withdrew in disgust. Almost all Party leaders gave full, if perhaps not always enthusiastic, support to the new "line." The Party quickly launched a major campaign to keep the United States out of the "imperialist war" and to denounce the alleged perfidy and warmongering of the Western allies, particularly Great Britain. Those Party leaders who had been less than enthusiastic in their acceptance of the Popular Front, including William Foster, now felt vindicated and were free once again to employ the old revolutionary rhetoric.[21] Soon the Party press was again filled with condemnations of American imperialism and vitriolic attacks on the Roosevelt administration, which was condemned as pro-fascist and "Hitlerian." Dismay and consternation over the Party's apparently slavish attachment to the Soviet Union and abandonment of the struggle against Nazi Germany led not only to a drop in Party membership, especially among Jews, but also to a loss of the public goodwill that had been gained during the last half of the 1930s. Nonetheless, the majority of CPUSA members, seeing no real alternative, remained loyal to the movement.[22]

Realizing the unpopularity of the Party's new policies and noting the growing tendency of writers and political observers to lump together Nazis and Communists as dangerous and subversive groups, CPUSA leaders anticipated that increased intimidation and persecution of the Party was imminent. Federal officials now seemed intent on prosecuting those Communists who, as the U.S. attorney general put it at a Cabinet meeting, had "violated the criminal laws in any respect."[23] The October 23 indictment and arrest of Earl Browder on charges of passport fraud was a great blow to the CPUSA and caused "severe cases of nerves" among Party officials, since most of those who had traveled abroad had done so, as Browder had, on fraudulent passports.[24]

The outbreak of the war, the rise of anti-Communist sentiments, and the heightened police surveillance and intimidation convinced Party leaders that the time had come for the implementation of the "illegal apparatus" that J. Peters had created in the first half of the 1930s.[25] Although CPUSA records for the war years beginning in 1939 are sparse, the available evidence suggests that responsibility for the implementation of the "illegal apparatus" was shared by three individuals: Alexander Stevens, "Brown" (Mario Alpi), and Jack Stachel.[26] Their work was complicated by the fact that both Stevens and Stachel had gone underground and feared arrest. Furthermore, over the years of the Popular Front the leaders of even those districts that had made a serious effort to establish the framework of the "illegal apparatus" had often become lackadaisical. Not all districts had functioning mail drops; few had followed Peters's guidelines and cached a printing press or duplicating machine to be used in times of emergency. In these difficult circumstances Stevens probably was in the best position to coordinate the operation since he had maintained good ties with many of those Party officials who had remained active in district leadership throughout the 1930s.

CP district organizers all across the country were thus advised by Peters to "tighten up" the "illegal apparatus" in their areas. Funds and resources were made available to purchase mimeograph machines and to enable key Party leaders to go underground.[27] One Communist official, John Gates, later characterized the steps taken in the 1939–41 period to implement the "illegal apparatus" as "amateurish, romantic, and stupid."[28] Some of the measures undertaken were perhaps "amateurish," but those Communists who were the targets of government intimidation would hardly have agreed that the steps they took to defend themselves were "romantic" or "stupid." True, it turned out that fears the Communist Party would be outlawed and its members arrested en masse proved unrealized. Ordinary Party members did, however, have to contend with a public opinion that was increasingly hostile, for many Americans had come to view Communists as unpatriotic and even seditious. But for the most part, American Communists were able to continue their work along traditional lines at the local level in the factories and unions. Actions by state and federal officials against the CPUSA tended to be focused on high-level leaders, especially those who were aliens. Earl Browder was a convenient target because he was the Party leader, but the most vulnerable Party leaders were those who had never become citizens, like Jack Stachel, William Weiner, and J. Peters.

J. Peters had thus been quite prescient in the summer of 1939 when he decided that the time had come to go underground and become Alexander Stevens. Beginning shortly after the outbreak of World War II, several other CPUSA leaders followed his example, though most did not go so far as to create for themselves an entirely new identity. J. Peters had to become Alexander Stevens because he was much more vulnerable than the others: not only had he traveled on a false passport, but he had been the mastermind behind the whole Communist fraudulent passport operation. Furthermore, in his supervision of the Washington spy ring and his close collaboration with Soviet intelligence agents he had committed very serious crimes. So, even while contributing to the implementation of the "illegal apparatus" in 1939 and 1940, Stevens kept a very low profile. He rarely if ever appeared at the CPUSA headquarters on East Thirteenth Street and he did not attend the Party national convention held in New York in May 1940.

During 1940 and early 1941, Stevens continued to take steps to strengthen his new identity. He and his common-law wife, who now took the name Sophie Stevens, filed a federal income tax form for 1940, although they had not done so for 1939. In 1940 Stevens applied for a learner's permit and in time obtained a New York State driver's license.[29] At that point he must have felt a certain amount of confidence that his project to transform himself into an entirely new person would succeed, for he had at least one government document, his driver's license, that he could use to prove that he was who he claimed to be, Alexander Stevens. He knew, however, that he had to remain constantly vigilant and avoid any actions that might alert the authorities to his true identity. In mid-1940, Stevens received what previously would have been good news: his preliminary petition for naturalization had been approved. However, in order to continue the process and become an American citizen, he had to present himself to an INS agent for an interview and the completion of additional forms. No doubt he would be asked questions to which he could not give honest answers. Stevens must have struggled over how to respond to this summons from the INS. Was this a trap? If he showed up for the interview, might he be arrested on the spot by the FBI? After consideration he apparently decided that a personal interview with an INS agent was simply too great a risk. He failed to respond to the letter, and on February 20, 1941, the INS determined that the "subject seemed uninterested in becoming a U.S. citizen." Stevens's application was canceled and the application fee was refunded to him.[30]

In the summer of 1940, the U.S. Congress passed the Alien Registration Act (known as the Smith Act), which sought to weaken and undermine those organizations, primarily the Communist Party and domestic Nazi groups, that were deemed to be subversive. The law made it illegal for anyone in the United States to "advocate, abet, or teach the desirability of overthrowing the government." A key provision of the law was the requirement that all resident aliens had to register with the federal government within four months and provide information about their personal status, occupation, and political beliefs. This development posed a new dilemma for Alexander Stevens. Should he join the millions of other resident aliens who proceeded quickly to register? In this case Stevens decided that though there was a definite risk in registering as an alien, his fate would be worse if he failed to register and later was apprehended by the police. Alexander Stevens thus appeared at a Jamaica, Long Island, post office on December 5, 1940, filled out the registration form, had his fingerprints taken, was photographed, and denied that he had membership in any subversive group.

Having successfully solved the immediate problem posed by the Alien Registration Act, Stevens could now focus on his Party duties. In the absence of relevant CPUSA documents, little is known of his activities in 1941. He certainly continued to play some role in directing the "illegal apparatus," which seems to have required numerous trips by car to Chicago and other cities. He also continued to make suggestions and give advice on various problems, using intermediaries like V. J. Jerome to take his letters and memorandums to Party headquarters.[31] It is possible that he remained a member of the Central Control Commission, the most secretive of Party committees and the one that was thus least subject to public scrutiny. There is also evidence suggesting that he attempted to reestablish some sort of connection with the remnants of the Ware group in Washington, which was being supervised by Victor Perlo. But Alexander Stevens's most important new Party assignment in 1941–42 took him not to Washington but to the West Coast, where he served as the Party's representative to a group of secret Party members and fellow travelers in Hollywood who had previously been supervised by Otto Katz, the Comintern agent.[32]

Alexander Stevens, who as J. Peters had had such great success in instilling Party loyalty in the intellectuals, artists, and civil servants he had worked with in New York and Washington, was a logical choice to serve as Katz's successor in Hollywood. Stevens had close ties with several members of the film community, including Joseph Losey and John Lawson, both of whom had worked in Peters's "Arts Project" in New York in the early 1930s and then embarked on successful careers in Hollywood later in the decade. Lawson, the first president of the Screen Writers Guild, gave passionate personal and financial support to Party causes. He was, according to one of his biographers, the "face of Red Hollywood."[33] During Stevens's first trip to Los Angeles (probably in early 1941), Lawson introduced the man he referred to as his "Hungarian friend" to other key Party members and sympathizers in Hollywood, including Herbert Biberman and Lester Cole.[34] Stevens's work in Hollywood remained entirely behind the scenes. His visits were never announced publicly and he met only with trusted Party officials, key Hollywood Communists, and fellow travelers who were potential donors. His responsibilities as the representative of the CPUSA apparently included maintaining morale (especially in the difficult period of the Nazi-Soviet Pact), offering ideological guidance, collecting dues, and fund-raising.[35]

Stevens's work in Hollywood was greatly eased by Germany's attack on the Soviet Union in June 1941 and America's entry into the war after the Japanese attack on Pearl Harbor in December. Making a radical shift that in effect took it back to policies advocated between 1935 and 1939, the CPUSA now threw its full and enthusiastic support to the Allied war effort and the defense of Russia. For Alexander Stevens this development must have provided considerable relief. Even during a time of growing public anti-Communism and increased harassment of CP leaders by government agencies, he had managed to remain undetected in his newly fashioned underground existence. He sensed, however, that he had to remain constantly vigilant, for the public image of Communists as patriots might not endure for long. Thus in 1941, following the normal Communist conspiratorial practice of frequently changing addresses and places of work, he acquired a new fictitious occupation as a sales representative of Modern Age Physicians Supply, a company based in Newark, New Jersey. This seems to have been a legitimate company run by a Communist Party sympathizer willing to affirm that Alexander Stevens was one of his employees. However, he did no actual work for the company.

Alexander Stevens took two other steps in 1942 that were seemingly designed to demonstrate that he was an upstanding, patriotic American. The first involved the publication, early in that year, of a booklet of song lyrics entitled "America Sings for Victory." Alexander Stevens was listed as the compiler of this collection of over forty songs, which included patriotic selections like "The Star-Spangled Banner" and "When Johnny Comes Marching Home," as well as traditional or recently composed songs of the Left such as "The Internationale," "Red Partisans," and, no doubt a particular favorite, "Round and Round Hitler's Grave." Although Alexander Stevens is not known to have had any special interest or expertise in music, he might very well have been the Party functionary who pointed out the need for an inexpensive booklet of songs that emphasized the Party's newly proclaimed patriotism and full support for the Allied effort in the war. He might even have actually selected some of the songs to be included. But the main reason for listing him as the compiler was undoubtedly to create further evidence of the existence of an individual named Alexander Stevens who had no discernable connection to J. Peters.[36]

A second initiative undertaken by Stevens early in 1942 pertained to his relationship with Sophie (Silver) Stevens, with whom he had lived in a common-law marriage since the mid-1930s. Although some CPUSA leaders were legally married, many American Communists denigrated traditional marriage as an outmoded bourgeois institution. Nonetheless, Alexander Stevens and Sophie Stevens now decided that they should legalize their marriage. Perhaps Stevens reasoned that it was wise to have another official document, like a marriage license, that used his assumed underground name. Or he might have worried that someday their common-law marriage would be questioned by neighbors or that somehow the police would charge them with bigamy. For in fact neither Sophie nor Alexander had ever been legally divorced from their previous spouses. For reasons that thus remain somewhat murky, Sophie Silver and Alexander Stevens decided early in 1942 that before marrying they must obtain a legal divorce from their spouses. But because the grounds for divorce in New York, as in most states, were quite stringent, their only recourse was to the "divorce mills" of Nevada. Divorce was fairly easy to obtain in Nevada, but there was one onerous requirement: the applicant must reside in Nevada for at least six weeks. Accordingly, Stevens and Sophie Silver traveled by train to file divorce papers in Reno, where they resided from January 9 to February 20, 1942. During their stay in Reno, Alexander and Sophie were careful not to draw any undue attention. Their landlord found them to be a "nice couple," who were planning to get married soon. They received no mail and spent almost all their time in their separate apartments reading nonpolitical books borrowed from the local library. Stevens thus had a chance to catch up with the latest mystery novels of his favorite author, Rex Stout.[37] They departed for New York after the required six weeks, with Stevens returning again alone in late April to be on hand for the final divorce proceedings.[38] They were married on May 19, 1942, in Newark, New Jersey, and from that time the former Sophie (Sprecher) Silver began using the name Ann Stevens.[39]

In May 1942, Alexander Stevens might well have felt quite secure in the undercover identity he had adopted three years earlier. He had complied with all relevant government regulations and laws, including those dealing with alien registration and military conscription.[40] He had a driver's license, a marriage license, a bank account, and business cards that affirmed his identity as Alexander Stevens, a resident since October 1940 at 83-46 118th Street, Kew Gardens, Queens. With luck and constant vigilance perhaps he could maintain himself in this undercover existence until the public memory of J. Peters had faded away and government investigators had lost interest. But in fact the luck of this man of mystery had run out. In early May the FBI had, almost by accident, stumbled upon Alexander Stevens, an individual previously unknown to them. When on May 19 the Stevens returned to their apartment as a newly married couple, they had as yet no inkling that the FBI had just begun an intensive surveillance. Their mail was intercepted, their backgrounds were checked, and their daily movements were traced. Before long their telephone would be tapped.

For most of the 1930s, the FBI had taken no notice of J. Peters and knew nothing of his activities in Washington, D.C. In 1932 J. Edgar Hoover had stated that he had no interest in investigating the "Communistic inner circles."[41] No notice was taken in 1934 when John L. Lewis, head of the United Mine Workers, publicly accused J. Peters of operating a Communist underground based in Peekskill, New York.[42] Only in the tense political atmosphere accompanying the outbreak of war in September 1939 did governmental agencies begin more intensive investigations of the CPUSA. The first mention of J. Peters at a government forum came at hearings of the House Un-American Activities Committee, known at the time as the Dies Committee. In the fall of 1939 two witnesses, Andrew Smith and William Odell Nowell, testified that they had known Peters in Moscow while he was serving as the CPUSA's representative to the Comintern in 1932.[43] Another witness, the chairman of the Radical Research Committee of the American Legion, submitted to the Dies Committee materials that he argued demonstrated that the Communist Party sought to overthrow the American government by force and violence. Among the publications he drew attention to was J. Peters's *A Manual on Organization*.[44]

Another ominous development for J. Peters/Alexander Stevens was the decision of Whittaker Chambers finally to tell his story to an official of the American government.[45] The impetus for this action was the Nazi-Soviet Pact, which convinced Chambers that in effect Stalin would now be able to pass on to Hitler intelligence from the spy ring he, Chambers, had helped establish in Washington. Chambers had hoped to speak personally with President Roosevelt, but agreed when offered the opportunity to talk with Adolf A. Berle, the assistant secretary of state and the president's liaison with the intelligence agencies. In their meeting on September 2, Chambers gave an extensive, if somewhat disjointed, account of his underground activities. He mentioned the names of more than twenty individuals he knew to have engaged in underground work or espionage, including Alger Hiss, Lawrence Duggan, and Noel Field. But he attributed special importance to J. Peters, whom he described as the head of the "CP underground" and "responsible for [the] Washington sector." Chambers also provided additional information about Peters: that he had participated in the Communist revolution in Hungary, had worked for the Hungarian-American Communist newspaper (*Új Előre*), and lived in Woodside Park, Long Island, under the name "Silver." Berle included this information in a memo on his conversation with Chambers that he titled "Underground Espionage Agent." At the end of the section on Peters he added: "Went to Moscow—Where is he now?"[46]

Preoccupied by events surrounding the outbreak of war in Europe, neither President Roosevelt nor Adolf Berle seemed to think that the information provided by Whittaker Chambers was important enough to warrant close attention and immediate action. Thus, it was only a year and a half later, in March 1941, that Berle informed J. Edgar Hoover of his meeting with Chambers and offered to share his notes on the information Chambers had provided.[47] But for unknown reasons the FBI delayed another year in seeking an interview with Chambers, and, perhaps because of a bureaucratic mix-up, did not in fact receive Berle's memo, "Underground Espionage Agent," until 1943.[48] As a result, the FBI's own investigation of J. Peters, which had been underway for over a year, was hampered by ignorance of the firsthand information that Whittaker Chambers could have offered.

The name "J. Peters" first appears in FBI records in November 1939, in a report that J. Edgar Hoover sent to President Roosevelt on the "current activities of the Communist Party."[49] Hoover informed the president that the FBI had learned that plans for the Communist Party to go underground were being formulated by three individuals, one of whom was "a Hungarian Jew" named Peters. As the FBI investigation and surveillance of the Communist Party accelerated in 1940 and 1941, the shadowy J. Peters figured as one of the main targets. Yet FBI agents concerned with the CPUSA did not follow all the leads available to them. For example, they apparently did not pay close attention to the Dies Committee hearings in 1939, for no one thought to interview the two witnesses who had mentioned J. Peters. They also were unaware of Whittaker Chambers and the valuable information he could offer about J. Peters. Nonetheless, in 1940 and 1941 the FBI was able to locate several ex-Communists who had known Peters and were willing to serve as informants. One, James S. Glaser, was interviewed in June 1940 and provided the first information the FBI received that suggested Peters had engaged in conspiratorial activities. Glaser was a journalist, who in 1934 quit a job at the *New York Times* to become managing editor of the *Daily Worker*, where he remained until 1936. On the basis of the frequent contact and conversations he had had with Peters, Glaser concluded that he was a Soviet agent and a representative of the Communist International.[50] Peters, according to Glaser, was an important Party figure. He had written a manual on CP organization and "decided on those who were to be expelled from the Communist Party." Glaser recalled that Peters had boasted to him that the Party had contacts in the Immigration Service and other branches of the federal government that "could aid the Communists in practically any way desired."

In October 1940, the FBI interviewed an unnamed, but apparently quite knowledgeable, former Party member who had attended a CP training school at both the district and national level in the mid-1930s. This informant recalled that Peters gave instruction in both schools on conspiratorial work. In one class he told the students that in case of war or revolution, it would become necessary to sabotage ships, for example, by pouring sand into the oil cups to burn out the bearings.[51] On the basis of this allegation and similar reports the FBI subsequently received, J. Edgar Hoover in April 1941 placed Peters high on the list of those whom he recommended for "custodial detention in the event of a national emergency." In justifying this step, the FBI described Peters as a member of the National Committee of the Communist Party, a representative of the Comintern in the United States, and the author of a Communist manual on organization. The only direct evidence Hoover provided of Peters's seditious activities was a 1934 article in the *Party Organizer* in which he advocated infiltration of National Guard units and urged Communists to "fight back the attacks of the armed forces either legal or extra-legal."[52] Clearly, the FBI had as yet only an incomplete and in part inaccurate picture of J. Peters and his activities as a Communist activist and no inkling of the role that he had played in espionage and the production of false passports.

Shortly after the United States' entry into World War II, the Special Defense Unit of the federal government placed J. Peters in Group A of the custodial detention program, which consisted of those individuals "believed to be the most dangerous and who in all probability should be interned."[53] Once J. Edgar Hoover learned of this action, he ordered that the FBI's investigation of J. Peters be given "preferred and expeditious attention."[54] But locating J. Peters was to prove no easy task, especially since they could find no photograph of him for purposes of identification.[55] But just as the agents assigned to the case were concluding that they had reached a dead end, new information on the mysterious J. Peters was received from Whittaker Chambers, who was finally contacted by the FBI.

In an interview conducted on May 13, 1942, Chambers was much more wary and circumspect than he had been when he talked with Adolf Berle nearly three years earlier.[56] Chambers had become perplexed and frustrated by the fact that the American government had apparently not acted on the information he had provided to Berle. His anxiety increased when, shortly into the interview with the FBI, he sensed that the agents were not aware of the revelations he had made to Berle. Since he was unsure about the FBI's intentions and whether the government would grant him immunity from prosecution, Chambers resolved to provide the FBI with only a very hedged account of his career as a Communist, with no mention at all of espionage or other illegal activities.[57] He did identify J. Peters as "the head of the Communist Underground Movement" and a Party member who had connections with Soviet agents. On the other hand, Chambers claimed that he had seen Peters "only from time to time" and had never learned much about him. In fact, their connection was more like "a personal friendship" than a "formal Party relationship." Chambers supplied some of the same factual information about Peters that he had given to Berle, and in addition offered a detailed description of Peters's physical appearance, including the suggestion that he had a "lively and intelligent" expression.

The information that Whittaker Chambers provided was potentially very useful, but could not directly aid in the effort to discover Peters's undercover identity. But in fact, two weeks before Chambers was interviewed, FBI agents in California had stumbled upon Alexander Stevens, and although it was quickly apparent to Hoover and his assistants in Washington that Stevens was an important Communist engaged in some sort of underground work, nearly a year would pass before they deduced that Stevens and J. Peters were the same person. In May 1940, President Roosevelt had authorized the FBI to use telephone wiretaps in cases involving spies or domestic subversives.[58] One of the first uses to which the FBI put this new authority was in an investigation of certain Hollywood Communists, particularly Herbert Biberman, who was suspected of receiving and laundering money from Comintern agents in Mexico. By the spring of 1942 an intensive surveillance of Biberman was underway: his phone was tapped, his mail was opened, agents watched his house, and one of the members of his household staff was an FBI informant. Yet nothing of substance was learned until May 2, when a person who did not identify himself telephoned from Union Station in Los Angeles to tell Biberman he had arrived.[59]

Although the FBI in time learned that Biberman's visitor was Alexander Stevens/Alexander Goldberger, this was not evident during Stevens's two-day visit. It was clear from the interactions between Stevens and the Hollywood Communists and Party sympathizers with whom he consulted that he had met with them a number of previous times and had instructed them on the precautions they needed to take in order to thwart any possible police surveillance. In inviting friends and colleagues to meetings with Stevens, Biberman never referred to the visitor as Alexander Stevens or J. Peters, but instead as "the Hungarian with a mustache," "our weekend guest," or (to screenwriter Madeleine Ruthven) "your boyfriend." During his visit Stevens consulted most closely with Biberman, John Lawson, and Waldo Salt, at whose home he stayed. In addition to several officials of the Los Angeles CP, Stevens met about twenty people, most of them prominent Hollywood screenwriters. In addition to Biberman, Lawson, Salt, and Ruthven, they included Les Cole, Sidney Buchman, Hyman Kraft, Paul Jarrico, Robert Rossen, and Lou Harris. The FBI was unable to listen in on these meetings, but its informant in the Biberman household apparently rifled through Stevens's suitcase and discovered notes suggesting that the main purpose of his visit was to raise funds to aid in the campaign to free Earl Browder.[60] In all, Stevens collected well over $5000, including $1,500 from Louise Bransten, a wealthy Party sympathizer who had ties to a number of Soviet intelligence agents.[61] He transferred a portion of these funds to the local Party, and retained the rest for the "Free Browder" campaign.

Alexander Stevens departed by train on May 4 and arrived back in New York four days later. Throughout his journey he was tailed by a series of FBI agents. During a layover in Chicago, he was observed having a long talk in a restaurant with Morris Childs, secretary of the Illinois CP.[62] Stevens also spent an hour in a movie theater, during which time an FBI agent seized the opportunity to search his suitcase, which had been stored at the train station. Nothing incriminating was found.[63] Meanwhile, information obtained from railroad officials led FBI agents to Reno, where they learned not only that Sophie Silver and Alexander Stevens had been there to file for divorce from their spouses, but that Stevens's real name was Goldberger. Armed with this information, the FBI was able to begin an intensive security check on Alexander Stevens/Goldberger even before his arrival in New York on May 8. They gathered information from his alien registration file (along with a photograph), applications for citizenship, and bank account. None of these sources threw light on Stevens's apparent link to the Communist movement, but a review of Alexander Goldberger's travel documents for his trip to Europe in 1928 revealed that on his return he had lied about his place of birth and claimed to be a German citizen.[64] How did Alexander Stevens earn a living? The agents who searched his suitcase in Chicago found a business card for Modern Age Physicians Supply in Newark, but an FBI investigation found that the company had gone out of business in 1941 and no one associated with it could now be located. Equally unproductive was a month-long interception of mail at Stevens's residence in Kew Gardens that was initiated on May 14. Of course Stevens, a seasoned veteran of years of conspiratorial work, would never have used the open mail for any CP-related activity. However, from letters sent by an insurance company they did discover that Stevens's car had been in an accident while being driven by Emerich Goldberger, one of his brothers. Through a background check on Emerich Goldberger the FBI discovered that he was a chauffeur who worked for Amtorg, the Soviet trade agency that was under intensive FBI surveillance because of its suspected role in facilitating Soviet espionage.[65]

Initially it appeared that the FBI would have better luck with the owner and porter of Stevens's apartment house, each of whom seemed at first willing to cooperate with the investigation. But the agents who interviewed the owner left with the impression, which was fully justified, that he had "purposely withheld information concerning the subject." The only information that the African American porter provided was that the Stevens were a quiet couple who spent a good deal of time carrying out some sort of work involving typing in their apartment.[66] In fact, both the owner, who had known Stevens for many years, and the porter were Communist Party sympathizers. The porter immediately told Stevens that FBI agents had been snooping around and asking about him.[67] This must have greatly alarmed Stevens, and his first impulse may have been to flee and create a new identity in a different location. But if the FBI was indeed watching him closely, an attempt to escape might precipitate an immediate arrest. So he and Sophie decided to stay put, be even more cautious than normal in their conversations on the telephone and in their apartment, and avoid any direct contact with the Party. This seemed the best strategy so long as it remained unclear how much the FBI knew about him and what their intentions were. Perhaps the evidence that had led them to launch their investigation was inaccurate or flimsy, in which case he might still be able to sustain his identity as Alexander Stevens.

One immediate problem needed to be addressed. Although the Modern Age Company had ceased operations in May 1941, Stevens had continued to use his business card as proof of employment. Since the FBI was sure to check on this, Stevens apparently reasoned that he needed an actual job to divert attention from the fact that he had been a paid CP functionary since 1924. Stevens could not risk going to the Party headquarters, but by using the time-tested method of phone calls at public telephone booths or messages sent through intermediaries he was able to alert Party leaders to his predicament. By early June a job had been secured for him as an assembler of phonographs at the Dynavox Company, which was owned by a Party sympathizer. The company was located on East Eleventh Street in Manhattan, conveniently close to CP headquarters. Peters performed the same work as other assemblers in the Dynavox plant and received a salary, although his schedule seemed irregular and he often spent weekdays at home in his apartment.

When the FBI background check and "spot" surveillance in May and June failed to discover anything incriminating about Stevens and his ties to the Communist movement, J. Edgar Hoover authorized a full-time "physical" surveillance beginning on July 18. This involved considerable manpower, since it meant that Stevens would be followed and observed throughout the day. Yet this more intensive surveillance also proved disappointing. The agents did learn, of course, that Stevens was now employed by the Dynavox Company. Before and after his work hours, Stevens occasionally entered the nearby Albert Hotel, where he sometimes remained for long periods. This was suggestive, since that hotel was known to the FBI as "a meeting place for members of the Communist Party." Otherwise, Stevens and his wife seemed almost to be recluses, not venturing out even for family gatherings.[68] The only people they met frequently were John Abt and his wife Jessica Smith (the former wife of Hal Ware), whom they frequently visited at their residence on Long Island.[69] On several occasions the Stevens also took a train ride to Croton-on-Hudson, where they visited James Proctor and his wife. The FBI had information suggesting that both Proctor, a successful theatrical agent, and Abt were closely tied to the Communist Party.

In their frustration, FBI agents decided to try to take advantage of an absence of Stevens and his wife from their apartment to carry out a "surreptitious entry." This practice was illegal but frequently used by the FBI. Normally a "surreptitious entry" or "bag job" required authorization from J. Edgar Hoover, but agents in the field often felt justified in acting on their own when they could arrange to accompany someone, such as an apartment manager, who was otherwise authorized to enter a residence.[70] On one occasion when the Stevens's apartment was apparently empty, the agents placed several "fake phone calls" that were unanswered. It was laundry pick-up day, and the laundryman was unable to rouse anyone in the apartment when he rang the doorbell. The manager then gave him permission to enter the apartment to pick up the laundry, and the FBI agents waited cautiously in the hall, ready to enter if the coast was clear. But when the laundryman entered he found Alexander Stevens quietly reading a newspaper, a broad smile on his face. When they tried again a few days later the FBI agents had better luck. They persuaded the manager to allow them to join him as he "inspected" the Stevens's apartment. This time no one was at home, and the agents were free to search. But the only material of interest that they found were records indicating that over the past two years Stevens had made extensive out-of-town car trips, particularly to Chicago.[71]

The results of the three-month-long investigation of Alexander Stevens were thus quite meager. Oddly, no one in the FBI suspected that Stevens had been tipped off and had thus deliberately adopted tactics aimed at thwarting the investigation. Dismayed by the lack of progress, J. Edgar Hoover decided that a telephone wiretap was needed. In late September he wrote to the attorney general, Francis Biddle, requesting authorization to use "technical surveillance" against Stevens, whom he described, somewhat cryptically, as possibly "the payoff man for the Communist Party in this country." Stevens, he wrote, is "particularly secretive in his activities" and for that reason it was "especially difficult to conduct a thorough check of him."[72] Biddle quickly approved the request, and soon agents were dutifully monitoring all incoming and outgoing conversations. Predictably, however, they learned nothing, since Stevens scrupulously avoided making any incriminating comments and had long ago alerted his comrades to the probability that his phone was tapped. Perhaps he did broach sensitive topics when speaking with one of his brothers, but this did not help the FBI, since, as one flustered agent complained, they spoke "in some foreign language" (Hungarian).[73]

At the end of 1942, after nearly eight months of surveillance, the FBI had learned very little about Alexander Stevens/Goldberger. There were, to be sure, strong indications that he had some leadership role in the Communist Party. He had raised funds for the Party in California and conferred with the leader of the Illinois CP. There were, in addition, certain bits of circumstantial evidence. Stevens met frequently with John Abt and Jessica Smith, both of whom were regarded as Party members or fellow travelers. He spent a good deal of time at the Albert Hotel, a frequent gathering place of Communist officials. His brother Emerich was employed by Amtorg. But the physical and technical surveillance of Stevens had added almost no evidence supporting the suspicion that he was involved in subversive activity. He held a regular, nonpolitical job and spent almost all of his free time quietly working or reading in his apartment. There seemed no compelling reason to continue to devote extensive resources and personnel to an investigation that, to all appearances, had reached a dead end.

By late 1942 the FBI surveillance of Stevens was reduced and only spot checks were made on his movements.

Similarly, the investigation of J. Peters, which so far had not in any way overlapped with that of Alexander Stevens, made little progress in 1942. To be sure, one ex-Communist did provide the FBI with a fairly accurate description of the security procedures that had been implemented by Peters in the 1930s as part of the CP's "illegal apparatus."[74] This information helped the FBI to form a fuller picture of J. Peters's role in the CPUSA, but was of no help in actually locating him. But early in 1943 a group of FBI analysts in Washington assigned the general task of searching for CP leaders who had "never been definitely identified except by their Communist Party names," achieved a breakthrough. One of them noticed that the detailed description of J. Peters that Whittaker Chambers had supplied in his May 1942 interview was quite similar to the description of Alexander Stevens/Goldberger drawn up by FBI agents involved in his surveillance. In addition, Chambers had mentioned that Peters lived with a woman named Silver or Silvers. Before her recent divorce Alexander Stevens's wife was known as Sophie Silver. Unless this was a remarkable coincidence, it seemed that Alexander Stevens was in fact J. Peters.[75]

To test this hypothesis, FBI agents showed a recent photograph of Alexander Stevens to Whittaker Chambers, who immediately said: "That's Peters, head of the Communist underground movement in the United States." When similar responses were received from Benjamin Gitlow and another ex-Communist informant, agents in charge of the cases of J. Peters and Alexander Stevens/Goldberger agreed that the two files should be merged into one investigation.[76] The question now was: What should be done about this Communist, who had been assigned the highest priority on the custodial internment list, was accused of directing the CP underground, and was suspected of being a Comintern agent?

8

Dueling with "the Feds,"
1943–48

Once the FBI concluded that J. Peters and Alexander Stevens were one and the same person, the agents on the case hoped to intensify their efforts to uncover incriminating evidence that would justify his arrest. Having learned from a new informant that Peters was "undoubtedly the strongest and most direct link between the Communist Party in the United States and the Comintern,"[1] J. Edgar Hoover approved several new initiatives in the spring of 1943 that were designed to build a case that would justify the arrest of this elusive but apparently important Communist. In late March, Hoover approved a request from the agents on the case in New York to rent a room in Stevens's apartment house. This, they argued with undue optimism, would allow them to "conduct a proper surveillance" and bring the investigation to a "logical conclusion."[2] A few days later Hoover authorized "microphone surveillance" of Stevens's apartment. A listening device was duly installed and FBI agents, huddled in apartment J1, were soon listening in on all conversations in apartment C3. In May, Hoover authorized "technical surveillance" at Stevens's workplace, the Dynavox Company.[3]

Yet the fruits of this intensified investigation proved once again to be exceedingly meager. Alerted by the apartment house porter to the presence of FBI agents in J1, Alexander and Ann Stevens were careful to limit their conversations to innocuous topics. Well into the summer an FBI agent was on duty around the clock monitoring the conversations in C3. In time it became clear that they would not likely overhear anything of value and that the Stevens were probably aware that a listening device had been installed. Frustrated and bored, the agents began to resort to petty harassment in the form of prank telephone calls to the Stevens's apartment at 2:00 A.M.[4] In mid-August the microphone surveillance was discontinued, since "no information of any value" had been obtained and the deployment of two agents was deemed a waste of personnel. The wiretap at

Dynavox Company was similarly unproductive.[5] Stevens had seemingly out-foxed "the Feds," as he later boasted in his memoir.[6]

Despite these setbacks, J. Edgar Hoover had no intention of slowing down his investigation of those Communist leaders who, like J. Peters, had been high on his custodial detention list. But in order to take any direct action against Peters the FBI would need to produce evidence that criminal acts had been committed. By 1943 the FBI had collected a good deal of evidence that Peters/Alexander had been and was still involved in various Communist Party activities that could be construed as subversive. But there was as yet no real proof that he had engaged in sabotage or espionage; moreover, it remained unclear whether the FBI even had the authority to investigate individuals suspected merely of "subversive activities."[7] In April 1943, espionage had been added as a "descriptor" to Alexander Stevens's FBI file, but this apparently was just a tactical step to justify the major effort that had been undertaken to keep him under surveillance.

Ironically, it was precisely in 1943, as the FBI frantically searched for incriminating evidence to prove their speculation that Peters/Stevens was an espionage agent, that the elusive Hungarian man of mystery severed his last, tenuous ties to the spy network he had established in Washington during the 1930s. In the immediate aftermath of Whittaker Chambers's defection in 1938, J. Peters had withdrawn from all activities connected with his "Washington set-up" and ended his collaboration with GRU, NKVD, and OMS agents, with the exception of Boris Bykov, who in any case departed from the United States early in 1939. But by late 1939 and early 1940, when it began to appear unlikely that Chambers would become a government informer, Peters apparently cautiously reestablished contact with some former Ware group members in Washington, sometimes using Maxim Lieber as an intermediary.[8] The remaining members of the Ware group and its sub-units had continued their activity under the supervision of Victor Perlo. What Soviet intelligence agents would soon be calling the "Perlo group" consisted of a few Ware group veterans (Perlo, Charles Kramer, Harold Glasser), new members who might have been recommended by Peters (such as Edward "Ted" Fitzgerald), and others who were probably unknown to Peters. They now resumed the former practice of sending to CPUSA headquarters government documents and other materials they had procured. At first this material apparently went, as in the past, by courier directly to "Peter" or "Steve" (names that Perlo group members continued to use). Once Alexander Stevens came under FBI surveillance, however, John Abt became the liaison with the group. He would pass on the material he received to Earl Browder, for the general understanding was that the purpose of this "information gathering" was to assist the work of the CPUSA. Browder, for his part, retained those documents or reports that were of use to the CPUSA, and probably passed along to the NKVD (via Jacob Golos) items he thought would interest Soviet intelligence.[9]

There is evidence suggesting that between 1940 and 1942 Peters even traveled from time to time to Washington to affirm his interest in the Perlo group, offer guidance in their underground operations, and recruit new members.[10] In this period, GRU and NKVD agents were vaguely aware that the Washington information group that "Storm" (J. Peters) had established in the 1930s continued to operate, but there was considerable confusion over the group's status. In 1940 or 1941 a GRU agent made an attempt to recruit Harold Glasser, but desisted when he concluded that the group that formerly had been "under the leadership of secret PB [PolBuro] member 'Peter'" was now being transferred to the NKVD. This seemed to be confirmed when Gayk Ovakimyan, the NKVD resident in New York who supervised all Soviet intelligence work at the time, instructed the GRU to "leave this entire group alone."[11] But, even though the NKVD evinced an interest in recruiting one or more of the members of the Perlo group, nothing was done for some time, probably because of the long-standing reluctance of NKVD operatives to interfere with the information-gathering activity of the CPUSA and lingering concerns that one or more members of the group might still have a connection with the GRU.

The situation was transformed in June 1942, when the FBI began its intensive surveillance of Alexander Stevens, who naturally broke off any remaining contact with the Washington group. For the rest of 1942 and into 1943, the Perlo group was apparently left to drift on its own. Material continued to be sent to the CPUSA headquarters, but John Abt and Earl Browder were no doubt wary of communicating directly with the members of the Washington underground unit, fearing that the FBI was investigating not only J. Peters/Alexander Stevens, but also those who had cooperated with him in his conspiratorial work. Early in 1943, a GRU agent once again encountered the Perlo group and, apparently unaware of previous discussion among Soviet operatives,[12] reported to his superior that the group was responsible to the "American ComParty" and was headed by a "CC worker known as Peter." However, certain members of the group were unhappy with "Peter," since he was paying "almost no attention to informational work and takes no interest in the information received."[13]

In 1943, NKVD officials decided that the time had come to recruit some or all of the members of Storm's "lost tribe." Eventually the Perlo group was annexed to the Soviet intelligence network, but not without considerable difficulty. When Earl Browder was approached early in 1943 with a proposal that Perlo ("Eck" or "Raid") be placed under the jurisdiction of the NKVD, the CPUSA leader readily agreed, although he seemed to know little about the Perlo group except that its members were all "secret, reliable fellowcountrymen working at various government institutions in 'Carthage' [Washington]."[14] Browder instructed John Abt to arrange this matter, but when Soviet agents contacted Abt, he refused to cooperate. In this matter, he told them, Browder's instructions were not binding on him and he could only "do something when he had received orders from his superior, 'Peter.'" When apprised of Abt's response, Browder could only shrug his shoulders and declare that "there was nothing he could do in this situation."[15]

In the following months, however, Browder looked more closely into the matter. Having spent over a year in prison in the early 1940s, Browder perhaps had not been able to keep track of J. Peters's activities as Alexander Stevens. He now discovered that Stevens had been underground since 1939, had come under intensive surveillance by the FBI, and since 1942 had been working in a factory and had had no direct connection with the Perlo group. In light of this information, Browder took formal action. In late summer he instructed Stevens to discontinue any connection he might still have with the Washington group, while at the same time hinting that perhaps a way could be found now for him to return to open Party work. He then informed the NKVD that he had determined that "Storm" had "long since drifted away from these matters, did not have communications with that group [the Perlo group] and had nothing to do with the fellowcountrymen's special work at all anymore." There were the further complications that he was an alien and that he might be under surveillance by American counter-intelligence because "the neighbors [GRU] used to use him a great deal." Browder insisted, however, that he continued to regard Stevens as "a reliable person and a good fellowcountryman."[16]

In the circumstances, Alexander Stevens could hardly object to his final removal from "special work" and contact with the Perlo group, which could now be brought under the supervision of the NKVD.[17] At a meeting in John Abt's Central Park West apartment early in 1944, Elizabeth Bentley, the NKVD agent who was to serve as the group's new handler, was told by those members in attendance that for some time the group had felt abandoned and "nobody was interested in their possibilities."[18] By the spring of 1944 the Perlo group had been fully integrated into the NKVD network and its members were to remain a major source of information for Soviet intelligence until the end of World War II. In a sense the group was J. Peters's final legacy to Soviet intelligence. He had recruited and trained many of its members, whom their new handler now praised as trustworthy CP members who were "highly developed politically and have a desire to help us with information."[19]

Completely unaware of these developments in the complex relationship between the CPUSA and Soviet intelligence, the FBI continued its investigation of Alexander Stevens into 1944, but with diminishing intensity, since month after month the agents involved had little of significance to report. When the Dynavox Company closed down late in 1943 because of poor sales of phonographs, Stevens found new employment with the All-American Playthings Corporation in Long Island City, also owned by a CP sympathizer. He was hired as foreman of the plant, which employed forty workers and specialized in the production of wooden toys, the most popular of which was a machine-gun.[20] But before long Stevens began to contemplate the possibility of returning to full-time work in the Party, an idea that Earl Browder had broached. American public opinion seemed in 1944 to be much less hostile to the Communist Party, which since July 1941 had given strong support to the Roosevelt administration in the war effort. Many Americans now had a more favorable view of Soviet Russia because of its valiant resistance against the Nazi German invaders. One sign of this changed national mood had been President Roosevelt's commutation of Earl Browder's prison sentence as a gesture of good will toward the Communist Party and the Soviet Union.[21] Perhaps Alexander Stevens noticed that in the first half of 1944 the FBI had reduced its surveillance of him, and concluded that he no longer had to fear arrest.

Early in June, John Williamson, a member of the Central Committee, contacted Stevens, with whom he had not talked for almost a year. Williamson suggested that conditions had changed and he saw no reason why Stevens should not "come around," that is, why Stevens should not appear once again openly at Party events. The two men agreed that as a first step Stevens should attend the upcoming national convention. Williamson also responded favorably to Stevens's proposal that he return to full-time, open work in the Party, which had recently been renamed the Communist Political Association (CPA): "Why don't you look up our old mutual friend, Will, sometime? There may be something in his outfit."[22] The reference was apparently to William Weiner, with whom J. Peters had worked in the Organization Department. When in mid-August the All-American Toy Company closed down because of a large drop in sales, Stevens pressed more vigorously for a full-time position in the Party. After a short delay he was appointed organizational secretary for New York County, a position similar to the job he had held in 1929–31. In preparation for his new responsibility, Stevens spent much of his time in the early fall of 1944 in his apartment, working on what he called his "debut report," apparently a study of recruitment and retention of members based on his experiences in the 1930s. In November he began to appear daily at the Party headquarters. At this time he assumed yet another alias, Steve Miller, although he kept Alexander Stevens as his public name.[23]

The Party Steve Miller now reentered had recently undergone a dramatic transformation. Early in 1944 Earl Browder had done what previously would have been unthinkable: without informing or seeking the approval of Moscow, he pushed through a plan for changing the Communist Party into a kind of left-wing pressure group that would henceforth work for reform within the existing American political system. Greatly impressed by the appearance of allied unity at the Teheran Conference late in November 1943, Browder predicted that after the war there would be a long era of peaceful coexistence between the Soviet

Union and the Western Powers. "Class divisions and political groupings" would therefore lose their significance, and Communists could best contribute to the building of a just and prosperous society by allaying fears that they sought a Socialist revolution.[24] Browder had sufficient backing in the Party to win apparently solid approval for this radical change in strategy and for the renaming of the CPUSA as the Communist Political Association (CPA), but there were several dissidents who were horrified at the changes, which they regarded as outright heresies. Orthodox Communists like William Foster believed that Browder was advocating the abandonment of several of the core principles of Marxism.[25] Foster might well have quoted from J. Peters's *A Manual on Organization* to bolster his claims. There Peters had stipulated several principles of Communist orthodoxy that could never be questioned, including the inevitability of class struggle and the necessity of revolutionary change in order to achieve the forceful overthrow of capitalism and create a proletarian dictatorship.

But just as J. Peters in 1935 had quietly acquiesced in and embraced a new Comintern "line" that was completely antithetical to the ideas propounded in his recently published *Manual*, Steve Miller a decade later found it expedient to give apparently enthusiastic support to Browder's restructuring of the Party, even though he had come to dislike his former mentor and privately probably shared the apprehensions of Browder's critics.[26] In January 1945, shortly after assuming his new duties as organizational secretary for New York County, Miller gave an important speech to a large group at the county training school. Reminiscing about his earlier days in the Party, he recalled a time when it was necessary to operate secretly because of the repressive policies of the FBI and the Department of Justice. But, Miller asserted, "that day is gone." Quoting the words of Earl Browder, he suggested that the goal of the CPA was "to develop unity which will guarantee legalization of the organization in the community." The CPA, he said, could work to exert its influence without fear of repression: "There is nothing about the present party line that will permit or invite investigations. Without question we are loyal patriots. We are no longer advocating force or violence, only taking a strong and forceful place in the political life of the country." Miller added that he could speak openly about such matters, even if there was a spy in their midst, since "we are no longer afraid."[27]

In the early months of 1945, Steve Miller continued to offer support for the transformation of the Party that Browder had championed.[28] But by May there were strong indications that the Soviet leadership, which had silently observed the significant changes Browder had introduced, in fact regarded his initiatives as wrongheaded and dangerous. This emboldened Browder's critics, led by William Foster, to accuse him openly of having violated sacred Marxist and Leninist principles. Once it became clear that Browder no longer had support in Moscow, American Communist leaders turned quickly, and often viciously, against him. At a special national convention in July, Browder was ousted as Party leader and replaced by a secretariat headed by Foster. By unanimous vote the CPUSA was reestablished and the CPA sank into oblivion. Earl Browder, who only a few months earlier had basked in the adulation of the great majority of Party activists, was now denounced as "an enemy of the working class," a "renegade," and "an apologist for American imperialism." Literally overnight he had become a pariah.[29]

In the 1930s, J. Peters had generally refrained from joining openly in critical policy debates involving major shifts in Party strategy. In similar fashion, Steve Miller chose not to voice his opinions during the meetings in which Browder's fate was being decided. Yet it seems certain that Miller, despite his outspoken support for the CPA, welcomed Browder's downfall and in this period felt ideologically much closer to William Foster.[30] For the remainder of his tenure as organizational secretary for New York County, which lasted until early 1947, Miller was free once again to use the kind of militant terminology and methods he seemed to prefer. In a long and important speech in late January 1946 at the "New York County Convention on the Reconstitution of the Communist Party," Miller sounded very much like the J. Peters of old.[31] "We are proud," he announced, "to be able to say that for the first time in a very long time . . . the Communists are where they should be—in the midst of the fighting workers." Citing with approval recent comments by William Foster, Miller argued that there were still some "opportunistic methods of thinking and working" that were left over from the Browder regime. The reconstituted CP thus had to become once again a "militant Marxist Party," the vanguard of the working class. Miller warned that it took real courage for members to "show the Party's face" in the factories, but it was necessary and would bring real rewards: "Our liberal friends sneer when they hear us saying this, but whether they like it or not, we are the vanguard, we are the only working class organization which is armed with a knowledge of the laws of the life of the society, the laws of its development and the laws of the class struggle. It is our historic task to explain these laws to the working class. . . . Our big job is to make the American worker really class conscious, to make him hate not only the trusts, but capitalists, individually and the whole class, and the system."

Miller pointed out to the Communist activists in the audience that as members of the Party's largest district they had a special obligation to "show initiative, imagination, and boldness in our approach to problems." He ended with a rhetorical flourish very much in the spirit of J. Peters's *A Manual on Organization*: "The American worker is not the happy, contented worker that he has been pictured to the people of the world and that has been portrayed in our movies and radio. . . . Ours is the historic mission to lead the workers of America toward realization of their dreams. . . . We are taking the first steps.

Let us step out firmly, boldly, as only Communists know how, to achieve our goal—socialism."

Steve Miller applied himself to the job of organizational secretary in New York County in 1945 and 1946 with the same fervor and dedication that he, as J. Peters, had approached the job more than a decade earlier. He met frequently with union organizers; planned strikes, rallies, and marches; issued newsletters and reports; and experimented with ways to increase membership. He attempted to inspire unit leaders with his own enthusiasm and often exaggerated optimism. This was an exciting time for activists like Miller, for in the immediate post–World War II period the Party was near its peak in membership and influence. In his memoirs, József Péter was to look back on this phase of his career with particular fondness and a sense of pride. He felt he had played some role, for example, in establishing and maintaining the Party's foothold in numerous CIO unions and in promoting Communist candidates for political office.[32] In fact, it was in the New York district that the CPUSA had some of its greatest success in getting members or strong Party sympathizers elected to important posts in local and national government. Steve Miller was particularly gratified when Benjamin J. Davis, an African American Communist with whom he worked closely in 1945–46, was reelected to a seat on New York's City Council that he had initially won in 1943.[33]

However, Steve Miller's tenure as organizational secretary of New York County also brought him some disappointments. He must have been dismayed to discover that some of the same problems of recruitment and retention of members that he had grappled with in the 1930s still bedeviled the Party. In 1945, New York County had a net loss of two thousand members over the past year, due mainly to the large number of dropouts.[34] Miller tried to use the same methods that he, as J. Peters, had employed in the 1930s, to inspire the club leaders to meet their recruitment quotas. But Miller's approach, a mix of encouragement, didacticism, and badgering, was apparently not well received by some of the club leaders, who were part of a younger generation in the Party. To them, Steve Miller was a stranger who possessed no special aura of authority. This caused some confusion and embarrassment in July 1945 at a New York County meeting at which delegates were to be chosen to represent the district at the upcoming state convention. Normally those nominated by the Party leadership were unanimously elected. But in this case when Steve Miller was nominated, opposition was voiced by several members, who pointed out in the ensuing debate that Miller was practically unknown in the district. In the end Miller was nominated and elected, but only after it was made clear that this was strongly desired by state officials.[35]

Even those younger Party leaders who knew something of the role that J. Peters had played in the 1930s were sometimes disappointed when they met and worked with Steve Miller. When George Charney, a rising figure in the Party, returned from military service in 1945, he was appointed organizer for New York County. He was excited to learn that his organizational secretary, Steve Miller, was in fact J. Peters, for he had always imagined Peters as an imposing Party leader and a "legendary Bolshevik." But after meeting and working for a time with Peters, Charney became disillusioned. He discovered that this "noble figure in the movement" was in fact very reluctant to join in Party discussions or debates, preferring instead to sit quietly with Charney and surreptitiously slip him notes with advice on what to say. Charney observed that Peters seemed at his best when he could "sit in a back room and compose a blueprint on party organization and write articles for internal party publications like a sage." But he shrank from taking a firm stand on controversial Party problems because he feared "exposing himself to criticism for deviationism." All in all, Charney later concluded, J. Peters was "a man who could shift with the winds of political doctrine."[36]

Charney's comment on Peters's ideological opportunism was incisive, but his feeling that Peters did not live up to his "legendary" status was based on the mistaken assumption that his only contributions to the Party had been as an organization specialist who wrote an important but dull *Manual*. Charney, along with virtually all CP leaders in the post–World War II period, knew nothing of Peters's previous activity in the 1930s as head of the secret apparatus. One can see how Steve Miller, reduced to the humdrum world of an organizational secretary, might cut a less than imposing figure. No doubt Miller missed the intrigue of underground work, but his relinquishing of all ties to the secret apparatus meant that his work schedule was much less hectic and demanding. For the first time in his career he could ease up a bit and allow more free time for reading and socializing with Party friends.

When the wartime gasoline rationing ended in 1945, the Stevens often drove up on weekends to Lake Peekskill, where they had use of one of a group of cabins owned by Alexander's brother, Joseph Goldberger.[37] Many other weekends were spent at the Jackson Heights home of their close friends, John Abt and Jessica Smith. These were convivial gatherings consisting of "roast beef, drinks, and poker." Among the frequent guests, along with their spouses and children, were veterans of the Ware group like Nathan Witt, George Silverman, and Charles Kramer, as well as Joe Freeman and Gerhardt Eisler. Though he drank alcohol only in moderation, "Pete" (as Stevens was known to these friends) was the life of the party. He told funny jokes, amused the children who called him Uncle Peter, and played a wicked hand at the card game of "Baseball."[38] The Stevens were also frequent guests at John Abt's country home. In fact, "Pete" had in 1940 been the first to suggest to John Abt that he should buy a country retreat where he and Jessica could find solitude and relaxation and "where no one can see your belly" (a reference to Abt's increasing girth). Abt and "Pete" pored over the real estate ads in the Sunday *Times,* drove out on weekends to inspect the most interesting prospects, and eventually selected a large log cabin in a rural area of the Connecticut Berkshires. Over the years "Pete" helped in the remodeling of the home and the building of a terrace, from which the spectacular autumn foliage in the area could be viewed. Soon "Pete" began to call the Berkshire retreat "October Hill," a name that John Abt and Jessica Smith readily adopted.[39]

The period stretching from the end of World War II in 1945 to the autumn of 1946 represented for the "red conspirator" a relatively tranquil time. Especially when he was at the Lake Peekskill cabin or October Hill, he could feel free from snooping FBI agents. In this period American attitudes towards the CPUSA were still favorably influenced by the strong support the Party had given to the war effort. But dark clouds were definitely on the horizon. American policy toward the Soviet Union began to harden when it became apparent that Stalin did not intend to honor his wartime declarations that the countries of Eastern Europe would be reconstructed on the basis of national independence and democratic principles. By the time Winston Churchill coined the term "iron curtain" in his speech at Fulton College in March 1946, there were many signs that the wartime collaboration between the United States and the U.S.S.R. had been transformed into an emerging cold war. For Alexander Stevens the most ominous development came late in 1946, when Louis Budenz, a former editor of the *Daily Worker,* defected and began making strong, and often sensationalist, anti-Communist public statements. In testimony before the House Committee on Un-American Activities, or HUAC (formerly called the Dies Committee), Budenz declared that in its aim to establish a Soviet government in the United States, Moscow relied on the assistance of the CPUSA, which was "a puppet fifth column of the Soviet dictatorship." Each CP member was "a potential spy agent," and he himself had collaborated in the 1930s with the NKVD, which was actively at work in the United States.[40]

Budenz's often exaggerated testimony, combined with other revelations about alleged Soviet espionage, greatly contributed in 1947 to the resurgence of a virulent popular hostility toward the CPUSA and the Soviet Union. Alexander Stevens had good reason to fear that Budenz might soon begin to tell the HUAC what he knew about the CP secret apparatus, for Budenz had worked with Peters and Soviet agents in the campaign against the Trotskyites. When they were Party comrades, Peters must have viewed Budenz as trustworthy, for he had confided to him certain information about his activity in the secret apparatus that few other Party officials ever learned.

At a HUAC hearing on February 6, 1947, Budenz mentioned J. Peters for the first time, identifying him as a "high level Comintern operative" who collaborated with Gerhardt Eisler, whom Budenz identified as a "Kremlin agent." Budenz did not elaborate on this, other than to establish Peters in the public

mind as a mysterious and sinister Communist agent who used so many different aliases that it had been difficult even for his comrades to remember at any
given time which was the correct one.[41] Although Budenz did not speak more
extensively about Peters at a HUAC hearing until more than a year later, he almost certainly was the main source for an important article that appeared in the
New York World Telegram on February 13, 1947. The title of this piece by Nelson
Frank, "Another Stalin Agent Is Smoked Out Here," set the tone for American
newspaper coverage about J. Peters that was to continue right up to his departure
from the United States in 1949. Frank reported that Peters, whom he incorrectly
described as a German, was currently using the alias of Steve Miller and was
serving as the "membership director" of the Party's New York district. Peters
was identified in the article as an influential Party leader who "directed affairs
from the background." The only evidence Frank offered was J. Peters's *Manual
on Organization,* which, he declared, "since 1935 [has] been the party's guide to
its ultimate aim, the overthrow of the American system of society." The article
contained numerous quotes from the more strident sections of the *Manual,*
including Peters's call for "the revolutionary overthrow of capitalism and for
the establishment of a new world, a Soviet America."

Louis Budenz's HUAC testimony and subsequent public statements and publications and Nelson Frank's article were instrumental in creating the public
image of J. Peters as a man of mystery and a dangerous "Kremlin agent" and a
"red conspirator."[42] Frank's suggestion that the *Manual on Organization* offered
proof of the revolutionary aims of the CPUSA was to be particularly influential
in shaping Cold War attitudes in the United States. Only a few days after the
appearance of Frank's article, Monsignor Fulton J. Sheen, whose weekly radio
program, "The Catholic Hour," had an extensive national audience, illustrated
the evils of Communism by reading excerpts from Peters's *Manual.*[43] In a 1948
documentary produced by the ABC television network entitled "Communism—
American Brand," a reference was made to the oath for new Party members that
Peters had reproduced in the *Manual.* A writer for the *Daily Worker* criticized
the documentary filmmakers for their distortions, pointing out, for example,
that Peters's pamphlet had for many years not been used as a Party guide.[44] But
few Americans at the time gave much credence to articles in the *Daily Worker* or
disclaimers made by Communist officials. Writers and public figures who were
convinced that the CPUSA was a grave threat to national security continued
to cite the more extreme passages in Peters's work, for they found that a more
convincing case against the CPUSA could be made by citing the *Manual* rather
than simply the works of Marx, Lenin, and Stalin, in which the focus was on
Europe and the United States received only occasional mention. Peters's pamphlet seemed more relevant to American society, since it had been composed
as recently as 1935 and focused on the need for the creation of a Soviet-style

dictatorship specifically in the United States. Moreover, the author of the *Manual,* using a variety of aliases, apparently continued to carry on his nefarious, if ill-defined, activities. By 1948, interest in Peters's *Manual* in anti-Communist circles was so strong that used copies, if obtainable at all, were selling for as much as ten dollars.

The mounting fury of anti-Communist sentiment seems to have convinced Alexander Stevens that his arrest by the FBI was imminent. On the same day that the *Journal American* reported that J. Peters/Steve Miller was another Soviet agent who had been "smoked out," Stevens and his wife abruptly left their apartment and went into hiding. Although a month later Ann Stevens returned to live in the Kew Gardens apartment, Alexander remained on the run, moving from one safe house to another in the greater New York area.[45] During this time he could not risk an appearance at Party headquarters, but remained in touch with John Williamson by telephone or through intermediaries. Meanwhile, J. Edgar Hoover, somewhat miffed by the fact that a reporter for the *Journal American* had been able to learn so much about J. Peters without the assistance of the FBI, instructed his agents that the locating of Alexander Stevens was "vitally important" and should be "pursued vigorously [and] without delay."[46] Hoover's sense of urgency was driven also by an important breakthrough in the investigation of J. Peters/Alexander Stevens. By early 1947, J. Edgar Hoover was confident that he now had strong evidence that Stevens had at least on one occasion committed passport fraud. This discovery was made when an FBI agent, assigned to collaborate with the State Department on another case, was by chance shown a group of passport application photos of individuals suspected of being Communists. As he perused these photos he immediately recognized one of them, bearing the name Isadore Boorstein, as Alexander Stevens. The passport seemed conclusive evidence that Stevens "used the name of another individual who evidently answered the same description and was born approximately the same date, a clear violation of the U.S. statutes."[47] Everything previously known about the trip to the Soviet Union taken by Alexander Stevens/J. Peters in 1931–32 now fell neatly into place, for the passport records showed the exact dates of his departure and return.

For several months after Alexander Stevens's disappearance in February 1947, FBI agents made frequent but fruitless spot checks at his apartment in Kew Gardens, CP headquarters, and his brother Joseph's residence in Brooklyn. Finally, in June an informant in Lake Peekskill reported that Stevens's blue Chrysler sedan had been spotted parked near one of the cabins owned by his brother. From this point on the FBI was able once again to keep Stevens under constant surveillance. He was observed meeting his wife at prearranged rendezvous points, moving from one safe house to another, and making frequent telephone calls from public phone booths. By the summer months of 1947, Stevens began to spend longer periods at Lake Peekskill, doing handyman jobs at cabins owned by his brother. As each month passed, however, the news became increasingly grim for this Communist on the run. The hunt for Communist "subversives" was now in full swing. In June a grand jury was impaneled in New York City to determine if the CPUSA was a conspiratorial organization whose purpose was to overthrow the American government. J. Peters was soon placed on the list of individuals who would be summoned to testify. On July 8, Gene Dennis, national secretary of the CPUSA, was given a one-year prison sentence for refusing to appear when summoned to a HUAC session.[48] In August, Stevens learned that investigators for HUAC had been staking out his apartment in order to serve a subpoena requiring his appearance before the Committee on October 30.[49]

In their effort to locate Alexander Stevens, HUAC investigators sought the help of the FBI, but J. Edgar Hoover was not inclined to lend his assistance to the congressional committee, preferring instead to work with the Department of Justice and the Immigration and Naturalization Service (INS) to arrange for the arrest of the mysterious Communist he and his agents had been tracking for many years. On September 18, 1947, he sent to the INS a memorandum summarizing what was known about J. Peters/Alexander Stevens, with an emphasis on his status as an alien, his alleged subversive activities, and his overseas travel in 1931–32 on a fraudulent passport.[50] He sent a similar memorandum to the attorney general, Tom Clark, asking for his suggestions on how to proceed. In his response, Clark stated his opinion that, provided it didn't interfere with any of the bureau's other investigations, Stevens could be deported "on either of two grounds, one as a functionary of the Communist Party and second as perpetrating a passport fraud." He pointed out that the statute of limitations would prevent the prosecution of an American citizen for passport fraud committed more than ten years ago, but that statute did not apply to aliens at INS deportation hearings.[51]

The attorney general's office, the FBI, and the INS were now in agreement on how to proceed against Alexander Stevens. He was to be arrested and, after an INS hearing, compelled to leave the country and return to Czechoslovakia. Later events suggest that some in the Department of Justice were open to the possibility that Stevens might be induced to turn state's evidence and cooperate in ongoing investigations of Soviet intelligence. If he did so, some sort of plea bargain might be arranged that would allow him to remain in the United States and perhaps be granted citizenship. But FBI and INS officials were unwilling to collaborate with HUAC, which was dominated by Republicans, including Richard Nixon and Karl Mundt, who seemed eager to gain a political advantage and national acclaim by exposing Communists like Alexander Stevens. By early October, the INS, relying on material provided by the FBI, prepared a deportation warrant charging Stevens with a violation of the Immigration Act of 1924.

On October 8, a group of nine INS agents surrounded Stevens and his wife as they left his brother's cabin in Lake Peekskill and were about to drive off in their car. Stevens, who had no doubt feared that this would be the outcome of his long duel with the FBI, remained calm and offered no resistance. However, he refused to answer any questions, and when searched was found to have on his person his driver's license and a small amount of money, but no incriminating material. When Stevens was taken away in an INS vehicle, his wife was permitted to keep possession of their car. She proceeded directly to New York and informed the CP leadership of her husband's arrest.[52]

Stevens was taken first to the INS office in Manhattan, where he was fingerprinted and photographed, and then was transferred later in the day to a detention facility on Ellis Island. There he was allowed to meet with the lawyer the CP had provided, Carol Weiss King, who specialized in the defense of left-wing (in practice, almost always Communist) aliens at deportation hearings.[53] Noted for her knowledge of immigration law and her often abrasive style, King instructed Stevens to refuse to answer any questions posed by INS agents and asserted that the action against her client was illegal and politically motivated.[54] Furthermore, she needled INS officers by asserting that in any case they would never succeed in deporting her client because Czechoslovakia, where she claimed to have more influence than the INS, would never agree to accept him.[55] King hoped to move quickly on the posting of bond so that her client would not have to spend the night in detention. But she was irate when told the bond would be set at five thousand dollars, an amount that could not be raised that day.[56] As a result, Stevens had to spend the night in a detention cell on Ellis Island, the only incarceration that he would ever suffer in the United States. Later that day King told CP officials that she was inclined to fight to lower the bond, which would tie up too large an amount of Party funds for an indefinite period of time. She was even prepared to travel to INS headquarters in Philadelphia in order to get the bond reduced. But to her dismay Party leaders ("the people upstairs") rejected her proposal, arguing that it was best to free Stevens as soon as possible.[57]

On the following day Ann Stevens received from a Party official five $1000 U.S. Treasury bonds to be used to meet her husband's bail. When Stevens was released later that day, Carol Weiss King complained that a large and unruly group of reporters and photographers were camped out at the front gate of the INS facility, presumably tipped off by INS officials to what was happening. She demanded that Stevens be allowed to exit the building so as to avoid the reporters. The INS was not averse to this suggestion, since it was known that a representative of HUAC was also at the front gate, ready to issue a subpoena requiring Stevens to appear at a hearing later in October. Stevens and his wife were thus taken through a basement passageway that led to an exit at the rear of the building. Stevens then proceeded with his wife to the CP headquarters in

Manhattan, where Party leaders urged him to go underground again in order "to avoid Nixon's subpoena."[58] Since it was to take an abnormally long time for the INS to make preparations for and schedule his deportation hearing, Stevens had to spend the next ten months in hiding.

Although reporters had been thwarted in their attempt to interview and photograph Alexander Stevens, New York City newspapers gave prominent coverage to his arrest and release. Given the lack of hard information, these reports tended to be a garbled mixture of a few facts, many inaccuracies, and a good deal of creative speculation. There was a general consensus that the individual who had been arrested was the J. Peters who had written a notorious manual on Communist organization. Only the *Daily Worker* persisted in identifying him simply as Steve Miller, although it was conceded that he was "an active worker in the Communist and labor movement."[59] Beyond the fact that he had been charged with illegal entry into the country in 1932, reporters had very little evidence on which to construct a story about this Communist "man of mystery." Since the INS was seeking to deport Stevens to Czechoslovakia, it was assumed that he was by origin Czech or Slovak ("Czech Seized Upstate as High Russian Agent"). Only the writer for the *New York Sun*, apparently relying on a source in the FBI, got the basic facts right: the individual arrested by the INS was a "Hungarian of many aliases" (including Alexander Goldberger) who had been living in the United States for twenty-five years.[60] The terms used to identify Alexander Stevens in these press reports reflected the Cold War mentality that had begun to permeate the American media. He was variously referred to as a "Red Conspirator," "Kremlin stooge," a "top Stalin spy," and an "elusive and mysterious agent of the Communist International."[61] One reporter suggested that since his arrival in the United States, J. Peters had operated out of Peekskill, which was one of the "hideouts in the Kremlin's underground stretching from Moscow via Newfoundland into Canada, then into the United States." Another wrote confidently about the existence of a Communist Party military committee, headed by J. Peters, which organized espionage related to the Army and Navy and sent the information gathered "by courier to Moscow where it was turned over to Russian scientists and the Red Army."[62]

Although there was a kernel of truth in some of the newspaper allegations, FBI and INS officials in 1947 had no convincing evidence to prove that Stevens had engaged in espionage and sabotage. In fact, at that point federal investigators had only the sketchiest information about the "Ware group," and no knowledge at all of J. Peters's false passport operation and his espionage ring in Washington, D.C. In order to build their case against Alexander Stevens, INS investigators began at the end of 1947 to seek out and interview any ex-Communists who were willing to offer relevant testimony about Stevens's Party career. Most of these informants had earlier cooperated with the FBI, but the INS on its own discovered a few other individuals who were able to provide useful information. Ironically, although the FBI and the attorney general's office were initially in agreement that Whittaker Chambers would likely be a key witness at Stevens's deportation hearing, in fact he was interviewed but never called to testify by the INS. In this period Chambers, the only potential witness who had a comprehensive knowledge of J. Peters's underground activities, remained reluctant to speak publicly about his conspiratorial past. Not only was he fearful of being prosecuted and sent to prison, but he also retained enough of a Communist mentality to view with repugnance the idea of betraying the individuals with whom he had worked in J. Peters's "Washington set-up."[63] Chambers thus told only part of what he knew in several FBI interviews in this period, and he managed for a time to avoid speaking with INS agents or testifying at the New York grand jury that was investigating the Communist Party.

As the INS continued in 1948 to build its case against Alexander Stevens, the Hungarian alien continued his precarious underground existence. Moving from one Communist safe house to another, never staying more than two or three weeks at each, Stevens managed to escape detection by government agents or newspaper reporters. He spent the longest period of time in a Long Island beachfront cabin owned by his friend John Lautner, whom Party officials had given the assignment of coordinating Stevens's underground movements.[64] Although he never dared to appear at CP headquarters, he was able to confer by telephone from time to time with Party leaders, including Gene Dennis and John Williamson. They may have given him assignments to compose reports on various issues affecting the Party.[65] Using various subterfuges and prearranged phone calls from public phone booths, he was able to keep in touch with his wife and even meet her occasionally. Otherwise he had a good deal of time on his hands and was thus able to read, no doubt with increasing trepidation, press reports about the rising tide of anti-Communist sentiment in the country. Late in 1947 the HUAC held a series of hearings to investigate Communist influence in the Hollywood film industry. Among the directors and scriptwriters who were forced to appear were several with whom Stevens had collaborated in Party activities, including John Howard Lawson, Herbert Biberman, and Lester Cole. All of the hostile witnesses (later known as the Hollywood Ten) cited their constitutional rights under the First Amendment in refusing to answer questions about alleged ties to the Communist Party. Stevens may have taken some delight in the histrionic defiance of the witnesses, particularly of his friend John Lawson, who succeeded in making a mockery of the proceedings. But the final result was sobering: Lawson and the others were cited for contempt of Congress and were given one-year prison sentences.[66]

In July 1948, the New York grand jury that had spent more than a year investigating the Communist Party issued indictments against twelve leaders of the

CPUSA, including William Foster, Gene Dennis, and John Williamson. They were charged under the Smith Act with conspiring to advocate the overthrow of the United States government. Fearing that he too would soon be indicted, Stevens decided to find a safe haven farther removed from New York City. Soon he and John Lautner were on their way by Greyhound bus to Riegelsville, Pennsylvania, where a Party sympathizer owned a farm. There Stevens was to remain during most of August, while FBI and HUAC agents continued their search for him in and around New York. Stevens enjoyed this sojourn in rural Pennsylvania, where he helped out with farm chores and listened each day to radio broadcasts to see if his name was mentioned.[67]

In Washington, meanwhile, momentous events were unfolding. On August 3, Whittaker Chambers was summoned to testify at a HUAC session. Chambers's appearance before the Committee was by no means voluntary, but once there he seemed resolved to demonstrate his anti-Communist credentials. In his opening statement he asserted that Americans were "at grips with a secret, sinister, and enormously powerful force whose tireless purpose is their enslavement." He then proceeded to repeat, for the first time publicly, the account of the Communist underground apparatus in Washington that he had first described to Adolph Berle in September 1939.[68] Chambers discussed the organization of the Ware group and named its members, with a particular emphasis on Alger Hiss. However, in describing the Washington underground operation he chose his words carefully: its purpose was "not primarily espionage" but infiltration of the government, although espionage "was certainly one of its eventual objectives." When asked what he could tell the Committee about an individual named J. Peters, Chambers responded without hesitation that Peters was, "to the best of my knowledge, the head of the whole underground United States Communist Party." In a quick sketch of the career of his erstwhile handler, Chambers mentioned his origins in Hungary, service as an officer in World War I, and participation in the short-lived Hungarian Communist government. When a committee member asked how J. Peters, an alien, could have obtained an American passport to travel to the Soviet Union in 1931, Chambers offered, for the first time publicly, a description of Peters's fraudulent passport operation. Peters, he said, had once told him all about it "with great amusement because of the simplicity of the scheme."

Although Chambers did not explicitly state that J. Peters had engaged in espionage, some HUAC members immediately jumped to that conclusion. Karl Mundt expressed outrage that Peters, an alien who had formerly served as an officer in a foreign army and as a member of a foreign government, had presided over "espionage activities carried on throughout our governmental departments." It seemed even more important now that the elusive J. Peters be found and forced to testify at a HUAC session. Mundt asked rhetorically why this had not yet been done, despite the fact that a subpoena demanding his appearance had been issued nearly a year earlier. Robert Stripling, chief investigator for the committee, explained that the FBI apparently had no information as to his whereabouts. To which Mundt responded sarcastically: "They will have to modify that statement that they always get their man and add 'with the exception of Mr. Peters.'"

Ensconced on the farm in Riegelville, Alexander Stevens could hope to continue for some time to evade the HUAC and FBI investigators who were on his trail. But, as he told John Lautner at the time, he was deeply concerned about Chambers's HUAC testimony, which "is one of the most serious things that could happen to the party. . . . We are really in trouble at this time."[69] But there was still a possibility that the full story of the Washington espionage ring would not come to light. Stevens was one of the very few people in the country who knew that in his HUAC testimony Chambers had not been entirely forthcoming. To protect himself and others, he had not revealed that he and J. Peters had created an espionage apparatus that cooperated closely with Soviet military intelligence. He had carefully avoided mention of the names of Soviet agents (Bill, Col. Bykov, Richard Ikal) and of those who had worked in Apparatus B, such as Henry Wadleigh and David Carpenter, and though he had named Alger Hiss a Communist, he had not accused him of espionage. And he had not, of course, given the slightest hint to the HUAC committee that he had stowed away a group of stolen State Department documents.

Throughout August, HUAC held a series of hearings to which the individuals named by Chambers as members of the Communist underground in Washington were summoned to testify. Most of them (including Abt, Perlo, Silverman, Collins, Pressman, Kramer, and Witt) refused to answer any questions relating to the accusations Chambers had made, citing their constitutional rights under the Fifth Amendment. Only two of those named by Chambers were willing to respond directly to his charges, Donald and Alger Hiss. Both forcefully denied that they had ever had any connection to the Communist Party or had known Chambers or J. Peters.[70] This placed the Committee members in a quandary, since it was obvious that either Chambers or the Hiss brothers were lying. To try to clarify the situation, Chambers was recalled and was asked further questions about his alleged relationship with Alger Hiss. How, for example, did he know that Hiss had been a Communist? Chambers replied: "I was told that by Mr. Peters . . . [who] was head of the entire underground."[71] Committee members were now even more convinced that the mysterious J. Peters, who was such a central figure in Chambers's narrative, must be found and compelled to testify.

As it happened, the INS was completing its investigation of Alexander Stevens precisely as the dramatic events were unfolding at the HUAC hearings. On August 20 a letter was sent to Stevens at his Kew Gardens address, with copies to his wife and Carol King, summoning him to his deportation hearing, which was scheduled to begin on August 30. Stevens might have been briefly tempted to ignore this summons and remain in hiding indefinitely. But CP officials insisted that nothing would be gained in that way, and the consequences would be even worse when, eventually, the FBI tracked him down. Furthermore, the Party did not want to lose the five thousand dollar bond it had posted.[72] Stevens thus returned by bus to New York City, consulted with Party leaders and Carol King, and showed up on August 30 at the INS building on Columbus Avenue at precisely the deadline stipulated in the INS summons. Shortly after his arrival, Stephen Birmingham, a representative of HUAC, was finally able to serve the subpoena that had been issued over a year earlier. August 30 was truly to be a day of ordeal for the Hungarian man of mystery: in the morning his INS deportation hearing would begin, and in the afternoon he would have to contend with Richard Nixon and relentless HUAC investigators who for some time had wanted to interrogate the individual they believed was the mastermind behind the subversive activities of the CPUSA.

9

Trial and Deportation

One reflection of the heightened fear of Communism that began to convulse American society in 1947 was the decision of INS officials to begin a major campaign to identify, arrest, and deport aliens who were Communist Party members. The legislation on which they based their campaign was the Immigration Act of 1917 (also known as the second Alien Exclusion Act), which stated that aliens who advocated the violent overthrow of the American government were subject to deportation. In the course of 1947 nearly a hundred Communist aliens were arrested on this basis. An INS official stated publicly that the agency was determined to "rid the country of such undesirable aliens as expeditiously as possible."[1] At first Alexander Stevens's case seemed to be in a slightly different category. In the arrest warrant that was served on him in October 1947, he was charged only with a violation of a provision of the Immigration Act of 1924, which stated that an alien entering the United States must possess a valid immigrant visa.[2] After nearly a year investigating this charge, the INS was able to build an incontrovertible case against Stevens, who had left and reentered the country in 1931–32 using a fraudulent passport. It seemed a certainty that the presiding inspector at his hearing would find him guilty of illegal entry into the country and order him deported.

Yet shortly before Stevens's hearing on August 30, INS officials decided to add two new charges based on violations of the Immigration Act of 1917. When Stevens and Carol King arrived at the hearing, they discovered that he was now also accused of being a member of an organization that advocated "the overthrow by force and violence of the Government of the United States" and of assisting that organization in the dissemination of seditious literature. Why did the INS add these two new charges when they had such a clear-cut case on the initial charge and only a short hearing would have been needed to prove Stevens's guilt? Almost surely the INS decision was politically motivated. By August it was becoming clear that of all the Communist aliens that the INS had targeted, Alexander Stevens (J. Peters) was the most important and controversial. His INS hearing would surely attract a good deal of media attention. Here was a good opportunity to steal some of the thunder from the House Un-American Activities Committee and counter Republican accusations that the Truman administration was "soft on Communism."[3] In this way Stevens's hearing was transformed from a straightforward prosecution of passport fraud by an alien posing as an American citizen into an exposé of the evils of the Communist Party and the seditious activities of one of its most important functionaries.

Stevens's attorney, Carol King, faced a formidable challenge in devising a defense for her client. The INS was asserting that Alexander Stevens was in fact J. Peters. She knew this to be true, and in fact even before her client's hearing had admitted it to a *New York Times* reporter, who had promptly published the fact.[4] She also undoubtedly had been told by Stevens that he had in fact traveled to and from the USSR in 1931–32 using a fraudulent passport. In the circumstances, she must have realized that any attempt to refute the initial charge about illegal reentry into the country would be hopeless. She dared not allow Stevens to testify on his behalf, since any explanations he might offer would likely just lead to further legal problems. King thus decided to shift attention away from the charge of illegal reentry and the use of a false passport by challenging the legality of the proceedings against her client and asserting that the whole process was politically motivated. At the beginning of the three-day hearing and frequently thereafter, she asserted that the hearing "was not properly constituted" and that her client did not wish "to participate in any way in this illegal proceeding."[5] When King's protest was rejected by the presiding inspector, Ralph Farb, she instructed Stevens to remain silent through the proceedings, and she refused to cross-examine witnesses, although she did make occasional comments and interject protests during the hearing.

The legal wrangling between Carol King and the presiding inspector that dominated the morning session of Stevens's hearing on August 30 was interrupted by one dramatic development. Steven Birmingham, a process server for HUAC, was permitted to enter the chamber in order to present "a rose-colored subpoena" that required Stevens's appearance at a hearing scheduled for 1:00 that afternoon. Carol King vehemently denounced this "trick devised at the insistence of the House committee" and questioned the good faith of the INS officials who had connived in it. Bemoaning the fact that her client was treated like a "football between two Federal agencies," she requested and received a postponement of the INS hearing so that Stevens could prepare for the HUAC session scheduled to begin in just a few hours.[6] No doubt Stevens's spirits were briefly lifted when, on leaving the INS building, he saw that the Party had arranged for a group of pickets who carried signs demanding that he be freed and denouncing the witnesses as "spies" and "renegades."[7]

The HUAC hearing that afternoon in the Federal Building in Manhattan was fraught with tension and anticipation. The decision to allow photographs to be taken through most of the hearing created a circus-like atmosphere, with an almost constant popping of flashbulbs and chattering among the reporters. Two HUAC members (John McDowell and Richard Nixon) and two investigators comprised the subcommittee that had made its way to New York to interrogate the Communist alien about whom so much had been speculated in the press and whom the committee had proclaimed to be a major figure in their investigation of Communist-led espionage. The government officials, newspaper reporters, photographers, and newsreel cameramen crammed into a fairly small meeting room were curious to have a look at this Hungarian man of mystery. Most were probably surprised to find him to be, in Whittaker Chambers's words, a "small, undistinguished man" whose testimony, in colloquial but accented English, was soft-spoken and even polite. His attorney, Carol King, might have struck some as a stereotypical Communist, "with bobbed grey hair, bulging brief case clutched under her arm and a cigarette drooped from her lips."[8] But Stevens, dressed in a natty suit and polka-dot bow tie, did not fit the stereotype. Earlier in the day at the INS hearing one witness thought Stevens, with his "large blue eyes and dark curly hair," looked like "a grown up Eagle Scout who helped old ladies across the street."[9] At the HUAC session the reporter for *Time* magazine noted a strong resemblance between Stevens and Groucho Marx.[10] On first impressions, Alexander Stevens/J. Peters thus hardly seemed to fit the description of a menacing Soviet spy.

In his response to initial questions from the committee, Stevens seemed willing to cooperate, unlike his friend John Lawson, who had been hostile and disruptive from the start at his appearance before HUAC a year earlier.[11] He gave accurate answers to such questions as his address, place of birth, and his status as an alien. After some hesitation he even admitted that he knew Earl Browder. But when he was asked whether he was a member of the Communist Party, Stevens replied, for the first of many times: "I decline to answer that question under the first and fifth amendments to the Constitution, on the ground that my answer might tend to incriminate or degrade me." Stevens proceeded to give the same response to a series of questions about whether he had served as a Comintern representative, had used the name "J. Peters" or other aliases, or had directed an underground apparatus aimed at infiltrating the federal government. Then, in a moment of high drama that was to be featured in newsreels and in photographs on the front page of many newspapers the next day,[12] Whittaker Chambers was escorted into the room. He immediately identified the witness as J. Peters. When asked if he recognized Chambers, Stevens glared at him and refused to answer because, he said, it might incriminate and degrade him.[13] There then followed what was becoming a HUAC ritual: the reading of a list of names, one by one, and asking the witness if he knew that person. Since the list was quite long, from Solomon Adler to Nathan Witt, the committee's chief investigator, Robert Stripling, agreed that Stevens could simply reply "same answer" whenever he wished to invoke his constitutional rights. By the end of this roll call, Stevens had repeated his stock answer thirty-nine times.

Frustrated and irritated, Richard Nixon now declared that he was losing patience with Communist Party members who appeared before the Committee. He lamented the fact that Stevens and all the other alleged Communists had used the U.S. Constitution as "a shield for their failure to give Congress the information to which the Congress was entitled." He pointed out that the alleged espionage had occurred so far in the past that the statute of limitations applied and their answers could not in fact legally incriminate them. Yet J. Peters, a "key witness" in the committee's investigation, "insolently refused to answer questions." Nixon expressed his disgust that a person who was "a guest of the country" and not even a citizen had been "working to overthrow the very government that has been working to protect him." It was incumbent on the committee, Nixon concluded, to cite the witness for contempt. Hoping that this threat might induce Stevens to cooperate, Nixon tried a new tact in his final questions to Stevens.

> NIXON: Mr. Stevens, I would like to ask you this question. Although you are not a citizen of the United States, you certainly are interested in doing everything you can to protect the security of the country, are you not?
> STEVENS: Sure.
> NIXON: You are. You, for example, do not believe that it is in the interests of the country that confidential information from Government files be furnished to representatives of other governments in an unauthorized manner, do you?
> STEVENS: [After some hesitation and shuffling of the papers before him] I am not interested to get these materials in a way you describe.[14]

Encouraged by these answers and concluding that "now we are getting some place," Nixon then asked Stevens to discuss his relationship to Alger Hiss, but Stevens once again invoked his constitutional rights to remain silent. Since it was now clear that nothing more was to be gained by further questioning, Stevens was dismissed.

Alexander Stevens thus survived the political theatrics of his HUAC hearing, and, since he in fact was never cited for contempt, might even be said to have scored a minor victory.[15] He had been fortunate that the HUAC inquisitors had not even raised the allegation that he had presided over a fraudulent passport operation. But the INS hearing, to which Stevens was immediately returned after the HUAC session, was a different matter. For the remainder of the afternoon on August 30 and on the following two days, the INS prosecutor called on six witnesses, all former Communists, who testified that they had known and had dealings with J. Peters in Moscow and/or New York.[16] Three of the witnesses, George Hewitt, Charles H. White, and William Nowell, all African Americans, had been students at the International Lenin School in 1931 and 1932. They related how Peters, then serving as the CPUSA representative to the Comintern, had cooperated with ECCI officials in suppressing a protest initiated by African American students.[17] Another witness, Andrew Smith, not only confirmed that he had met J. Peters in Moscow, but also submitted as evidence two original documents signed by Peters in 1932 in his capacity as the Party's representative to the ECCI.[18] All four of these witnesses asserted that Alexander Stevens was the person they had known as J. Peters and that the passport photograph of Isadore Boorstein was in fact Peters. Experts who studied handwriting samples of J. Peters and Alexander Stevens testified that they had concluded they were written by the same person. In short, only a few hours into the first day of the hearing, the INS had presented a very strong, indeed conclusive, case that Stevens, an alien, had used a fraudulent passport made out in the name of an American citizen when he left the country in 1931, had resided in Moscow and served as the CPUSA representative to the Comintern, and had returned in 1932 without being in possession of a valid immigrant visa.

The rest of the three-day INS hearing was devoted to an attempt to prove the additional charges relating to Stevens's membership in the Communist Party and his role in advocating the overthrow of the U.S. government. Here the prosecution relied largely on the testimony of two other ex-Communists, Maurice Malkin and Louis Budenz, both of whom had at different times from 1931 to 1945 worked closely with J. Peters. Each of them had some accurate information to relay about Peters's role as director of the secret apparatus, but they both had a tendency to embellish their accounts with suppositions and speculations that played to the anti-Communist sentiments of the day. From his testimony on the first day of the hearing it was clear that Malkin had ambivalent feelings about Peters. He spoke highly of his skills in organizational work, but related with some resentment the story of how Peters had played the leading role on the Control Commission that expelled him from the Party in the late 1930s. The most sensational part of Malkin's testimony was the somewhat garbled account he gave of Peters's project in the 1930s for infiltrating the armed forces. Malkin may well have been present at the Central Committee Plenum in early 1934 at which Peters had outlined his plans, which he had warned were "absolutely illegal" and should never be discussed "out of this room" because of the great harm that could be done to the Party. Now, fourteen years later, Malkin seemed to relish the opportunity to relate what he remembered about the "anti-militarist" wing of Peters's secret apparatus. During the 1930s, he testified, Peters was the "big boss" of "action committees" that were designed to penetrate into the National Guard and "create and organize riots." These "action committees" received their training in the basement of the Party headquarters in New York. In the event of war or grave economic crisis, the committees would be prepared to seize power and "arrest such officials as governor, mayor, and congressmen and set up a Soviet government in the city or state." Those who resisted, Malkin said, would be "put against the wall" and liquidated.[19]

Since Carol Weiss King had declared at the outset that she and her client would not participate in the "illegally constituted" hearing, Malkin's sensational account was not subjected to cross-examination. At the end of the first day of the hearing, however, Stevens was besieged by reporters and he agreed to an impromptu news conference. Hoping to capture Stevens in a provocative pose, the photographers who were present yelled out to him: "Wave the subpoena, Mr. Peters!" Stevens looked for advice to his attorney, who was standing nearby. Carol King cried out sarcastically: "Do as you damn please, Mr. Peters!"[20] Stevens complied, but insisted to the reporters that his name was Stevens, not Peters, and that he was not a paid official of the Communist Party. In fact, he said, he was currently unemployed and had found it impossible to get a job ever since his arrest a year earlier. The witnesses against him, he insisted, were "all confused" and had "false ideas about me and my work." Since he was innocent of the charges the INS was making against him, he would fight against deportation "to the very end." Sensing that it would be a mistake to try to challenge the evidence that he had traveled on a fraudulent passport in 1931–32, Stevens instead focused on the more sensational accusations made by Maurice Malkin, for which, as far as he knew, the INS had no substantiating evidence. He scoffed at the idea that he been involved with underground operations or "action committees": "I never heard of them. I don't take that story seriously."[21]

As his deportation hearing continued on August 31 and September 1, Alexander Stevens listened in silence, "calmly polishing his glasses and smiling," as the INS prosecutor presented evidence that Stevens had been an active member of the CPUSA throughout his twenty-four-year sojourn in the United States.[22] Louis Budenz, who was the only witness to testify on the third and last day of the hearing, repeated the major accusations he had previously made at HUAC hearings and in a recently published book.[23] Peters, he said, had told him at some point in the mid-1930s that he served as the "link between the Communist International apparatus here and the Soviet secret police." According to Budenz, Peters once explained to him that his secretiveness and frequent changes of aliases were necessitated by "the work he was doing in Washington and elsewhere." Budenz also related at some length the story of how he had assisted Peters and Soviet agents in spying on American Trotskyite groups.[24]

In order to prove the charge that the Communist Party sought violent revolutionary change, and that Stevens, as a member of the party, had assisted in the dissemination of literature that advocated the "the overthrow by force and violence of the Government of the United States," the INS prosecutor introduced as evidence numerous pamphlets and books by Karl Marx, Lenin, and Stalin, as well as articles from such CPUSA publications as *The Communist* and the *Daily Worker*.[25] This tedious and time-consuming process added nothing of substance to the case against the defendant, especially since, as Stevens would later sarcastically point out, the INS prosecutors were not particularly well versed in the history of Communism or in political theory. Not surprisingly, the prosecutors paid much attention to Peters's *Manual on Organization,* many excerpts of which were entered into the hearing record. Particular emphasis was placed on a passage in which Peters wrote that the Communist Party, as the "trusted vanguard" of the working class, was leading the fight for "the revolutionary overthrow of capitalism, for the establishment of the dictatorship of the proletariat, for the establishment of a Socialist Soviet Republic in the Untied States, for the complete abolition of classes, for the establishment of socialism, the first stage of the classless Communist society" (pp. 8–9).

One can only wonder what thoughts went through Alexander Stevens's mind during his three-day hearing as he listened and observed in silence. He realized, of course, that most of the allegations made against him were true. He had in fact traveled on a false passport; had been a link between the Party and Soviet intelligence agencies; and had been involved in attempts to infiltrate the armed forces. True, some of the testimony of the witnesses may have been mistaken because of faulty memories or a tendency to exaggerate. For example, it is quite possible that the term "action committees," which Maurice Malkin used to describe the Party units that were allegedly involved in attempts to infiltrate the armed forces, had never been employed by J. Peters. There may also never have been any explicit plans to arrest government officials, as Malkin alleged. Yet Alexander Stevens surely recognized that Malkin was referring to the Party units that were part of his "work in the armed forces" in the mid-1930s. Yet he could never engage in any kind of legal argument or public exchange about this and other accusations made against him, since one of the firmest rules governing the conduct of Communists, especially those who had been involved in clandestine activity, was that a Party member who was being interrogated by the police or placed on trial must "deny everything." A corollary to this rule was that any ex-Communists who testified against their former comrades were, ipso facto, "stool pigeons" and liars. Thus the *Daily Worker* claimed that Stevens's

INS hearing was based on "tailor-made evidence" from a "parade of expelled Communists and FBI finger-men who wove fantastic and repetitious tales of 'action committees,' killings and 'underground rings.'"[26] When looking back on his INS hearing many years later, József Péter took the same line: it was all the work of despicable, lying "renegades."[27]

There is some reason to believe that Stevens was not completely candid about his past Party activities even with his attorney, who may have been ignorant, as were most of the current leaders of the Party, of the work he had done in the secret apparatus. Her conduct and occasional utterances during the hearing suggest that she may truly have believed that the testimony of the witnesses was the imaginings of anti-Communist zealots. As soon as the hearing ended, both Stevens and King issued public statements that were intended to be an explanation of why Stevens had refused to answer questions at the HUAC session and INS hearing and a rebuttal of the testimony of the witnesses.

In her press release and response to reporters' questions, King did concede that her client had used the name J. Peters and that he had been and was a Communist Party functionary.[28] These facts, she said quite disingenuously, were never in "serious dispute" and Alexander Stevens had never denied them. She implied that the only charge against her client at the INS hearing was that he was a Communist, and that none of the other issues raised ("spy scares, etc.") were relevant. In fact, she insisted, the only purpose of the hearing was to increase "the present anti-Red tension." Nowhere in her statement did King mention the initial and primary INS charge against her client, namely that he had used a forged passport to depart from and return to the United States in 1931–32. There was good reason for her to wish to divert attention from this issue, for there was overwhelming evidence that her client was guilty, and she could hardly argue that aliens had a legal right to enter and leave the United States at their own convenience without proper travel documents.

Alexander Stevens offered similar arguments in his press release, although he still refused to concede that he had ever been known as J. Peters.[29] It was his "duty to the American people," he insisted, "to refute the false and ridiculous statements made about me at the hearings." He had refused to answer questions because the HUAC and INS were "not interested in facts and the truth" but desired only to "smear and defame, to discredit all that is decent in our country." In the circumstances "no honest man has a fair chance when forced to appear." Stevens portrayed himself as an innocent victim of a campaign of "outrageous slanders, falsehoods, [and] distortions" by a warmongering congressional committee, an illegally constituted INS panel and "their stoolpigeons," and "the more notorious newspapers." Furthermore, he was being threatened with a contempt charge by individuals who wished to "trample upon the Constitution" and "drag the American people down the road to fascism as the Nazis did in Germany."

Why did they focus their wrath on him? Why had they made Alexander Stevens their "new 'mystery' man, the new 'number one' Communist?" He suggested that there was an obvious reason: HUAC had launched a campaign of "spy scares and frame-ups" in order to cover up the failure of Congress to solve the nation's pressing economic problems, to prevent a rapprochement with Russia, and to "take away from the people the protection of the fifth amendment." Thus, it was not really Alexander Stevens that "they are after," but "the American people and the United States Constitution."

Having offered this highly partisan and self-centered analysis of the American political scene, Stevens also felt obliged to refute the widespread idea that he was a "mystery man." This false notion, he suggested, had been deliberately propagated by his enemies and the anti-Communist media. In fact, he stated, "There is no mystery about me."

> I immigrated to this country, like millions of others who came from other lands. I came from Czechoslovakia, a young man of 29, a university graduate, a veteran of World War I. . . . Twice I applied for my final citizenship papers. They were denied through no fault of my own. Since my arrival in this country, I have been working for a living at various occupations, again like so many generations of immigrants. I participated in work among my fellow Hungarian Americans, whose loyalty to our adopted country is second to none. I fought for the working people to the best of my abilities. For many years I was an active member of the Communist Party and elected to various committees, all of which is publically known. Thousands and thousands of Communists and non-Communists knew me, heard my lectures, and read my articles. I am married to an American citizen and am a resident of New York City. I have lived at my present address for the past 8 years.

This brief biographical sketch, which Stevens suggested would clear up the "'mystery' which the Un-American Committee has manufactured," was notable for its obvious omissions and several misleading assertions. He was not a university graduate, and his failure to become a citizen was a result not of some arbitrary government decision but of his failure in 1929 to meet a deadline and in 1940 to complete the application by appearing for a personal interview. Stevens did admit here for the first time publically that he had been active in the Communist movement. But he attempted to soften this by stressing that he was an immigrant like many others, a hard worker with an American wife, and a New Yorker who had lived in the same apartment for eight years. In short, though an alien, he was nonetheless loyal to his "adopted country."

Having survived a whirlwind week in which he appeared in the newsreels and his photograph was published in *Time, Newsweek,* the *New York Times,* and countless other newspapers across the country, Alexander Stevens (for he continued to use this name) now hoped to return to the "normal" life he had enjoyed before it had been interrupted by the sensational newspaper reports about J. Peters that first appeared in February 1947. Once he was off the "front pages" he would be able to live in relative peace with his wife in their Kew Gardens apartment and return to his work at CP headquarters, where he continued to use the name Steve Miller. Perhaps in recognition of his status as one of the most prominent victims of the current government campaign against the CPUSA, Miller was once again given an office on the ninth floor and was made a member of the National Committee.[30] He and Ann could now once again join social gatherings with their friends and make weekend jaunts to "October Hill." But Stevens could not so easily escape his recently gained notoriety. Strangers sometimes accosted him on the sidewalks and asked in a threatening way: "Don't I know you from somewhere?" When riding the subway people (who, József Péter later recalled, were "usually reading the *Daily News*") would look up and stare at him in a hostile way, forcing him to get up and walk away.[31]

Furthermore, there was no way that Alexander Stevens could prevent the growing use of J. Peters's *Manual on Organization* by anti-Communist organizations intent on weakening or abolishing the CPUSA. When the Smith Act trial against Party leaders began in March 1949, the prosecutor cited two books as key texts for understanding the subversive plans of the Communist movement: Stalin's *The Fundamentals of Leninism* and J. Peters's *Manual*. The latter, it was argued, contained a clear call for revolution.[32] At some point in 1948 or 1949, a right-wing group, the Bi-Partisan League of Ohio, decided it would be useful in their campaign against Communism to reprint Peters's *Manual* and add their own commentary and illustrations. The pamphlet purported to offer the American public the "amazing, revealing, and shocking" secret Communist Manual, in which one learned of the Party's plans to "organize the United States and the world under a totalitarian regime" and "attain world conquest." In addition, according to the editor in his introduction, the pamphlet revealed how the Communist Party "pits the negro race against the white race, citizens against their government, employee against employer, and the farmer against the city worker."[33]

At the end of the INS hearing, the presiding inspector had indicated that he would issue his ruling in about ten days. But no decision was announced by that deadline and Stevens and his attorney heard nothing from the INS all through October and November. Was this a good sign? Perhaps Carol King's objections and legal arguments were being given serious consideration by the INS commissioner or even by the attorney general. But any optimism Stevens might have felt about the INS decision was balanced by new concerns over developments in the Chambers-Hiss controversy. In late September, Alger Hiss filed suit against Chambers for slander, claiming that the latter's accusation that he was a Communist had damaged his public reputation and brought him into "public odium."[34] At some point in early or mid-November Stevens learned, probably from Nathan Witt, that Hiss's lawyers had demanded that Chambers turn over any correspondence and written or typed materials that he had ever received from Alger Hiss or his wife. Stevens immediately realized that such a request could have disastrous consequences. It was quite possible that Chambers still had in his possession typewritten copies of stolen State Department documents, a sample of which he had enclosed in the warning note he had sent to Peters and Col. Bykov in 1938. If, in response to this demand from the Hiss defense team, Chambers were to hand over the incriminating documents he had retained, the impact would be devastating, not only for Alger Hiss and J. Peters/Alexander Stevens, but also for the Communist Party.

Desperate to find a way to induce Chambers to continue to remain silent about Peters's "Washington set-up," Stevens came up with a plan that was clearly a long shot. Stevens summoned his friend John Lautner to the "ninth floor" and told him there was a "sensitive task" he wanted him to undertake as a favor.[35] Lautner was instructed to see Witt at his law office in midtown Manhattan and "do whatever he wants." Witt took Lautner to a nearby bar and explained that the Party was worried about Whittaker Chambers and a way had to be found to intimidate him and persuade him not to reveal certain incriminating information. He suggested that Lautner find out if Chambers was currently working in his *Time Magazine* office in New York. If so, he was to arrange to send him a bouquet of flowers. Puzzled by this strange scheme, Lautner asked if Chambers would consider the flowers "a warning from the Party." Witt replied that, yes, he "thought it will have that effect," since Chambers was, by nature, "a very scary fellow and he will understand the nature of the intimidation." The two agreed that the flowers should be white lilies, and Witt gave Lautner a hundred dollars to cover expenses. The next day Lautner, working with a Party organizer based in Manhattan, determined that Chambers was not in New York but somewhere in Maryland. Lautner was preparing to travel to Baltimore to complete his mission, but before he could depart a story broke in the newspapers that Chambers had already turned over to the Hiss defense team copies of stolen State Department records (which became known as the "Baltimore documents"). Witt then called Lautner and told him "to forget about the whole thing" since "it was too late now anyway."

Having finally decided to make use of the documents he regarded as his "life preservers," Chambers no longer felt that he could or should refrain from telling the full story of Apparatus B and Peters's "Washington set-up." At HUAC sessions and in testimony at the Hiss grand jury, Chambers now gave a full description of the espionage operation J. Peters had created and he named those who had been involved, including Hiss, Henry Wadleigh, Ward Pigman, and

David Carpenter. Many reasonable-minded Americans were at first skeptical of Chambers's new revelations. After all, he was now admitting that he had per-jured himself in previous testimony, no doubt to conceal his own complicity in espionage. Why should anyone believe that he was now telling the truth? But Chambers's credibility was greatly enhanced when in early December Henry Wadleigh broke down and made a full confession to the FBI, and a few days later to the Hiss grand jury, about his involvement in the Washington spy ring. In his testimony Wadleigh corroborated key elements of Chambers's new account.

For Alexander Stevens these developments were truly worrisome. He feared that he would soon be receiving another subpoena from the HUAC and would be subjected to renewed grilling by Richard Nixon and his colleagues. As it turned out, the HUAC never did summon him again, but he did have to testify in another setting that in some ways was even more challenging: the New York grand jury (the Hiss grand jury) that was now focusing on Chambers's allega-tions concerning Hiss's role in espionage. In his two appearances before the grand jury on January 27 and February 1, 1949, Stevens had to contend with a hard-nosed federal prosecutor, Tom Donegan, who had considerable experi-ence in dealing with uncooperative witnesses.[36] Attorneys for witnesses are not permitted to be present during grand jury testimony, but Stevens apparently was advised beforehand by his attorney that, just as at the HUAC session, he should invoke the Fifth Amendment and refuse to answer questions relating to his activity in the Communist Party and Whittaker Chambers's allegations about underground activity.

In the first part of his testimony on January 27, Stevens was asked general questions about his background, marital status, and the factory jobs he had held. Most of these questions he answered truthfully, including an admission that he had left his first wife in Czechoslovakia and had later divorced her. But about halfway through the session the mood abruptly changed, with Donegan, the chief prosecutor, announcing that they needed now to "get to the merits of this thing." Stevens was asked: "Have you ever been known as J. Peters?" His reply was the familiar one: "I decline to answer that question, because it may incriminate me." His response was the same to a long list of questions now posed to him. Do you know Whittaker Chambers? Alger Hiss? Pricilla Hiss? Colonel Bykov? Ward Pigman? Franklin Reno? Harry Dexter White? Donald Hiss? Felix Inslerman? Eventually Donegan addressed the witness sternly, warn-ing him that the only grounds for declining to answer a question were that it might incriminate him. "In other words, if you don't know a man, you have to give an honest answer that you don't know the man, do you understand that? You are subject to the laws of perjury here. . . . I want to point out to you again that if you honestly don't know a person under the name that he is identified here, you have to answer that you don't know him under that name."[37]

Stevens said that he understood this, and he insisted that "he was not trying to be frivolous in answering any of those questions." But he still maintained that if he followed the prosecutor's advice and declared that he did not know certain individuals mentioned, it could still have "certain incriminatory effects." When Donegan reiterated his position, Stevens became confused and asked if he could consult with his attorney: "It won't take an hour, it will take a second." But Donegan refused this request and was backed up by a stern warning from the jury foreman that if he continued to be uncooperative Stevens could be charged with contempt of court.

In the circumstances Stevens apparently decided that he had no recourse but to adhere as best he could to the rules as stipulated by the prosecutors. It appears that for the remainder of his testimony that day he responded truthfully when asked if he had met certain individuals. If he had in fact not met an individual named by the prosecutor, he answered, "I do not recollect that I ever met that person." If he had met the person in question, he took the Fifth Amendment. His answers proved of no value to the prosecutors, but do provide some intriguing evidence for the historical record. For example, Stevens denied that he had ever met Henry Wadleigh and Harry Dexter White, suggesting that only Chambers was in direct contact with these two members of Apparatus B. On the other hand, when he did take the Fifth Amendment Stevens was implicitly acknowledging having known certain individuals for whom there might otherwise not be conclusive evidence of a relationship with J. Peters, including Harold Glasser, Jacob Golos, Eleanor Nelson, David Carpenter, and "a Russian agent known as Bill."

During his second appearance before the grand jury on February 1, another challenge awaited Alexander Stevens. Donegan tried a new tack. Noting that Stevens was apparently resisting the INS's move to deport him, he asked if he really wanted to stay in the United States. Stevens replied: "Certainly. . . . I like this country." At this point Donegan began to probe to see if there was any way Stevens might be persuaded to turn state's evidence. Stevens was assured that "if you decide you want to cooperate in this secret Grand Jury room, it isn't going to hurt you." "The past is past," Donegan added, "and you are the only man who can say whether you want the future to be different."

In the ensuing exchange, Stevens tried to defend himself, asserting that he was doing his best to cooperate and was relying on his constitutional privilege to remain silent only when necessary to protect himself. At this point one of the jurors made a particularly persuasive plea:

> Mr. Stevens, you have expressed a desire to stay in this country because you like this country. I think you appreciate, as well as does everybody in this room, that with these deportation proceedings pending, that if you really had a strong de-

sire to stay, you would recognize that there is an opportunity, possibly the best opportunity that will ever be afforded to you, to put that thought into action. Regardless of what has happened in the past, this Grand Jury doesn't feel punitively inclined and I'm sure that the Grand Jury would take whatever action it thought necessary to help you if you, in turn, were prepared to help . . .

Stevens was given a moment to mull this over, before Donegan resumed questioning by asking the witness if he knew "Maxim Lieber, a literary agent." When Stevens once again declined to answer the question, he was dismissed and the session was ended.

Only a few days after Stevens's second appearance before the grand jury, Ralph Farb, the INS presiding inspector, issued a long report in which he reviewed the evidence presented at Stevens's deportation hearing. He found Stevens guilty of the charges brought against him and recommended that "the alien be deported to Czechoslovakia."[38] After receipt of the report, Carol King filed a brief listing a number of legal objections to the report. This led INS officials to believe that she fully intended to appeal the final decision if it called for her client's deportation.[39]

In late February and March, while the decision on Stevens's deportation remained pending, it appears that additional feelers were put out to him from the Department of Justice in the hope that some sort of deal could still be worked out. INS officials indicated that they were inclined to cancel the deportation proceedings if Stevens proved cooperative.[40] Was there any chance that Stevens might be "turned?" One thing seems fairly certain: Alexander Stevens was being honest when he told the grand jury that he liked America and did not want to be deported. After all, he had spent most of his adult life in the United States and, in many ways, had become Americanized. Of course he knew well, and had often railed against, the evils of American society: racial discrimination, social and economic inequalities, political corruption. Yet in his many trips across the country, by train and car, he could not have helped but notice that the United States was not, as the *Daily Worker* insisted, completely dominated by rapacious capitalists, the Ku Klux Klan, and corrupt police. Though he could never admit it publicly, and perhaps not even in a conscious way to himself, there was much that he could admire and like in American society. Though he too wore the blinders that hampered the vision of most Communists, Stevens was perceptive enough to notice, for example, that there was in fact social mobility in American society. He had seen this firsthand. Many of the poor Hungarian immigrants he had known in the 1920s had worked their way up, escaped poverty, and, in some cases, even entered the middle class. His own brother, Joseph, was a prime example. And the second generation of Hungarian Americans, the children of the immigrants, had attended public schools, become almost completely acculturated, and had before them many opportunities for further educational and economic advancement. Stevens also must have recognized the richness and diversity of intellectual and cultural life. He enjoyed reading the many newspapers available to him in New York, serious nonfiction books, and his favorite mystery novels.

If he were to be deported, Stevens would be forced to sever his ties to the CPUSA, an organization to which he had devoted almost all his time and energy over the past twenty-five years. It was in the Party that he had met his wife and all his friends. Now fifty-five years old, he was a seasoned veteran and knew all the ins and outs of the Communist movement. After all, he had been, and in his mind perhaps still was, the Party's leading organizational specialist. No doubt he could attach himself to the CP in another country, but he would be an outsider and the prestige he enjoyed in the CPUSA would not easily transfer to a new situation. One other factor that might have motivated Alexander Stevens to seek to remain in the United States was one that, as a committed Communist, he would never have spoken of openly or perhaps even consciously recognized. In fact, Alexander and Ann Stevens enjoyed a relatively comfortable standard of living, one that would have been the envy of Communist functionaries in any European country. Of course, by some measures Stevens and his wife were poor. They had almost no savings and faced bleak prospects once they retired. Yet John Abt was surely exaggerating when he later wrote that the Stevens "lived on the edge of starvation as long as I knew them."[41] Their home was a modest apartment in Kew Gardens, a pleasant middle-class area with easy connections by train to downtown Manhattan. They lived a frugal life style and had few material possessions, but their basic needs were met. In 1941 their joint income as reported to the Internal Revenue Service was $3,558, above the average for American families.[42] The Stevens had use of a 1943 Chrysler on permanent loan from the Party, could stay whenever they wanted at one of Joseph Goldberger's cabins at Lake Peekskill, occasionally ate out at restaurants (usually Stevens's favorite Hungarian places), and frequently were guests for dinner and social gatherings at the homes of their more affluent friends, the Abts, Proctors, and Witts. The lure of these "roast beef, drinks, and poker" parties must have been strong.

Stevens probably had other concerns related to his possible deportation. He certainly would not have wanted to live in Czechoslovakia, where he would be a stranger who did not speak the language. If he were to be deported, Hungary would have to be his destination. Yet even in that case there were problems. His wife would be forced to break all her ties in the United States and begin a new life in a country with an impenetrable language. Stevens himself would be a kind of stranger, though he had retained his fluency in Hungarian and had closely followed Hungarian events from afar. It would no doubt be an exhilarating experience to contribute to the building of the Communist regime in his native land, but he knew hardly any of the Communist leaders active in Hungary in the late 1940s. True, he had met and had dealings with Mátyás Rákosi during his stay in Moscow in the early 1930s. He almost surely met him again in New York during a visit that Rákosi made to the United States in 1946. In postwar Hungary, Rákosi emerged as the dominant figure in the Hungarian CP and thus the leader of the Communist dictatorship that was established in 1947–48. But Stevens may well have had some misgivings about Rákosi, who was known for his ruthlessness and styled himself as "Stalin's best pupil." By 1949, even observers in the United States saw signs that Rákosi was establishing for himself a cult of personality along the same lines as that of his Soviet patron. Remembering the horrible fate of many Soviet intelligence agents and diplomats when they returned to Moscow after spending time in the West, Stevens might well have pondered his own possible return to Hungary with a bit of trepidation.

For these reasons, Stevens continued to hope that some way could be found out of his dilemma that would allow him to avoid deportation. But he would never seek any solution to his problem that would entail cooperation with the FBI, for that would be a betrayal of everything that he had believed in and fought for during his entire adult life. After all, Stevens, as J. Peters, had been instrumental in reinforcing the aversion against informing that was an intrinsic part of Communist culture. In his *Manual* and in many speeches and articles Peters had railed against "stool pigeons" and "renegades." It was simply unimaginable that a Communist like Alexander Stevens would suddenly become a turncoat, admit that he had participated in subversive activities, and "name names." No, he must continue to "deny everything" and hope that Carol King would find some legal strategy that would forestall his deportation. In his despair he must have begun to rue the fact that, through his own procrastination and wariness, he had failed to complete the process of becoming an American citizen. As a citizen he could not have been deported, though he likely would have been targeted, along with the other prominent Communists, for prosecution under the Smith Act and like them would have been sentenced to several years in prison. Yet once released he could have returned to his work in the CPUSA.

By mid-April it had become clear to Department of Justice officials that there was no chance that Stevens would be persuaded to become an informer. There was still the possibility that Stevens might be called to testify again before the HUAC or at the Alger Hiss trial,[43] but INS officials apparently feared that if they procrastinated, Stevens might once again go into hiding. Another impetus for quicker action on Peters's deportation was the fact that the Truman administration had for some time been under attack from Republicans and anti-Communist organizations for the slow pace of the program to deport Communists. One newspaper editorial aptly summed up this critique: what the country needs now is "deportation, actual, prompt, and sure," for all members of the "Peters tribe."[44] On April 12, Carol King was informed that the INS commissioner had upheld the ruling of the presiding inspector and that a warrant for deportation of Alexander Stevens had been issued. He was to be deported to "Bremen, Germany, if that place will accept him, otherwise to Czechoslovakia," with all expenses paid by the INS.[45]

In a public statement, King deplored the action of the INS, which she interpreted as punishing a person simply "for membership in the Communist Party."[46] She immediately began the process of appealing the INS decision, and the ACPFB intensified its publicity campaign in support of Stevens and several other Communist aliens who were about to be deported. They invited other organizations to join them in protesting the actions of the INS, which they condemned as a threat to "the democratic rights of foreign born Americans and the liberties of the American people."[47] Privately, however, Carol King may well have told Stevens that the chances for a successful appeal were slim and that he should prepare for the worst. In this period the policy of the CPUSA was to give full support and encouragement to all aliens protesting against an INS deportation order. Yet at some point in April, Party leaders decided that it would be best for Stevens to leave the country voluntarily and on his own terms. Apparently they feared that the longer Stevens remained in the country, the greater the chance that he would be summoned to testify once again at a session of the HUAC or at the Smith Act trial of Party officials. Such a development could have dangerous consequences, for it likely would focus attention once again on J. Peters's work in the secret apparatus. Stevens was thus informed that the Party preferred that he discontinue his fight against deportation. Now reconciled to his fate, Stevens authorized King to contact the INS and the Hungarian government to make the necessary arrangements for him to leave voluntarily.

Accordingly, in late April King advised the INS that Stevens and John Santo, another Hungarian American Communist she was representing, both wished to leave the United States voluntarily and at their own expense and return to their native land, Hungary. Stevens had reached this decision because he had come to realize that "a quiet and useful life in this country was now impossible."[48] It did not take long for INS officials to decide that Stevens and Santo should be granted permission to leave the country voluntarily, on the condition that they would not be permitted to return. In fact, INS lawyers welcomed this development as a way out of an unexpected predicament. It had been assumed all along that Stevens could be deported to Czechoslovakia, or if that proved impossible at least to Germany. But when the matter was more closely studied, it was concluded that since Stevens had been absent from Czechoslovakia for more than ten years, it was "very unlikely that the Czechoslovakian government would issue travel documents for his entry into that country." Nor was it likely that he could be sent to Germany, since, it was now discovered, American military authorities there refused to accept aliens who were not German nationals. That Stevens might in fact prefer to go to Hungary seemed not to have occurred previously to INS officials, but they quickly realized that it was the best solution to the problem. If no other place could be found that would accept Stevens, there was no existing legislation that would have permitted any additional punitive action against him. It is true, as some contemporary observers noted, that allowing Peters to leave would mean that the person perhaps most knowledgeable of CPUSA underground activities and Soviet-sponsored espionage would no longer be available to testify at various trials and congressional hearings.[49] But, as one INS official later wrote when attempting to justify the approval of Stevens's request, if self-deportation had not been granted "this alien would have been free to roam the United States at his will and carry on his activities regarding the Communist apparatus." There was no reason to believe that he would ever have been willing to answer questions about his conspiratorial past.[50]

Having been assured of the cooperation of the INS, Carol King met on May 3 in Washington with Endre Sik, the chief envoy at the Hungarian Embassy. She informed him that Alexander Stevens (whom she identified as J. Peters) and John Santo wished to leave voluntarily and return to Hungary. CPUSA officials approved this and requested quick action. As the question of the repatriation of Hungarian-born Communists who had lived in the West for many years was a somewhat delicate matter that could not be dealt with unilaterally by the Hungarian embassy, Sik reported on the matter that same day to László Rajk, the Hungarian foreign minister. He also wrote directly to his friend, Mátyás Rákosi, and enclosed a copy of his letter to Rajk, with the explanation that since Rajk and others in the Foreign Ministry might not know of the role "Peters" had played in the CPUSA, it would be desirable that the Hungarian leader offer an opinion on how to proceed in a matter "of such importance."[51] Here, it seems, Sik may have been hinting about Peters's contributions to Soviet intelligence work, of which he may have been aware, since he himself had served as a KGB agent.[52] Both Rajk and Rákosi gave their approval, and after only a short delay Sik was able to inform Carol King that both Stevens and Santo would be given Hungarian passports and would be welcomed back in their native land.

Now that all parties were in agreement, Stevens made preparations for his journey. At this time most East European Communists returning to their homelands from the United States went by ship. It was in recognition of his more exalted status that Stevens was provided with tickets to travel by Lufthansa airplane to Budapest, via Amsterdam and Prague. The necessary arrangements for vacating their apartment were left to Ann Stevens, who was to follow her husband to Hungary a month later. Endre Sik personally presented the passports to Stevens and Santo at a small party at the home of a Hungarian American

Communist in the Bronx.[53] Stevens's passport bore the name József Péter, the alias he had adopted when he first began to work in the Hungarian Federation in the 1920s. This was to be the last of his name changes. In his last few days in the United States, Stevens spent most of his time at the CP headquarters and in Hungarian restaurants, reminiscing with friends about his twenty-five years in Party work. On May 6 the Party held a farewell dinner for Stevens, which was attended by over fifty of his friends, among them most of the members of the National Committee. Gus Hall served as toastmaster, and several speakers offered tributes, among them John Williamson, the current organizational secretary, who said of Stevens that he could think of no individual who "had made a more significant contribution to the growth and development of the Communist Party." Several speakers, while regretting that he was leaving, expressed their happiness that Stevens was able to return to a "New Hungary, the Hungary of the People's Democracy," where he would undoubtedly "make a notable contribution to the struggle for peace, democracy, and socialism."[54]

On May 8, the day of his departure, Stevens was accompanied to Idlewild Airport by his wife, Joseph Goldberger, and Carol King. But even on his last day in the country the "red conspirator" could not avoid one last brush with the FBI. From a phone booth at the airport he decided to call Gerhardt Eisler's wife to inform her about his decision to return to Hungary and to send his greetings to her husband. Because the Eisler's home phone was being wiretapped, a transcript of the conversation ended up in J. Peters's FBI file. Eisler's wife was surprised to hear the news, but, perhaps thinking of her husband's troubles, remarked on how "some people have such luck." Stevens laughed and responded in a bittersweet tone: "Luck you call it?"[55] He was clearly ambivalent about the return to his native land, and perhaps even a bit nervous about the flight, since he had never traveled by airplane before. When reporters plied him with questions before he boarded the plane, Stevens smiled and merely said it seemed a fine day for flying. However, once the plane had taken off, Carol King announced that Stevens had left behind a statement that would be released the following day.[56]

Stevens's statement was meant to be his valedictory to the American people, although there is some evidence that he still held out some hope that his stay in Hungary would not be permanent.[57] In it he repeated the arguments he had made after his appearance before the HUAC and his deportation hearing, but with a few added distortions and emphases. Now he claimed that in 1924 he had been exiled from the land of his birth by "the post-war reaction which was preparing the way for fascist dictatorship and national subjugation to the Nazis." Though he had wanted to become an American citizen, this had been denied to him by the immigration authorities because he had "served the American and Hungarian working class and people in their post-war anti-fascist struggle."

But in the end that didn't matter, since his membership in the American Communist Party was his true "certificate of citizenship." The charges made against him, he insisted, were "ridiculous" and the American authorities knew this. But these attacks had made it impossible for him to continue his work on behalf of American workers, so he had chosen voluntarily to return to his native land, where he hoped to contribute to the "great work of reconstruction and advance toward socialism." Nonetheless, he would remain true to the interests of the American workers, which "lie with the victory of the world camp of peace, progress, and socialism."

With his departure from the country, interest in the notorious "red conspirator" quickly ebbed. The HUAC found other targets, neither prosecutors nor defense lawyers in the Hiss or Smith Act trials found it useful to emphasize the role of J. Peters, and Senator Joe McCarthy was more concerned with identifying alleged Communists still active in the government. As a result, Peters's photo never again appeared in the newspapers and as time passed anti-Communist writers rarely mentioned him. The FBI continued for some years to maintain a file on Peters, and some relevant information was obtained from new informers, but before long most of the new material consisted of "sightings" of Peters in such unlikely locales as Argentina, Florida, and Texas.[58] The *Manual on Organization* was cited from time to time at Smith Act trials and in political debates that arose in the Cold War era,[59] and was even reprinted in 1975 by the Revolutionary Communist Party, a radical organization founded in the San Francisco Bay area.[60] Historians sometimes referred to the mysterious Hungarian Communist, but it was not until the renewal of interest in the Chambers-Hiss controversy in the late 1970s that the career of J. Peters began again to receive close attention. Yet for many years he remained an enigmatic figure, since many observers believed there was insufficient evidence to judge whether there was any merit to the accusations against Peters made by Whittaker Chambers, Louis Budenz, and others, especially since Peters continued right up to his death in 1990 to brand such charges as ridiculous.

Epilogue and Assessment

In the first few months of his return to Hungary, József Péter was treated like an honored soldier returning home after many years of combat. Upon his arrival he was greeted by Mózes Simon, whom he had met in Party work in the CPUSA. Simon, who served as a host of comrades newly arrived from the United States, put Péter up in a nice hotel room and gave him an orientation on life in a Hungary that had undergone a rapid social and political transformation since the end of World War II. Within days of his arrival, Péter was invited to a meeting with Mátyás Rákosi, general secretary of the Communist Party (called the Hungarian Workers Party,) to discuss his future employment. A few days later, in a letter to his friend John Lautner he expressed satisfaction over his hour-long talk with Rákosi, whom he referred to as "the boss" and "a great guy." Péter was given to understand that he would work in the Party central office, probably in cadre development. Since he had a good deal of experience in that sort of work, he felt confident that he "could make a contribution."[1]

While awaiting word on his Party assignment, Péter was given the opportunity to travel around the country with Lajos Bebrits, minister of the railroads and transportation, as his tour guide. Bebrits was a friend from the old days, having worked for years with Péter on the *Új Előre*. Bebrits was in the position to arrange a deluxe tour for Péter, using special trains and chauffeured cars. He got to see everything: the major cities, villages, the puszta, Lake Balaton. It was an exhilarating experience: "I saw more of Hungary in 3 weeks than [in] all my life before." Back in Budapest, still not having received any word from Rákosi's office, he spent his free time exploring the city on foot. Although Hungary had by no means fully recovered from the devastation of the war, Péter professed to see store windows "overflowing with goods." He was also impressed by the enthusiasm he encountered when he made a tour of Party offices and polling stations during the Parliamentary election that was held shortly after his arrival in Hungary. If Péter noticed that the election, in which the Hungarian Workers Party and its allies garnered 95.6 percent of the votes, was far from democratic in character, he did not venture to comment on this in a report to his friend John Lautner.[2]

Although everything seemed to be auguring well for József and Ann Péter, who joined her husband in June, at some point during the summer there were several disturbing developments. Péter was informed by one of Rákosi's confidantes that it had been decided he would not be given a position in the cadre department, since comrades returning from the West could not, for a while at least, be employed in the Party central office. Some job, however, would be found for Péter in one of the Party's publishing agencies.[3] In the meantime he was offered the opportunity to give lectures on the United States at various Party functions.[4]

During this period Péter and John Santo, who arrived in Hungary in late May, were required by the Party to fill out numerous questionnaires and write brief autobiographies, which were returned to them several times for corrections or rewriting of certain sections. To Santo this was merely annoying paperwork, but Péter became "extremely nervous," for he knew the "dangers inherent in the situation."[5] His uneasiness must have been increased by clear indications that some sort of Stalinist purge was underway in Hungary. On May 30, László Rajk was arrested by the state security police and accused of traitorous activity as a spy for foreign imperialist powers and Tito's Yugoslavia. From newspaper reports and the Communist Party grapevine, Péter and Santo learned that numerous individuals were being arrested as "accomplices" of Rajk. There was a definite pattern that knowledgeable observers like Péter could discern in the emerging purge trial. Those most vulnerable to arrest were Communists who had spent considerable time in the West and were of petit bourgeois and/or Jewish origin (which raised suspicions that they were "Zionists" or "cosmopolitans"). Péter could not have failed to notice that he fit into these categories. And given his own orthodox Communist mindset, he could easily imagine that Rákosi might regard him with suspicion because during twenty-five years in the United States he had perhaps become infected by "Browderism" or been recruited by the FBI.

In late summer, Péter's nervousness must have been substantially increased as he learned further details about the impending show trial. Noel Field was to play a key role in the script of the trial as the intermediary between the "traitors" in the Hungarian Communist Party and the United States Office of Strategic Services (OSS) and the CIA. Péter's friend John Lautner, who remained in the United States, was also implicated because of his alleged collaboration with Rajk and agents of Marshall Tito during World War II.[6] Furthermore, it was becoming clear that Hungarian Communists who had worked in the United States were being specifically targeted. In September, Mózes Simon was arrested and accused of being a spy for British Intelligence. This happened just hours after he had dined with Péter and his wife. In a letter to John Abt in this period, Péter took the risk of hinting that he himself was under suspicion and unable to gain employment.[7]

Because of the general unavailability to researchers of the records of the Hungarian secret service, it is impossible to determine how close József Péter was to being arrested. In the end, however, though he no doubt dreaded the late night knock on the door, the security police never appeared to arrest him. Perhaps Rákosi simply decided that there were other more suitable targets. Or someone in the KGB may have been apprised of what was afoot and privately informed the Hungarian leader that Péter had made valuable contributions to Soviet intelligence work and should not be molested. In any case, Péter must have been greatly relieved when in late 1949 or early 1950 he was finally given a permanent job as the director of the editorial department at Szikra (later called Kossuth), the Party's major publishing house for political literature. The assignment made some sense, since he did of course have considerable experience from his days with the *Új Előre*.

At Szikra, Péter made a good impression on his co-workers, who found him "quiet, even dignified," not at all "stuffy or pompous."[8] He was treated with the respect due to Party veterans and even regarded, especially by the younger members of the staff, as a "romantic" figure because he had supposedly held his own in confrontations with Nixon and the FBI. Péter revealed little about his past, and no one knew much about his career as J. Peters or anything of his origins as Sándor Goldberger. Because he was acknowledged to be the "house expert" on all things relating to the United States, he was frequently consulted by his comrades who had questions or needed help in translating English-language materials. He was always generous in giving his assistance.

Yet even though Péter now had what appeared to be a secure and respectable position in an important Party organization, he must have realized that he was by no means out of danger. There remained his troublesome connection with John Lautner. Péter had of course broken off communication with his former friend, but he undoubtedly learned that, on Rákosi's instigation, Lautner had been expelled from the CPUSA as "an imperialist agent" and, in his bitterness and resentment, had become one of the FBI's most important witnesses at trials of Communist leaders.[9] It would be difficult to explain his friendship with Lautner if, for whatever reason, Rákosi's suspicions were again aroused. The end of the Rajk show trial in late September 1949 did not by any means bring an end to state-sponsored terror, which continued for several years in the form of numerous arrests, forced relocations, secret trials, and executions.[10] At some point in 1950 or 1951, the chief editor of Szikra, Péter's boss, was arrested.[11] Several of Péter's personal friends were caught up in this continuing campaign of terror. In October 1950 the wife of Louis Weinstock was in Hungary to participate in an international congress of Communist women's federations. Immediately upon her arrival Rose Weinstock visited Ann and József Péter, who were old friends. Several weeks later, however, security agents made a midnight visit and forced her and her eleven-year-old daughter to relocate to a town far from Budapest, where they remained for several months under house arrest.[12] When Rose Weinstock was finally able to make a trip to Budapest, she sought help from her friends. But the Péters, aware of the danger of showing solidarity with those who were being targeted by the secret police, refused even to open their apartment door when Weinstock showed up.[13]

By 1951, Péter's position at the Szikra publishing house was becoming more secure. He was quickly gaining the reputation as Hungary's best authority on the United States and as a result he began to receive invitations to contribute articles on American topics to some of the leading Hungarian journals. By the mid-1950s he was a regular contributor to a variety of journals and newspapers, particularly *Társadalmi Szemle,* for which he became the resident expert on the United States. In the articles he wrote in this period, Péter described American government and society in the 1950s using the same rigid, Bolshevik terminology he had employed twenty years earlier in his *Manual on Organization.* Another indication that Péter was no longer under any suspicion came in November 1953, when he received one of the Party's awards of merit, the "Szocialista munkáért" (For Socialist Work).[14] This was to be the first of many such awards that Péter was to receive over the next two decades.

After Stalin's death in February 1953, the wave of terror that had swept over Hungarian society began slowly to recede. In time a process of de-Stalinization began. Some of the victims who had survived the horrors of state security prisons were gradually released, among them Noel Field. But the powerful political currents unleashed by de-Stalinization in Hungary could not easily be contained. Revulsion against the Rákosi regime and Soviet Russia was one of the main contributing factors to the revolutionary uprising that occurred in Hungary in 1956. Nothing is known of József Péter's contemporary reaction to that shattering event, but he clearly supported the suppression of the revolt by Soviet troops and the restoration of a Communist regime loyal to Moscow under János Kádár. He fully identified with the Kádár regime and supported its depiction of the events of 1956 as a counter-revolution. In his one known comment about the 1956 uprising, he made the dubious assertion to an American visitor that thousands of Jews "fled the 'counter-revolutionaries' . . . because they were starting up an anti-Semitic program."[15]

After several years of repressive policies designed to punish the main leaders of the 1956 uprising, the Kádár regime began in the early 1960s a slow but steady program of social, cultural, and political liberalization. In time the country enjoyed the fruits of what came to be called "goulasch communism." This meant much more stable conditions, an improved standard of living, greater cultural freedom, and enhanced contacts with the West through travel and educational exchanges. This liberalization opened up new opportunities for József Péter, as it did for many Hungarians. He continued to work in the Kossuth publishing house, where he was responsible for editing books on political and international topics. The main focus of his work soon became the *Nemzetközi Szemle* (*International Review*), a prestigious journal established in 1957 that reprinted articles from foreign publications that were translated into Hungarian. He began as group leader, became department head, and in the last years of his career was chief editor. Péter made a point of telling visitors from abroad that his journal contained pieces from many sources, "including the capitalist press—articles representing all viewpoints."[16] In recognition of his service to the Party and to Hungarian journalism over many years, Péter began to receive many awards and decorations, including one honoring those who had participated in the Hungarian Soviet Republic forty years earlier.[17]

By the 1960s, József and Ann Péter were living a reasonably comfortable life in a small home they had moved into on the Buda side of town. Their standard of living was on a par with higher-level Party officials. Theirs was an ideologically correct home: sets of the works of Marx and Lenin lined the bookshelves and a bust of Lenin had a place of honor in the living room. Ann had never really learned to speak Hungarian with any fluency, but she had a good Party job as head of the English-language section of Hungarian state radio and had acclimated herself to conditions in a strange land. Up to and beyond 1974, the year in which he officially retired, Péter played the role of a kind of elder statesman in the Party. He attended congresses, took part in symposiums, and, alas, attended many funerals as one by one all of the comrades of his generation began to pass away.

Péter also sought to take advantage of the increasing intellectual freedom and greater opportunities for contacts with the West that resulted from the liberalized atmosphere permitted by the Kádár regime in the 1960s and 1970s. His friends in the United States could now more easily send him books and journals that allowed him to keep abreast of American political and social developments. In 1969, Péter was invited by Gus Hall to attend the fiftieth anniversary celebration of the founding of the CPUSA, and he gave serious thought to making a return visit to the country from which he had been deported. But when he went to the American Embassy in Budapest and began filling out the necessary forms to obtain a visa, he discovered that he would have to list all the aliases he had ever used. This convinced him of the futility of the venture, which "would have raised all the fuss again."[18] But if he could not travel to the United States, his American friends certainly now could visit him in Hungary.

Beginning in the late 1960s, a steady stream of visitors was welcomed to the Péters' home on a hillside in Buda with a view of the Danube River. It was, an American historian later recalled, a "very old home, well worn, old soft couches, chairs, books in English and Hungarian, lots of books."[19] Among the most frequent visitors were John Abt and Jessica Smith and Lewis Fraad and his wife. Left-wing American artists and scholars who happened to be in Budapest were invariably invited to the Péters' home. Among them were Paul Robeson, the famous actor and musician,[20] and Péter's old friend and collaborator, Joseph Losey. In 1971, upon learning that Losey was planning to make a film about the assassination of Trotsky, Péter telephoned him in London and suggested, perhaps tongue in cheek, that he might make a good historical consultant for the film. It is unclear whether the director took him up on this offer, but it was definitely Losey who was responsible for arranging for Péter to have a real brush with celebrity. In 1972 Richard Burton (who played Trotsky in the film) decided to have a grand birthday party for his wife, Elizabeth Taylor, in Budapest. Losey managed to wrangle an invitation to the party for the Péters, who found themselves in exalted company. In addition to Losey himself, among those who flew in were Princess Grace of Monaco (Grace Kelly), Ringo Starr, Michael Caine, and Raquel Welch.[21] After the party, Losey and his wife were invited for tea at the Péters' cottage. Later that year Losey gave a report on his visit to their mutual friend, Frederick Vanderbilt Field: "Our friends are well . . . old . . . and a little sad . . . not so much changed as one might have imagined."[22] One change not mentioned by Losey but noted by other American friends was that "Pete" had become severely overweight, indeed almost obese.

The Péters also socialized with and welcomed into their home various expatriates and other English-speaking visitors who were staying in Hungary for extended periods of time. They became good friends of Noel and Herta Field, although privately Péter spoke condescendingly of Field, calling him "naïve . . . like all the other Quaker Communists."[23] The Péters were especially welcoming of young Americans who came to Hungary in connection with various left-wing projects or organizations. One such visitor, Dan Rosenberg, who was working with the World Federation of Democratic Youth, came to know the Péters well while residing in Budapest in 1976 and 1977. He found the eighty-two-year-old Péter, whom he was soon calling "Pete," to be a "congenial and likeable man, very easy to talk to." He was, Rosenberg later suggested, "the last person you would ever have suspected of writing such a doctrinaire book" as J. Peters's *Manual on Organization*. To American guests like Rosenberg, Péter spoke in glowing terms about the progress socialist Hungary had made, although he did gripe about the health care system, which he complained was rife with "corruption and expectation of favors and gifts."[24]

József Péter was pleased with almost all his visitors, perhaps because they were mostly all old friends and Communist Party members or sympathizers. The one exception was Allen Weinstein, an American historian doing research for what would be a very controversial book, *Perjury: The Hiss-Chambers Case.* Hopeful of interviewing all surviving participants in the dramatic story he was chronicling, Weinstein was able to track down the address of the former J. Peters in Hungary and overcome his reluctance to speak about his career.[25] Péter finally agreed to be interviewed, perhaps assured by American friends that Weinstein, who was thought by fellow academics to be sympathetic to Alger Hiss, was ideologically reliable. At their meeting in March 1975 in a Budapest hotel, Weinstein had a very favorable first impression: "He is a handsome, white-haired man of eighty-one, short and somewhat chunky but still sturdily built. He has an imposing mane of hair . . . [and] looks decades younger than his years."

Péter began their conversation by suggesting that his visitor was probably wasting his time, since "he had nothing of consequence to tell . . . about the absurd charges made by Chambers." Péter willingly talked about his organizational work in the Party and acknowledged that he had written the *Manual on Organization,* which unfortunately got him into trouble because it brought him to the attention of the federal authorities. Otherwise, "he might have been left alone." In listing a number of accomplishments of which he was proud, he mentioned such things as successes in union organization (especially the CIO), strikes (Flint, San Francisco), his role in the growth in Party membership, work with intellectuals and artists, and, above all, of having been "a loyal Party functionary." But he denied having known Hiss, and if he had met Chambers at all, it was only in passing, perhaps in the offices of the *New Masses.* He had never engaged in any sort of "secret work." Indeed, he knew of no such "secret work," and as for espionage, although he assumed that some Americans probably did assist the Soviets in their spying, "it would have been stupid for the open Party people such as myself to get involved." In response to a question from Weinstein about the Ware group, Péter insisted that he had had no involvement with such a group and in fact had never been in Washington, except to participate in the Bonus March. Whenever Weinstein gently probed into sensitive areas, Péter either issued blanket denials without any attempt to prove his point, or brushed away any incriminating evidence. Thus, when Weinstein pointed out that Lee Pressman had told a congressional committee that he had met J. Peters in Washington in connection with the Ware group, Péter responded that Pressman was mistaken, since they had met not in Washington but only later in New York.

To Weinstein's remark that not only Whittaker Chambers but also Louis Budenz and several other informers had expressed some admiration for him,

Péter's response was indignant: "It disturbs me that all these bastards liked me." Chambers, he opined, was "not entirely normal," and, he had heard, was a homosexual. For that matter, he believed that J. Edgar Hoover, Roosevelt, and even Harry Hopkins were also homosexuals. Weinstein did not attempt to challenge such remarkable statements, but instead tried to gain Péter's cooperation in discovering any as yet unknown evidence on the Hiss-Chambers affair. Would he, for example, have any objection to Weinstein's examining Péter's FBI file if it could be obtained? This question greatly disconcerted Péter, who, after a pause, suggested that what Weinstein proposed would be undesirable and unwise. He seemed unable to explain his opposition, other than to suggest that other people might be harmed. Later in the conversation, staring at Weinstein with what the American historian regarded as "a cold look in his eyes," Péter spoke more firmly: "Be very careful. I am here and nothing can happen to me—be very careful that the Party shall in no way be hurt by it [Weinstein's book]."

Despite this rather blunt warning, Péter maintained throughout the conversation a friendly manner and smile. In parting he expressed the hope that Weinstein would be able to visit again: "Come back in June or July with your family. We will show you Hungary, my wife and I." Weinstein, it seems, left with a feeling of accomplishment, though he must have realized that Péter had provided little in the way of new evidence. The wish being the father to the thought, Weinstein concluded that he and the former J. Peters had been talking in a kind of coded language: "I think it was assumed throughout our conversation that he wasn't telling me the real story, and that I knew this, and that it didn't matter. Twice, I repeated the statement that I knew if he had done all the things Chamber said he did, that he couldn't tell me about it, and twice he smiled and nodded!" Similarly, Weinstein observed that when Péter referred several times to the "open" Party, he did so with a smile, which Weinstein interpreted as a tacit admission of the existence of a "secret" Party as well.

Whether or not Péter had intentionally been giving the visiting American historian a "wink and a nod," he seemed genuinely outraged when he was informed by some American friends of the content of Weinstein's book, which appeared in 1978. After evaluating the massive amount of new evidence he had collected, Weinstein concluded that Whittaker Chambers had by and large told the truth, and that consequently Alger Hiss had indeed been a member of the Communist Party and had been an important cog in the espionage network that J. Peters had established and later turned over to a GRU operative. Weinstein had not in fact been able to procure Peters's FBI file, but on the basis of the records of his INS deportation hearing and other new evidence, he concluded that Peters had been "a gray eminence who held important posts for twenty-five years at both the 'open' organizational level and in the Party's secret work."[26]

In the debate stirred by the appearance of *Perjury*, Weinstein's critics argued that he had misinterpreted or distorted the evidence, in particular as it pertained to J. Peters. In an essay in which he asserted that *Perjury* settled nothing about the Hiss-Chambers case, Victor Navasky, editor of *The Nation* argued that Weinstein surely was placing far too much significance on the fact that Peters had smiled during his interview. "If," he asserted, "anything more than Peters's smile was involved in his confirmation of Chambers's activities, we are given no evidence of it."[27] Even historians who were persuaded by Weinstein's main thesis and now believed that Hiss was probably guilty were troubled by Weinstein's use of his interview with Peters, which Ronald Radosh, in a review of the book, deemed the author's "weakest use of such material." He concluded that Weinstein had "foolishly and unnecessarily sought to gain great mileage out of this now famous smile, a smile whose substance is an enigma."[28]

In Budapest, József Péter reacted with surprise and chagrin when he learned that his enigmatic smile had become a topic of debate among academics and literati in the United States. Once he received from American friends photocopies of those sections of *Perjury* that related to J. Peters, he realized he had blundered in speaking with a historian whose ideological orientation he had clearly misjudged. Péter had assumed that Weinstein would share his view that nothing should be published that would harm the CPUSA or damage the reputation of Alger Hiss, and that the main purpose of his book would be to depict the evils of the McCarthy era.[29] Now he must do whatever he could to discredit Weinstein and limit the damage. The first, and as it turned out, only opportunity to do so in a public way came in the spring of 1978, when Donald Kirk, a writer for *The Nation* (who was not well versed in the issues but happened to be passing through Hungary), was commissioned by Navasky to seek an interview with Péters in order to check up on "Peter's smile." Ann Péter seemed, if anything, more indignant than her husband about Weinstein's "treachery." When Kirk mentioned Weinstein's interpretation of Péter's smile, she became irate: "I ask how the dickens will my husband remember if he smiled. Isn't that ridiculous? My husband is terribly annoyed that his name is mentioned as verifying what Weinstein wrote."

Péter himself was more subdued, and seemed wary of having to talk once more about the issues that had long bedeviled him. He greeted Kirk with his now famous smile, which the writer described, quite perceptively, as "the half-smile of a skeptic, an intellectual who cannot help but perceive humor in the posturing and maneuvering." Péter proceeded to give what by now were pro forma answers to Kirk's questions. What Weinstein wrote about him was "nonsense." He had never met Hiss, and had certainly not done the things Chambers described in *Witness*. Did he engage in espionage? "Spy network—I deny it. It's nonsense."

At Kirk's prodding, Péter offered a brief sketch of his life in the United States, emphasizing his previous argument that he wanted to become a citizen but had been thwarted by the INS. But as Kirk went on to ask Péter what he knew about certain individuals, the Hungarian seemed to become bored: "What nonsense. Let's stop it." Péter proceeded to show his guest around the house and muse about his life in Hungary, the joys of retirement, and the pleasure he took in reading. Soon Kirk found himself being politely ushered out the door, with the vague sensation that he "had intruded upon the inner contentment they [the Péters] have known since the turmoil of their lives in America."

After the conversation with the writer from the *The Nation,* there is no evidence that Péter ever again made public comments about his controversial past. Almost nothing is known about the last decade of his life. At some point in the 1980s Ann, his companion of over forty years, died. As he began to ponder his own mortality, Péter may have remembered a suggestion that the "despicable" Alan Weinstein had made to him. He (Péter) should write his memoirs, because "his perspective was a fascinating one: from the Hungarian Revolution of 1919 to the Czechoslovakian Party until 1924, then to the United States until 1949, and now back in Hungary."[30] In his determination to honor the "code of silence" expected of all Communists who had engaged in "special work," Péter had always refused to write about his career. One of the main reasons he would never reveal the truth about his involvement in the secret apparatus was that he might thereby do great harm to individuals who had never revealed their own membership in and contributions to the Communist Party, such as Alger Hiss and John Abt. Now, however, as he approached the age of ninety, Péter seemed to have second thoughts. Perhaps he could in fact compose an autobiography that emphasized his accomplishments in the "open" Party and omitted (or perhaps obliquely hinted at) his conspiratorial work, without naming any names. In that way he would not endanger those friends and comrades who were still alive, but at the same time would ensure that future generations of Hungarian Communists would, as a historian has aptly put it, "one day appreciate the work he had performed for the 'Cause.'"[31]

An opportunity for Péter to write just such a memoir came in 1983, when the Institute of Party History in Budapest invited him to join other prominent Hungarian Communists who were contributing materials to be placed on deposit in the institute's archives. In this way the recollections and reminiscences of participants in, and eyewitnesses to, major events in the history of the Hungarian Communist Party would be preserved for future study. Péter, perhaps confident that material deposited in the institute's archive would never be available to the general public, agreed to compose a brief memoir for this project. The manuscript he submitted in parts over a two-year period from 1983 to 1985 was by no means a full and objective description of his life and career.[32] But this is no surprise, since in their autobiographies Communists, whether in Hungary or elsewhere, have always felt the need to practice a kind of self-censorship, omit sensitive topics, and "ignore the personal dimension of experience in favor of the collective."[33]

It is therefore not surprising that in his memoir József Péter provided very little information about his personal life. He made no mention of his first marriage in 1923, his common-law wife of the late 1920s, or even of Sophie Frommer (Ann Péter), his wife and close companion for more than four decades. He did briefly describe his family life in Csap and education in Debrecen, depicting his parents as poor and hardworking. But he wrote nothing of his Jewish origins and did not mention that until the age of twenty-nine the only name he used was Sándor Goldberger. He passed quickly over the awkward fact that he served for four years in World War I as an infantry officer. The period from 1918 to 1929 was more fully covered, but here too there were intentional omissions. No proper explanation was offered for the decision that resulted in his emigration to the United States. No mention is made of the challenges to his leadership of the Hungarian Federation in the 1920s.

In that part of his memoir devoted to his work in the national headquarters of the CPUSA in the 1930s, Péter accurately described his role as that of an expert in organization matters and author of the *Manual*. He even allowed himself a mild boast when he declared that he had been involved "in the organization of all of the more important actions" undertaken by the CPUSA in the 1930s. He was far more circumspect, however, in his discussion of the "special work" that he now admitted, for the first time, he had performed for the American Party. He did not elaborate on the nature of this "special work," other than to imply that part of it involved creating an "illegal apparatus" that would allow the CPUSA to operate in times of severe political repression. However, he hinted at its importance by stating that he received "very useful" training in illegal work in both Moscow and Berlin. Péter went on to suggest that he was the innocent victim of persecution by the FBI and INS, who harassed him only because he was a member of the Communist Party. However, he did admit that serious accusations were made against him by "the informer Whittaker Chambers" at sessions of the HUAC. These included involvement in espionage, along with Alger Hiss, and the production of fraudulent passports. Péter did not state that Chambers's accusations were false, but merely that on the instructions of Party leaders he refused to answer any questions about them when he appeared before HUAC and at his INS hearing. Nor did he attempt in his memoir to refute the main accusations made against him. Instead, he emphasized that Chambers was a "renegade," thus implying that he had committed the cardinal sin of deserting the Party and breaking the "code of silence." It would seem that Péter hoped that future readers of his memoirs would all be loyal Party members who would be able to read through the lines and grasp what he was implying but could not state openly: I received training in and carried out "special work" for the CPUSA. Enemies of the Party accused me of espionage and other crimes. Of course, I had to deny those charges (though they were true) in order to protect the Party and the comrades with whom I worked.[34]

Nothing is known of the last few years of József Péter's life or of his reaction (assuming he was still of clear mind) to the collapse of the Communist regimes in Hungary and elsewhere in Eastern Europe in 1989. He died on December 9, 1990, at the age of ninety-six and was buried in the Budapest Public Cemetery. Péter had outlived all his close friends and comrades, except John Abt, who died four months later.[35] In the Hungarian press, which was preoccupied with the momentous events surrounding Hungary's transition from Communism to a multi-party democracy, only a few brief obituaries appeared.[36] And why should Hungarians take notice of the death of an obscure middle-level Communist functionary and journalist? Only a handful of them could have been aware that this fellow Hungarian had once been known as J. Peters, the "red conspirator," and had been a major and mysterious figure in one of the most important political controversies in twentieth-century American history.

* * *

In his long career as a Communist organizer, writer, and specialist in conspiratorial work, J. Peters was an observer of and participant in many important events and developments in the rise and fall of world Communism. During his twenty-five years of work in the Communist Party of the United States, he was involved in a great diversity of activities and organizations: the ethnic federations; relations with the Comintern; work in the national headquarters; union organization; cadre recruitment and development; Party schools; and the secret apparatus. In his native Hungary, he participated in the creation of the first Communist regime outside of Russia, survived the Stalinist terror that gripped the country in the Rákosi era, and lived long enough to see the rapid collapse of Communist regimes all across Eastern Europe in 1989. A study of J. Peters's career can thus provide some useful insights into the nature and impact of Communism in the twentieth century. His career is also a case study of that distinctive group of European Communists who as young men or women experienced the revolutionary events of 1917–19, left or were expelled from their native lands, and spent the rest of their lives in the service of world Communism while living in Moscow, Berlin, New York, or elsewhere.

Much of the work J. Peters did in the CPUSA was of the kind that has not frequently received the attention of historians. The years he spent as an organizer and journalist in the Hungarian Federation throw some light on the role that the ethnic or language organizations played in the CPUSA of the 1920s.

The leaders of the Hungarian Federation were dedicated individuals who were willing to endure great personal hardship and frustration in the effort to win new recruits to the Party. Their task was formidable, as Peters learned when he was sent in 1925 to organize Hungarian-speaking workers in the steel mills, auto factories, and mines of the Midwest. The reality, which Peters must have observed but, like his colleagues in the leadership of the Hungarian Federation, found impossible to accept, was that Hungarian American workers by and large rejected the radical policies advocated by the Communist Party. The number of Hungarian Americans who were members of the CPUSA actually plummeted from 1925 to 1929. Peters and his colleagues either found ways of explaining away the dismal membership statistics, or simply ignored them.

Although the national leadership of the CPUSA fretted over the constant infighting and factionalism in the language federations, they also came to realize their importance as a training ground for talented comrades who could be promoted to positions in the national Party. By 1929, J. Peters had been identified by Party leaders as one such ethnic Communist who showed considerable promise. Having maneuvered successfully through the factional struggles, Peters made a name for himself in national headquarters by proposing a creative solution to the financial problems of the *Daily Worker*. When the Party was thrown into turmoil in 1929 and Moscow anointed a new leadership for the CPUSA, Peters showed his opportunism and shrewdly followed the example of Max Bedacht by denouncing his former sponsor, Jay Lovestone, and swearing his allegiance to the Comintern.

As his reward for supporting the new CPUSA leadership, Peters was made the organizational secretary for the New York district and, after returning from additional training in Moscow, was placed in a leadership position in the Organization Bureau along with other aliens with similar backgrounds. It turned out that Peters had a real aptitude for cadre development and organizational work. He helped to expand the network of Party schools, became one of the more popular instructors in those schools, and made an important contribution to the increase in Party membership in the mid-1930s. As the Party's acknowledged expert on such matters, it was only natural that he was assigned the task of writing an organizational manual that members could consult to understand the Party's complex structure and objectives.

As the Cold War developed in the late 1940s, the more vociferous opponents of the CPUSA often cited Peters's *Manual of Organization* as proof that the Party was a subversive organization that aimed to overthrow the American government. Party leaders dismissed such arguments, pointing out that the *Manual* had been withdrawn shortly after its publication and suggesting that it had never really represented the true position of the CPUSA. No doubt, most CPUSA members at the local level in the late 1930s and 1940s were unaware of Peters's *Manual* and did not really think in terms of creating a "proletariat dictatorship." They had more practical, short-term goals: building powerful unions, improving the lives of workers, eliminating racial and social injustices. But, as J. Peters would no doubt have argued, it was the responsibility of Party leaders to think of long-term objectives, and what was the purpose of a Communist Party if not to seek revolutionary change, the overthrow of capitalism, and the establishment of a government run by the workers? It is worth noting that when Earl Browder was expelled from the Party in 1946 and the CPA was disbanded, Party leaders like William Foster began publicly, and J. Peters privately, to describe the Party's policies in a spirit quite compatible with that found in the *Manual on Organization*.

Among his many contributions to the growing influence of the CPUSA in the 1930s was J. Peters's success in winning support from artists, intellectuals, and professionals. With his charm, affability, and soft-spoken demeanor, Peters was an impressive representative of the Communist movement. He was sufficiently well educated to feel comfortable in the company of artists, economists, and lawyers, many of them graduates of the finest universities. He was able to persuade such Americans, some of whom were quite affluent, to make substantial donations of their time and money to the Party. In fact, he had the knack of convincing at least some of these otherwise staid and law-abiding individuals to join him in his clandestine operations.

J. Peters was best known to other CPUSA members as a specialist in organizational matters and for his work among intellectuals and artists. However, many Party members came to know, or at least surmised, that upon his return from Moscow in 1932 he began to work in some capacity as a representative of the Comintern. Few knew, however, the details of Peters's work as the supervisor of the Party's secret apparatus. His initial responsibilities appear to have been twofold: to serve as the liaison between the Comintern's intelligence service (OMS) and the CPUSA, and to coordinate efforts to establish, or reinvigorate, a functioning "illegal apparatus." To Peters in 1933 it must have seemed self-evident that the CPUSA urgently needed an effective "illegal apparatus" because American Communists faced the same dangers that Russian Communists had in the tsarist era and German Communists were experiencing as a result of Hitler's coming to power. Certainly this was the clearly stated position of the Comintern. What Peters did not realize was that an operation designed for particular conditions in Europe could not easily be transplanted to the United States. Most American Communists at the local level did not place a high priority on building the "illegal apparatus," probably because they sensed that the American government would never resort to the same repressive policies that had been employed by tsarist Russia and Nazi Germany. Perhaps some might even have privately harbored the heretical view that the national headquarters paid too much attention to what a historian would later call the "formulaic gibberish that came their way from Moscow."[37] In fact, the one notable example of the efficacy of the "illegal apparatus" was Peters himself. Using the conspiratorial methods he had long preached, he was able to go underground in 1939, create an entirely new identity, and elude the FBI for several years.

When J. Peters was placed in charge of the secret apparatus in 1932, it was not automatically assumed by Earl Browder and other informed Party leaders that he would coordinate the CPUSA's relations with Soviet intelligence agencies other than the OMS. Quite quickly, however, Peters expanded his bailiwick to include the GRU and, to a lesser extent, the NKVD. In developing the secret apparatus, Peters displayed very effective managerial skills, much creativity, and an entrepreneurial spirit. On his own initiative he proceeded for the next several years to involve the Party in a series of operations that were clearly criminal in nature, including the amalgamation and expansion of the fraudulent passport operation, a more systematic arrangement of safe houses and business fronts to be used by Soviet agents, and military and political espionage. When J. Peters came to the attention of the American media and public in the late 1940s, he was often referred to by such epithets as a "top Stalin spy" and a "Kremlin agent." This was misleading, however, for such terms suggested Peters was under the supervision of Soviet intelligence agents and, in theory, ultimately of Stalin himself. In fact, although he received payments from the GRU and NKVD for fraudulent passports, Peters's foray into espionage was conducted largely on his own initiative and no Soviet agent ever served directly as his handler. Throughout the 1930s and even later, Soviet operatives in the United States had only sketchy reports about the "fellow countryman" called "Peter" or "Peters" who was the handler of a number of productive government employees. The one Soviet intelligence agent who had a fairly good idea of what J. Peters had accomplished was Iskhak Akhmerov, who realized during World War II that most of the members of the Perlo group, who proved of such value as intelligence sources, had originally worked with Peters or been recommended by him.

Recent revelations of the extent to which members of the CPUSA cooperated with Soviet agents in espionage and other criminal activity have prompted historians to rethink some important and controversial questions. Although few would subscribe to Louis Budenz's blanket assertion that every American Communist was a "potential spy agent," there has been a developing consensus that the CPUSA functioned in the 1930s and 1940s as "an auxiliary to Soviet intelligence."[38] Scholars disagree, however, about the significance of this. Was such cooperation natural and inevitable, given the Party's intimate ties with the Soviet Union and its long-stated ambition to overthrow the capitalist system? Or should it be considered more as an incidental sideshow, the significance of which pales compared with the Party's truly important work on behalf of workers and minorities? In addressing such questions, one must take into account the fact that very few Party leaders, even at the highest level, were privy to the details of the cooperation with Soviet intelligence agencies carried out by Earl Browder, J. Peters, and Jacob Golos. Other than the participants themselves, only a handful of Party members knew that J. Peters supervised a spy ring in Washington. Almost certainly the vast majority of CPUSA members had no idea that some Party leaders were engaged in such subversive, indeed criminal, activity. Could one not conclude, then, that the few "conspiracy-minded" individuals in the national leadership who cooperated with Soviet agents in espionage operations did so more or less unilaterally, and that such activity was alien to the methods and objectives of most Party members?

As has been seen, J. Peters was not some sort of Comintern "outsider" when he returned from Moscow in 1932. Though not an American citizen, he had been a CPUSA member since 1924 and had served as secretary of the Hungarian Federation and organizational secretary for the New York district. Even as he was supervising the Party's secret apparatus in the 1930s, Peters was also deeply involved in such traditional Party activities as union organization, recruitment, and cadre development. Furthermore, Peters's conspiratorial operations were by no means carried out unilaterally. In his fraudulent passport operation, the attempt to infiltrate the armed forces, and information gathering and espionage in Washington, Peters needed the cooperation of hundreds of Party members, none of whom could have been in any doubt that these were criminal activities. Yet the evidence suggests that Peters had no difficulty in finding Party members to contribute to his conspiratorial work. Only a few cases are known of a Party member declining to participate in, or withdrawing from, one of Peters's clandestine operations. For example, of the original Ware group members only one, Nathaniel Weyl, seemed to have had any serious misgivings about the Washington underground organization. Feeling vaguely that something about the Ware group was "duplicitous," Weyl opted to withdraw and pursue other Party work. Sylvia Castleton (who later married Nathaniel Weyl) was another Party member who resisted being drawn into Peters's conspiratorial world. When Peters suggested that she serve as manager of a travel agency that he proposed to set up as a business front for his underground apparatus, she declined. And, with the notable exception of Whittaker Chambers, no individual with knowledge of Peters's "Washington set-up" ever sought to inform government authorities.

On the whole, then, the "red conspirator" was successful in recruiting all the foot soldiers he needed to ensure a proper functioning of his many underground enterprises, including librarians, photographers, lawyers, economists, and government bureaucrats. This seems to suggest that even though most CPUSA members never learned anything about the Party's secret apparatus, almost none showed any ethical inhibition about fabricating and using false passports or participating in criminal activity if they were urged to do so by Peters, who was seen as a representative of the "ninth floor." Of course, it is likely that Peters, who was a shrewd judge of the political reliability of individual Party members, would have tried to recruit only those whom he believed would be open to the idea of clandestine work. He was very adept at using the most efficacious and appropriate arguments to persuade individual Party members. He was perhaps the first CPUSA official to recognize and exploit the "romantic anti-fascism" that motivated many young, well-educated Americans in the early 1930s. He also sensed that many Party members were fascinated by the idea of covert work, which they thought of as a risky but exciting adventure. Others wished to prove their credentials as dedicated "professional revolutionists" who, as Peters had stated in his *Manual,* were "ready to go whenever and wherever the Party sends him."

Not all of J. Peters's operations in the secret apparatus were successful. His only known attempt at military espionage misfired, and the program to infiltrate the armed forces and proselytize soldiers and sailors was an almost complete failure. On the other hand, his fraudulent passport mill was an efficiently run enterprise that supplied the CPUSA, Comintern, GRU, and NKVD with perhaps thousands of travel documents in the 1930s. And the spy ring he established in Washington has been described as one of the first successful attempts to establish an "agent beachhead within the Roosevelt Administration."[39] Although he had been trained in Soviet conspiratorial methods in Moscow and Berlin, there is no reason to believe that Peters received instruction specifically in the tradecraft of espionage. In fact, Peters was very much an amateur, and a part-time one at that, since in the mid-1930s he had numerous other Party responsibilities to attend to. Similarly, Whittaker Chambers, Alger Hiss, and the other agents Peters recruited had no prior experience in clandestine work, which explains their tendency on occasion to flout traditional Soviet principles of conspiratorial work. The methods they used were loosely based on Soviet models, but Peters and Chambers often had to improvise and conform to conditions in Washington. Yet the results were impressive. By late 1936, Peters was supervising a corps of agents in several government agencies, most notably the State Department. A highly efficient procedure had been established for procuring and photographing documents. Dozens of other government employees in a variety of agencies were, under Peters's direction, also providing the CPUSA with reports, and were poised to proceed to more serious information gathering if and when the opportunity arose. Thus Peters was perhaps justified when he boasted to Whittaker Chambers, "Even in Germany under the Weimar Republic, the party did not have what we have here."[40]

Certainly Peters's success both in the passport operation and espionage was in part a reflection of his ingenuity, effective organizing skills, and deft handling of

Party workers and sympathizers. There are, however, certain other factors that were at work. In the early and mid-1930s, the Soviet intelligence agencies were undergoing various organizational problems and were under certain restraints that made it possible for an outsider from the CPUSA to seize the initiative in attempting to infiltrate the U.S. government. It is noteworthy that in these circumstances Peters was able to circumvent one of the most important guidelines of Soviet intelligence work in that era: namely, that the Soviet agencies (NKVD, GRU, and OMS) should operate completely independently and avoid interfering with each other's operations and agents. Certain CPUSA leaders and members cooperated with the NKVD, others with the GRU. But J. Peters was the only one known to have managed to forge ties with not only the GRU and OMS, but the NKVD as well.

J. Peters's success was also made possible by the fact that American government agencies in the 1930s were not greatly concerned about the Communist Party and its conspiratorial activities. Peters's passport operation flourished because the State Department was not alert to the possibility of widespread passport fraud and did not oversee the issuance of passports with much vigilance. Alger Hiss and Henry Wadleigh discovered that State Department procedures were so lax that it was a relatively simple matter to gather up documents of interest, take them home to be photographed, and return them the following morning. Finally, through most of the 1930s neither the FBI nor any other U.S. government agency had a counter-intelligence program to combat espionage conducted by the CPUSA or Soviet agents.

There remains the broader question of whether J. Peters's conspiratorial operations had a significant impact. Did they actually benefit the Soviet Union and do significant harm to the security interests of the United States? Certainly it was Peters's intention that his work in the secret apparatus would aid Soviet Russia and, indirectly, pave the way for the hoped-for workers' revolution in the United States. That was his motive in his attempts to obtain the blueprints of submarines and information about American military weapons and installations. Had such attempts succeeded, the damage to American security could have been substantial. Peters's highly successful fraudulent passport operation greatly assisted the work of Soviet and Comintern intelligence agents, who, using forged American passports, were able for most of the 1930s to travel with impunity in and out of the United States and all across the globe. Peters also facilitated the work of Soviet agents by providing safe houses, mail drops, and such business fronts as the American Feature Writers Syndicate.

The impact of Peters's espionage work in Washington, however, is more difficult to assess. Were the intelligence materials obtained by the Soviets in the United States in this period truly important and did any of it make "much difference in the long run"?[41] A definitive answer to this question will probably be possible only when, and if, the records of the GRU become available for research. It is probably safe to conclude tentatively that none of the documents obtained by the agents in Peters's "Washington set-up" contained major revelations. The material passed on to the Soviet Union is likely to have been similar to the two State Department documents from 1937 that found their way into the CPUSA archive. Such information would have been useful to Soviet leaders in making general assessments of American foreign and trade policy. From time to time, Peters's agents may have been able to provide documents containing nuggets of useful information obtained by American diplomats or military attachés in Berlin, Rome, Tokyo, or elsewhere. In addition, having access to original State Department documents might well have been invaluable to Soviet cryptographers working on the decoding of American diplomatic correspondence. Finally, even if the immediate harm done to American security interests by Peters's espionage exploits was not great, the longer term impact was significant. He had demonstrated that even someone without thorough training in espionage work could place agents in "old-line agencies" and that there was a corps of dedicated and idealistic Party members and sympathizers in the federal government who were prepared, without any monetary compensation, to assist Soviet intelligence agencies. Moreover, even after Peters himself was forced to withdraw from participation in the Washington underground, some of his acolytes, under the direction of Victor Perlo, supplied the NKVD with important military, economic, and political intelligence during World War II.[42]

Despite the limited kinds of primary sources available, a reasonably complete narrative of the career of J. Peters can be constructed. Much more difficult is the task of penetrating the inner life of the "red conspirator." To what extent were his life and career shaped by his family origins, his early years and education in Hungary, his embrace of Communism, and his long sojourn in the United States? And what of his self identity? If someone had asked him who and what he was, no doubt he would have called himself simply a Communist functionary. But the historian must also take into account his identity as a Jew, a Hungarian, and even an American.

When he arrived in the United States in 1924, Sándor Goldberger was already firmly committed to the Communist cause. The Marxist ideology that he had encountered and embraced at the end of World War I provided the compass that guided him through the remainder of life. Radicalized by the events of 1918–19, he had become a fervent Communist and had immersed himself in the works of Marx and Lenin. Goldberger was convinced that history was moving inexorably toward a revolutionary uprising of the workers under the direction of the Communist Party and the ultimate collapse of capitalist regimes. During his career in the United States, J. Peters encountered problems and obstacles that would have led to disillusionment in a person less determined and confident in the justice of the cause to which he had devoted his life. Like many of his comrades, Peters lived in what Arthur Koestler, another Jewish-Hungarian Communist, would later call an "intellectually closed world" that dulls the critical faculties and "refuses to be modified by newly observed facts."[43] If he had been a more objective observer, one less shackled by the "scientific laws" posited by Karl Marx, he might have had a more realistic view of the prospects of the CPUSA. Instead, he found ways to rationalize the overall failure of the Party's recruiting of Hungarian American workers and the rapid turnover of Party membership in the 1930s. He was likewise blind to any faults or shortcomings of the "Soviet experiment."

Having absorbed the prevailing political culture of the Soviet Union in the early 1930s and received instruction in conspiratorial work, J. Peters returned to the United States as an adherent of a rigid, orthodox Communism. He described his vision of the Communist Party in painstaking detail in his *Manual on Organization*. Many people who met Peters in later years were surprised to discover that he was the author of the infamous *Manual*. They could not imagine that such an affable, soft-spoken, and tactful person could have written such a doctrinaire and imperious political tract. In praising Peters's *Manual* upon its appearance in 1935, the CPUSA leaders could hardly have anticipated that within months the Comintern "line" would be changed and the "Popular Front" launched, thus rendering Peters's pamphlet instantly obsolete. Although the Bolshevik principles to be found in the *Manual* were more to his taste, Peters realized that the principle of "democratic centralism" must prevail and he acquiesced quietly as the Party declared the *Manual* no longer operative. Peters realized at the time, and on other similar occasions, that a Communist must not be tied so firmly to any particular ideological position that he would find it difficult to adjust should the Party "line" change. He had successfully made such an adjustment in 1929, when he denounced his former patron, Jay Lovestone, and pledged loyalty to Stalin and the Comintern. He was to execute similar flip-flops at the time of the Communist Political Association in 1945, at first greeting the change with enthusiasm and later quickly denouncing it when the Soviet leadership branded Earl Browder an ideological heretic. George Charney, observing Peters's opportunism at the time, made the shrewd observation that he was "a man who could shift with the winds of political doctrine."

Probably quite early in his career as a Communist functionary J. Peters discovered that he would often have to resort to prevarication and duplicity as part of the struggle against the ruthless enemies of the Party. He took very seriously the "discipline of apparatus" that required those who had done "special Party work" to honor the code of silence and denial. This meant that even as the evidence against him steadily mounted, Peters had to continue throughout the remainder of his life to deny that he had engaged in espionage or other criminal activity and to continue to brand his accusers as "renegades" and "stool pigeons." Even in his last years he could not bring himself to tell the truth and set the record straight, as did, for example, Morton Sobell, an American Communist who, after many years of public denials, finally admitted in 2009 that he had engaged in espionage.[44]

J. Peters was born in Hungary and lived the first twenty-four and last forty-one years of his life there. During his residence in the United States he often spoke and wrote in Hungarian, preferred Hungarian food, and closely followed events in Hungary. But up to his deportation from the United States in 1949 his attitude toward his native country seemed to be very ambivalent. Although in his memoir he carefully avoided any discussion of the subject, it is quite possible that as a young man Sándor Goldberger felt himself to be Hungarian and was optimistic about his future life in his native land. Young Jews like himself, even if they came from poor families, were being given the opportunity to acquire an excellent education and enter the professions. For this reason the eruption of virulent state-sponsored anti-Semitism in 1918–19 must have been a great shock and caused profound alienation. How could he any longer identify with a Hungary in which hatred of Jews was now so openly expressed? By the same token, he was now convinced that he and others like him could have a secure place only in a socialist society, which would eliminate the pernicious influence of anti-Semitism and exaggerated nationalism.

It was perhaps a profound disgust with what had become of his native land, Hungary, and a desire to seek a new Communist identity that eventually motivated him to emigrate to the United States. When he left in 1924, almost surely he did so with the conviction that he would never return to his native land. In the United States, especially in the 1920s, he continued to speak and write in Hungarian, but in time he mastered English and slowly became assimilated. After World War II, J. Peters showed no interest in returning to Hungary and offering his support to the Communist Party in the establishment of a socialist society. Ultimately, of course, he had no choice but to agree to depart "voluntarily" from the United States and return to the only country that would then welcome him, Hungary. After the first perilous years when he rightly feared arrest by the secret police, J. Peters, now József Péter, apparently found a Communist-dominated Hungary a congenial place to spend the last decades of his life.

In his retirement years the former "red conspirator" may have reached a state of inner contentment, even though the pesky problems relating to the Hiss-Chambers controversy still intruded from time to time. Yet it would not be surprising if, on reflecting over his life, Péter regretted that he had not persevered in his two applications to become a citizen of the United States. In the 1930s, having been removed from the milieu of the Hungarian Federation and other Hungarian-American organizations, Peters had become increasingly

Americanized. He learned to speak a good, colloquial American-English, eagerly read American popular literature and newspapers, and made many American friends. When not on the run from the FBI, he was able to lead a secure, even at times quiet, life in a pleasant suburb of New York City. He enjoyed socializing with his Party friends, some of them quite affluent. In his public statements and testimony before congressional committees or grand juries, the one statement he made that seems most truthful and sincere is: "I like this country." In 1948–49, even with the threat of prosecution for membership in the Communist Party, Peters probably would have preferred to stay in the United States and, if still possible, become a citizen, so long as this did not require that he become a traitor to the CPUSA.

There is considerable pathos in Peters's insistence, in the statement he issued as he departed for Hungary in 1949, that though he had never legally become an American citizen, he regarded his membership in the CPUSA as his "certificate of citizenship." In fact, this and other related public utterances of Peters in 1948–49 suggest that he sincerely believed that his Party work on behalf of American workers and support of the war effort (such as his sponsorship of the pamphlet "America Sings for Victory") proved that he was a loyal and even patriotic American. Conveniently ignoring the crimes he had committed while supervising the secret apparatus and the harm that may have been done to national security, Peters even had the audacity to claim that he was a victim of government persecution. In the late 1940s and 1950s many individuals were in fact harassed and prosecuted simply because they were CPUSA members. But this was not true of J. Peters, who had actually committed serious crimes. Convinced that his best strategy would be, as he himself had written in the *Manual,* to "put up a defiant aggressive Party attitude" and to "accuse the authorities, the bourgeois state, [and] the capitalist society," Peters even tried to portray himself as a champion of civil rights and the American Constitution.

There remains the question of whether J. Peters's Jewish origins had any impact on his political career. As has been seen, Peters never referred to or acknowledged his Jewish past and did not consider it necessary to mention it in his memoir. In his long career in the Communist movement Peters never showed any special interest in Jewish affairs or in combating anti-Semitism. He was, to use an apt phrase coined by the historian Isaac Deutscher, a "non-Jewish Jew," an individual who grew up in a Jewish milieu but as an adult tried to eradicate all traces of his Jewish past. Had he been asked directly if he was a Jew, Goldberger might have responded in the same way that Béla Kun did to that question: "My father was a Jew but I am no longer one, for I became a socialist and a communist."[45] Perhaps, like Leon Trotsky, he believed that becoming a Marxist was such an all-encompassing experience that all traces of his Jewish origins should and would be eliminated.[46]

When the Hungarian Communist government collapsed in 1919, almost all its leaders fled the country and, in time, ended up in Moscow. There they offered their services to the Soviet government and the Comintern. During the interwar period these Hungarian Communist émigrés, most of them "non-Jewish Jews," proved particularly valuable to the Comintern as international cadres involved in propaganda and clandestine activity. These émigrés usually spoke German, the lingua franca of the world Communist movement, and, like most educated Hungarians of that era, already knew or quickly learned other languages. Perhaps because in Hungary many of them had already coped with the problems of name changes and attempts to assimilate, they did not find it difficult to undertake assignments that required the use of many aliases and operating undercover in strange and usually hostile societies. Many of them also seemed to have a knack for creating effective propaganda, using both the spoken and written word.

It was only in 1931 that Sándor Goldberger, then known as Joe Peter, made his way to the Soviet capital city for an extended visit. Quite quickly, Comintern officials decided that here was another Hungarian Communist with the requisite skills and personality to succeed in conspiratorial work. Having received the appropriate training, he returned to the United States and, as J. Peters, embarked on his remarkable career in the secret apparatus. Perhaps Peters noticed and wondered about the presence of so many Hungarians of Jewish origin who were to be found carrying out Comintern missions all across Europe and North America. He was less likely to have been aware of an even more remarkable phenomenon: the large number of Hungarian "non-Jewish Jews" of his generation who in the interwar period were making impressive contributions to American life in the spheres of science, music, philosophy, and entertainment.[47]

J. Peters felt very little affinity with the numerous Hollywood Hungarians, who were usually anti-Communist and passionately devoted to their adopted country. Yet in some ways Peters had a good deal in common with people like Adolph Zukor, Peter Lorre, and Michael Curtiz. They had all grown up in Jewish families in pre–World War I Hungary, had benefited from the excellent Hungarian educational system, and had experienced, with shock and dismay, the virulent anti-Semitism that arose after the war. Perhaps it was only by chance that, for example, the careers of the famous film director Michael Curtiz and J. Peters diverged so greatly, for in fact they had many similar traits, talents, and early ideological proclivities. Curtiz's only surviving Hungarian film, made in Hungary in 1919 during the Béla Kun regime, was a sympathetic treatment of the story of a returning Hungarian POW who becomes a Communist.[48] In 1942, the year in which Peters made his fateful visit to Los Angeles to coordinate the work of Party members and sympathizers, Curtiz directed *Yankee Doodle Dandy* and *Casablanca,* two films that have endured because they portrayed and celebrated the myths and dreams of American society in so compelling a fashion. As he had demonstrated in his *Manual on Organization* and other publications, J. Peters, the "red conspirator," was also adept at creating and manipulating myths, but his objective, unlike that of Curtiz, was to denigrate American democracy and pave the way for a Communist revolution.

Notes

Introduction

1. FBI interview of Nathaniel Weyl, November 15, 1950, in the FBI file of J. Peters, 100-184255. Cited hereafter as "Peters FBI File."

2. Peters, *The Communist Party: A Manual on Organization*.

3. Testimony of John Lautner, Records of the Subversive Activities Control Board, 1950–72 (hereafter RSACB) (Frederick, Md.: University Publications of America, 1988), microfilm reel 17, 9551. See also *Daily Worker*, May 3, 1949.

4. Schrecker, "Before the Rosenbergs," 328. On anti-Communism in the pre–Cold War era, see Sibley, *Red Spies in America*, 242–43.

5. *New York World Telegram*, February 13, 1947.

6. Testimony of Whittaker Chambers, *Hearings before the Committee on Un-American Activities* (hereafter HUAC), 80th Congress, Second Session (Washington, D.C.: Government Printing Office, 1948), 1283; "Budenz Calls Stevens Chief Link with Soviet Secret Police Machine," *New York Times*, September 2, 1948.

7. Chambers, *Witness*, 309.

8. The Senate Judiciary Committee compiled a brief study entitled "The Career of J. Peters." This is found in *Scope of Soviet Activity in the United States*, Hearings before the Subcommittee to Investigate the Administration of the Internal Security and Other Internal Security Laws of the Committee on the Judiciary. United States Senate, 84th Congress, Second Session, part 27 (Washington, D.C.: Government Printing Office, 1956). Cited hereafter as "Career of J. Peters."

9. Klehr, *Heyday of American Communism*, 25.

10. Dallin, *Soviet Espionage*, 412.

11. Weinstein, *Perjury*.

12. For Weinstein's notes on his interview with Peters, see "Interview with Jozsef Peter," in the Allen Weinstein Papers (AWP), box 18, folders 1–4, Hoover Institution, Stanford, California.

13. Weinstein, *Perjury*, 62.

14. Theodore Draper, *The Roots of American Communism* (New York: Viking Press, 1957) and *American Communism and Soviet Russia*.

15. See Isserman, "Three Generations," 539–40; and Haynes and Klehr, *In Denial*, 27–46.

16. Ottanelli, *Communist Party*, 129.

17. Buhle et al., *Encyclopedia of the American Left*.

18. See Browder, *Reminiscences of Earl Browder*, 295. In fact, Browder and several of his family members were deeply complicit in Soviet espionage operations. See Ryan, "Socialist Triumph."

19. Bedacht, "Path of Life."

20. See Bedacht's statement and FBI interrogation in the Sam Tanenhaus Papers, box 36.

21. One of the earliest references to the code of silence and denial can be found in a letter dated January 2, 1931, from the CPUSA Organization Department to district leaders. Records of the Communist Party of the United States of America from the Comintern archive held by the Russian State Archive of Social and Political History (cited hereafter as RGASPI), 515/1/2299 (from the microfilm collection: Files of the Communist Party of the United States, Leiden: IDC Publishers, 2000). These records will hereafter be cited as RCPUSA, followed by file and reel number.

22. Herbert L. Packer, the one scholar who made a thorough study of the testimony of ex-Communists, concluded that, "on a fair appraisal," Lautner was a reliable witness. Packer, *Ex-Communist Witnesses*, 219.

23. For a discussion of the nature and impact of the newly accessible material, see Haynes and Klehr, *In Denial*, 59–80.

24. Klehr, Haynes, and Firsov, *The Secret World of American Communism*; Klehr, Haynes, and Anderson, The *Soviet World of American Communism*; Haynes, Klehr, and Vassiliev, *Spies: The Rise and Fall of the KGB in America*.

25. Klehr et al., *Secret World*, 18–19. See also Isserman, "Notes from Underground."

26. Of particular importance was a brief autobiographical sketch Peters composed for the Comintern in 1931, printed in Klehr et al., *Secret World*, 74–79. My references will be to the original, apparently clearer, copy of this document that I examined. RGASPI, 495/261/5584; henceforth cited as "Comintern Autobiography."

27. On the Venona project, see Haynes and Klehr, *Venona: Decoding Soviet Espionage in America*, and Romerstein and Breindel, *The Venona Secrets: Exposing Soviet Espionage and America's Traitors*.

28. Tanenhaus, *Whittaker Chambers*.

29. For a brief sketch of the career of J. Peters using the newly available archival material, see Haynes and Klehr, *Venona*, 60–62. See also McKnight, *Espionage and the Roots of the Cold War*, 130–32; and Weinstein and Vassiliev, *The Haunted Wood: Soviet Espionage in American*, 38–39, 302–3.

30. Isserman, "Notes from Underground," 853.

31. Buhle, "Spies Everywhere," 190.

32. Ellen Schrecker, *Many are the Crimes: McCarthyism in America* (Boston: Little, Brown, 1998), 132.

33. "Péter József visszaemlékezése" (Memoir of József Péter), Politkatudományi Intézet (Budapest), 867, f. p-235. This document (referred to hereafter as "Péter Memoir") was first used by the Hungarian historian Mária Schmidt. See her *A titkosszolgálatok kulisszái mögött: Hirek, ideológiák és hirszerzö a XX. században* (Behind the Scenes of the Secret Services: Ideas, Ideologies, and Intelligence Agents in the Twentieth Century) (Budapest: XX. Század Intézet, 2006), 90–100. An English translation of an excerpt from the Péter Memoir has been circulating for some time among American historians, and can be found at a Web site devoted to Alger Hiss (The Alger Hiss Story, http://homepages.nyu.edu/~th15/peters.html; accessed July 1, 2010). It must be noted, however, that this excerpt can be misleading because it omits those sections of the Péter Memoir in which he conceded (despite his adamant previous denials) that during visits to Moscow and Berlin he had received training in illegal work and applied this training in the United States.

34. It was while writing a biography of Admiral Miklós Horthy, one of the most important figures in twentieth-century Hungarian history (*Hungary's Admiral on Horseback, Miklós Horthy, 1918–1944*), that I first became acquainted with a cohort of virulently anti-Horthy Communist émigrés living in the Soviet Union and the United States. J. Peters was a prominent member of this cohort.

35. Until recently, Hungarians have been largely unaware of the true identity and Hungarian origins of J. Peters. My article in a Hungarian journal of history in 2007 was the first to bring this to the attention of Hungarian historians. Thomas Sakmyster, "J. Peters (Goldberger Sándor) és az amerikai kommunista mozgalom" (J. Peters, Sándor Goldberger, and the American Communist Movement), *Századok*, no. 1 (2007): 185–202.

Chapter 1. Sándor Goldberger: From Hungary to the New World

1. On Hungarian immigration patterns before and after World War I, see Puskás, *Ties That Bind*, 192–93.

2. Várdy, *Hungarian Americans*, 89. Among these notable Hungarians were Leo Szilard, Eugene Ormandy, Karl Mannheim, and Michael Curtiz.

3. Deák, "Communism's Appeals," 321.

4. Frank, "Pioneers Welcome," 237.

5. Deák, "Communism's Appeals," 321–22.

6. Ignotus, *Hungary*, 93.

7. Perlman, *Bridging Three Worlds*, 44; Pataki, *Jews of Hungary*, 437–38.

8. In northeastern Hungary, Jews often retained Yiddish as their home language, but a Yiddish heavily German in vocabulary and grammar. See Perlman, *Bridging Three Worlds*, 65.

9. Comintern Autobiography, 1.

10. Ibid.

11. Péter Memoir, part 1, p. 1.

12. Comintern Autobiography, 1.

13. Pataki, *Jews of Hungary,* 442.

14. Béla Kohn became Béla Kun; József Schwarz became József Pogány (and later John Pepper).

15. Borsányi, *Life of a Communist Revolutionary,* 8.

16. Comintern Autobiography, 1.

17. Deák, *Beyond Nationalism,* 195.

18. Ibid., 196.

19. J. Peters told this story to Whittaker Chambers and no doubt others. See "The Career of J. Peters," 1487.

20. Ibid.

21. Rang-und Einteilungslisten, k. u. k. Infanterieregiment Nr. 66, October 1918, in Kriegsarchiv (Vienna), AT-OeStA/KA Pers REL.

22. Péter Memoir, part 1, p. 1.

23. Comintern Autobiography, 2.

24. Ibid.; Péter Memoir, part 1, pp. 1–2.

25. Péter Memoir, part 1, p. 2

26. Frank, "Between Red and White," 107.

27. Sakmyster, *Hungary's Admiral,* 29–57.

28. Comintern Autobiography, 1.

29. Magocsi, *Shaping of National Identity,* 195.

30. Comintern Autobiography, 3.

31. Ibid.; Péter Memoir, part 1, p. 3.

32. Péter Memoir, part 1, p. 3.

33. Ibid., p. 2.

34. Cited in Frank, "Patterns," 5.

35. See Goldberger's responses on the passenger manifest for the ship on which he and his family traveled, the Andania, at http:/www.ellisisland.org/search/shipManifest .asp?MID=1287166644025992, accessed August 2, 2010.

36. Ibid.

37. Péter Memoir, part 1, p. 5.

38. A copy of Goldberger's "first papers" can be found in Peters FBI file.

39. Affidavit of Louis Rethy Reed (his Communist Party alias had been Leo Rostovsky), n.d. (but probably 1950 or 1951), Records of the Internal Security Subcommittee of the U.S. Senate, RG646, National Archives (Washington, D.C.). Reed recalled that Goldberger told his new colleagues "some very tall tales" about his exploits in the Hungarian Communist government. Cited hereafter as "Louis Reed Affidavit."

40. FBI interview of Andrew Smith, March 4–5, 1943, in Peters FBI File; John Lautner's testimony, cited in "The Career of J. Peters," 1486.

41. Abt, *Advocate and Activist,* 46.

42. FBI interview of Andrew Smith, March 4–5, 1943, in Peters FBI File; Louis Reed Affidavit.

43. Péter Memoir, part 1, p. 6.

44. Sakmyster, "Hungarian in the Comintern."

45. Péter Memoir, part 1, pp. 6–7.

46. Hungarian Section questionnaire, February 3, 1925, RCPUSA, 515/1/560; and report by Kövess, late 1929, RCPUSA, 515/1/1810.

47. For a perceptive analysis of the problems posed by the ethnic federations, see Storch, "'Their unCommunist Stand.'"

48. "Career of J. Peters," 1487.

49. Minutes of the National Conference of the Hungarian Fractions, December 2–3, 1926, RCPUSA, 515/1/897; "Career of J. Peters," 1487–88.

50. FBI interview of Nathaniel Wehl, November 15, 1950, in Peters FBI File.

51. Sakmyster, "Communist Newspaper," 49–51.

52. Péter's report to the Central Committee, March 26, 1927, RCPUSA, 515/1/1179 (reel 179).

53. Péter Memoir, part 1, p. 9.

54. See the Új Előre article "Horthyellenes tüntetés a szoborleleplezésnél" (Anti-Horthy Demonstration at the Unveiling of the Statue), March 17, 1928; and "Two Nations Unveil Statue of Horthy," New York Times, March 16, 1928.

55. Péter Memoir, part 1, p. 9.

56. Vörös, American Commisar, 186; Sakmyster, "Communist Newspaper," 44–51.

57. "A sajtó bolsevizálása (Bolshevization of the Press), Új Előre, September 22, 1925.

58. Testimony of Louis Rethy Reed (Rostovsky), "The Career of J. Peters," 1487.

59. FBI interview of Andrew Smith, March 4–5, 1943, in Peters FBI File.

60. "Szegények és gazdagok Mikulása" (The St. Nicholas of the Poor and the Rich), December 24, 1925; "Karácsony hetében" (During Christmas Week), December 26, 1926.

61. "Ma" column of September 11, 1926. One wonders if, at least in this column, Péter was writing with tongue in cheek.

62. "Ma" columns of June 25, 1927, and November 3, 1928.

63. For the plan as outlined to the Central Committee, see the February 1, 1927, letter to Charles Ruthenberg, RCPUSA, 515/1/1049. Further details were worked out at a Daily Worker business meeting that Péter attended. March 15, 1927, RCPUSA, 515/1/1019 (reel 75).

64. Comintern Autobiography, 4.

65. Daily Worker, May 5, 1928.

66. Louis Reed Affidavit; report of August 30, 1949, in FBI file of Leo Rostovsky, 100-364414.

67. RCPUSA, 515/1/954 (reel 71).

68. Chambers, Witness, 244. See also Louis Reed Affidavit.

69. See, for example, the list of contributors in the Új Előre of October 10, 1929.

70. Engdahl to Anglo-American Secretariat, July 6, 1928, RCPUSA, 515/1/1250; and memo in Péter's Comintern cadre file, RGASPI, 485/261/5584.

71. See "Ma" column of November 3, 1928; "A világkongresszus vendégségében, a

Vörös Hadsereg nyári táborában" (Visiting the World Congress, At the Summer Camp of the Red Army), November 8, 1928.

72. Louis Kövess to Lovestone, February 18, 1929, box 224, Lovestone Papers, Hoover Institution Archive (Stanford, California).

73. These events are succinctly described in Klehr and Haynes, *American Communist Movement*, 46–50.

74. Memo of Frank Walker, September 30, 1947, Deportation File of Alexander Stevens, Immigration and Naturalization Services, Department of Justice (obtained by the author through a FOIA request to the Homeland Security Agency). Referred to hereafter as Stevens INS File.

75. For Bedacht's comments, see RCPUSA, 515/1/1627 (reel 125).

76. *Daily Worker*, May 24, 1929, 1.

77. In August 1929 he spoke and made a proposal for the first time at a CC meeting, an indication that his spoken English was now good enough to enable him to engage in high-level discussions. Minutes of Central Committee meeting, August 30, 1929, RCPUSA, 515/1/1619 (reel 124).

78. Minutes of March 20, 1930, meeting of the Secretariat, RCPUSA, 515/1/1941 (reel 150). In the minutes Péter is referred to as "Peters."

79. Comintern Autobiography, 5.

80. Malkin, *Return to My Father's House*, 117.

81. District Bulletins of Organization Department, District no. 2, May 14, June 12, June 26, and July 3, 1930, RCPUSA, 515/1/2072 (reel 158).

82. Israel Amter described Péter's approach as one of "military discipline" at a PolBuro meeting, February 20, 1931, RCPUSA, 515/169/2249 (reel 169).

83. Peter later posed this question at a meeting of the Comintern's Anglo-American Secretariat, January 7, 1932, RGASPI, 495/72/168.

84. Ottanelli, *Communist Party*, 43.

85. Peter's speech at meeting of the Anglo-American Secretariat, January 7, 1932, RGASPI, 495/72/168.

86. Ibid.

87. See Peter's description of the use of "shock troops" in a report he composed in November 1931: "Material on Org. Situation CPUSA," RCPUSA, 515/1/2624 (reel 199).

88. J. P., "Getting a Contact," *Party Organizer* no. 6 (May–June 1932), 5.

89. The PolBuro declared the approach of the New York District in this matter to be incorrect, since food raids "must be a real expression of the mood of the masses." See the discussion at the PolBuro meeting of February 16, 1931, RCPUSA, 515/1/2249 (reel 169).

90. Peter's speech at the meeting of the Anglo-American Secretariat, January 7, 1932, RGASPI, 495/72/168.

91. In a later interview with the FBI, the student related this story and admitted that he had carried out Peter's instructions. FBI report of March 16, 1943, NY100-24753, in Peters FBI File.

92. Malkin, *Return to My Father's House*, 143–45.

93. Klehr and Haynes, *American Communist Movement*, 60–62.

94. "Resolution on the New York District," dated March 31, 1931, is found at RCPUSA, 515/1/2252 (reel 170).

95. Comintern Autobiography, 4.

Chapter 2. The Making of J. Peters, 1931–32

1. McKnight, *Espionage,* 56–60. For an explanation of the Commission on Illegal Work and its various proposals in 1925, see RGASPI, 495/27/2.

2. Haynes and Klehr, *Venona,* 60. In a report of the Comintern Commission on Illegal Work, undated but probably from the mid-1920s, it was stated that "the Party [CPUSA] has had very little experience in illegal work." RGASPI, 495/27/17.

3. PolCom minutes of December 3, 1930, RCPUSA, 515/1/1934 (reel 149).

4. Klehr, *Soviet World,* 138.

5. RCPUSA, 515/1/2299 (reel 174).

6. The term "conspirative work" was a somewhat awkward rendering of the Russian word "konspiratsiya," which can simply be translated as "conspiratorial work" or "clandestinity." Mitrokhin, *KGB Lexicon,* 231.

7. Comintern Autobiography, 4.

8. FBI interview of John Lautner, December 6, 1951, Peters FBI file, 100-AQ 16177.

9. Late in 1930 Peter was named secretary of the subcommittee on organization of the National School Committee. RCPUSA, 515/1/2003 (reel 154).

10. Péter Memoir, part 2, p. 17.

11. Peter's report is quoted extensively in a January 1938 memo by a Comrade Belov, Cadre File of William Foster, RGASPI, 495/261/15. See also Barrett, *William Z. Foster,* 187; Johanningsmeier, *Forging American Communism,* 286; and Péter Memoir, part 2, p. 17.

12. Hathaway to Browder, August 26, 1931, RCPUSA, 515/1/2290 (reel 174). Those chosen to become practicants were promising cadre who had considerable experience and were deemed ready for advanced training.

13. FBI interview of John Lautner, June 14, 1954, Peters FBI file, 100-24753.

14. Gitlow, *I Confess,* 316.

15. See Paul Crouch's comments on sexual mores in the CPUSA in chapter 10 of his unpublished memoir, "Broken Chains," Hoover Institution Archive (Stanford), box 17; and Dennis, *Autobiography,* 77.

16. See Hathaway's memo of November 26 reporting on Peter's arrival, RGASPI, 495/261/5584.

17. Louis Reed Affidavit. See also the minutes of the District 2 Bureau, January 30, 1930, RCPUSA, 515/1/2066 (reel 158), where Peter and Manya Reiss are listed among the eleven members of the Org Department.

18. Peter's cadre file, RGASPI, 495/261/5584.

19. Comintern Autobiography, 1–6.

20. "Division of Work among Referents," RGASPI, 495/72/143.

21. "Material on Org. Situation CPUSA," November 6, 1931, CPUSA, 515/1/2624 (reel 199).

22. See reports of February 7, 1932, March 7, 1932, April 3, 1932, June 8, 1932, and June 15, 1932, RCPUSA, 515/1/2623 (reel 199).

23. RGASPI, 495/72/164.

24. "The Growth of the CP United States and Membership Fluctuation," April 3, 1932, RCPUSA, 515/1/2623 (reel 199).

25. RGASPI, 495/72/165.

26. For the power struggle in the CPUSA in this period, see Ryan, *Earl Browder*, 45–56.

27. Transcript of discussion before the Anglo-American Secretariat, RGASPI, 495/72/168. An excerpt from this discussion appears in Klehr, *Soviet World*, 163–64.

28. Comintern PolCom to CPUSA, February 22, 1932, RCPUSA, 515/1/2600 (reel 197).

29. It is also interesting to note that in a report submitted to the Comintern on January 13 and signed by Browder, Stachel, and Hathaway, the American leaders echoed Peter's comments when they acknowledged that the CPUSA had a tendency "to hide the face of the Party and its leading role in the course of mass struggles." RCPUSA, 515/1/2597 (reel 196).

30. Ibid. Also Ryan, *Earl Browder*, 50–51.

31. Minutes of Political Secretariat meetings, February 10 and March 15, 1932, RGASPI, 495/4/170.

32. Zinkin, *Man to be Watched*, 87–88.

33. Smith, *I Was A Soviet Worker*, 62.

34. Foreign Communists serving in Moscow as representatives to the Comintern were provided "living quarters, special food privileges, and a comfortable monthly salary." Gitlow, *I Confess*, 232.

35. Dennis, *Autobiography*, 60.

36. For the responsibilities of the CPUSA representative to the ECCI, see Klehr, *Soviet World*, 200–202.

37. Report on the International Lenin School, March 10, 1932, RCPUSA, 515/1/2602 (reel 197). An unnamed informant later told the FBI that Peters had "generally won the enmity of every Negro." FBI report of March 31, 1944, NY100-247531, Peters FBI File. See also Péter Memoir, part 2, p. 26.

38. Smith, *I Was A Soviet Worker*, 159–62. See also FBI interview of Andrew Smith, March 4–5, 1943, in Peters FBI File.

39. Chambers, *Witness*, 263–64. Several years later the two men discussed this incident and Chambers concluded that Peter's interpretation had been correct, for "Communism may never make truce with the spirit of man."

40. In June 1932, Peter wrote a letter to the editor of *Pravda* in which he introduced Golos. June 3, 1932, RGASPI, 495/72/201.

41. Minutes of Anglo-American Secretariat meeting, June 26, 1932, RCPUSA, 495/72/152.

42. Louis Reed Affidavit; and Rostovsky's FBI FOIA file, 100-364414.

43. At the time, Clarence Hathaway called "Manya" one of the "strong elements" in

an otherwise weak contingent of American women at the Lenin School. See his letter of August 19, 1931, to the Central Committee, RCPUSA, 515/1/2225 (reel 167).

44. On Manya Reiss (Maria Aerova), see Klehr, *Soviet World*, 254–55.

45. Péter Memoir, part 2, p. 26.

46. Peggy Dennis, who was in Moscow in the early 1930s, recalled in her memoirs how she was called before a Comintern committee, the members of which had clearly been studying her cadre file, and recruited for work in the Comintern's "illegal apparatus." Dennis, *Autobiography*, 77–79.

47. On this see the information provided by Walter Krivitsky, a Soviet agent who defected in the late 1930s, to the British Military Intelligence, in Kern, *Walter G. Krivitsky*, 120.

48. Since the records of the OMS are not accessible for research, scholars have been able to draw only a sketchy picture of the history and functioning of this shadowy Comintern agency. Among the most important sources and secondary studies are Krivitsky, *In Stalin's Secret Service*; Kern, *Walter G. Krivitsky*; Rosenfeldt, *Stalin's Secret Chancellery*; and McKnight, *Espionage*.

49. West, *Mask*, 291.

50. The apt phrase is that of Ruth von Mayenburg, *Hotel Lux*, 119.

51. Rosenfeldt, *Stalin's Secret Chancellery*, 27–30.

52. Krivitsky, *In Stalin's Secret Service*, 58–59.

53. RGASPI, 495/27/2.

54. In the 1930s, the British Security Service had an agent who had penetrated deep into the Comintern apparatus in Moscow. See his important report of May 29, 1933, on the OMS training school, Records of the Security Service, KV3/127, National Archives (London).

55. Ibid.

56. Péter Memoir, part 1, p.18; part 2, p. 26.

57. Dallin, *Soviet Espionage*, 92–101. See also Leonard, *Secret Soldiers*, 140.

Chapter 3. J. Peters in the 1930s: The Organization Man

1. An indication of how widespread this practice was can be gained from a perusal of a useful list of pseudonyms compiled by Jeffrey B. Perry in "Pseudonyms: A Reference Aid for Studying American Communist History."

2. Rudy Baker, "Brief on the Work of the CPUSA Secret Apparatus," Klehr, *Secret World*, 92. A Soviet document from 1947 also provides a brief sketch of Peters's career. Here Peters is described as a "worker in the secret apparatus of the CPUSA CC" in 1936–38. Klehr, *Secret World*, 81.

3. Massing, *This Deception*, 154.

4. Peters told Louis Budenz, whom he came to know in the 1930s when the latter served as editor of the *Daily Worker*, that he was "the link—the liaison—between the Soviet secret police and the Comintern apparatus here." Budenz, *Men Without Faces*, 247. On the basis of his dealings with Peters, James S. Glaser, a managing editor of the *Daily Worker*

in the mid-1930s, also became convinced that he was a representative of the Comintern. FBI interview of Glaser, January 27, 1940, NY 100-24753, in Peters FBI File.

5. See unsigned letter of April 22, 1932 (in German), RCPUSA, 515/1/2616 (reel 198).

6. Testimony of Louis Budenz, RSACB, reel 1, 0879.

7. On one occasion Peters gently chided one of his colleagues, Louis Budenz, who had used an incorrect name when greeting him. Later Budenz told his wife of the incident: "I am getting dizzy trying to keep Peters's name before me." Testimony of Louis Budenz, August 24, 1947, HUAC, "Hearings Regarding Communist Espionage in the United States Government" (Washington, D.C.: Government Printing Office, 1948), 1041.

8. Ibid. Budenz, *This Is My Story*, 139.

9. According to Comintern practice, the leader of the "illegal apparatus" in each Communist Party was invariably a member of the Central Committee. Report of British agent on the Comintern, KV#/127, National Archives (London).

10. Weinstein, "Interview with Jozsef Peter," AWP, 5.

11. Péter Memoir, part 1, p. 12.

12. PolCom to CPUSA, May 31, 1932, RCPUSA, 515/1/2600 (reel 179).

13. Péter Memoir, part 2, p. 30.

14. Peters's report of September 21, 1932, 515/1/3132 (reel 244).

15. Keeran, *Communist Party*, 15–20.

16. See, for example, Peters's letter to F. Brown, November 3, 1933, RCPUSA, 515/1/3150 (reel 246).

17. Péter Memoir, part 2, p. 30.

18. Peters report of August 30, 1932, 515/1/2654 (reel 204).

19. See minutes of the Secretariat, September 6 and 29, 1932, RCPUSA, 515/1/2695 (reel 209).

20. Peters to "Dear Comrades," September 23, 1932, RCPUSA, 515/1/2713 (reel 212).

21. For evidence of a more systematic approach to membership records, see organizational records from 1932–33, RCPUSA, 515/1/3146 (reel 246).

22. See his article "Organizational Problems in the Light of the Open Letter"; a two-part article entitled "Strike Wave Is Opportunity to Recruit Party Members"; and "A Study of Fluctuation in the Chicago District."

23. Peters's speech of July 30, 1933, RCPUSA, 515/1/3105.

24. For a review of the Party's approach to the problem of membership fluctuation, see Alperin, "Organization in the Communist Party," 194–211.

25. Klehr, *American Communist Movement*, 73.

26. Stachel at Special Conference on Organization, February 22, 1937, RCPUSA, 515/1/4069 (reel 306).

27. PolBuro meeting of July 19, 1933, RCPUSA, 515/1/3131 (reel 244).

28. At the Eighth National Convention in April 1934 he served as both the reporter (along with Browder and Stachel) and as chairman of the Org Commission. RCPUSA, 515/1/3414 (reel 263) and 515/1/3447 (reel 269).

29. Budenz, *Men Without Faces*, 102.

30. Testimony of John Lautner, who was asked to write autobiographies every two or three years. RSACB, reel 17, 9560-9561. James Glaser, a journalist who entered the Party in 1934 as managing editor of the *Daily Worker*, was required to submit his "life story" to J. Peters for review. FBI interview of Glaser, January 27, 1940, NY 100-24753, in Peters FBI File.

31. When he returned in 1933 from Russia, where he had attended the International Lenin School, Charles H. White reported to Peters, who assigned him to lecture to Party members in Poughkeepsie, New York. "Stevens Is Called Communist 'Boss' at Alien Hearing," *New York Times*, September 1, 1948.

32. Peters, *Manual*,112; and Vörös, *American Commisar*, 450–51.

33. Interview of James Glaser, former editor of the *Daily Worker*, June 1940, Peters FBI File. See also the testimony of a well-informed former CPUSA member, June 8, 1942, FBI, 65-10519, in Peters FBI File.

34. The *Daily Worker* reported in June 1936 that "Comrade Peters has just finished an interesting day of classes on Party organization." Jim Hill, "From the Krumbein Training School," June 8, 1936, p. 5.

35. William Odell Nowell claimed that Peters had mentioned the idea of writing such a pamphlet during one of their conversations in Moscow in 1932. See Nowell's testimony in RSACB, reel 10, 2617.

36. A previous pamphlet, published in 1928, focused on organization only at the lower levels. See Jenks, *Communist Nucleus*.

37. Peters, "Organizational Structure of the Party."

38. *Daily Worker*, August 19, 1935, 5; Peters, *Manual*, 3.

39. The full text of Peters's *Manual* is available online at http://www.marxists.org/history/usa/parties/cpusa/1935/07/organisers-manual/index.htm (accessed July 18, 2010).

40. Tim Rees and Andrew Thorpe, eds., *International Communism and the Communist International, 1919-43* (Manchester: Manchester University Press, 1998), 4–5; Ottanelli, *Communist Party*, 18–19.

41. Peters did not claim that this pledge was regularly taken by all new members, and it is unclear whether in fact it was regularly required of new members. In her account of her experience as an informant for the FBI, Angela Calomiris recalled that at her induction into the Party in 1942, the pledge was read to her. Angela Calomiris, *Masquerade: Undercover for the F.B.I.* (Philadelphia: Lippincott, 1950), 270.

42. Abt, *Advocate and Activist*, 46.

43. *Party Organizer* 8, no. 10 (October 1935): 24–29.

44. This was true, for example, of the Hungarian newspaper *Új Előre*. See Sakmyster, "Communist Newspaper," 61–65.

45. Minutes of Eighth National Convention, April 3–7, 1934, RCPUSA, 515/1/3414 (reel 263).

46. Ottanelli, *Communist Party*, 49–80.

47. "5 Thousand Reds Battle with Socialists at Garden Rally," *New York Times*, February 17, 1934, 1. See also Klehr, *American Communist Movement*, 70–71; and Ottanelli, *Communist Party*, 56–57.

48. Barrett, *William Z. Foster*, 178–80.

49. Information provided by an informant in a report on "Communist Activities," December 5, 1940, FBI report 39-915-659, in Peters FBI File.

50. Testimony of Lou Rosser, December 1, 1953, J. Peters file, Internal Security Subcommittee of the U.S. Senate, RG46 (National Archives); testimony of William Odell Nowell, RSACB, reel 10, 2390. John Lautner recalled using the *Manual* in classes he taught as late as the mid-1940s. Testimony of Lautner, RSACB, reel 17, 9549-50.

51. District 23 (which included Kentucky) ordered fifty copies in October. See literature order of District 23, October 11, 1935, 515/1/3898 (reel 298).

52. Charney, *Long Journey*, 31.

53. Péter Memoir, part 2, p. 15; Weinstein, "Interview with Jozsef Peter," AWP, 3.

54. Ottanelli, *Communist Party*, 77–81; Klehr, *American Communist Movement*, 77–79.

55. Klehr, *American Communist Movement*, 84.

56. Literature Department report, February 5, 1936, RCPUSA, 515/1/3989 (reel 303).

57. Testimony of an ex-Communist who was present at the meeting, Peters INS hearing. The discussion of Peters's pamphlet does not appear in the surviving minutes of PolCom meetings in the RCPUSA collection. Records of PolCom meetings from 1935 on are increasingly sketchy and sporadic.

58. Literature Department report, February 5, 1936, RCPUSA, 515/1/3989 (reel 303).

59. The offer came from Marian Abt. See Abt, *Advocate and Activist*, 46.

60. Charney, *Long Journey*, 94.

61. FBI report of October 10, 1940, 39-915-307X3, in Peters FBI File.

62. Weinstein, "Interview with Jozsef Peter," AWP, 4.

63. Upon his return from service in the Abraham Lincoln Brigade in Spain, Sándor Vörös, who had known Peters from his days in the Hungarian Buro, reported to him at CPUSA headquarters and was surprised to find that he had grown a potbelly. Vörös, *American Commisar*, 451.

64. In a letter to "Edwards" on November 3, 1933, Peters wrote: "All your things are in my place. Write to me whether your original proposal about the apartment stands or not." RCPUSA, 515/1/3150 (reel 246).

65. For Sophie Silver/Ann Peters, see the affidavit of John Lautner, J. Peters file, Internal Security Subcommittee of the U.S. Senate, National Archives, RG46; Abt, *Advocate and Activist, 178*; and Peters FBI File.

Chapter 4. J. Peters and the Secret Apparatus

1. Agenda for CC meeting of August 30, 1932, RCPUSA, 515/1/2653 (reel 204).

2. A 1938 CPUSA report to the Comintern named as one of Peters's major successes as director of the secret apparatus the "satisfactory and secure safeguarding" of Party membership rolls and of the most confidential of Central Committee records. Rudy Baker, "Brief on the Work of the CPUSA Secret Apparatus," in Klehr, *Secret World*, 87.

3. Org Commission to "Dear Friends," November 2, 1934, RCPUSA, 515/1/3459, in Klehr, *Secret World*, 35.

4. Klehr, *Secret World*, 35–36. See also an undated document entitled "Instructions for Special Mailing," attached to an FBI report dated June 8, 1942, 65-10519, Peters FBI File. For the use of mail drops in the Baltimore district, see Pedersen, *Communist Party in Maryland*, 72.

5. For an explanation of this cipher system as used in the California district, see a document describing steps needed to implement the illegal apparatus in District 13. April 24, 1933, RCPUSA, 515/1/3296, in Klehr, *Secret World*, 38. For a fuller description of the book cipher used by Peters, see the testimony of Paul Crouch, RSACB, reel 11, 3134.

6. FBI interview of an informant, February 26, 1943, 100-24753, in Peters FBI file. The same informant regarded Peters as "the highest and best versed instructor," on a level with Earl Browder and Robert Minor.

7. In this Peters was heeding the advice of B. Vassiliev, "Problem of Organization," 15: "All Communist Parties must without fail have an extensive apparatus for the publication of illegal Party literature: printing plant, various kinds of rotary machines, copying machines, mimeographs, and simple hectographs in order to publish illegal literature, newspapers, leaflets, etc."

8. In his National Training School classes Peters taught students how to operate the stencil machines and mimeographs. FBI interview of an informant, February 26, 1943, 100-24753, in Peters FBI file.

9. Peters's speech, which lasted one and one half hours, is found in the minutes of the plenum of January 16–17, 1934, RCPUSA, 515/1/3427 (reel 265).

10. B. Vassiliev had warned that Communist parties in Western Europe or North America, which enjoyed what seemed to be great "democratic freedom" to organize and publish literature, should not be lulled into a false feeling of security. Vassiliev, "Problem of Organization," 28.

11. J. Peters, "Strengthen the Fighting Ability of the Party"; Peters's speech at CC plenum, RCPUSA, 515/1/3427 (reel 265).

12. Peters's speech at CC plenum.

13. Peters, "Mass Defense," 30.

14. Peters's speech at CC plenum; J. Peters, "Strengthen the Fighting Ability," 26.

15. J. Peters, "Strengthen the Fighting Ability," 26.

16. Klehr, *Secret World*, 36.

17. Memorandum on "special preparations for illegality" (undated, but probably May 1933), RCPUSA, 515/1/3296 (reel 255). See also reports from the districts on their efforts to build the "illegal apparatus," RCPUSA, 515/1/3547 (reel 276); 515/1/3540 (reel 276).

18. Crouch told his story on several occasions, most fully in RSACB, reel 11, 3128–3136; and in an unpublished manuscript, "Brief History of the Communist Party in North and South Carolina," Paul Crouch Papers, box 1, Hoover Institution Archives (Stanford, Calif.).

19. For implementation of the "illegal apparatus" in Buffalo, Pittsburgh, and New York City, see RCPUSA, 515/1/3296 (reel 255), 515/1/3547 (reel 276); 515/1/3540 (reel 276); and 515/1/2811 (reel 294).

20. Klehr, *Secret World*, 34.

21. Letter to Org Commission from District 17, December 10, 1935, RCPUSA, 515/1/3885.

22. See, for example, a letter (July 13, 1935) of Paul Crouch to the Org Commission in which he refers to an attached coded message (not found) in which he supplied the name and background of a local Party member who was moving to another country and was available to do Party work. RCPUSA, 515/1/3882 (reel 298). Manning Johnson also recalled that he frequently used the book cipher when communicating with J. Peters and the Org Commission. RSACB, reel 13, 5240-5245.

23. Testimony of John Lautner, RSACB, part 1, reel 17, 9209.

24. Sibley, *Red Spies in America*, 19–20, 45.

25. Isserman, "Notes from Underground," 851.

26. In an article he wrote in 1934, Peters did assert that "only with mass agitation and organized self-defense groups can they [the Communist Party] fight back the attacks of the armed forces, either legal or extra-legal" ("Mass Defense," 31). It is not clear whether the phrase "legal or extra-legal" was meant by Peters to refer to the nature of the attacks by the armed forces or the methods used to counter these attacks.

27. Peters's letter to AWM (A. W. Mills), March 21, 1933, RCPUSA, 515/1/3146 (reel 246). This episode is fully discussed in Pedersen, *Communist Party in Maryland*, 71–72.

28. John Lautner later testified that Peters "made frequent trips to Washington and these things just got around among leading party functionaries, that J. Peters was in charge of that segment of the Washington organization which is in the Government" ("Career of J. Peters," 1501).

29. Benjamin Gitlow, an important leader of the Party in the 1920s, later declared that Party leaders "greatly cherished every opportunity to be of service to the G.P.U., aid its work, and be in its confidence" (*I Confess*, 303).

30. Romerstein and Breindel, *Venona Secrets*, 69, 111. On Bedacht, see Chambers, "Faking of Americans," part 1, pp. 17–19; and Gitlow, *Whole of Their Lives*, 146.

31. Maya and Nadezhda Ulanovskaya, *Istoriya Odnot Semyi* (One Family's Story), 95–104. In this memoir, Nadezhda Ulanovskaya confirmed the accuracy of Whittaker Chambers's account of the way in which he was recruited to work for Soviet intelligence. In his unpublished memoirs Bedacht did not mention any ties to Soviet intelligence agencies and denied that there was such a thing as a CPUSA secret or underground apparatus. Bedacht, "On the Path of Life," 323. When questioned by a federal grand jury in 1949, Bedacht stated categorically: "I have never had anything to do with underground work, with illegal work." Testimony of Max Bedacht, January 11, 1949, "Transcripts of Grand Jury Testimony in the Alger Hiss Case," 5174.

32. On Mikhelson-Manuilov, whose years of service in the United States (1933–38) coincided almost exactly with Peters's most active years in the secret apparatus, see Klehr, *Soviet World*, 186–87; and Haynes and Klehr, *Venona*, 24.

33. On Bedacht's trip to Moscow, see RCPUSA, 515/1/3150 (reel 244).

34. FBI memorandum on Chambers's statements concerning Peters, p. 10, compiled in April 1949, Peters FBI File.

35. Ibid. Chambers asked his GRU handler, Ulrich (Alexander Ulanovskaya) whether he should report to Bedacht or Peters. Ulrich replied: "When dealing with wolves, choose the one who has eaten." This presumably meant Bedacht, but by this time he had already "passed out of the picture."

36. Weinstein and Vassiliev, *Haunted Wood*, 304, 310. See also Ryan, "Socialist Triumph," 125–42.

37. Rudy Baker mentioned Weiner's secret fund in his report on the secret apparatus in 1939, and it is likely this was a continuation of the practice during Peters's tenure. See Klehr, *Secret World*, 90. Baker's report confirms that Louis Budenz was accurate when he later identified Weiner as the supervisor of a secret fund that was used for conspiratorial operations. See Budenz's testimony on June 9, 1949, United States Senate, *Hearings before the Subcommittee on Immigration and Naturalization of the Committee on the Judiciary*, 81st Congress (Washington, D.C.: Government Printing Office, 1950), 221–25.

38. Baker, "Brief on the Work of the CPUSA Secret Apparatus," in Klehr, *Secret World*, 87.

39. One such OMS agent, given the code name "Roberts" for his work in the United States, arrived in the fall of 1935. Intercepted Comintern radio message, Moscow to United States, October 24, 1935, MASK collection, National Cryptologic Museum (Fort Meade, Md.). Peters facilitated the work of Roberts, whose primary mission seems to have been to infiltrate Trotskyite groups. Budenz, *This Is My Story*, 254–62.

40. Klehr, *Secret World*, 87.

41. FBI blind memo of August 3, 1938, 61-7559-3008, in Peters FBI File. There is evidence that Feierabend was again engaging in "special work" in 1936. Klehr, *Secret World*, 297. See also "Soviet Agent Held in Passport Fraud," *New York Times*, April 12, 1933, 13.

42. Rosenfeldt, *Stalin's Secret Chancellery*, 29–30; Klehr, *Heyday*, 159. A special Comintern department was created in 1933 to provide training in illegal party work and to "instruct personnel on illegal work in the army." McKnight, *Espionage*, 60.

43. On the GRU's interest in covert penetration of the armed forces, see Kern, *MI5 Debriefing*, 186–87. This book deals with the debriefing of Walter Krivitsky by the British military intelligence agency.

44. Minutes of the CC plenum (January 16–17, 1934), RCPUSA, 515/1/3427 (reel 265).

45. For the meeting at Camp Unity in June 1935, see the testimony of John Lautner, RSACB, 9195 (reel 17). When rumors later spread of a Communist training school for maritime saboteurs, Camp Unity became known in anti-Communist circles as the "Red Annapolis."

46. Peters, "Mass Defense," 30.

47. Serge Jarama (Robert Gladnick), "I Was a Fifth Columnist," 5–7. Some "anti-militarist" work of this kind had apparently been conducted in the 1920s by Paul Crouch, under the supervision of Max Bedacht. See Romerstein and Levchenko, *KGB against the "Main Enemy,"* 64–65.

48. In 1933, the Young Communist League made available to those involved in the anti-militarist operation a "Manual for Work in the National Guard." The language of this six- page document closely resembles that used by Peters at the time, and he may well have been the author. RCPUSA, 515/1/3331 (reel 257).

49. Jarama (Gladnick), *I Was a Fifth Columnist*, 6.

50. Several sailors in the U.S. Navy attended the course, in civilian clothes, while on furlough in June 1934. Testimony of Robert Gladnick (no date), J. Peters File, Internal Subcommittee of the United States Senate, RG46. National Archives (Washington, D.C.).

51. Velson worked at the Brooklyn Navy Yard from 1931 to 1938. At some point in the late 1930s, he began, apparently under Peters's supervision, to provide assistance to the GRU in matters relating to naval intelligence. Several Soviet intelligence messages from World War II, deciphered by American military cryptographers as part of the Venona Project, document Velson's connection to the GRU. Haynes and Klehr, *Venona*, 185–86.

52. FBI interview of "confidential informant" (Gladnick), December 20, 1948, 65-694-29, in Peters FBI File. In an earlier interview Gladnick had stated that he knew a lot about Peters's underground work but he would never testify about this publicly because he feared for his life. FBI report of November 4, 1948, NY100-9448.

53. Sibley, *Red Spies in America*, 34–35 ; Weinstein, *Perjury*, 210; FBI memorandum on Chambers's statements concerning J. Peters, p. 24, compiled in April 1949, Peters FBI File.

54. Romerstein and Levchenko, *KGB against the "Main Enemy,"* 17.

55. Gladnick, "I Was a Fifth Columnist," 7.

56. Chambers, "Faking of Americans," part 2, p. 7.

57. On this, see Benjamin Gitlow's testimony about Communist production and use of false passports. United States Congress, House of Representatives, *Hearings before the Committee on Un-American Activities*, 4677–79; and Dallin, *Soviet Espionage*, 92–101.

58. Haynes and Klehr, *Venona*, 79.

59. For Lovestone's knowledge and use of illegal passports, see Klehr, *Secret World*, 131. On Bedacht, see Chambers, "Faking of Americans," part 1, p. 19.

60. Daniel P. Hornstein, *Arthur Ewert: A Life for the Comintern* (Lanham, Md.: University Press of America, 1993), 149–50.

61. Testimony of Joseph Zach Kornfeder, RSACB, reel 9, 412–13; Haynes and Klehr, *Venona*, 80.

62. Chambers, "Faking of Americans," part 1, p. 17.

63. For example, John Lautner, a leader in the Hungarian Bureau and district organizer in West Virginia from 1936, was often asked by Peters to supply citizenship papers and birth certificates. Lautner did so on several occasions. Lautner's testimony, RSACB, reel 17, 9555.

64. Chambers, "Faking of Americans," part 2, p. 15. The following is based for the most part on Chambers's unpublished 1939 article.

65. Testimony of John Lautner, RSACB, reel 17, 9555.

66. Chambers, "Faking of Americans," part 1, p. 6. Chambers, *Witness*, 399.

67. Peters also used his Atlantic City source to provide Whittaker Chambers and William Weiner (Wiener), his colleague in the Organization Buro, with passports. See "Birth Record Shown in Wiener's Trial. U.S. Contends Entry in Atlantic City Ledger is Forgery," *New York Times*, February 10, 1940, 7; and Chambers, *Witness*, 356.

68. Among them was the Hungarian Louis Gibarti (László Dobos), whom Peters assisted in 1937 when he needed to travel to France. FBI interview of Louis Gibarti, January 5, 1951, 66-6629, in Peters FBI File.

69. The following is based, except where otherwise indicated, on Chambers, "Faking of Americans," part 1, pp. 17–22.

70. The GRU budget for overseas intelligence work was substantial in this period, in fact twice as large as that of the OGPU. Suvorov, *Inside Soviet Military Intelligence*, 17–18.

71. OGPU report of January 1, 1933, Vassiliev Notebooks (VN), "White Notebook" no. 1, p. 140.

72. Chambers, "Faking of Americans," part 1, p. 22.

73. Ibid., 23.

74. Tanenhaus, *Whittaker Chambers*, 127–28.

75. The following is based on Massing, *This Deception*, 158–59. Massing also told her story, with slight variations, to the FBI. Interview of Hede Massing, July 8, 1949, in Peters FBI File.

76. Massing, *This Deception*, 159.

77. Akhmerov later reported to the Moscow center that "when the need arises for us in cases involving . . . certificates of naturalization, we resort to this 'Peter' for help." Akhmerov's report of May 18, 1936, VN, "Yellow Notebook" no. 2, p. 6. In this report he mentioned that this was the same "Peter" whom "I described to you orally when I was home."

78. FBI interview of Hede Massing, July 8, 1949, in Peters FBI File.

79. Massing, *This Deception*, 159.

80. Ibid.

81. This is based on a brief autobiographical statement written by Fitzgerald for the NKVD's New York station, February 17, 1945, VN, "Yellow Notebook," no. 2, p. 63. See also Weinstein and Vassiliev, *Haunted Wood*, 261–62; Haynes and Klehr, *Venona*, 117–19.

82. FBI interview of Sylvia (Castleton) Weyl (the name is blacked out on the FOIA copy, but internal evidence makes the identity as Sylvia Weyl certain), December 15, 1950, 100-184255, in Peters FBI File. Like her husband Nathaniel Weyl, Sylvia Weyl, for a time organizational secretary in the Texas/Oklahoma district, worked closely with Browder, Peters, and other Party leaders. Once Field was working with Peters, the latter ordered him not to contact Sylvia Weyl again, a step she interpreted as a way "to get Fred Field into the habit of obeying orders without question." Letter of Nathaniel Weyl to Hope Hale Davis, August 20, 1979, Hope Hale Davis Papers, Schlesinger Library, Harvard University.

83. Chambers, *Witness*, 382. In his autobiography, Field admitted that he had been an active member of the Communist Party, but did not mention J. Peters or any con-

nection with the secret apparatus (Field, *From Right to Left*). However, he told defense lawyers in the Alger Hiss trial that he knew J. Peters well, had invited him to his home, and called him "Pete." Undated memorandum, Hiss Defense Files, in AWP, 22/6.

84. Péter Memoir, part 2, p. 31.

85. One of Peters's operatives in the secret apparatus, John Sherman, once expressed the desire to meet Agnes Smedley, who was residing in New York at that time. Peters persuaded Smedley to meet him, hinting that he was an important underground figure. Later Smedley expressed disappointment, since she had expected that she would be meeting Gerhardt Eisler. FBI memorandum on Chambers's statements concerning J. Peters, p. 11, compiled in April 1949, Peters FBI File.

86. Tanenhaus, *Whittaker Chambers*, 100.

87. Abt, *Advocate and Activist*, 78; Caute, *Joseph Losey*, 48–49. The mutual friend was Lewis Fraad, a medical doctor and CP member, who had been James Proctor's roommate in college. When Peters registered for the draft in 1942, he listed Dr. L. Fraad as the person who "will always know your address." Peters's registration form (under the name Alexander Stevens) is in FBI report 100-184255-257, in Peters FBI File.

88. Allen Weinstein's interview of Maxim Lieber, May 10, 1975, in AWP, box 69. According to Whittaker Chambers, Peters knew Lieber "from earlier days in the American Communist Party" (*Witness*, 44). On Lieber, see Haynes et al., *Spies*, 16.

89. FBI interview of Sylvia (Castleton) Weyl, December 15, 1950, 100-184255, in Peters FBI File.

90. Whittaker Chambers described this business front in an interview with the FBI, 100-24753 in Peters FBI File.

91. Péter Memoir, part 2, p. 31.

Chapter 5. Whittaker Chambers and the "Washington Set-up"

1. In fact, he later insisted to the American historian Allan Weinstein that he had been to Washington only one time in his life, to join in the Bonus March in 1932. Weinstein, "Interview with Jozsef Peter," AWP, 2.

2. Testimony of John Lautner, January 24, 1952, RSACB, reel 17, 9554-59. In 1937 or 1938 Peters apparently also told Louis Budenz, then editor of the *Daily Worker*, that he was involved in work designed to infiltrate the government in Washington and to persuade government workers to cooperate with Soviet intelligence agencies. Interview of Louis Budenz, August 27, 1948, Peters INS File.

3. Shover, "Communist Party," 254.

4. Latham, *Communist Controversy*, 76.

5. On "romantic anti-fascism" see Weinstein, *Perjury*, 123; and Isserman, "Disloyalty," 4.

6. Minutes of May 15, 1933, PolBuro meeting, RCPUSA, 515/1/3131 (reel 244). Ware also attended PolBuro meetings on November 2 and 30, at which time he would have been able to report to Peters and Browder on the successful launching of the Washington underground group. RCPUSA, 515/1/3132/3133 (reels 244 and 245).

7. Undated KGB Moscow Center memorandum (likely 1946), VN, "White Notebook," no. 2, p. 41. See also Weinstein and Vassiliev, *Haunted Wood*, 302.

8. Peters's position seemed to be similar to that of Jacob Golos, who worked with the OGPU/NKVD in the 1930s and 1940s. On the basis of their relationship with him, NKVD operatives described Golos's position as follows: "'Helmsman' [Browder] did not interfere in his affairs at all and did not control his work. 'Sound' [Golos] was able to manage his affairs as he wished." Report on NKVD activity in the United States, 1942–44, an NKVD report of V. M. Merkulov, August, 1944, VN, "White Notebook" no. 1, p. 10.

9. Weyl, *Encounters*, 28.

10. Abt, *Advocate and Activist*, 42.

11. Weyl, *Encounters*, 28–29; Weyl, "I Was in a Communist Unit," 23.

12. For an excellent discussion of the development of the Ware group, see Haynes and Klehr, *Venona*, 62–67.

13. One other person, John Donovan, may also have been present, but if so he soon proved erratic and unreliable and was quietly removed from the group. Weyl, *Encounters*, 31. In 1953, Donovan admitted that he had attended CP meetings in 1934 in Washington. Among those he remembered seeing at some of these meetings were Hal Ware, Nathaniel Weyl, Henry Collins, and Victor Perlo. Testimony of John L. Donovan, May 6, 1953, Executive Sessions of the Senate Permanent Subcommittee on Investigations of the Committee on Government Operations, vol. 2 (Washington, D.C.: Government Printing Office, 2003), http://www.gpo.gov/congress/senate/mccarthy/83870.html (accessed July 13, 2010). Cited hereafter as "Testimony of John Donovan."

14. There remains some uncertainty about the extent to which Donald Hiss participated in the Ware group. He is the only one identified by Whittaker Chambers for whom there is no confirming evidence from other sources. Chambers, *Witness*, 469.

15. Weyl, *Encounters*, 30; Chambers, *Witness*, 342–43.

16. Josephine Herbst, the wife of John Hermann, later remembered how members of the Ware group "took pride in their sense of conspiracy." Weinstein, *Perjury*, 121.

17. Davis, *Great Day Coming*, 329. This secrecy was in compliance with Comintern guidelines outlined in "Report of Comintern Commission on Illegal Work" (ca. 1925) RGASPI, 495/27/2, p. 72.

18. For example, the wife of Charles Kramer was used by Peters as a courier and in other positions in the Washington underground and in New York. See the autobiographical statement of Charles Kramer (using the cover name "Mole") received by the NKVD on March 25, 1945, in VN, "White Notebook" no. 3, p. 90.

19. Isserman, "Disloyalty," 2.

20. In his memoir Peters admitted, in what may have been an allusion to the Ware group, that one of his Party responsibilities was to organize "semi-legal" groups of Communists and Party sympathizers and to give them instruction in Marxism. Péter Memoir, part 2, p. 31.

21. FBI interview of Hope Hale Davis, March 3, 1954, 100-29100, in Peters FBI File. Nathaniel Weyl stated that he had not seen Peters at any of the Ware group meetings he attended before he left Washington in the summer of 1934. Weyl's letter to Allen Weinstein, April 14, 1978, in AWP, box 116, folder 13.

22. "Steve Lapin" was one of the aliases Peters used in this period. James Glaser, the managing editor of the *Daily Worker* in the mid-1930s, knew Peters by this name. Undated FBI interview (probably 1940) of James Glaser, Peters FBI File.

23. Louis Budenz, an editor of the *Daily Worker* in the mid-1930s, later recalled that Peters had a kind of permanent "artificial smile," like a Cheshire cat. "Career of J. Peters," 1486.

24. In an autobiographical statement written in 1945, Kramer described how he and Peters had become close personal friends and "discussed all matters pertaining to [special] work." Kramer's statement of March 25, 1945, VN, "White Notebook" no. 3, p. 92.

25. Weyl, *Encounters*, 35; Davis, *Great Day Coming*, 329–30.

26. Weinstein, *Perjury*, 118–19.

27. Weyl, *Encounters*, 28–29.

28. Abt, *Advocate and Activist*, 41–42.

29. Letter of Davis to Nathaniel Weyl, July 21, 1979, in Nathaniel Weyl Papers, box 2, Hoover Institution Archive.

30. Weinstein, *Perjury*, 121; Chambers, *Witness*, 342.

31. Schlesinger Jr., *Coming of the New Deal*, 40.

32. Even so, some of his comrades in the Organization Bureau seemed to resent the fact that Peters spent so much time on projects in the secret apparatus and not enough on his regular work. In late 1933, Peters was upbraided for not meeting deadlines and was warned not to offer any "flimsy explanations" or "back talk." Memo of December 29, 1933, from W. W. (William Weiner) to Peters, RCPUSA, 515/1/3150 (reel 286).

33. Chambers, *Witness*, 32.

34. Chambers, "Faking of Americans," part 1, p. 21.

35. Massing, *This Deception*, 122.

36. Chambers related this incident in FBI interviews, April 4, 1949, 62-31468-23, and April 25, 1949, 100-92303-29, in Peters FBI File.

37. Chambers, FBI interview, April 25, 1949, 100-92303-29.

38. FBI interviews of one of the workers, Clayton B. Darrow, in May and June 1934, 100-354455-17, in Peters FBI File.

39. On another occasion in late 1933 or early 1934, Peters told Chambers that Ned Sparks, then a Party organizer in Boston, had some contacts at the Torpedo Base in Narragansett Bay. Peters suggested that Chambers get in contact with Sparks, but this never came about. FBI report of April 4, 1949, 62-31468-23, in Peters FBI File.

40. On the limitations and failings of the OGPU/NKVD in the United States in the early 1930s, see Haynes et al., *Spies*, 483–500, 534–38.

41. Undated NKVD memorandum (likely 1946), VN, "White Notebook," no. 2, p. 41.

42. Ibid., p. 33.

43. Leonard, *Secret Soldiers*, 119.

44. Chambers, *Witness*, 315.

45. FBI memorandum on Chambers's statements concerning J. Peters, p. 10, compiled in April 1949, Peters FBI File.

46. Ibid., p. 13.

47. Chambers, *Witness*, 336–37.

48. Weyl, *Encounters*, 29–30.

49. Chambers, *Witness*, 335–36.

50. Ibid., 338–39.

51. Weinstein and Vassiliev, *Haunted Wood*, 36.

52. Chambers, *Witness*, 354. The identity of Chambers's new handler has long been a mystery. Some historians have assumed that he must have been Iskhak Akhmerov, an NKVD officer who arrived in the United States in April 1934 and often used the cover name "Bill." See Weinstein and Vassiliev, *Haunted Wood*, 35. But the known facts about Akhmerov and his subsequent career as the chief NKVD illegal in the United States demonstrate that he could not have been the Soviet operative who became Chambers's handler. For an interesting speculation on this question, see H. B. Laes, "Who was Bill?" at http://essaysonespionage.blogspot.com (accessed July 13, 2010).

53. Chambers, *Witness*, 354; and FBI memorandum on Chambers's statements concerning J. Peters, p. 10, compiled in April 1949, Peters FBI File.

54. Chambers, *Witness*, 354.

55. Ibid., 354–55. For a fuller description of the planning for the London apparatus, see Tanenhaus, *Whittaker Chambers*, 99–100; and Weinstein, *Perjury*, 111.

56. Chambers, *Witness*, 364.

57. In 1975, Lieber confirmed that he had agreed to serve as a "cover" for the newspaper syndicate: "Chambers and Chase [Sherman] and I set up that syndicate on orders from J. Peter." Allen Weinstein's interview of Maxim Lieber, May 10, 1975, in AWP, box 69. See also Weinstein, *Perjury*, 111–12.

58. Tanenhaus, *Whittaker Chambers*, 100–101; Weinstein, *Perjury*, 112–13. On Chambers's request for help from Peters to find a suitable person to be Sherman's assistant, see FBI interview of Chambers, November 11, 1951, 65-59091-89.

59. Chambers, *Witness*, 357. Chambers later recalled that in this period the "activities for Bill and those in Washington were so intermingled that I am unable to be specific as to dates or chronological order." FBI memorandum on Chambers's statements concerning Peters, p. 12, compiled in April 1949, Peters FBI File.

60. Murphy, "Memorandum of Conversation."

61. Hope Hale Davis letter to Nathaniel Weyl, June 1, 1978, in Hope Hale Davis Papers, Schlesinger Library, Radcliffe Institute, Harvard University. Davis herself later became the head of one of the sub-units. The total number of members in the secret Washington units, according to estimates later made by Chambers and Josephine Herbst, was probably about seventy-five. Haynes and Klehr, *Venona*, 62.

62. Chambers, *Witness*, 335; FBI memorandum on Chambers's statements concerning J. Peters, p. 16, compiled in April 1949, Peters FBI File. Two group members, Lee Pressman and John Abt, later confirmed that Peters met with the group from time to time. Gall, *Pursuing Justice*, 60; Abt, *Advocate and Activist*, 45.

63. Davis, *Great Day Coming*, 108–11; Tanenhaus, *Whittaker Chambers*, 105.

64. Chambers, *Witness*, 378–79.

65. Pressman stated that Peters "showed up, announced that he was taking Ware's place, and continued, thereafter, to act more-or-less as the leader of the group." FBI

interview of Lee Pressman, October 12, 1950, 100-11820-503. See also Abt, *Advocate and Activist*, 45.

66. Chambers later recalled that Peters "was in Washington constantly in 1937" (*Witness*, 429).

67. Davis letter to Nathaniel Weyl, May 24, 1978, in Nathaniel Weyl Papers, box 2, Hoover Institution Archives. See also Davis, *Great Day Coming*, 98.

68. Davis, *Great Day Coming*, 98–99. Sidney Hook was a Socialist who had become interested in, and offered some support to, the Communist Party in the early 1930s. In 1933, however, he became a strong critic of Stalin and the international Communist movement. He instantly became a béte noire of the CPUSA, and of Peters in particular.

69. Ibid., 252–53.

70. Ibid., 163, 167, 188.

71. Ibid., 329–30.

72. FBI interview of Hope Hale Davis, March 1954, BS100-29108, in Peters FBI File; Davis, *Great Day Coming*, 331–32.

73. Chambers, *Witness*, 383; FBI memorandum on Chambers's statements concerning J. Peters, p. 23, compiled in April 1949, Peters FBI File.

74. When Nate Witt was selected to head the Ware group, Perlo had tried unsuccessfully to promote his own candidacy. Chambers, *Witness*, 378–79.

75. This candid assessment of Pressman is found in an undated (though likely 1950 or 1951) and unsigned (probably Henry Collins) memo in the CP's Central Control Commission Records, microfilm reel 2, Tamiment Library.

76. Gall, *Pursuing Justice*, 60–62. Chambers later claimed that he had encouraged Pressman to flout the decision of the CC.

77. See ibid., 286–88.

78. Klehr, *Secret World*, 98–99.

79. Undated (but probably 1946) KGB report, VN, "White Notebook" no. 2, p. 42.

80. In a January 1945 report by Anatoly Gorsky to the Moscow Center, he wrote concerning the remnants of Peters's Washington underground groups: "Konspiratsia both among the members of Raid's [Perlo's] former group and, unfortunately, among oth[er] info[rmation] groups here, leaves a lot to be desired." Gorsky's report of March 20–21, 1945, VN, "White Notebook" no. 3, p. 77.

81. FBI memorandum on Chambers's statements concerning J. Peters, p. 18, compiled in April 1949, Peters FBI File.

82. Weinstein, *Perjury*, 18–19, 41–42, and 46–47. The strongest evidence for the accuracy of Chambers's recollections of this incident is found in a statement made to Hiss's defense attorneys by the lawyer representing one of the defendants in the alleged transaction. He confirmed that in fact a "dummy transaction" had taken place, that a "very high Communist" (presumably Peters) was involved, and that the person who ultimately got the car was a Communist. Ibid., 47.

Chapter 6. J. Peters's Espionage Ring, 1934–38

1. Undated message (probably June 1934) of Moscow Center to Valentin Markin on the "plan of work" for the second half of 1934, VN, "Black Notebook," p. 35. See also Weinstein and Vassiliev, *Haunted Wood*, 33–34.

2. April 1934 memorandum from the New York station of the NKVD to the Center, VN, "Black Notebook," p. 3. Actually, the NKVD did have one valuable source in the State Department in the mid-1930s, David Salmon ("Willy"). But "Willy" proved a problematical source, and was dropped in 1937. Haynes et al., *Spies*, 196–200.

3. Weinstein and Vassiliev, *Haunted Wood*, 38.

4. FBI memorandum on Chambers's statements concerning J. Peters, p. 25, compiled in April 1949, Peters FBI File; Chambers, *Witness*, 38.

5. Chambers later reported that when told the nature of the apparatus he was entering, Hiss was "perfectly agreeable to it." FBI memorandum on Chambers's statements concerning Peters, p. 15, compiled in April 1949, Peters FBI File. It may well be, of course, that Hiss struggled privately over this decision, as did two of his contemporaries, Noel Field (a friend of Hiss) and Henry Wadleigh.

6. Romerstein and Breindel, *Venona Secrets*, 115–16.

7. FBI memorandum on Chambers's statements concerning J. Peters, p. 20, compiled in April 1949, Peters FBI File. On the confidential nature of the State Department records obtained by the Nye Committee, see Weinstein, *Perjury*, 127.

8. Chambers, *Witness*, 375.

9. Noel Field, "Geschichte meiner politischen Tätigkeit," in *Der Fall Noel Field*, ed. Barth, Schweizer, and Grimm, vol. 1, 393.

10. Report from "Redhead" (Hede Massing) appended to a letter to NKVD headquarters, April 26, 1936, in VN, "Yellow Notebook" no. 2, p. 4.

11. *Der Fall Noel Field*, vol. 1, 393, 753; Chambers, *Witness*, 381; Massing, *This Deception*, 147–49; and Weinstein and Vassiliev, *Haunted Wood*, 5–7. The independent accounts offered by Chambers, Massing, and Field have been confirmed, except for minor details, in VN, "Yellow Notebook" no. 2, pp. 4–6.

12. Hede Massing's superior, Iskhak Akhmerov, later reported on the incident and acknowledged that Peters had acted correctly but "rather ineptly," since he should not have spoken so freely to Hiss about Hede Massing's connection to the NKVD. Report of Iskhak Akhmerov (using code name "Jung"), May 18, 1936, VN, "Yellow Notebook" no. 2, p. 6.

13. Chambers, *Witness*, 339–41.

14. Hede Massing's account in VN, "Yellow Notebook" no. 2, p. 4. See also Haynes et al., *Spies*, 4–6.

15. The recruitment of Duggan can be traced in VN, "Yellow Notebook" no. 2, pp. 4–6, where Frederick Field is described as belonging to "the Washington group of leftists"; and in Chambers, *Witness*, 489–90.

16. *Der Fall Noel Field*, vol. 1, 393; and Weinstein and Vassiliev, *Haunted Wood*, 6.

17. Moscow Center to NKVD New York Station, May 3, 1936, VN, "Yellow Notebook" no. 2, p. 5. See also Haynes et al., *Spies*, 8–9, and Massing, *This Deception*, 147–49.

18. Report of Iskhak Akhmerov, May 18, 1936, VN, "Yellow Notebook" no. 2, p. 6.

19. Akhmerov's report of July 31, 1938, VN, "White Notebook" no. 3, p. 119. From the context of Akhmerov's report, in which Hiss is referred to by his real name, it seems that his conversation with Peters had occurred some time earlier, perhaps in 1937. See also White, *Alger Hiss's Looking-Glass Wars*, 230.

20. Chambers, *Witness*, 370.

21. Chambers later told the FBI that he had a vague recollection that the documents might have included lists of Japanese agents. But it would seem unlikely that White would have had access to such material. FBI memorandum on Chambers's statements concerning J. Peters, p. 21, compiled in April 1949, Peters FBI File.

22. Chambers, *Witness*, 370; FBI memorandum on Chambers's statements concerning J. Peters, p. 21, compiled in April 1949, Peters FBI File.

23. Chambers, *Witness*, 370. See also Craig, *Treasonable Doubt*, 44.

24. Tanenhaus (*Whittaker Chambers*, 106) places this in the fall of 1935, but the detailed narrative of Henry Julian Wadleigh, discussed below, makes the later dating much more probable.

25. Romerstein and Breindel, *Venona Secrets*, 131.

26. Chambers, *Witness*, 31, 385. John Donovan, who was recruited to the Party by Nelson, testified that he saw her at one small group meeting with Hal Ware, Bob Coe, Victor Perlo, Henry Collins, George Silverman, and Nathaniel Weyl. "Testimony of John Donovan."

27. Wadleigh told his story in a series of newspaper articles in July 1949. Wadleigh, "Why I Spied," July 12, 1949, 3, 30. See also his FBI interview of December 9, 1948, in Sam Tanenhaus Papers, box 64, Hoover Institution Archive.

28. See the brief, handwritten autobiographical sketch that Carpenter provided to the Central Control Commission in the late 1940s. Records of the Communist Party of the United States, Central Control Commission Records, reel 2, Tamiment Library, New York University.

29. Pederson, *Communist Party in Maryland*, 72–73; Wadleigh, "Why I Spied," July 13, 1949, 3.

30. Wadleigh, "Why I Spied," July 12, 1949, 30.

31. Testimony of Henry Julian Wadleigh, December 11, 1948, "Transcripts of Grand Jury Testimony in the Alger Hiss Case," 4076.

32. FBI interview of Chambers, November 20, 1951, 65-59091-89.

33. In fact, Bill had been temporarily recalled to Moscow, where he stayed from July until the end of 1935 or early 1936. Felix Inslerman, who had been instructed by Bill to travel to Russia for training, saw Bill numerous times in Moscow in this period. See the detailed account given by Inslerman, an Estonian American Communist, to the FBI in February and March 1954, as summarized in an FBI report of May 14, 1954, in Sam Tanenhaus Papers, box 46, Hoover Institution Archive.

34. Wadleigh, "Why I Spied," July 12, 1949, 30. In an autobiographical sketch that Carpenter later composed for the Central Control Commission, when he reached the point where he would have described his Party activities in the mid-1930s, he wrote simply: "will discuss orally." This was almost surely a guarded reference to his espionage work, which, in accordance with the rules of conspiratorial work, he did not wish to set down in writing. Central Control Commission Records, reel 2, Tamiment Library, New York University.

35. Wadleigh, "Why I Spied," July 13, 1949, 3. Noel Field also recalled the lax security at the State Department and how easy it was to steal important documents: "The institution, and consequently the mentality, of the State Department was rather provincial

in my day. . . . This was evident from the careless manner in which state secrets were managed. The most secret documents, sometimes in multiple copies, circulated from hand to hand." Cited in Schmidt, *Battle of Wits*, 109.

36. Wadleigh recalled Carpenter telling him that his "superior in the Party" (Peters) had ordered him to be "more 'tactful' with me." Wadleigh, "Why I Spied," July 13, 1949, 30.

37. One person who later admitted to having assisted Chambers and Peters by acting as a courier in their espionage operation was David Zabladowsky, whom Chambers had met at Columbia University. Weinstein, *Perjury*, 109. Another was William Edward Crane ("Keith"), who was one of three photographers used in Apparatus B. When Crane decided to withdraw and take on other Party work on the West Coast, Chambers arranged for him to meet Peters, who needed to approve Crane's request. On the basis of that meeting, Crane concluded that "Chambers knew Peters very well." Undated (but apparently 1949) FBI interview of Crane, in Peters FBI File.

38. In 1949, Wadleigh confessed that he had been involved in espionage, but William Ward Pigman, who later became an eminent biochemist at the New York Medical College, denied that he had known Whittaker Chambers, supported the Communist Party, or engaged in espionage. In FBI interviews, however, he did admit that he had known David Carpenter and that he had had "leftish" views in the 1930s. FBI reports, January 24 and February 8, 1945, in Sam Tanenhaus Papers, box 52, Hoover Institution Archive. Furthermore, Pigman (with the code name "114th") is identified as a member of Chambers's espionage ring in the so-called Gorsky memo of December 1948. See the text of this memo, annotated by John Haynes, at http://h-net.msu.edu/cgi-bin/logbrowse .pl?trx=vx&list=h-hoac&month=0503&week=b&msg=ycrsVT7M1e2L9EECiLFskg& user=&pw= (accessed July 24, 2010).

39. FBI memorandum on Chambers's statements concerning J. Peters, p. 21, compiled in April 1949, Peters FBI File.

40. Ibid.

41. Chambers, *Witness*, 405.

42. Suvorov, *Inside Soviet Military Intelligence*, 21–23.

43. Ibid., 398.

44. Inslerman gave his testimony in 1954 to the FBI and before the House Un-American Activities Committee. FBI report of May 14, 1954, on interviews of Inslerman in February and March 1954, in AWP, box 7, folder 3.

45. Interview of John S. Dickey by defense lawyers in the Hiss trial, cited in Weinstein, *Perjury*, 189.

46. RCPUSA, 515/1/4077. The copy of Dodd's letter to Roosevelt bears a date-stamp of January 5, 1937, the day on which the item was officially registered as received by an unknown CPUSA official. Both documents can be found in Klehr, *Secret World*, 110–18.

47. Any espionage activity carried out by CPUSA members in Washington would have been under the supervision of Peters. At this time the NKVD had several sources in the State Department, including Larry Duggan, but none of the documents obtained by that apparatus would have been passed to the CPUSA.

48. As for the source of the documents, the only plausible candidates are Henry Wadleigh and Alger Hiss. However, Wadleigh apparently confined his espionage activity to the handling of original documents to be photographed, whereas it would later be shown that the preparation of handwritten or typed extracts and summaries was part of Hiss's modus operandi in the State Department. See Weinstein, *Perjury*, 215–22.

49. Chambers, *Witness*, 402.

50. Tanenhaus, *Whittaker Chambers*, 110; Chambers, *Witness*, 408. Chambers, who spoke German fluently, often had trouble understanding Bykov, but Peters, who was more familiar with Yiddish, apparently did not.

51. FBI memorandum on Chambers's statements concerning J. Peters, p. 23, compiled in April 1949, Peters FBI File.

52. Chambers, *Witness*, 405–6.

53. Only years later did Chambers learn that the real name of his handler was Boris Bykov. It is not clear whether Peters knew him as Bykov, Peter, or some other alias.

54. Chambers, *Witness*, 414–15. See also Weinstein, *Perjury*, 189–92.

55. FBI memorandum on Chambers's statements concerning J. Peters, pp. 23–24, compiled in April 1949, Peters FBI File.

56. Ibid.; Tanenhaus, *Whittaker Chambers*, 115.

57. Chambers, *Witness*, 429–30. On Glasser, see Craig, *Treasonable Doubt*, 96–99. Glasser (under the code name "Ruble") described his activity in Apparatus B under Chambers's supervision in an autobiographical statement he provided to the NKVD in December 1944, VN, "White Notebook" no. 3, pp. 47–48.

58. On Adler, see Weinstein, *Perjury*, 211; Craig, *Treasonable Doubt*, 86–88; and Haynes et al., *Spies*, 11–12. Adler later denied that he had been a CP member or had assisted the Party in any way, but NKVD records and U.S. intercepts of Soviet wartime messages (Venona) show that he was a recruiter for the CP and supplied information to Soviet intelligence. Haynes et al., *Spies*, 538; Weinstein and Vassiliev, *Haunted Wood*, 78, 158.

59. Budenz, *Men Without Faces*, 250. There is no evidence that Peters actually proceeded to establish such an apparatus.

60. At the District 34 (Baltimore) Buro meeting of January 13, 1938, it is stated that "Comrade Peters" was to be in charge of the Washington, D.C., and Baltimore delegations at the upcoming national conference. The Buro minutes for the meeting of January 27 list among the attendees "Peters (invited for report)." Apparently Peters reported on the national conference. RGASPI, 495/14/104. I am grateful to John Haynes for calling my attention to these documents.

61. Weinstein, "Interview of Jozsef Peter," 5.

62. Paul Crouch, "Broken Chains," chapter 15, box 17, Paul Crouch Papers, Hoover Institution Archive. See also the FBI interview of an unnamed informant, who stated that Peters had been in charge of financial matters relating to the Abraham Lincoln Brigade. Interview of May 23, 1949, in Peters FBI File.

63. FBI interview of Louis Gibarti, March 22, 1951, in Peters FBI File. Gibarti did not take up Peters's offer, but he did end up in Spain during World War II and spent the last years of the war in prison there.

64. FBI interview of an unidentified female informant who had had several dealings with Peters in the 1930s, November 10 and 18, 1950, 100-184255, in Peters FBI File; FBI memorandum on Chambers's statements concerning J. Peters, p. 23, compiled in April 1949, Peters FBI File; Weinstein, *Perjury,* 117–18.

65. Undated report (probably 1946), KGB Moscow Center report, VN, "White Notebook" no. 2, pp. 41–42.

66. "Budenz Links Peters to Red Secret Police," *New York Herald Tribune,* September 1, 1949, 1; "Budenz Calls Stevens Chief Link with Soviet Secret Police Machine," *New York Times,* September 2, 1948, 4. See also Romerstein and Breindel, *Venona Secrets,* 342–44. It is likely that the material acquired by Budenz was part of the document collection that Peters asked Hope Hale Davis to store in her apartment.

67. Akhmerov's reports of July 5, 1937, and October 26, 1938, VN, "Yellow Notebook" no. 2, pp. 70–72.

68. Letter of Akhmerov (Jung), April 4, 1939, VN, "White Notebook" no. 3, p. 66.

69. Craig, *Treasonable Doubt, 60–62;* Weinstein and Vassiliev, *Haunted Wood,* 226–27.

70. Chambers, *Witness,* 139.

71. Perhaps Chambers read the *New York Times* story: "16 in Soviet Admit to Two Plots to Kill Stalin and Others," August 20, 1936, 1.

72. Chambers, *Witness,* 75–76. Although Chambers remembered Peters's warning as referring to a male, it is possible that Peters actually had in mind a woman, Juliet Stuart Poyntz, whose case is discussed in this chapter.

73. Chambers, *Witness,* 398–99.

74. Chambers, "Faking of Americans," part 1, p. 33. Chambers suggested that by this oblique reference to the Stalinist terror Peters "risked something himself."

75. FBI memorandum on Chambers's statements concerning J. Peters, p. 22, compiled in April 1949, Peters FBI File.

76. Tanenhaus, *Whittaker Chambers,* 128–29.

77. See, e.g., "Passports Issued as Political Favor in Robinson Case," *New York Times,* December 31, 1937, 1, 5.

78. Chambers, *Witness,* 401.

79. When in his first talk with Bykov, Chambers admitted that he knew Richard Ikal, the Russian said, "Too bad for you." Ibid., 406.

80. An account of this PolCom meeting is found in "Report on Subversive Activities," January 31, 1938, *U.S. Military Intelligence Reports: Surveillance of Radicals in the United States, 1917–41* (Frederick, Md.: University Publications of America, 1984), reel 30, 0595–97. In the late 1930s, U.S. Military Intelligence was far more successful than the FBI in infiltrating the Communist Party. For a time in 1937 and 1938 they seem to have had an informant at the highest level of the Party who provided them with accurate reports on some PolCom and Central Committee meetings.

81. On the disappearance of Juliet Poyntz, see Tanenhaus, *Whittaker Chambers,* 131; Weinstein, *Perjury,* 276.

82. Chambers, *Witness,* 78.

83. Henry Wadleigh, thinking over the matter later, recalled that Chambers had brooded over the "Spanish tragedy" and had shown other "signs of misgivings and doubts." Wadleigh, "Why I Spied," July 17, 1949, 3.

84. Chambers, *Witness*, 40; FBI memorandum on Chambers's statements concerning J. Peters, p. 24, compiled in April 1949, Peters FBI File. See also Tanenhaus, *Whittaker Chambers*, 125.

85. Tanenhaus, *Whittaker Chambers*, 125.

86. Ibid., 137. Chambers later speculated on why Peters so quickly understood what had happened: "Perhaps some trifling change in my manner, which I always feared might betray me in the days when I was preparing to break, had registered on Peters's mind, and he had dismissed it, but now it hardened into certainty." Chambers, *Witness*, 44–45.

Chapter 7. From Peters to Stevens: Life in the Underground

1. Weinstein, *Perjury*, 281.

2. Ibid., 280.

3. Rudy Baker, "Brief on the Work of the CPUSA Secret Apparatus," January 28, 1939, in Klehr, *Secret World*, 87.

4. Ibid. At another point in this "Brief" (91–92), Baker admitted that, although he had worked closely with Peters in 1930–31, he did "not know the details of his [current] situation." Baker here erroneously calls Peters a "Jew from Vienna."

5. Remarkably, when asked by the NKVD in 1944 for information about Peters's activity in Washington in the 1930s, Browder professed an inability to recall much about the nature of Peters's operation. He stated that Peters had been sent by the Party to Washington, but could not remember "by whom and for what purpose." Since it seems improbable that Browder would not be able to remember what Peters was doing in Washington, it may be that for some unknown reason he chose to withhold this information from the NKVD. Memorandum of Vasily M. Zarubin, May 1944, VN, "White Notebook" no. 2, p. 38.

6. Baker, "Brief," 87–90. Baker listed as the main priorities "document safe-keeping, communications, and the exposure and weeding out of enemies," especially "Trotskyists and Lovestoneists." In this connection he found fault with Peters's direction of the secret apparatus, which he claimed had not addressed "the problem of exposing enemies within the party" (87).

7. RCPUSA, 515/1/4708.

8. For example, in August the *Daily Worker* reported that the enlarged plenum of the Party in Pennsylvania heard "J. Peters of the National Committee calls for more vigilant recruiting to the Communist Party from the basic industries." "Anti-New Deal Aim of Pa. Probe," August 25, 1938.

9. Weinstein, *Perjury*, 282; Tanenhaus, *Whittaker Chambers*, 141–43.

10. Tanenhaus, *Whittaker Chambers*, 139.

11. Weinstein, *Perjury*, 285–86.

12. Ibid., 286; and Radosh and Radosh, *Red Star*, 47–54.

13. Weinstein, *Perjury*, 287.

14. FBI report on interviews of Felix Inslerman in February and March 1954, in AWP, box 7, folder 3, Hoover Institution Archive.

15. "Seven More Indicted in Passport Fraud," *New York Times*, March 4, 1939, 32; "Jailed Witness in Passport Fraud," *New York Times*, March 30, 1939, 22; "Spy's Data Clue in Passport Trial," *New York Times*, April 27, 1939, 13

16. "Red Link Revealed in Passport Trial," *New York Times*, April 21, 1939, 7; "Lawyer's Kinsman Links Him to Spy," *New York Times*, April 21, 1939, 3.

17. FBI report, NY100-1400, in Peters FBI File.

18. See the "Declaration of Intention" forms of Alexander Stevens, July 1, 1939, in Peters INS File.

19. Péter Memoir, part 2, p. 32.

20. According to a brief survey of Peters's career drawn up on October 15, 1947, by a Soviet official (possibly a member of the International Department), at this time Peters was "relieved of his duties in the CPUSA CC as a non-American citizen and performed special assignments for the party CC." Klehr, *Secret World*, 81.

21. See the comments Foster made at a November 7 meeting of the executive committee of the Illinois CP. A detailed report on this meeting, dated November 17, 1939, was obtained by the FBI. (probably from U.S. military intelligence) and forwarded by J. Edgar Hoover to General Edwin Watson, President Roosevelt's personal secretary. FBI reports 10B, no. 3, Franklin D. Roosevelt Library (Hyde Park, N.Y.).

22. Ottanelli, *Communist Pary*, 204; Klehr, *American Communist Movement*, 92–95.

23. Isserman, *Which Side Were You On?* 49.

24. Comments of Morris Childs, leader of the Illinois CP, at a meeting of the Illinois CP executive committee, October 25, 1939. *U.S. Military Intelligence Reports: Surveillance of Radicals in the United States, 1917–41* (Frederick, Md.: University Publications of America, 1984), reel 31, 014.

25. Hoover to General Edwin Watson, November 17, 1939, FBI reports 10B, no. 3, Franklin D. Roosevelt Library. See also Storch, *Red Chicago*, 229.

26. Peters later recalled that despite the fact that he was living underground at the time, the Party entrusted him with the supervision of the "illegal apparatus" throughout this period. Péter Memoir, part 2, p. 32.

27. Testimony of Paul Crouch, RSACB, reel 12, 4863-65, 5006-07; Isserman, *Which Side Were You On?* 51–52.

28. From an interview of Gates in 1977, cited in ibid., 52.

29. Peters drove a Chrysler, which he had purchased new in 1937 with funds generated by the secret apparatus.

30. Memo of Frank Walker, September 30, 1947, Peters INS File.

31. Budenz, *Men Without Faces*, 45–46.

32. Radosh and Radosh, *Red Star*, 47–54.

33. Horne, *Final Victim*, 132.

34. In the late 1940s, Lawson, Biberman, and Cole joined other directors and writers in refusing to cooperate with the House Un-American Activities Committee in its investigation of Communist influences in the film industry. The group became known as the "Hollywood Ten."

35. Peters later recalled that one of his most important responsibilities in supervising groups of artists and intellectuals, like those in Hollywood, was "Marxist formation." Péter Memoir, part 2, p. 31.

36. Copies of *America Sings for Victory* were sold at Party functions, for example at a local unit meeting in New York in August 1942. FBI report of August 31, 1942, 100-3-4720, in Peters FBI File.

37. Stevens may have found it amusing that the master sleuth in Stout's novels, Nero Wolfe, could read Hungarian poems in the original Magyar. See Rex Stout, *The Rubber Band* (1936).

38. The FBI later made a thorough investigation of Stevens's trip to Reno, which included interviews of the landlord and divorce court officials. Records of the Reno Public Library were checked to determine what books Stevens had borrowed. FBI report of May 14, 1942, 100-3039, in Peters FBI File.

39. FBI report of June 1949, 100-347268-53, in Peters FBI File.

40. Stevens registered for the draft on April 25, 1942. Here he stated that he was unemployed. FBI report (undated), 100-1400, in Peters FBI File.

41. Sibley, *Red Spies,* 20.

42. Edward Nellor, "Red Plot Charge Investigated," *New York Sun*, October 10, 1947, 1.

43. Smith testified on October 25, Nowell on November 30. House of Representatives, *Investigation of Un-American Propaganda Activities in the United States*, vol. 10, 6436, vol. 11, 7030 (Washington, D.C.: Government Printing Office, 1940).

44. Ibid., vol. 3, p. 1868.

45. The following is based on the accounts of Tanenhaus, *Whittaker Chambers,* 159–63, and Weinstein, *Perjury,* 291–95.

46. For the text of Berle's memorandum, with marginal notes by John Earl Haynes, see http://www.johnearlhaynes.org/page100.html (accessed July 15, 2010).

47. Tanenhaus, *Whittaker Chambers,* 169–70, 203–4.

48. On the FBI's failure to make timely use of Chambers as an informant, see Sibley, *Red Spies,* 80–81.

49. Hoover letter of November 17, 1939, FBI reports 10B, no. 3, Franklin D. Roosevelt Library (Hyde Park, N.Y.).

50. A summary of Glaser's June 1940 interview is contained in a memorandum of Warren R. Hearn, February 1, 1942, 100-24783, in Peters FBI File.

51. Interview of unnamed informant, October 21, 1940, in Peters FBI File.

52. Hoover to L. M. C. Smith, Chief, Special Defense Unit, April 1, 1941, 100-HQ-184255, in Peters FBI File.

53. Letter of Hoover to "Special Agent in Charge," February 23, 1942, 100-184255, in Peters FBI File.

54. Ibid.

55. It had long been the practice in the CPUSA that the *Daily Worker* would not publish photographs of most of the Party's top leaders, with the exception of the national secretary and those who ran for public office. Thus, J. Peters's photo had never appeared in that newspaper or any other. Budenz, *Men Without Faces,* 17–18.

56. FBI report of Warren R. Hearn, February 1, 1943, 100-184255-54, in Peters FBI File.

57. Tanenhaus, *Whittaker Chambes,* 170.

58. Sibley, *Red Spies,* 59.

59. The following is drawn from a description of Alexander Stevens's visit to Los Angeles found in a lengthy FBI report on the surveillance of Herbert Biberman, one section of which is entitled "Conferences with Alexander Goldberger." Report of John R. Vicars, September 15, 1942, 100-6769, in Peters FBI File.

60. Stevens apparently solicited contributions as a gift for Browder, whose birthday was May 20. The funds would help finance the "Free Browder" campaign. The note found in Stevens's suitcase read in part: "E.B. 5/20—Birthday gift to get him out—Big meetings, Radio."

61. Haynes and Klehr, *Venona,* 232–33.

62. Photographs of Childs and Stevens walking along a Chicago street are found in Peters FBI File, 100-184255-257.

63. FBI report of John C. Bills, May 19, 1942, 100-5149, in Peters FBI File. Illegal searches of this kind were commonly employed by FBI agents during World War II, especially in cases, as here, that were designated "Internal Security." Gentry, *J. Edgar Hoover,* 281–84.

64. Report of FBI agent Warren R. Hearn, December 23, 1942, 100-24753, in Peters FBI File.

65. The FBI also intercepted and read the mail of Stevens's two brothers, Emerich and Joseph, but discovered nothing of value. Ibid.

66. Report of Warren R. Hearn, May 28, 1942, 100-1400, in Peters FBI File.

67. Weinstein, "Interview with Jozsef Peter," AWP, 4.

68. In March 1943, when Stevens's brother Emerich telephoned and informed him that their brother's wife had died and when the funeral would be held, Stevens replied: "I don't want to and can't go there—don't tell them you told me. You can tell them afterwards." FBI phone surveillance, March 20, 1943, NY100-34753, in Peters FBI File.

69. The results of the physical surveillance are detailed in a report by FBI agent Warren R. Hearn, December 23, 1942, 100-24753, in Peters FBI File.

70. Gentry, *J. Edgar Hoover,* 281–83.

71. Memorandum for Mr. Ladd, July 17, 1942, in Peters FBI File.

72. Hoover's "Memorandum for the Attorney General," September 30, 1942, 100-184255, in Peters FBI File.

73. On the technical surveillance, see FBI memo of October 30, 1942, 100-184255; and report by Warren R. Hearn, December 23, 1942, 100-24753, in Peters FBI File.

74. The informant also gave the FBI an original copy of a CP document entitled "Instructions for Special Mailing," as well as a questionnaire Peters had required all Party functionaries to fill out. P. K. Foxworth to Director, June 8, 1942, 65-10519, in Peters FBI File.

75. Memorandum of Warren R. Hearn, February 1, 1943, 100-24753, in Peters FBI File.

76. FBI reports of March 5, 1943, 100-7596; (undated, but clearly March 1943), 100-24753, Peters FBI File.

Chapter 8. Dueling with "the Feds," 1943–48

1. Report on interview of an unnamed ex-Communist in Detroit (probably William Odell Nowell), April 12, 1943, 100-24753, in Peters FBI File.

2. E. E. Conroy to Hoover, March 24, 1943, 100-24753, in Peters FBI File.

3. "Memorandum for Mr. Ladd," April 3, 1943, and Hoover to Communications Center, May 29, 1943, 100-24753, in Peters FBI File.

4. Weinstein, "Interview with Jozsef Peter," AWP, 2.

5. "Memorandum for Mr. Ladd," August 18, 1943, 100-24753, in Peters FBI File.

6. Péter Memoir, part 2, p. 30.

7. Theoharis, *Spying on Americans*, pp. 75–76.

8. It appears that in June 1940 Stevens had sent Maxim Lieber, using the cover name "Paul," to Washington to contact Harold Glasser and to identify himself as the replacement for "Karl" (Whittaker Chambers), his former handler. Glasser related this incident in an autobiographical statement he provided to the NKVD in December 1944, VN, "White Notebook" no. 3, pp. 47–48. In his autobiography, Chambers stated that Maxim Lieber sometimes used the cover name "Paul." Chambers, *Witness*, 40.

9. The roles played by Abt and Browder in the collection and distribution of material from the Perlo group were discussed in an NKVD report of V. M. Merkulov, August 1944, VN, "White Notebook" no. 1, pp. 10–11; and a report of "Vardo" (Elizabeth Zarubin), November 11, 1944, VN, "White Notebook" no. 3, p. 44.

10. Elizabeth Bentley, a courier for the NKVD who had worked with Jacob Golos, told the FBI that she had learned from one of her Washington contacts, Gregory Silvermaster, that Peters had been in Washington at some point in the early 1940s and had attempted to infiltrate into the Silvermaster group, that is "to secure information from some of the members." Statement of Elizabeth Bentley, November 30, 1945, 65-56402-220, in Peters FBI File.

11. NKVD report, May 1944, "White Notebook" no. 3, p. 45; Report of Anatoly Gorsky, May 4, 1944, VN, "White Notebook" no. 3, p. 67.

12. There was considerable disarray and little institutional memory among Soviet NKVD and GRU agents in the United States in this period, largely because many agents continued to fall victim to Stalin's campaign of terror. Andrew and Mitrokhin, *Sword and the Shield*, 106–7. See also Haynes et al., *Spies*, 489–500.

13. This report was sent on to Moscow, where in March 1943 a GRU official inquired of Georgi Dimitrov, head of the Comintern, whether the "Peter group" was attached to the OMS. The inquiry was repeated in May, but there is no indication how and when Dimitrov responded. Klehr, *Secret World*, 107–9.

14. NKVD report of V. M. Merkulov, August 1944, VN, "White Notebook" no. 1, p. 11.

15. Letter to the Moscow Center, May 8, 1943, VN, "White Notebook" no. 3, p. 67.

16. Memo of Vasily Zarubin, May 1944, VN, "White Notebook" no. 2, 37; NKVD report of V. M. Merkulov, August 1944, VN, "White Notebook" no. 1, p. 11; and NKVD memo, June 1, 1944, VN, "White Notebook" no. 3, p. 68.

17. As a further precaution, the NKVD asked Browder to warn "Storm" once again not to have any contact with the Perlo group or with the GRU. Iskhak Ahkmerov was advised not to renew his ties with "Storm." NKVD report, June 1, 1944, VN, "White Notebook" no. 3, p. 68.

18. Kessler, *Clever Girl*, 97–98; Weinstein and Vassiliev, *Haunted Wood*, 224–35.

19. Ahkmerov's report of May 19, 1944, VN, "White Notebook" no. 3, p. 68.

20. FBI report of Edward Hummer, March 31, 1944, 100-24753, in Peters FBI File.

21. Ryan, *Earl Browder*, 204–5. Upon Browder's release, the Citizens' Committee to Free Earl Browder donated the $20,000 that had been raised to the United States military. Thus, at least some of the funds that Alexander Stevens raised in Hollywood ended up supporting the war effort.

22. Information on the conversation between Stevens and Williamson was obtained from one of the informants the FBI now had in the CP headquarters. Report of E. E. Conroy, June 8, 1944, 100-24753, in Peters FBI File.

23. The FBI was able to keep track of these changes through informants and spot checks on Stevens's movements. See reports of October 31, 1944, 100-24753 and January 27, 1945, 100-184255, in Peters FBI File. CP records for this period are not available.

24. Ryan, *Earl Browder*, 218–23.

25. Klehr, *American Communist Movement*, 98.

26. Many years later, József Péter spoke with bitterness about Browder's "mistaken" policies, including his insistence that only U.S. citizens should be allowed to occupy highly visible leadership positions in the Party. Weinstein, "Interview with Jozsef Peter," AWP, 5.

27. In fact, there was an FBI informant in the audience, who had a hidden device that recorded Miller's speech. Informant's report of January 11, 1945, 100-284255. Peters FBI File. It is noteworthy that Miller here in effect admitted that the Party did at one time advocate force and violence.

28. See his speech of April 2, 1945, recorded verbatim in FBI report of April 25, 100-24753, in Peters FBI File.

29. Ryan, *Earl Browder*, 249–61; Klehr, *American Communist Movement*, 103.

30. Later József Péter would declare that at the time he had regarded the CPA as a "serious political mistake" that threatened to destroy "the Party organization." Weinstein, "Interview with Jozsef Peter," AWP, 5.

31. Miller's speech was once again captured verbatim by an FBI informant who brought a secret microphone to the meeting. FBI report of April 25, 1945, NY100-24753, in Peters FBI File.

32. Péter Memoir, part 2, p. 29.

33. On Miller's frequent meetings with Davis and his role in Davis's reelection campaign in 1945, see the FBI report of December 18, 1945, 100-232047-8, in Peters FBI File.

34. Miller's report on recruitment to club (unit) leaders on April 2, 1945, FBI report of April 25, 100-24753, in Peters FBI File.

35. New York office to Hoover, July 23, 1945, 100-3-4-4698, in Peters FBI File.

36. Charney, *Long Journey*, 66–67.

37. Though friendly with his brother and sympathetic to the CP, Joseph Goldberger was not directly involved with the Communist movement. He had worked his way up in the United Doll Company and by 1945 was vice president. He and his wife were sufficiently prosperous to be able to purchase a group of land plots and cabins at Lake Peekskill.

38. Abt, *Advocate and Activist,* 178–79.

39. Ibid., 95–96, 178.

40. "All Communists Here are Spies, Budenz, Once Red, Tells Hearing," *New York Times,* November 23, 1946, 1. See also Klehr, *American Communist Movement,* 107–8.

41. "Hearings on Proposed Legislation to Curb or Control the Communist Party of the United States," February 6, 1947 (Washington, D.C.: Government Printing Office), 45–50. Published records of the House Committee on Un-American Activities will hereafter be cited as HUAC, followed by title of the hearings, date, and page number. See also "Communist Chief in U.S. Is Accused of Revolution Plot," *New York Times,* February 7, 1947, 1.

42. Eric Johnston, president of the Motion Picture Association, was probably thinking of Peters when in a speech on March 27, 1947, he said: "My concern is the red conspirator, the man who uses the freedoms of democracy to destroy democracy." HUAC, 8th Congress, first session, http://www.archive.org/stream/investigatonofun1947unit/investigatonofun1947unit_djvu.txt (accessed July 16, 2010).

43. Memo of D. M. Ladd to Director, February 17, 1947, 100-3-74-426, in Peters FBI File.

44. Bob Lauter, "Around the Dial," *Daily Worker,* August 5, 1948, 13. And FBI report of August 5, 1948, 100-340922-A, in Peters FBI File.

45. Stevens found refuge in the homes of Party sympathizers, particularly Hungarian-Americans. Péter Memoir, part 2, p 35.

46. Hoover to New York Station, April 7, 1947, 100-24753, in Peters FBI File.

47. Guy Hottel to Director, June 6, 1946, 100-24753, in Peters FBI File.

48. "Red Party Leader Gets Year in Jail," *New York Times,* July 9, 1947, 48.

49. Memo of Donald Appell to Robert Stripling, Chief Investigator, August 22, 1947, HUAC records, Investigative File on J. Peters, RG233, National Archives (Washington, D.C.).

50. Hoover to Commissioner of INS, September 18, 1947, 100-104255, in Peters FBI File.

51. Hoover's memorandum of September 30, 1947, 100-104255, in Peters FBI File.

52. An account of Stevens's arrest can be found in the report of FBI agent Raymond Firth, October 8, 1947, 100-184255, in Peters FBI File.

53. Peters later described King as "a liberal attorney who sympathized with the Party and who volunteered her services to defend Communists." Péter Memoir, part 2, p. 36. Whittaker Chambers aptly called her "a habitual attorney for Communists in trouble" (*Witness,* 635). For a sympathetic biography of King, see Fagan, *Carol Weiss King.*

54. The American Committee for Protection of the Foreign Born (ACPFB), a Communist Party front organization, also condemned the deportation proceedings against

Stevens as an "attack on the Bill of Rights." Memo to Director, October 16, 1947, 100-7046-271, in Peters FBI File.

55. FBI report of November 26, 1947, NY100-24753, in Peters FBI File.

56. In fact, in the initial arrest warrant for Stevens the bond was set at one thousand dollars. Later, apparently in response to the intensive media coverage of the arrest, the bond was raised to five thousand dollars. "Warrant for Arrest of Alien," October 6, 1947, Peters INS File.

57. The FBI learned of this incident from an informant in CP national headquarters. FBI report of November 26, 1947, NY100-24753, in Peters FBI File.

58. Péter Memoir, part 2, p. 36.

59. "Steve Miller Arrested," *Daily Worker*, October 10, 1947, 3. Carol Weiss also admitted to journalists that Stevens was a Communist, claiming that "he has never denied it." "Writer Arrested, Faces Deportation," *New York Times*, October 10, 1947, 2.

60. Edward Nellor, "Red Plot Charge Investigated," *New York Sun*, October 10, 1947, 1.

61. Only the *New York Times* managed to avoid this sensationalist, anti-Communist tone. It reported simply that Stevens, a writer and "reputed member of the Communist Party," had been arrested. "Writer Arrested, Faces Deportation," October 10, 1947, 2.

62. Howard Rushmore, "Reveal Red Spy was Saboteur," *New York Journal American*, October 10, 1; "Red Revolutionary Leader Arrested, Faces Deportation," *New York World Telegram*, October 9, 1947, 1.

63. Tanenhaus, *Whittaker Chambers,* 206.

64. Undated affidavit of John Lautner, Internal Security Subcommittee of the U.S. Senate, J. Peters file, RG46, National Archives (Washington, D.C.).

65. Peters later claimed that in this period he worked on the Platform Committee for the presidential campaign of Henry Wallace. Weinstein, "Interview with Jozsef Peter," AWP, 5.

66. Radosh and Radosh, *Red Star,* 153–59.

67. Lautner identified the farm owner as Joe Herman, "an old time Party member." Testimony of John Lautner, RSACB, 9564-5 (reel 7); and Péter Memoir, part 2, p. 37.

68. HUAC, "Hearings Regarding Communist Espionage in the United States Government," August 3, pp. 563–84. A transcript of Chambers's testimony on August 3 can be found at http://www.law.umkc.edu/faculty/projects/ftrials/hiss/8-3testimony.html (accessed July 16, 2010).

69. Undated affidavit of John Lautner, Internal Security Subcommittee of the U.S. Senate, J. Peters file, RG46, National Archives (Washington, D.C.); and FBI report of June 19, 1956, 100-184255, in Peters FBI File.

70. White, *Alger Hiss's Looking-Glass War,* 54–55; Weinstein, *Perjury,* 9–12, 22.

71. HUAC, "Hearings Regarding Communist Espionage in the United States Government," August 7, 1948, p. 662.

72. Péter Memoir, part 2, p. 37.

Chapter 9. Trial and Deportation

1. Statement of John P. Boyd, deputy commissioner of the INS, "Stevens Admits He Is Communist," *New York Times*, September 3, 1948, 4.

2. Arrest warrant for Alexander Stevens, October 6, 1947, in Peters INS File.

3. Tom Clark, the Attorney General, likewise tried to exploit the controversy over Alexander Stevens/J. Peters to demonstrate that the Democrats were doing a better job than the Republicans in dealing with the Communist Party. In a speech on September 18 he asserted that because the Republicans had failed to tighten immigration law, J. Peters "roams our streets and carries on his sinister Communist activities." Cited in Richard M. Fried, *Nightmare in Red: The McCarthy Era in Perspective* (New York: Oxford University Press, 1990), 82–83.

4. "House Unit to Get Alleged Spy Chief," *New York Times*, August 29, 1948, 2.

5. "Two More Charges against Stevens," *New York Times*, August 31, 1948, 4.

6. Charles Grutzner, "Chambers Faces Key Inquiry Figure and Calls Him Spy," *New York Times*, August 31, 1948, 1; "Two More Charges against Peters," *New York Times*, August 31, 1948, 4.

7. Malkin, *Return to My Father's House*, 188.

8. Chambers, *Witness*, 718.

9. Malkin, *Return to My Father's House*, 188.

10. "Burden of Proof," *Time*, September 6, 1948, 17. Illustrating the article was a photo of a grinning J. Peters, looking, indeed, much like Groucho Marx.

11. HUAC, "Hearings Regarding Communist Espionage in the United States Government," August 30, 1948 (Washington, D.C.: Government Printing Office), 1267–77.

12. For example, the *New York Times* on August 31 gave the following heading to the photo: "A Dramatic Moment at Spy Inquiry."

13. Chambers, *Witness*, 718.

14. HUAC, "Hearings Regarding Communist Espionage in the United States Government," August 30, 1948 (Washington, D.C.: Government Printing Office), 1275.

15. Louise Mitchell, writing in the *Daily Worker*, seemed to think that Stevens had scored a victory against HUAC and Chambers, "a small pudgy man with effeminate manners and shifty colorless eyes" who spun "a hopped-up story about a J. Peters who he claimed was Stevens." "Un-American Threats on Stevens with Reprisals," *Daily Worker*, August 31, 1948, 1.

16. The INS had earlier decided not to use Whittaker Chambers "unless his testimony is the only testimony that can save [the] government's case." "Memo for File" by E. Emanuel, August 37, 1948, in Peters INS File.

17. The verbatim transcript of Stevens's deportation hearing is not part of his INS file and has apparently not survived. However, it can be reconstructed from press accounts and from the extensive commentary on the hearing provided by Ralph Farb in "Opinion of the Presiding Inspector," January 9, 1949, in Peters INS File.

18. Farb, "Opinion of the Presiding Inspector," 3–4.

19. "Man From Moscow," *Newsweek*, September 10, 1948, 23; "Swears Peters Taught

Bloody U.S. Downfall," *New York Herald Tribune*, August 31, 1949, 1; Péter Memoir, part 2, p. 38.

20. This exchange was reported on in an issue of a virulently anti-Communist magazine, *Counterattack: Facts to Combat Communism*, no. 67, September 3, 1948, 1. The editors of the magazine raised the question of whether the American people would now "insist on taking hard, effective action to stop Peters and the rest of the Communists from doing as they 'damn please' any more."

21. "Stevens Is Called Communist 'Boss' at Alien Hearing," *New York Times*, September 1, 1948, 1; *Daily Mirror*, August 31, 1948, 1; "Man from Moscow," *Newsweek*, September 10, 1948, 23.

22. "Shadowy Portrait of Red Big Shot, J. Peters," *New York Herald Tribune*, August 30, 1949, 2.

23. Budenz, *This Is My Story*.

24. Farb, "Opinion of the Presiding Inspector," 10–11; "Budenz Calls Stevens Chief Link with Soviet Secret Police Machine," *New York Times*, September 2, 1948, 4.

25. More than half of Ralph Farb's summation of the hearing was taken up with lengthy quotes from Communist material submitted as evidence. Farb, "Opinion of the Presiding Inspector."

26. "Stoolies on Parade at Stevens Hearing," *Daily Worker*, September 1, 4.

27. Péter Memoir, part 2, p. 39.

28. "Press Statement of Carol King, Attorney for Alexander Stevens," September 2, 1948, Records of the American Committee for the Protection of the Foreign Born, the Labadie Collection, University of Michigan Library, Ann Arbor.

29. "Press Statement of Alexander Stevens," September 2, 1948, Records of the American Committee for the Protection of the Foreign Born, the Labadie Collection, University of Michigan Library, Ann Arbor.

30. In a private letter obtained by the FBI, Max Bedacht complained that Steve Miller had been placed on the National Committee only because he was believed "to be sufficiently incapable of doing anything" and because of his "willingness to play stooge." FBI report of May 17, 1949, citing Bedacht's letters of February 16, 1949, 100-3-3009, p. 37, in Peters FBI File.

31. Weinstein, "Interview of Jozsef Peter," 3.

32. Walter Arm, "Stalin's Books Call for Violence in U.S. Is Read at Trial of Reds," *New York Herald Tribune*, March 25, 1949, 1, 4.

33. C. W. Reinig, ed., *The Secret Manual of the Communist Party: A Manual on Organization* (Columbus, Ohio: State Publishing Company, ca. 1948). Each section of the text of Peters's *Manual* was illustrated with satirical cartoons in which a Party organizer is depicted as a scruffy figure with a long, Pinocchio-like nose.

34. Tanenhaus, *Whittaker Chambers,* 283. Commenting on these events years later, József Péter suggested that Hiss's libel suit had been "misguided and unwise." Weinstein, "Interview of Jozsef Peter," AWP, 6.

35. For Lautner's account of this incident, see RSACB, 9574-75 (reel 17); and FBI interview of June 14, 1956, in Peters FBI File.

36. Grand Jury Testimony of Alexander Stevens in Alger Hiss Case, RG118, Harry Truman Library (Independence, Mo.). Hereafter cited as "Stevens's Grand Jury Testimony," followed by page number.

37. Ibid., 5795–96.

38. Farb's eighty-page report, entitled "Opinion of the Presiding Inspector," is found in Peters INS File.

39. "Exceptions to Opinion of the Presiding Inspector," February 28, 1949, in Peters INS File.

40. FBI report of February 7, 1949, in Peters FBI File.

41. Abt, *Advocate and Activist,* 179.

42. Although not legally authorized to do so, the FBI obtained a copy of the Stevens' income tax form for 1941 by conniving with a cooperative IRS worker. FBI report of January 23, 1943, 100-7166, in Peters FBI File.

43. A lawyer from the Hiss defense team contacted Carol King to ask if Stevens could provide any information that would help in the defense of his client. King was noncommittal: she said some "items" might be forthcoming. Later, however, she informed Hiss's lawyers that Stevens was unwilling to get involved. Undated memo in Hiss Defense Files, in AWP; Weinstein, *Perjury,* 60, 141.

44. *New York Herald Tribune,* August 31, 1949, 18.

45. Letter of assistant INS Commissioner to Carol King, April 12, 1949, with enclosed twenty-two page ruling of the "Chief Examiner," in Peters INS File.

46. "U.S. Orders Peters Deported, Gives Him 15 Days to Appeal," *New York Herald Tribune,* April 14, 1949, 14.

47. An undated press release of the American Committee for the Protection of the Foreign Born, "Presiding Inspector Recommends Deportation of Alexander Stevens," in Records of the American Committee for the Protection of the Foreign Born, in Labadie Collection, University of Michigan Library, Ann Arbor.

48. King to New York District Director, April 27, 1949; and unsigned INS memo of May 2, 1949, in Peters INS File.

49. Chambers, *Witness,* 617.

50. INS memos of April 27, April 28, and May 3, 1949, in Peters INS File.

51. Endre Sik's letters of May 3, 1949, to Rajk and Rákosi, Magyar Országos Levéltár (Hungarian National Archives, hereafter cited as MOL), Magyar Szocialista Munkáspárt (Hungarian Socialist Workers Party, MszMP), 276-G5, pp. 14–15.

52. Sik (code-named Shumsky) is mentioned in a KGB memo of March 1949 on "connections with agents," VN, "Black Notebook," p. 74.

53. HUAC, *A Communist in a Workers' Paradise: John Santo's Own Story,* 9. Hereafter cited as *John Santo's Own Story.*

54. Testimony of John Lautner, RSACB, roll 17, 9551, 9560; "Farewell Dinner Held for Alexander Stevens," *Daily Worker,* May 11, 1949, 4.

55. FBI memo of May 8, 1949, RR-3106-1, in Peters FBI File.

56. "Alien Communist Deports Himself, Leaving behind Wife and Message," *New York Times,* May 9, 1949, 5. Stevens's statement is found in records of the ACPFB, Labadie

Collection, University of Michigan, Ann Arbor. The *Daily Worker* published the full text of Stevens's statement on May 11, 1949, 4.

57. In early June, as she was preparing to depart for Hungary, Ann Stevens told a reporter that her husband would be "very happy to get his citizenship and come back home." *New York World Telegram*, June 6, 1949, p. 4.

58. In 1951 the FBI received an anonymous letter from a person in a Bonita Springs, Florida, retirement community who was convinced that one of his fellow retirees was J. Peters. Report of April 2, 1951, in Peters FBI File.

59. Defense lawyers for Communist leaders placed on trial in the 1950s did their best to prevent J. Peters's *Manual* from being introduced as evidence, for, as one wrote in an internal brief, it contained "extreme prejudicial material." Unidentified associate of Mary Kaufman, undated brief (1952), in Mary Metlay Kaufman Papers, Sophia Smith Collection, Smith College, MS300, box 5, folder 2, p. 3.

60. When he learned of this, József Péter was indignant, for he had not been consulted and in fact regarded it as a kind of "provocation." He would do anything necessary to prevent any further reprints of the *Manual*. Weinstein, "Interview of Jozsef Peter," AWP, 3.

Epilogue and Assessment

1. Letter of "Pete" to "Johny" (Lautner), May 30, 1949, John Lautner file, records of the Central Control Commission of the CPUSA, reel 2, Tamiment Library, New York University.

2. Ibid.

3. Péter Memoir, part 2, p. 40.

4. Péter wrote to John Lautner telling him of his new assignment and asking for a steady transmission of clippings from American newspapers, especially those dealing with the "Chambers-Hiss matter." Undated letter (probably July 1949), in AWP, box 18, folder 4.

5. *John Santo's Own Story*, 15–17.

6. *John Santo's Own Story*, 19–20. Rákosi's suspicions about Lautner had been fueled by a report about Hungarian American Communists that the Hungarian leader had solicited and received from the CPUSA leadership. Memo of Louis Weinstock, August 8, 1949, MOL, MszMP, 276-G5, 1–15.

7. *John Santo's Own Story*, 20; Abt, *Advocate and Activist*, 179.

8. The following is based on the recollections of one of Péter's co-workers, Paul Lendvai, in a letter of August 25, 1971, to Theodore Draper, in Theodore Draper Papers, Manuscripts, Archives, and Rare Book Library (MARBL), MSS579, box 15, folder 21; and Lendvai's email message to the author, January 15, 2008.

9. For what came to be called the "Lautner affair," see Lautner's testimony, RSACB, reel 17, 9294-9417; Joseph R. Starobin, *American Communism in Crisis: 1943-1957* (Cambridge, Mass.: Harvard University Press, 1972), 218–19; Charney, *Long Journey*, 219–21.

10. Hodos, *Show Trials*, 65.

11. Lendvai's letter to Draper, Theodore Draper Papers, MARBL.

12. Rákosi had ordered the secret police to take this action because he had come to the conclusion that Louis Weinstock was also an FBI agent. Since he could not persuade Weinstock to make a visit to Hungary, he retaliated against his wife and daughter. Letter of Louis Weinstock, November 28, 1950, MOL, MszMP, 276-G5, 27; and interview of Susan (Weinstock) Gould, January 10, 2010.

13. Interview of Susan (Weinstock) Gould, January 10, 2010.

14. Péter Memoir, part 1, p. 18.

15. Weinstein, "Interview with Jozsef Peter," AWP, March 20, 1975, 3.

16. Péter Memoir, part 2, p. 40.

17. Péter Memoir, part 2, p. 40. In all, Péter was the recipient of twelve awards and medals.

18. Weinstein, "Interview with Jozsef Peter," AWP, 4.

19. Interview of Dan Rosenberg, February 23, 2007.

20. Schmidt, "A Rajk per és az amerikai kapcsolat," p. 17, n. 8.

21. Caute, *Joseph Losey,* 50; Weinstein, "Interview with Jozsef Peter," AWP, 3.

22. Caute, *Joseph Losey,* 50.

23. Weinstein, "Interview with Jozsef Peter," AWP, 3.

24. Interview of Dan Rosenberg.

25. The following is based on Weinstein, "Interview with Jozsef Peter."

26. Weinstein, *Perjury*, 54.

27. Navasky, "Case Not Proved Against Hiss," 396.

28. Ronald Radosh's review of *Perjury, American Historical Review* 84, no. 2 (April 1979): 587.

29. According to Ann Péter, Weinstein had told them that "what he wanted to prove was the horrors of the McCarthy period." Donald Kirk, "Checking Up on Peter's Smile," *The Nation*, May, 6, 1978, 526.

30. Weinstein, "Interview with Jozsef Peter," AWP, 4.

31. Schmidt, *Battle of Wits*, 100.

32. The material submitted by Péter was divided into two parts. The first consisted of a two-page summary of his career, several pages of lists, an index, and an eleven-page draft of his career up to 1929. The second part, forty pages in length, is the complete memoir, which repeats much of the material from part 1 and contains some handwritten additions and corrections.

33. Barrett, "Was the Personal Political?" 398.

34. For a persuasive argument along these lines, see Schmidt, *Battle of Wits*, 97–99.

35. In his autobiography, published posthumously in 1993, Abt revealed that, despite his previous vehement denials, he had been a secret member of the Communist Party most of his adult life and had participated in what he called a Marxist study group in Washington, D.C., under the supervision of J. Peters.

36. *Népszabadság*, January 21, 1990, p. 11; *Magyar Sajtó*, no. 2, 1991, p. 16.

37. Isserman, "Notes from Underground," 857.

38. Haynes, "Historiography of Soviet Espionage, 16.

39. Weinstein and Vassiliev, *Haunted Wood*, 38.

40. Chambers, *Witness*, 338–39.

41. Weiner, "Soviet Spies," 2–3.

42. On this, see Haynes et al., *Spies*, 271–85.

43. Koestler, *Arrow in the Blue*, vol. 1, 260.

44. Sam Roberts, "Figure in Rosenberg Case Admits to Soviet Spying," *New York Times*, September 11, 2008, 1.

45. Mendelsohn, *Jews of East Central Europe*, 95.

46. Service, *Trotsky*, 199–200.

47. An excellent recent treatment of the remarkable cohort of Hungarian-Jewish émigrés is Kati Marton's *The Great Escape: Nine Jews Who Fled Hitler and Changed the World.*

48. "My Brother Is Coming" can be viewed at http://www.europafilmtreasures.eu/PY/293/see-the-film-my_brother_is_coming (accessed July 17, 2010).

Bibliography

Primary Sources

UNPUBLISHED

Bedacht, Max. "On the Path of Life: Memoirs of Your Father." Unpublished memoir in Max Bedacht Papers, O72, Box 1. Tamiment Library, New York University.

Chambers, Whittaker. "The Faking of Americans." In the Herbert Solow Papers, Box 5, Hoover Institution Archives, Stanford, California.

Crouch, Paul. Papers. Hoover Institution Archives, Stanford, California.

Darcy, Sam. Papers. Tamiment Library, New York University.

Davis, Hope Hale. Papers. Schlesinger Library, Radcliffe Institute, Harvard University.

Draper, Theodore. Papers. Manuscript, Archives, and Rare Book Library (MARBL), Emory University, Atlanta, Georgia.

Federal Bureau of Investigation, FOIA file of J. Peters (184255).

FBI reports sent by J. Edgar Hoover to General Edwin Watson, 1939. White House Official Files, Department of Justice, Box 10. Franklin D. Roosevelt Library, Hyde Park, New York.

Files of the Communist Party of the United States in the Comintern Archives, 326 microfilm reels. Leiden: IDC Publishers, 2000.

Gladnick, Robert (Serge Jarama). "I Was a Fifth Columnist." Isaac Dan Levine Papers, Emory University Library, Atlanta, Georgia.

"Gorsky Memo." Text of a memorandum written by Anatoly Gorsky in 1948, annotated by John Haynes. http://h-net.msu.edu/cgi-bin/logbrowse.pl?trx=vx&list=h-hoac&month=0503&week=b&msg=ycrsVT7M1e2L9EECiLFskg&user=&pw= (accessed July 26, 2010).

Immigration and Naturalization Services, Department of Justice, Deportation File of Alexander Stevens (J. Peters). FOIA file obtained from the Homeland Security Agency.

MASK Collection (Intercepted Comintern radio messages). National Cryptologic Museum, Fort Meade, Maryland.

Murphy, Raymond. "Memorandum of Conversation [with Whittaker Chambers]." March 20, 1945, and August 28, 1946, homepages.nyu.edu/~th15/break45.html; and http://homepages.nyu.edu/~th15/break8_28.html (both accessed July 26, 2010).

"Péter József visszaemlékezése" (Memoir of József Péter). Politkatudományi Intézet (Budapest), 867, f. p-235, parts 1 and 2.

Rang- und Einteilungslisten, AT-OeStA/KA Pers REL, K und.K. Armee, Infanterieregiment Nr. 66, Kriegsarchiv, Vienna, Austria.

Records of the American Committee for the Protection of the Foreign Born, in Labadie Collection, University of Michigan Library, Ann Arbor.

Records of the Central Control Commission of the Communist Party, reels 1–2, Tamiment Library, New York University.

Records of the Communist International (Comintern), Russian State Archive of Social and Political History (RGASPI), Fonds 495 and 515, Moscow, Russia.

Records of the Internal Security Subcommittee of the U.S. Senate, RG646, National Archives, Washington, D.C.

Records of the Magyar Szocialista Munkáspárt (Hungarian Socialist Workers Party, MszMP), Magyar Országos Levéltár (Hungarian National Archives), 276/G5, Budapest, Hungary.

Records of the Military Intelligence Division, United States War Department, RG165, National Archives, Silver Spring, Maryland.

Records of the Security Service, KV3/127, National Archives, London, U.K.

Reuben, William A. Papers. Labadie Collection, Special Collections Library, University of Michigan, Ann Arbor.

Tanenhaus, Sam. Papers. Hoover Institution Archives, Stanford, California.

Transcripts of Grand Jury Testimony in the Alger Hiss Case, RG118. Harry S. Truman Library, Independence, Missouri.

Vassiliev, B[oris]. "How the Communist International Formulates at Present the Problem of Organization." Theodore Draper Papers, Emory University, Atlanta, Georgia, Box 1, folder 21, 12–28.

Vassiliev Notebooks (VN), Library of Congress, Washington, D.C.

Weinstein, Allen. Papers (AWP). Hoover Institution Archive, Stanford, California.

Weyl, Nathaniel. Papers. Hoover Institution Archive, Stanford, California.

PUBLISHED

Abt, John J. *Advocate and Activist: Memoirs of an American Communist Lawyer.* Urbana: University of Illinois Press, 1995.

Alperin, Robert Jay. "Organization in the Communist Party, U.S.A., 1931–1938." Ph.D. diss., Northwestern University, 1959.

Browder, Earl. *The Reminiscences of Earl Browder.* Columbia University Oral History Collection, pt. 2, no. 21. Glen Rock, N.J.: Microfilming Corp. of America, 1975.

Budenz, Louis Francis. *This Is My Story.* New York: McGraw Hill, 1947.

"The Career of J. Peters." *Scope of Soviet Activity in the United States*, Hearings before the Subcommittee to Investigate the Administration of the Internal Security and Other Internal Security Laws of the Committee on the Judiciary. United States Senate, 84th Congress, Second Session, part 27. Washington, D.C.: Government Printing Office, 1956.

Chambers, Whittaker. *Witness.* New York: Random House, 1952.

Charney, George. *A Long Journey.* Chicago: Quadrangle, 1968.

Davis, Hope Hale. *Great Day Coming: A Memoir of the 1930s.* South Royalton, Vt.: Steerforth Press, 1994.

Dennis, Peggy. *The Autobiography of an American Communist.* Westport, Conn.: Lawrence Hill, 1977.

Field, Frederick Vanderbilt. *From Right to Left: An Autobiography.* Westport, Conn.: Lawrence Hill, 1983.

Gitlow, Benjamin. *I Confess: The Truth about American Communism.* New York: Dutton, 1940.

———. *The Whole of Their Lives: Communism in America; A Personal History and Intimate Portrayal of Its Leaders.* New York: Scribner's, 1948.

Hearings before the Committee on Un-American Activities. United States Congress, House of Representatives, 80th Congress, Second Session. Washington, D.C.: Government Printing Office, 1948.

Hearings before the Committee on Un-American Activities. Investigations of Un-American Propaganda Activities in the United States (Communist Party), vol. 7. United States Congress, House of Representatives. Washington, D.C.: U.S. Government Printing Office, 1946.

Hill, Jim. "From the Krumbein Training School." *Daily Worker* (June 8, 1936): 5.

House of Representatives. *Investigation of Un-American Propaganda Activities in the United States,* vols. 10–11. Washington, D.C.: Government Printing Office, 1940.

House Un-American Activities Committee. *A Communist in a Workers' Paradise: John Santo's Own Story.* Washington, D.C.: Government Printing Office, 1963.

Jenks, M. *The Communist Nucleus: What It Is, How It Works.* New York: Workers Library, 1928.

Kern, Gary, ed. *MI5 Debriefing and Other Documents on Soviet Intelligence.* Grand Terrace, Calif.: Xenos Books, 2004.

Klehr, Harvey, John Earl Haynes, and Fridrikh Igorevich Firsov, eds. *The Secret World of American Communism.* New Haven: Yale University Press, 1995.

Klehr, Harvey, John Earl Haynes, and Kyrill Mikhailovich Anderson, eds. *The Soviet World of American Communism.* New Haven: Yale University Press, 1998.

Koestler, Arthur. *Arrow in the Blue,* vol. 1. New York: Macmillan, 1952.

Krivitsky, Walter G. *In Stalin's Secret Service.* Frederick, Md.: University Publications of America, 1985.

Massing, Hede. *This Deception.* New York: Duell, Sloan, and Pearce, 1951.

Peters, J. *The Communist Party: A Manual on Organization.* New York: Workers Library Publishers, 1935.

———. "Mass Defense Is the Only Answer to Terror." *Party Organizer* 7, no. 7 (July 1934): 30–31.

———. "Organizational Problems in the Light of the Open Letter." *The Communist* 12, no. 9 (September 1933): 948–54.

———. "The Organizational Structure of the Party." *Party Organizer* 8, no. 6 (June 1935): 21–25.

———. "Strengthen the Fighting Ability of the Party." *Party Organizer* 7, no. 9 (September 1934): 24–25.

———. "Strike Wave Is Opportunity to Recruit Party Members." *Daily Worker* (October 1933): 10–11.

———. "A Study of Fluctuation in the Chicago District." *Party Organizer* 6 (September 1933): 20–26.

Records of the Subversive Activities Control Board, 1950–1972, parts 1 and 2. Frederick, Md.: University Publications of America, 1988.

Scope of Soviet Activity in the United States, Hearings before the Subcommittee to Investigate the Administration of the Internal Security and Other Internal Security Laws of the Committee on the Judiciary. United States Senate, 84th Congress, Second Session, part 27. Washington, D.C.: Government Printing Office, 1956.

Ulanovskaya, Maya, and Nadezhda Ulanovskaya. *Istoriya Odnot Semyi* (One Family's Story). New York: Chalidze Publications, 1982.

U.S. Military Intelligence Reports: Surveillance of Radicals in the United States, 1917–1941. Frederick, Md.: University Publications of America, 1984.

Vörös, Sándor. *American Commisar.* Philadelphia: Chilton, 1961.

Wadleigh, Henry Julian. "Why I Spied for the Communists." *New York Post Home News,* July 11–15, 17–19, 21–23, 1949.

Weyl, Nathaniel. *Encounters with Communism.* Philadelphia: Xlibris, 2003.

———. "I Was in a Communist Unit with Hiss: Revelations of a Liberal." *U.S. News and World Report,* January 9, 1953, 22–40.

Zinkin, Peter. *A Man to be Watched Carefully.* Newcastle: People's Publications, 1985.

Newspapers and Periodicals

Counterattack: Facts to Combat Communism
Daily Mirror
Daily Worker
Magyar Sajtó
The Nation
Népszabadság
The New Republic
Newsweek
New York Herald Tribune
New York Journal American
New York Sun
New York Times
New York World Telegram
Party Organizer
Time
Új Előre

Secondary Sources

Andrew, Christopher, and Oleg Gordievsky. *KGB: The Inside Story of Its Foreign Operations from Lenin to Gorbachev*. New York: Harper Collins, 1990.

Andrew, Christopher, and Vasili Mitrokhin. *The Sword and the Shield: The Mitrokhin Archive and the Secret History of the KGB*. New York: Basic Books, 1999.

Barrett, James R. *William Z. Foster and the Tragedy of American Radicalism*. Urbana: University of Illinois Press, 1999.

———. "Was the Personal Political? Reading the Autobiography of American Communism." *International Review of Social History* 53, no. 3 (2008): 395–423.

Borsányi, György. *The Life of a Communist Revolutionary, Béla Kun*. Boulder: Social Science Monographs, 1993.

Budenz, Louis. *Men Without Faces: The Communist Conspiracy in the United States*. New York: Harper, 1948.

Buhle, Paul. "Spies Everywhere." *Radical History Review* 67 (Winter 1997): 187–98.

Caute, David. *Joseph Losey: A Revenge on Life*. New York: Oxford University Press, 1994.

Craig, Bruce. *Treasonable Doubt: The Harry Dexter White Spy Case*. Lawrence: University Press of Kansas, 2004.

Dallin, David J. *Soviet Espionage*. New Haven: Yale University Press, 1955.

Deák, István. *Beyond Nationalism: A Social and Political History of the Habsburg Officer Corps, 1848–1918*. New York: Oxford University Press, 1990.

———. "Communism's Appeals Revisited." *East European Politics and Societies* 16, no. 1 (2002): 314–22.

Der Fall Noel Field, vols. 1 and 2. Ed. Bernd-Rainer Barth, Werner Schweizer, and Thomas Grimm. Berlin: Basis Druck, 2005–7.

Draper, Theodore. *American Communism and Soviet Russia*. New York: Viking Press, 1960.

Encyclopedia of the American Left. Ed. Mari Jo Buhle, Paul Buhle, and Dan Georgakas. New York: Garland, 1990 (1st ed.) and 1998 (2nd ed.).

Fagan, Ann. *Carol Weiss King: Human Rights Lawyer, 1895–1952*. Niwot: University Press of Colorado, 1993.

Frank, Tibor. "Between Red and White: The Mood and Mind of Hungary's Radicals, 1919–1920." *Hungarian Studies* 9, nos. 1–2 (1994): 105–26.

———. "Patterns of Interwar Hungarian Immigration to the United States." *Hungarian Studies Review* 30, nos. 1–2 (2003): 3–27.

———. "Pioneers Welcome: The Escape of Hungarian Modernism to the US, 1919–1945." *Hungarian Studies* 8, no. 2 (1993): 237–60.

Fried, Richard M. *Nightmare in Red: The McCarthy Era in Perspective*. New York: Oxford University Press, 1990.

Gall, Gilbert J. *Pursuing Justice: Lee Pressman, the New Deal, and the CIO*. Albany: State University of New York Press, 1999.

Garber, Marjorie, and Rebecca Walkowitz, eds. *Secret Agents: The Rosenberg Case, McCarthyism, and Fifties America*. New York: Routledge, 1995.

Gentry, Curt. *J. Edgar Hoover: The Man and the Secrets*. New York: Penguin, 1991.

Hajdu, Tibor. "A Rajk-per háttere és fázisai" (The Background and Phases of the Rajk Trial). http://www.rev.hu/sulinet45/szerviz/szakirod/hajdutib.htm (accessed July 6, 2010).

Haynes, John Earl. "The Historiography of Soviet Espionage and American Communism: From Separate to Converging Paths." http://www.johnearlhaynes.org/page101. html (accessed July 6, 2010).

Haynes, John Earl, and Harvey Klehr. *In Denial: Historians, Communism, and Espionage.* San Francisco: Encounter Books, 2003.

———. *Venona: Decoding Soviet Espionage in America.* New Haven: Yale University Press, 2000.

Haynes, John Earl, Harvey Klehr, and Alexander Vassiliev. *Spies: The Rise and Fall of the KGB in America.* New Haven: Yale University Press, 2009.

Hodos, George H. *Show Trials: Stalinist Purges in Eastern Europe, 1948–1954.* New York: Praeger, 1987.

Horne, Gerald. *The Final Victim of the Blacklist: John Howard Lawson, Dean of the Hollywood Ten.* Berkeley: University of California Press, 2006.

Ignotus, Paul. *Hungary.* New York: Praeger, 1972.

Isserman, Maurice. "Disloyalty as a Principle: Why Communists Spied." http://www .afsa.org/fsj/octoo/isserman.cfm (accessed August 3, 2010).

———. "Notes from Underground." *The Nation,* June 12, 1995, 846–56.

———. "Three Generations: Historians View American Communism." *Labor History* 26 (Fall 1985): 517–45.

———. *Which Side Were You On?: The American Communist Party during the Second World War.* Urbana: University of Illinois Press, 1993.

Johanningsmeier, Edward P. *Forging American Communism: The Life of William Z. Forster.* Princeton: Princeton University Press, 1994.

Keeran, Roger. *The Communist Party and the Auto Workers Unions.* Bloomington: Indiana University Press, 1980.

Kessler, Lauren. *Clever Girl: Elizabeth Bentley, the Spy Who Ushered in the McCarthy Era.* New York: Harper Collins, 2003.

Kirk, Donald. "Checking Up on Peter's Smile." *The Nation,* May 6, 1978, 525–26.

Klehr, Harvey. *The American Communist Movement: Storming Heaven Itself.* NewYork: Maxwell McMillan, 1992.

———. *Communist Cadre: The Social Background of the American Communist Party Elite.* Stanford, Calif.: Hoover Institution Press, 1978.

———. *The Heyday of American Communism: The Depression Decade.* New York: Basic Books, 1984.

Latham, Earl. *The Communist Controversy in Washington: From the New Deal to McCarthy.* New York: Atheneum, 1966.

Leonard, Raymond W. *Secret Soldiers of the Revolution: Soviet Military Intelligence, 1918–1933.* Westport, Conn.: Greenwood Press, 1999.

Magocsi, Paul Robert. *The Shaping of National Identity: Subcarpathian Rus', 1848–1948.* Cambridge: Harvard University Press, 1978.

Malkin, Maurice L. *Return to My Father's House: A Charter Member of the American Communist Party Tells Why He Joined, and Why He Later Left to Fight Communism.* New Rochelle, N.Y.: Arlington House, 1972.

Marton, Kati. *The Great Escape: Nine Jews Who Fled Hitler and Changed the World.* New York: Simon & Schuster, 2006.

Mayenburg, Ruth von. *Hotel Lux.* Munich: Bertelsmann, 1978.

McKnight, David. *Espionage and the Roots of the Cold War: The Conspiratorial Heritage.* London: Frank Cass, 2002.

Mendelsohn, Ezra. *The Jews of East Central Europe between the World Wars.* Bloomington: Indiana University Press, 1983.

Mitrokhin, Vasiliv, ed. *KGB Lexicon: The Soviet Intelligence Officer's Handbook.* London: Frank Cass, 2002.

Navasky, Victor. "The Case Not Proved against Hiss." *The Nation,* April 6, 1978, 395–96.

Ottanelli, Fraser M. *The Communist Party of the United States: From the Depression to World War II.* New Brunswick, N.J.: Rutgers University Press, 1991.

Packer, Herbert L. *Ex-Communist Witnesses: Four Studies in Fact Finding.* Stanford, Calif.: Stanford University Press, 1962.

Pataki, Raphael. *The Jews of Hungary: History, Culture, Psychology.* Detroit: Wayne State University Press, 1996.

Pedersen, Vernon L. *The Communist Party in Maryland, 1919–57.* Urbana: University of Illinois Press, 1999.

Perlman, Robert. *Bridging Three Worlds: Hungarian-Jewish Americans, 1848–1914.* Amherst: University of Massachusetts Press, 1991.

Perry, Jeffrey B. "Pseudonyms: A Reference Aid for Studying American Communist History." *American Communist History* 3, no. 1 (2004): 55–126.

Puskás, Julianna. *Ties That Bind, Ties That Divide: 100 Years of Hungarian Experience in the United States.* New York: Holmes & Meier, 2000.

Radosh, Ronald, and Allis Radosh. *Red Star over Hollywood: The Film Colony's Long Romance with the Left.* San Francisco: Encounter, 2005.

Romerstein, Herbert, and Eric Breindel. *The Venona Secrets: Exposing Soviet Espionage and America's Traitors.* Washington, D.C.: Regnery, 2000.

Romerstein, Herbert, and Stanislav Levchenko. *The KGB against the "Main Enemy": How the Soviet Intelligence Service Operates against the United States.* Lexington, Mass.: D. C. Heath, 1989.

Rosenfeldt, Niels Erik. *Stalin's Secret Chancellery and the Comintern.* Copenhagen: C. A. Reitzels, 1991.

Ryan, James G. *Earl Browder: The Failure of American Communism.* Tuscaloosa: University of Alabama Press, 1997.

———. "Socialist Triumph as a Family Value: Earl Browder and Soviet Espionage." *American Communist History* 1, no. 2 (December 2002): 125–42.

Sakmyster, Thomas. "A Communist Newspaper for Hungarian Americans: The Strange World of the *Új Előre.*" *Hungarian Studies Review* 32 (2005): 41–70.

———. "A Hungarian in the Comintern: József Pogány/John Pepper." In *Agents of the*

Revolution: New Biographical Approaches to the History of International Communism in the Age of Lenin and Stalin, edited by Kevin Morgan, Gidon Cohen, and Andrew Flinn, 220–45. Oxford: Peter Lang, 2005.

———. *Hungary's Admiral on Horseback: Miklós Horthy, 1918–1944.* Boulder: East European Monographs/Columbia University Press, 1980.

———. "J. Peters (Goldberger Sándor) és az amerikai kommunista mozgalom" (J. Peters /Sándor Goldberger and the American Communist Movement). *Századok,* no. 1 (2007): 185–202.

Schlesinger, Arthur M., Jr. *The Coming of the New Deal, 1933–1935.* Boston: Houghton Mifflin, 1959.

Schmidt, Mária. *A titkosszolgálatok kulisszái mögött: Hirek, ideológiák és hirszerzők a XX. században* (Behind the Scenes of the Secret Services: Ideas, Ideologies, and Intelligence Agents in the Twentieth Century). Budapest: XX. Század Intézet, 2006.

———. *Battle of Wits: Beliefs, Ideologies, and Secret Agents in the Twentieth Century.* Budapest: XX. Század Intézet, 2007.

———. "Noel Field: The American Communist at the Center of Stalin's East European Purge: From the Hungarian Archives." *American Communist History* 3, no. 2 (2004): 214–45.

———. "A Rajk-per és az amerikai kapcsolat." http://www.hhrf.org/korunk/9805/5k15 .htm (accessed July 26, 2010).

Schrecker, Ellen. "Before the Rosenbergs: Espionage Scenarios in the Early Cold War." In *Secret Agents: The Rosenberg Case, McCarthyism, and Fifties America,* edited by Marjorie Garber and Rebecca Walkowitz, 127–42. New York: Routledge, 1995.

Service, Robert. *Trotsky: A Biography.* Cambridge: Harvard University Press, 2009.

Shover, John L. "The Communist Party and the Midwest Farm Crisis of 1933." *Journal of American History* 51, no. 2 (September 1964): 251.

Sibley, Katherine A. S. *Red Spies in America: Stolen Secrets and the Dawn of the Cold War.* Lawrence: University Press of Kansas, 2004.

Smith, Andrew. *I Was a Soviet Worker.* New York: Robert Hale, 1937.

Storch, Randi. *Red Chicago: American Communism at Its Grassroots, 1928–35.* Urbana: University of Illinois Press, 2007.

———. "'Their unCommunist Stand': Chicago's Foreign-Speaking Communists and the Question of Stalinization, 1928–1935." In *Bolshevism, Stalinism, and the Comintern: Perspectives on Stalinization, 1917–53,* edited by Nathan LaPorte, Kevin Morgan, and Matthew Worley, 263–67. New York: Palgrave Macmillan, 2008.

Suvorov, Victor. *Inside Soviet Military Intelligence.* New York: Macmillan, 1984.

Tanenhaus, Sam. *Whittaker Chambers: A Biography.* New York: Modern Library, 1998.

Theoharis, Athan. *Spying on Americans: Political Surveillance from Hoover to the Huston Plan.* Philadelphia: Temple University Press, 1978.

Várdy, Steven Béla. *The Hungarian Americans: The Hungarian Experience in North America.* New York: Chelsea House, 1990.

Weiner, Tim. "Soviet Spies: Did They Make a Difference?" *World Policy Journal* 16, no. 1 (1999): 2–3. http://www.fsa.ulaval.ca/personnel/vernag/eh/f/cons/lectures/weiner .html (accessed August 3, 2010).

Weinstein, Allen. *Perjury: The Hiss-Chambers Case.* New York: Knopf, 1978.

Weinstein, Allen, and Alexander Vassiliev. *The Haunted Wood: Soviet Espionage in America—The Stalin Years.* New York: Random House, 1999.

West, Nigel. *Mask: MI5's Penetration of the Communist Party of Great Britain.* London: Routledge, 2005.

White, G. Edward. *Alger Hiss's Looking-Glass Wars: The Covert Life of a Soviet Spy.* Oxford: Oxford University Press, 2004.

Index

Abraham Lincoln Brigade, 69, 105, 204n63, 218n62

Abt, John, 50, 163; friendship with J. Peters, 77, 127, 138–39, 171, 174; member of Ware group, 74, 76, 86–87, 89; and Perlo group, 132–33

Adler, Solomon, 104, 218n58

Agriculture Adjustment Agency (AAA), 74, 76

Akhmerov, Iskhak, 70–71, 95, 106, 209n77, 215n12

Alien Registration Act (Smith Act), 118–19, 146

Alpi, Mario ("Brown"), 43, 117

American Committee for Protection of the Foreign Born (ACPFB), 165, 226n54

American Feature Writers Syndicate, 85, 186

America Sings for Victory, 120, 190

Amersak, Francuska, 9, 121

Amter, Israel, 23, 52

Anglo-American Secretariat (of the Comintern), 30–32, 34, 109

anti-Communism, 120; as element of Cold War, xiv, 139–41, 144, 165–66

Anti-Horthy League, 13–14

anti-Semitism: in Eastern Europe, 8; in Hungary, 5–7, 189

Apparatus B, 83, 92, 94–95, 102–3, 218n57

"Arena," 106

Arts Project, 73, 119

Bachrach, Marion, 76, 88

Baker, Rudy, 23, 58; appointed director of

secret apparatus, 112–13; and "illegal apparatus," 26–28; report on secret apparatus, 40, 112

Baltimore documents, 159

Bebrits, Lajos, 169

Bedacht, Max, 19, 31, 181, 206n31; connection to Soviet intelligence, 61–62, 67, 69, 79; and J. Peters, xvii, 62, 229n30; and Whittaker Chambers, 61–62

Bell, Tom, 30

Bentley, Elizabeth, 133, 224n10

Berle, Adolf A., 122

Biberman, Herbert, 119, 125, 145, 221n34

Biddle, Francis, 128

"Bill," 161, 216n33; as handler of Whittaker Chambers, 83–85, 92–93, 95, 98–99, 103; identity of, 213n52; as victim of purges, 100

Boorstein, Isadore, 28, 39, 141, 153

Braman, Ruth, 69

Bransten, Louise, 125

Browder, Earl ("Campbell"), 17–18, 32–33, 43, 49, 53; arrest and imprisonment, 116–17, 125, 134; collaboration with NKVD, 62, 75, 105, 131–33; and Communist Political Association, 134–36; and Peters's Washington operation, 75, 102, 112, 133, 220n5; relationship with J. Peters, 40, 43, 62, 211n8; support of Joe Peter by, 28, 31, 33, 36

Browderism, 170. *See also* Browder, Earl

"Brown," 43, 117

Brunck, Hermann, 87

Budenz, Louis, 41, 106, 207n37; testimony about J. Peters, 139–40, 153–55
Buhle, Paul, xix
Bullitt, William, 102
Bykov, Boris, 103–5, 109–11, 114, 131

Calomiris, Angela, 203n41
"Campbell." See Browder, Earl
Camp Unity, 64
Carpenter, David, 97–101, 161, 216n34
Castleton, Sylvia, 72–73, 184, 209n82
Central Control Commission: of the Comintern, 29; of the CPUSA, 113, 116
Chambers, Whittaker, 35, 90, 94; begins underground work, 61–62; and Boris Bykov, 102–4; defection of, 108–11, 113–14; espionage activity of, 82, 92–93, 96, 98–103; and fraudulent passports, 67; and the GRU, 79–81, 83–85; identifies J. Peters, 129, 151–52; relationship with J. Peters, 62, 79, 106–8, 110, 176; and Stalinist show trials, 107–8; testimony about CP underground, xiv, 122–24, 145–46, 159–60; and Ware group, 78, 81–83
Chambers-Hiss controversy, xv, 158–59
Charney, George, 54, 138, 188
Childs, Morris, 125
Churchill, Winston, 139
Clark, Tom, 142, 228n3
Coe, Robert, 96
Cold War, public attitudes during, 139–41, 144
Cole, Lester, 119, 145
Collins, Henry, 76, 82, 86, 94, 211n31
Comintern (Communist International), 25–26, 32, 36–37, 40, 92; instructions to CPUSA, 63; launches Popular Front, 52–53. See also OMS
Commission on Illegal Work (in the Comintern), 25, 38
Communist International. See Comintern
Communist Party: A Manual on Organization, The, 135, 172, 175, 181–82, 188; content of, 48–50; genesis of, 47–48; impact in Cold War era, 48, 140–41; at J. Peters's deportation hearing, 155; in the Popular Front era, 53–54; as reflection of CPUSA views, 51–53, 122, 140–41; reprint of, 168, 231n60; used in CP schools, 52
Communist Party of the United States of America (CPUSA), 134–36; attitude toward A Manual on Organization, 51–53; attitude toward ethnic federations, 12–13;

cooperation with Soviet intelligence, 61–63, 105, 183–84; and the Depression, 20–21; electoral successes of, 137; and food riots, 22, 198n89; and fraudulent passports, 66–67; membership fluctuation in, 31, 42–45; prosecutions by U.S. government, 116–17, 158; publications of, 51–52; public opinion of, xiv, 51, 60, 134, 139; as recipient of government documents, 76, 101–2; and World War II, 116, 120
Communist Political Association. (CPA), 134–36. See also Communist Party of the United States of America
Congress of Industrial Organizations (CIO), 89
Crane, William Edward, 217n37
Crouch, Paul, 58–59
Csap, 1–3, 6
Curtiz, Michael, 191–92
Czechoslovakia, 7, 143, 163, 165

Daily Worker, xxi, 15–17, 19, 47, 140; and trial of J. Peters, 144
Dallin, David, xv
Davis, Benjamin J., 137
Davis, Hope Hale: admiration for J. Peters, 87–88; as member of Ware group, 78
democratic centralism, 48, 188
Dennis, Gene, 142
Dennis, Peggy, 201n46
Deutscher, Isaac, 190
Dies Committee. See House Un-American Activities Committee
District 2 (of CPUSA), 20, 23
Dodd, William, 101
Donegan, Tom, 160–62
Donovan, John, 211n13
Duggan, Larry, 94–95, 215n15

"Edwards." See Eisler, Gerhardt
Eisler, Gerhardt ("Edwards"), 35, 41, 139, 167; friendship with J. Peters, 39, 54
Electric Boat Company, 79–80
"Ewald," 67–70, 100–101, 108, 114

Faking of Americans, The (Whittaker Chambers), 113
Farb, Ralph, 150, 162
Federal Bureau of Investigation (FBI), 60, 80; attempts to make deal with J. Peters, 162; early lack of interest in CPUSA, 107, 121; illegal methods of, 125, 127–28, 230n42; interview of Whittaker Chambers, 145;

investigation of J. Peters, 123, 129–31, 168; pursuit of Alexander Stevens, 121, 124–27, 141–42
Feierabend, Albert, 63, 207n41
Field, Frederick Vanderbilt, 72, 73, 94, 174, 209n83
Field, Noel, 93–95, 170, 172
Fifth Amendment, invoked by Alexander Stevens, 152, 160–62
Fitzgerald, Edward ("Ted"), 71, 131
Foster, William Z., 18, 20, 31, 33, 135; as author of *In Soviet America*, 51, 53; Joe Peter's appraisal of, 28, 36
Fraad, Lewis, 174, 210n87
Frank, Nelson, 140
Freeman, Joe, 88, 138

Garber, Ossip, 69, 114–15
Gates, John, 117
Gellért, Hugó, 14
Gibarti, Louis (Dobos, László), 54, 105, 209n68, 218n63
Gitlow, Benjamin, 19, 67, 129, 206n29, 208n57
Gladnick, Robert, 65–66
Glaser, James S., 123, 203n30
Glasser, Harold, 104, 131–32, 161, 218n57, 224n8
Goldberger, Emerich (Goldberger, Imre), 2, 128
Goldberger, Imre, 2, 128
Goldberger, Joseph (Goldberger, József), 2, 8, 138, 162, 167, 226n37
Goldberger, József, 2, 8, 138, 162, 167, 226n37
Goldberger, Sándor (Goldberger, Alexander): applies for American citizenship, 10; changes name to József Péter, 11; conversion to Communism, 6; education of, 3; emigration to United States, 8–10; falsifies immigration application, 9; family origins of, 2–3; Jewish origins of, xxi, 2–3; joins Workers Party, 10; knowledge of Yiddish, 2; and law school, 4–5; marries Francuska Amersak, 9; military service in World War I, 4–5, 7–9; physical description of, 10–11; works in toy factory, 10, 11, 30. *See also* Peter, Joe; Péter, József; Peters, J.; Stevens, Alexander
Golos, Jacob, 35, 109, 161, 211n8; and fraudulent passports, 67
Gomperz, Hede, 40, 70–71, 91, 94–95
Granich, Grace, 41

Graze, Gerald ("Arena"), 106
GRU (Main Intelligence Directorate), 61, 81, 100, 111, 131, 132

Hall, Gus, 167, 173
Hathaway, Clarence, 29, 32, 51, 200n29
Haynes, John, xviii, 218n60
Herbst, Josephine, 76, 78
Hewitt, George, 34, 153
Hiss, Alger, 90, 159, 160–62; and confrontation with Whittaker Chambers, 146, 148; espionage activity of, 92, 94–95, 103; joins State Department, 101; as member of Ware group, 74, 76; and Nye Committee, 82, 92–94
Hiss, Donald, 76, 148, 160, 211n14
Hiss grand jury, 159, 160–62
Hollywood Ten, 145
Hook, Sidney, 87, 214n68
Hoover, J. Edgar, 121–23, 128, 130–31, 141, 176
Hotel Lux, 29, 33
House Un-American Activities Committee (HUAC), 122–23, 139, 145–47; Alexander Stevens's testimony before, 151–53; pursuit of J. Peters by, 142; Whittaker Chambers's testimony before, 146–47
HUAC. *See* House Un-American Activities Committee
Hungarian Federation (Hungarian Bureau), 10–12, 20; factionalism in, 13, 17–18, 180–81
Hutchins, Grace, 111

Ikal, Arnold ("Richard," "Ewald"), 67–70, 100–101, 108, 114
"illegal apparatus," 25–27, 40, 57; implemented by J. Peters, 57–60; reaction of CPUSA members to, 27, 58–60; relationship to secret apparatus, 60–61; revived by Alexander Stevens, 117–19. *See also* secret apparatus
immigrants, Hungarian, success in the United States, 1, 191–92
Immigration Act of 1917, 149
Immigration Act of 1924, 142, 149
Immigration and Naturalization Service (INS): and arrest of Alexander Stevens, 142; and deportation case against Alexander Stevens, 144–45, 153–57, 165–66; offers deal to Alexander Stevens, 162; plan to deport Communist aliens, 149–50
Inslerman, Felix, 101, 114

In Soviet America, 51, 53
International Lenin School, 34, 153, 203n31
International Liaison Section. *See* OMS
Isserman, Maurice, xvi, xix

Jerome, V. J., 119
Jews, Hungarian: assimilation of, 2; as
    Comintern agents, 188–89; as immigrants
    to the United States, 1, 191; prejudice
    against, 4–7; tolerance of, 2, 189
Johnston, Eric, 226n42

Kádár, János, 172–73
Katz, Otto, 114, 119
King, Carol Weiss, 143, 148, 151, 226n53;
    and deportation case of Alexander Ste-
    vens, 150, 153, 156–58, 162, 164–67; and
    Hiss trial, 230n43
Kirk, Donald, 177–78
Klehr, Harvey, xviii
Koestler, Arthur, 188
konspiratsia (also spelled "konspiratsiya"),
    90, 199n6, 214n80
Kramer, Charles (Krivitsky, Charles), 76–77,
    88, 131
Krumbein Training School, 47
Kun, Béla, 35, 109, 190, 196n14

Lautner, John, 59–60, 74, 159, 203n30; as
    friend of J. Peters, xvii, 145–46, 169; as
    victim of Hungarian show trial, 170–71
Lawrence, Bill, 50
Lawson, John, 119, 125, 145, 151
Lewis, John L., 121
Lieber, Maxim, 72, 84–85, 110, 113, 131,
    224n8
Losey, Joseph, 72–73, 119, 174
Lovestone, Jay, 17–19, 61, 67, 181
Lugosi, Béla, 14

Ma, 15–16
mail drops, 56, 59
Malkin, Maurice, 23, 153–55
Markin, Valentin, 80–81, 83, 93
Marx, Groucho, 151
Massing, Hede (Gumperz, Hede), 40, 70–71,
    91, 94–95
Mikhailov, Boris ("Williams"), 26–27, 39
Mikhelson-Manuilov, Solomon Vladi-
    mirovich, 62
Miller, Steve: appointed to National Com-
    mittee, 158; as organizational secretary,

134–37; speeches of, 135–36. *See also*
    Goldberger, Sándor; Peter, Joe; Péter, Józ-
    sef; Peters, J.; Stevens, Alexander
Mingulin, I. G., 109
Mink, George, 67
Minor, Robert, 31, 36, 51
Molotov, Vyacheslav, 30
Moore, R. Walton, 102
Moren, Mark, 105, 114
Moscow show trials, 87, 107–8
Mundt, Karl, 142, 146–47

Nation, The, 177–78
Navasky, Victor, 177
Nelson, Eleanor, 97–98
Nemzetközi Szemle, 173
New York County, Steve Miller's activity in,
    134–38
Nixon, Richard, 148, 151–52, 160
NKVD (People's Commissariat for Internal
    Affairs), 61, 62, 80, 93, 95, 101; and Perlo
    group, 131
Noda, Hideo, 72, 85
"non-Jewish Jews," 190–91
Nowell, William Odell, 33, 122, 153, 303n35
Nye Committee, 82, 92, 95, 96

"October Hill," 139, 158
Office of Strategic Services (OSS), 170
OGPU (State Political Directorate), 61. *See
    also* NKVD
OMS (International Liaison Department),
    37–38, 201n54; connection to CPUSA,
    62–63; program to infiltrate armed forces,
    63–64; training of J. Peters, 37–38
org practicant, 30, 33, 199n12
Osman, Robert, 65
Ottanelli, Fraser, xvii
Ovakimyan, Gayk, 132

Party Organizer, 47, 50, 57, 64
Pass Apparat, 38, 66
passport fraud, 61, 146; in Berlin, 38, 66; di-
    rected by J. Peters, 66–70; investigated by
    Department of Justice, 114
Pepper, John, 11, 196n14
Perjury: The Hiss-Chambers Case (Allen
    Weinstein), 175–78
Perlo, Katherine Wills, 106
Perlo, Victor, 119; collaboration with
    NKVD, 106; espionage work during
    World War II, 131, 187; as member of

Ware group, 76, 88, 103–4; relationship with J. Peters, 89

Perlo group, 131–32, 183

Péter, Ann, 170, 172–73, 177–78. *See also* Silver, Sophie; Stevens, Ann

Peter, Joe: advocacy of violence by, 22; attitude to "stool pigeons," 22; Comintern questionnaire of, 29–30; as CPUSA representative to Comintern, 33–36; and creation of "illegal apparatus," 25–26, 29, 40; and Earl Browder, 27, 36; food raid proposed by, 22; leadership style of, 20–22; and Lily Szirtes, 28; and Manya Reiss, 29, 36; meets Gerhardt Eisler and Jacob Golos, 35; and membership problems, 21; relationship with black American Communists, 35; and review of District 2, 23–24; speech before Anglo-American Secretariat, 31–32; studies of CPUSA membership by, 30–31; as trainee in Comintern, 29–33; training in Berlin, 38; training in illegal work in Moscow, 36–38; use of alias "J. Peters" and use of fraudulent passport by, 28. *See also* Goldberger, Sándor; Miller, Steve; Péter, József; Peters, J.; Stevens, Alexander

Péter, József: as activist in Workers Party, 11–12; and Allen Weinstein, 175–77; as alternate member of Central Committee, 17, 20; American visitors in Hungary, 174–75; career as editor in Hungary, 171–73; commitment to Communist ideals of, 12, 14–15; death of, 180; denunciation of Jay Lovestone by, 19; frugal life style of, 17; helps organize anti-fascist front group, 13–14; as Hungarian expert on United States, 172–73; and Hungarian show trial, 170–71; journalistic work of, 12, 14–15; leadership style of, 13; life style in Hungary, 173; his plan to rescue *Daily Worker*, 16–17; receives awards of merit, 172–73; his return to Hungary, 169–70; and revolution of 1956, 172; as secretary of Hungarian Federation, 13–14; and Soviet Russia, 15, 17–18; studies of CPUSA membership by, 30–31; as teacher in Party schools, 27; his ties to the Comintern, 27–28, 182. *See also* Goldberger, Sándor; Miller, Steve; Peter, Joe; Peters, J.; Stevens, Alexander

Peters, J.: and Alger Hiss, 82–83, 90, 95; Americanization of, 54, 189–90; and anti-

Trotsky campaign, 88–105; attempts to increase CP membership, 43–45; attitude toward "stool pigeons," 46–47; author of manual on organization, 47–54; book cipher used by, 57, 59–60; collaboration with Bill, 84–85, 92–93, 99–100; common-law marriage with Sophie Silver, 54–55; as Communist ideologue, 187–88; cooperation with OMS, 40, 62–63; as CP organizer in Detroit, 42–43; death of, 62, 180, 224n26; director of CP underground, 61; and Earl Browder, 40, 43, 62, 211n8; as editor in Hungary, 171–72; espionage operation in Washington, D.C., 82–83, 97–104, 131–33, 185–87; fraudulent passport operation, 66–71, 105, 107–8, 114–15, 185; and Frederick Vanderbilt Field, 72, 94; and Gerhardt Eisler, 54; and Hede Massing, 70–71; "illegal apparatus" built by, 58–60, 182–83; infiltration of armed forces, 63–66; involvement in "cadre affairs," 42–44; and Iskhak Ahkmerov, 71, 105–6; and Joseph Losey, 72–73, 119, 174; as "legendary Bolshevik," 138; and Maxim Lieber, 72, 110, 131; as member of Central Control Commission, 113; military espionage attempted by, 79–80; personality of, 71, 182; public image of, 140, 144; pursued by FBI, 123–24, 129; as recruiter for underground work, 71–73, 184–85; relationship with Whittaker Chambers, 79, 103–4, 106–11; reorganization of CP's governing structure, 45; replaced as head of secret apparatus, 111–12; role in CPUSA personnel decisions, 46; secret apparatus built by, 40, 56–57, 183; and Stalinist show trials, 87, 107–8; as teacher in Party schools, 64–65, 123; ties to Soviet intelligence agencies, 62, 67–70, 79–80, 99–100, 105; unpublished memoir of, xix, 178–80, 195n33; use of aliases, xiv, 41, 139–40; and Ware group, 74, 76–79, 86–89; work in Baltimore district, 104. *See also* Goldberger, Sándor; Miller, Steve; Peter, Joe; Péter, József; "Steve"; Stevens, Alexander; "Storm"

Pigman, William Ward, 99, 100, 103, 217n38

Popular Front, 52–54, 60, 87, 115

Poyntz, Julia Stuart, 109, 114, 219n72

Pressman, Lee, as member of Ware group, 74, 76, 78, 86; relationship with J. Peters, 88–89, 105, 175

Proctor, James, 72, 127

questionnaires, personal (in CPUSA), 46, 203n30

Rabinowitz, Gregory ("Roberts"), 39, 105, 207n39
Radosh, Ronald, 177
Rajk, László, 166, 170
Rákosi, Mátyás, 35, 164, 166, 169, 171
Red Front Fighters, 20, 23
Reiss, Manya (Aerova, Maria), 29, 36
Reno, Franklin Victor, 65, 103
"revisionists," xvii
"Richards," 67–70, 100–101, 108, 114
"Roberts," 39, 105, 207n39
Robeson, Paul, 174
Robinson/Rubens affair, 108, 114
"romantic anti-fascists," 75, 91, 103, 107, 185
Roosevelt, Franklin Delano, 101, 106, 122, 125
Rosenberg, Dan, 174
Rostovsky, Louis, 36
Ruthenia, 2, 3, 6
Ruthven, Madeleine, 125

Salt, Waldo, 125
Santo, John, 165, 166, 170
secret apparatus (of CPUSA), 40; cooperation with Soviet intelligence, 61–62; "illegal apparatus" as part of, 57–61; safeguarding CPUSA records, 56; secure communications, 57. See also illegal apparatus
Sheen, Msgr. Fulton J., 140
Shemitz, Reuben, 111
Sherman, John, 84–85, 210n85
Sik, Endre, 166
Silver, Sophie (Frommer, Sosse Frechman), 54–55, 129. See also Péter, Ann; Stevens, Ann
Silverman, George, 76, 88–89, 96, 104, 110, 147
Simon, Mózes, 169, 171
Smedley, Agnes, 72, 210n85
Smith, Andrew, 34–35, 122, 153
Smith, Jessica, 127, 128, 139, 174
Smith Act, 118–19, 146
Smith Act trials, 158, 168
"social fascists," 23, 51
Socialist Party, 23, 51
Sparks, Ned, 212n49
Stachel, Jack, 45, 47, 50, 52, 117; criticizes Joe Peter, 31–32
Stalin, Joseph, 49, 51

Stalinist show trials, 87, 107–8
"Steve" (J. Peters), 78, 105, 111, 131
Stevens, Alexander : and application for citizenship, 116, 118; arrest of, 142; attempt to silence Whittaker Chambers, 159–60; creation of, 115–18; his divorce, 120–21; farewell dinner for, 167; and Hiss grand jury, 160–62; his hope of avoiding deportation, 162–64, 231n57; his INS deportation hearing, 153–57; life style of, 163–64; his marriage, 121; public statements of, 156–57, 167–68; recreational activity of, 138–39; re-enters Party as Steve Miller, 134–35; returns to underground, 141, 145–46 ; revives "illegal apparatus," 117–19; and his self-deportation, 166–68; and Smith Act, 118–19; testimony at HUAC session, 151–53; under surveillance by FBI, 124–28, 130–31; work with Hollywood Communists, 119–20, 125. See also Goldberger, Sándor; Miller, Steve; Peter, Joe; Péter, József; Peters, J.
Stevens, Ann, 118, 120–21, 141, 143–44, 166. See also Péter, Ann; Silver, Sophie
"stool pigeons," 22, 157, 164
"Storm" (J. Peters), 105, 132–33, 225n17
Stripling, Robert, 147, 152
Szikra (Kossuth), 171–72
Szirtes, Lilly, 17, 28

Tanenhaus, Sam, xviii
Társadalmi Szemle, 172
"Ted," 71, 131
Toward Soviet America, 51–52. See also Foster, William Z.
Trotsky, Leon, 107, 190
Trotskyites, 14, 88, 106, 109, 157

Új Előre, xxi, 11–14, 16–17, 122, 169, 171
Ulanovsky, Alexander, 62, 79, 81, 207n35
Ulanovsky, Nadezhda, 62, 206n31
"Ulrich," 62, 79, 81, 207n35
underground (of CPUSA), xvii, 57
Uzhhorod (Ungvár), 8

Velson, Irving Charles, 65, 208n51
Venona project, xviii, 208n51
Vörös, Sándor, 54, 204n63

Wadleigh, Henry Julian, 97, 100, 103, 160
Ware, Harold, 74–77, 81–82, 86, 94
Ware group, 75–79, 81–82, 85–89, 103–4, 175

"Washington set-up," 74–75, 89–90, 145. *See also* Apparatus B; Ware group
Weiner, William, 62, 117, 134, 207n37, 209n67
Weinstein, Allen, xv, 175–78
Weinstock, Louis, 172, 232n12
Weinstock, Rose, 172
Weinstone, William, 18, 31, 33
Weyl, Nathaniel, 184; as member of Ware group, 74–75, 77, 82; opinion of J. Peters, xiii
Weyl, Sylvia, 72–73, 184, 209n82
White, Charles H., 33, 153, 203n31
White, Harry Dexter, 96–97, 104, 161
"White Terror," 6

Willert, Paul, 113
"Williams," 26–27, 39
Williams, Ed, 61
Williamson, John, xiv, 134, 141, 167
Witt, Nat, 159; friendship with J. Peters, 77; as member of Ware group, 74, 76, 86, 89
Wofsy, Isadore, 79–80
Workers Party, 10–12. *See also* Communist Party of the United States of America

Young Communist League, 64, 208n48

Zabladowsky, David, 217n37
Zimmerman, David, 97–101, 161, 216n34
Zinkin, Peter, 30, 33

THOMAS SAKMYSTER is a professor emeritus of history at the University of Cincinnati. He is the author of *Hungary, the Great Powers, and the Danubian Crisis, 1936–1939* and *Hungary's Admiral on Horseback: Miklós Horthy, 1918–1944.*

The University of Illinois Press
is a founding member of the
Association of American University Presses.

Composed in 10.5/13 Adobe Minion Pro
with Meta display
by Jim Proefrock
at the University of Illinois Press
Manufactured by Sheridan Books, Inc.

University of Illinois Press
1325 South Oak Street
Champaign, IL 61820-6903
www.press.uillinois.edu